Dynamics 365 Essentials

Getting Started with Dynamics 365 Apps in the Common Data Service

Second Edition

Sarah Critchley

Apress®

Dynamics 365 Essentials: Getting Started with Dynamics 365 Apps in the Common Data Service

Sarah Critchley
Cambridge, Cambridgeshire, UK

ISBN-13 (pbk): 978-1-4842-5910-8
https://doi.org/10.1007/978-1-4842-5911-5

ISBN-13 (electronic): 978-1-4842-5911-5

Managing Director, Apress Media LLC: Welmoed Spahr
Acquisitions Editor: Smriti Srivastava
Development Editor: Laura Berendson
Coordinating Editor: Shrikant Vishwakarma

Cover designed by eStudioCalamar

Cover image designed by Freepik (www.freepik.com)

Distributed to the book trade worldwide by Springer Science+Business Media New York, 233 Spring Street, 6th Floor, New York, NY 10013. Phone 1-800-SPRINGER, fax (201) 348-4505, e-mail orders-ny@springer-sbm.com, or visit www.springeronline.com. Apress Media, LLC is a California LLC and the sole member (owner) is Springer Science + Business Media Finance Inc (SSBM Finance Inc). SSBM Finance Inc is a **Delaware** corporation.

For information on translations, please e-mail rights@apress.com, or visit http://www.apress.com/rights-permissions.

Apress titles may be purchased in bulk for academic, corporate, or promotional use. eBook versions and licenses are also available for most titles. For more information, reference our Print and eBook Bulk Sales web page at http://www.apress.com/bulk-sales.

Any source code or other supplementary material referenced by the author in this book is available to readers on GitHub via the book's product page, located at www.apress.com/978-1-4842-5910-8. For more detailed information, please visit http://www.apress.com/source-code.

Printed on acid-free paper

For Joe, Jax, and Meg

Table of Contents

About the Author

Sarah Critchley is a Microsoft Dynamics Business Applications MVP, a published author, and an experienced technical consultant who has worked on numerous business system implementations, now working as lead architect for customer service in Hitachi Solutions, NA. She manages the strategy around all customer service–related technology, including Dynamics 365 Customer Service, Omni Channel Engagement, Forms Pro, Power Virtual Agents, and more.

Having led software projects in numerous industries, including healthcare and the public sector, she works across all areas of the project lifecycle from demonstrations, design, architecture, documentation, customization, and development. Sarah is heavily involved in community projects where she led and grew the Dynamics 365 and Power Platform UG in the United Kingdom for over three years, running technical events and presenting on a variety of topics at conferences around the world.

About the Technical Reviewers

Scott Durow is an experienced software architect and technologist with a passion for enabling business transformation through Microsoft technologies.

Scott is a Microsoft Business Applications MVP specializing in Dynamics 365. He is also the author of the Ribbon Workbench and Sparkle XRM.

Find him on Twitter as **@ScottDurow** and read his blog at **scottdurow.develop1.net**.

Shawn Tabor has been involved in the CRM community for over 15 years, working with Microsoft Dynamics solutions since Microsoft CRM version 3.0. Shawn has successfully implemented Dynamics 365 in various industries including financial services, manufacturing, healthcare, and sports/entertainment. Shawn also co-hosts several podcasts on the popular CRM Audio Podcast Network. Prior to working as a partner, Shawn managed a 4500-seat Dynamics CRM implementation for a large financial services firm. You can follow Shawn on his blog at https://atyourservicepod.com or subscribe to the CRM Audio podcast! In his spare time, Shawn enjoys collecting Star Wars Funko Pop! vinyl bobbleheads and spending time with his family.

Acknowledgments

I would like to express a huge thanks to the Apress team for taking the time and being so patient with me during the creation of this book. I talk quite a lot, have many ideas, and sometimes have a bucketload of enthusiasm that can be difficult to manage. The Apress team took this within their stride, and we all had a positive experience in the creation of this book! I would like to specifically thank Smriti Srivastava, Shrikant Vishwakarma, Matthew Moodie, and Laura Berendson for their absolute patience and diligence during the writing process.

Of course, I would like to offer thanks to Scott Durow, who reviewed the entire book and gave me sound advice and feedback (some of which was difficult to hear sometimes); without it, it would not be in the place it is today. Thank you for giving up your time and for all the effort you put into making this book a success.

Thank you to Shawn Tabor who reviewed this latest version of the book and had absolute patience with all of it (especially me!), the new chapters and working these into the existing content. Thank you, Shawn!

Absolute thanks also go to my husband, Joe, for putting up with my being on a computer much longer than usual (which is a long time anyway) and for offering a great deal of support and guidance where and when I needed it most – once again for putting up with this a second time around!

It would not be like me to forget to express a huge amount of gratitude to my cats, Jax and Meg. For those who have animals, you know how much they keep you calm during times of need, and mine are no exception. They continue to be an inspiration to me every day. It is my absolute privilege to watch you grow.

Introduction

The term *business applications* doesn't sound very interesting. It suggests gray, dull offices, computers with lots of spreadsheets, and the politics of a large organization. While this may have been true at one time, I want you to think of something different when you see or hear the term *business applications*. Think of a system that sends you notifications about your monthly bank statement. Think of engaging with your energy company on Twitter and getting a resolution to your problem in less than 30 minutes. Think of a real estate agent taking a couple on a tour of a home, entering information into their device, unconcerned that they have no Wi-Fi or 4G signal. Think of your doctor prescribing you your latest medication and the system on which that had to be carried out. Finally, think of vulnerable people seeking aid in a system that can help feed them, clothe them, and provide shelter, even giving them a safe home. *These* are business applications – applications that enable and empower human beings, organizations, and society to do more and to do better.

Microsoft Dynamics 365 is a suite of business applications that allow you to combine several different tools to create an infrastructure, a framework, and a core system within an organization. By doing so, it will enable organizations to meet the demands of an ever-changing industry as well as customer expectations. Dynamics 365 provides connectivity and enhancements to other applications, such as Office 365, to allow higher productivity using Outlook, SharePoint, Excel, Word, Teams, and even LinkedIn. Built on Microsoft Azure, Dynamics 365 can provide world-class reliability and performance, extending the capability of business applications even further in infrastructure, scalability, and serverless computing technology.

This book has undergone some significant updates to include the changes around the Microsoft Power Platform and how the Common Data Service (CDS) works together with Dynamics 365 Applications. Within that, we will look at how to create business solutions built upon the Common Data Service (CDS) for Applications. The CDS is at the core of Dynamics 365 and the business application platform that Microsoft offers, providing connectivity as a database across all areas, including talent, finance, and operations, as well as other third-party systems. Dynamics 365 Customer Engagement (CE) provides "first-party apps" for Field Service, Sales, Project Service, Customer

Service, Portals, and Marketing. Most of these apps can be licensed separately or can be purchased together in plan licenses, allowing organizations to tailor their business applications based on their needs.

Included within these pages will be the essential information on how to get started using these standard applications and their features. It will also cover how to extend those capabilities using Model-Driven Apps and a variety of no-code processes, including business rules, Business Process Flows, action steps, task flows, and more. At the end of the book, you (the reader) will be equipped with a solid understanding of how to get started with Dynamics 365 Apps, the Common Data Service, and Model-Driven Apps, being able to customize them to match your business needs.

Setting the Scene

Dynamics 365 and the Power Platform has undergone a number of updates in the past few years. At the time of writing the first edition of this book, the version (9.02) was where a user can choose to use the classic form, referred to as the "Classic UI," or the new user interface, which is called the Unified Interface (UI). There are some substantial differences between them. For clarity, this book will continue to refer to the Unified Interface (UI) where possible. However, in some experiences, especially those that are set up and administrative, the Classic UI will be used. In this updated edition of the book, I have reviewed where it made sense to update these experiences and done so. **For this reason, there may be some changes in the look and feel of the application according to what is available at the time of reading.**

This book purposefully doesn't cover a UI overview due to the nature of the changing releases and versions. Many of the elements are in flux, and while during the writing of the book I have been as descriptive as possible for walk-throughs, an extensive chapter on getting used to the user interface did not seem to be the best content to include.

Microsoft Power Platform

The Microsoft Power Platform has, in the last two years, revolutionized the extensibility platform that Dynamics has been built upon. The Power Platform includes Power Apps, Power BI, and Power Automate, including with it the Common Data Service and, more recently, Power Virtual Agents. The platform is the underlying technology that Dynamics

365 first-party Apps are built upon and used. While this book is not a primer, nor is it intended to be, for the Power Platform in its entirety, there will be a large amount of it covered relevant to Dynamics, including what it is and how these technologies work together. This includes the Common Data Service, which is at the center of Model-Driven Applications – in addition, Power Automate and creating automation processes, including Business Process Flows, within Model-Driven Apps and using this knowledge to modify Dynamics first-party Apps where required.

The Unified Interface (UI)

The Unified Interface, available in Model-Driven Apps in which Dynamics 365 is, has modernized the interface and reengineered the application to use a single interface across all devices and formats, from Web to mobile. A user can work on any form factor and ratio because the UI controls are designed to collapse into minified-style controls that are easier to use and take less of the form up. This responsive design has brought the application up to modern standards, allowing for further support to be added for screen readers and for easier navigation of forms using the Tab button. Satya Nadella, CEO of Microsoft, has consistently focused on the accessibility within technology, speaking at Ignite 2018 about the topic and actively participating in leadership teams with this as the focus.

The UI has a very similar interface to that of Office 365, such as Outlook and OneNote. The tabs and how the related items work in forms within the Dynamics 365 CE application, as well as the fonts and the look and feel of the application, allow users to get started in a more familiar environment as opposed to an entirely custom application. User experience is an important subtopic of software development and has a huge influence on user adoption of an application. This must be a consideration of Dynamics 365 CE and any additional customizations we make as customizers on the existing application.

Format of the Book

This book has two main sections - first being setup and the second being configuration. The book will introduce the Common Data Service, which underpins many of the core Dynamics 365 Apps, together with the ability to modify and create custom Model-Driven Apps. The first section is called "Setup" and focuses on the functionality within the first-party apps of Dynamics 365. Each chapter will cover what functionality is included within the app, how to set it up, and how to get started using the functionality. The book will focus specifically on the features of Dynamics 365 CE 9.0 Online and not earlier, except references to previous versions when discussing the Outlook Client Integration Capabilities in Chapter 1, which is done to give context surrounding a long and changing journey with the features.

The second part of this book is focused on Configuration. This section will look at ways in which a Model-Driven application can be created and configured to perform specific tasks and how this can be achieved using the native extensibility platform that the application provides. These same techniques can be used to edit many of the native features of the Dynamics 365 first-party apps. At the end of this section, readers will be confident in their knowledge of the extensibility platform, for example, what types of customizations can be used to modify the standard application. Both sections will provide considerations for real-life applications of the functionality where relevant, some of the potential shortcomings, and associated workarounds.

At the end of every chapter, there will be a section that gives up to ten suggested tasks for you to complete within the Power Platform and Dynamics 365 CE. These tasks will be based around the topics covered within the chapter and the further reading referenced at the end. They are aimed at expanding practical knowledge and applications regarding those topics that go beyond reading about them.

The strength of the Dynamics 365 application is in the standard configuration and customization capabilities that it provides. Even if readers know how to code, it is an established best practice to use out-of-the-box methods first before extending the application further. IT departments and system administrators who know these features of the application have greater ownership. This allows them to make more decisions and be more capable of analyzing and mitigating risk when changing processes. This allows for less overhead and for organizations to be more agile and adaptive to the changing needs of industries and customers.

Now, let's get started.

Second Edition Updates

In the last two years, much has changed within the Dynamics 365 Customer Engagement space. In this second edition, I wanted to take time to review the structure of the content and update it where it made sense to do so. The whole book has not been overhauled and is still very much the foundation of where it started in the first. Looking back at my ambition when I set out to create this book, it was to provide a solid foundation of Dynamics 365 capabilities that somebody could hold in the palm of their hand. That includes both a review of each "App" and how to configure those apps to suit specific needs.

The first edition certainly covered this ambition, but these second edition updates are at the core of the platform. The Microsoft Power Platform has emerged in the last 3 years and, at the time of writing the first version, was only a year old. Now having reached its third birthday, it is very much a core part of Dynamics 365, and the updates in this second edition have focused on setting the scene with where and how Dynamics 365 fits within this platform. Some functionality, such as workflows, and even apps, such as Social Engagement, have also been announced as being deprecated and so have been removed. This is so there is space for the technologies of the future, such as Power Automate, Power Virtual Agents, and the AI Applications now available.

Finally, what was important was to review the chapters on the Common Data Service and Model-Driven Apps. Configuration in these areas has been streamlined, and working within the Common Data Service has now proved even easier to create the apps of the future.

CHAPTER 1

The Common Data Service

The Common Data Service is a single place for apps. Data is stored in the Common Data Service that is served to many applications to be viewed and updated. Sounds like a basic definition, but really when it comes down to it, that is what is at the core of the Common Data Service, or CDS. The CDS is a data store, but it does more than simply store data in the same way as a SQL database, for example. The CDS reviews what data type is being stored, such as image data, and stores it in the correct type of storage based on the data type. Model-Driven Applications using Power Apps are built on top of the CDS, as the UI layer, or the "presentation" layer, and are designed for the user of the applications to interact with the data stored in the CDS.

In contrast to Model-Driven Applications, Canvas Apps are applications where the data store and the interface that the user of the apps interacts with are both created by the app maker. Both Canvas and Model-Driven Apps can utilize the CDS as their data store. The Common Data Service also acts as a data store and model for Dynamics 365 Customer Engagement data. Data entered through the user interface of any Dynamics 365 first-party Application gets stored within the Common Data Service. This results in the Common Data Service, or CDS, acting as one data store of information within the Power Platform. Included in the Power Platform are Power Apps, Power Automate, and Power BI. Within Power Apps, there are different types of applications that can be built, including Canvas, Model-Driven, and Portal. This book will focus on Dynamics 365 Apps and Model-Driven Apps. There is also a new chapter to introduce the new Power Platform Portal App type.

Model-Driven Apps utilize the Common Data Service as their default data store in the same way Dynamics 365 first-party Apps do. Dynamics 365 Apps are actually, at their core, Model-Driven Apps themselves that include extensive business logic and customizations created and managed by Microsoft. They have been designed so

© Sarah Critchley 2020
S. Critchley, *Dynamics 365 Essentials*, https://doi.org/10.1007/978-1-4842-5911-5_1

organizations don't have to create these apps themselves, which cover familiar industry-agnostic scenarios, accelerating the app's implementation time and increasing return on investment (ROI) value.

It is important to note that while Dynamics 365 Apps are Model-Driven Apps, Model-Driven Apps are not Dynamics 365 Apps – they are not mutually exclusive. A Model-Driven App uses the Unified Interface (UI). The UI is the presentation layer that is included in a Model-Driven App, prebuilt, so makers do not have to create it themselves and instead define the data (the "model") and add the required data to forms which are contained within the app. The scaffolding, such as navigation, sitemaps, basic CRUD operations, and responses to mobile and tablet, is already there ready to be put together based on whatever the essential need for an organization. A Model-Driven App is still classified as "custom" as the process behind it is a custom process being built and the app is simply the facilitator.

External data sources can be integrated with the Common Data Service so that the CDS can serve business applications of an organization with all the data stored and secured in a single space. The Common Data Service allows for a centrally controlled area to add and modify the structure (which reflects within the Dynamics 365 CE user interface) and for users to create canvas-driven applications that can utilize the data stored within the Common Data Service. Users would use Canvas Apps created in the Power Apps designer to link the Common Data Service as a data source so the users could retrieve and add new data. Changes in this data are always reflected in Model-Driven Apps without any integration or user intervention, as they are both using the same data store, the Common Data Service.

Organizations can begin with just the Common Data Service, which includes a core set of entities, such as Account, Activities, and more. The principal design of the Common Data Service is that the entities (record types) are added to the model based on other Model-Driven Apps being subscribed to them. An example of this would be that an Application using a custom "Event" entity would then allow this entity to be used by other Apps using the CDS. The Common Data Service is increasing in functionality every month, so this chapter aims to give an introduction to the service.

Power Automate is covered more extensively in Chapter 14, and can also utilize the Common Data Service from triggers when a record is created, deleted, or updated and then perform actions within the Common Data Service, such as creating new data. Power Automate and Canvas Apps are two of the core tools that can help construct automation and integration in the Common Data Service to enable organizations to benefit from a loosely coupled architecture of many different sources that form one operational database.

To summarize, no integration is required for the Common Data Service and Dynamics 365. Both applications use the same database. Users enter data, normally from a model or canvas-driven app, and the data is stored in a single common database that is visible in both Dynamics 365 interface and the Common Data Service.

Starting with the Common Data Service

The Common Data Service maker area, within the Power Platform maker experience (make.powerapps.com), is the same area users would go and make modifications to the Common Data Service whether they were creating a Model-Driven App or modifying a first-party App, such as Customer Service.

At the time of writing, there are two core ways to begin utilizing the Common Data Service, highlighted in the following:*

- Begin with Power Apps that include the Common Data Service, creating a "CDS-Only" environment and the capability to build Model-Driven Apps.

- Begin with a Dynamics 365 license, creating an environment licensed for Dynamics straight away which includes the Common Data Service and the capability to build Model-Driven Apps.

Before we get started, it would be useful to cover some terminology.

There is a concept called an "environment." An environment is a digital space which includes a single CDS data store. This environment is often categorized into a development, test, or production environment, very much like core software development methodology. A tenant is a collection of multiple environments. Dynamics 365 exists in one or more environments depending on if a user is licensed in the administration portal for one or more applications. This will direct if they see the core first-party Dynamics Apps. When Dynamics 365 CE is licensed and set up, the relevant applications are downloaded as solutions within the environment.

The Common Data Service manages the security of those applications using primarily Security Roles and, more recently, Azure AD Groups. There are multiple

---

*Note that this book will not be referencing licensing capabilities.

ways to secure and share an application, and these will be covered in later chapters. Model-Driven Apps can be created in the maker portal in the same way Canvas Apps are created – go to make.powerapps.com and select "Apps."

The Common Data Service exists per database per environment. An organization's sandbox and production Dynamics 365 CE environments will each have a separate database that is utilized and accessed using a different Common Data Service. The different environments can be accessed via `admin.powerplatform.com` which gives administrators the ability to review the current environments, modify various settings, and create new environments. *(At the time of writing, new environments created in the Common Data Service create an XRM-only instance of Dynamics 365 CE, with currently no upgrade path to add the customer service, sales, and other Model-Driven licensed apps into it.)* The XRM-only, or "CDS-Only," environment can be accessed in the same way via admin.powerpowerplatform.com.

Licensing is managed through the Office 365 Portal via Admins. It is expected that users' licenses attained through Dynamics 365 CE subscriptions and functionality will still be driven this way. Alternative routes are suggested for those organizations not requiring Dynamics 365 CE, where they can choose Common Data Service–only plans.

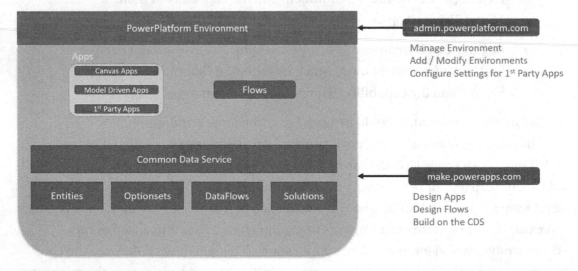

Figure 1-1. *Accessing the Dynamics 365 CE environment and Common Data Service*

All tenants have what is referred to as a "default" environment. This environment is often a personal productivity environment for all staff within an organization where they can review the features and functionality of the Power Platform. Additional environments are then created to create the dev, test, and production models (and more in some scenarios). The default environment establishes a way to foster adoption and build a community for the technology within the business. To further see what users are doing within this environment, organizations can utilize the (unofficial, open source) Center of Excellence (COE) kit. More information on the COE kit is available at the end of this chapter.

How Can the Common Data Service Be Accessed?

Administrators and customizers often referred to as *makers* within Microsoft documentation and learning material can access the Common Data Service by navigating to make.powerapps.com.

On the top right-hand side of the website, the environment selector is available for you to switch between accessible environments (Figure 1-2). Environments can contain different types of apps, including Dynamics 365, Model-Driven, and Canvas Apps. Administrators can also create new environments to be accessed from this dropdown at admin.powerplatform.com

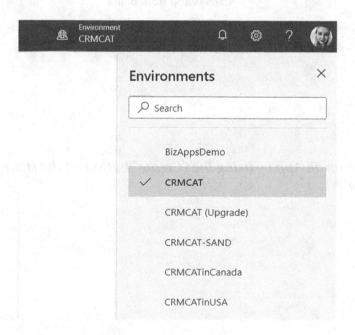

Figure 1-2. *Changing environments*

Once an environment is selected, provided you have the relevant permissions, you can either click "Create" on the left-hand-side panel and create an app from the screen based on the prompts or navigate to "Apps" also on the left-hand-side panel and a list of all Apps in this environment will be displayed. You can create new apps by selecting "New app" and choosing between the options available.

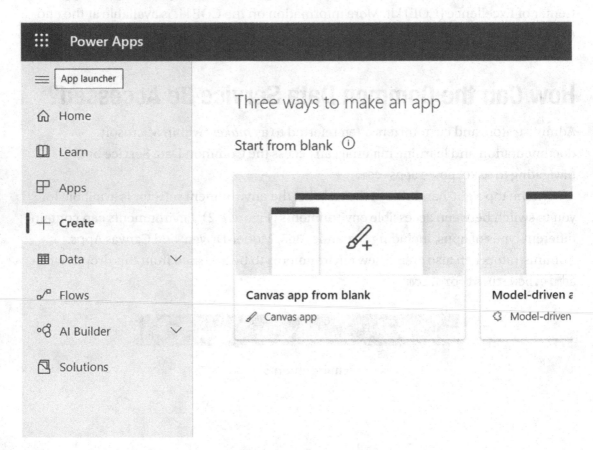

Figure 1-3. *Create an App by using the "Create" button on the sitemap in make. powerapps.com*

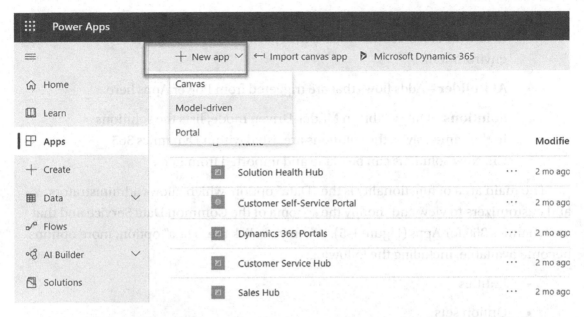

Figure 1-4. *Navigating to "Apps" and selecting "New app" will show available apps to be created in make.powerapps.com*

Navigation Within the Common Data Service

Navigating the Common Data Service is achieved by using the left-hand navigational pane. The left-hand navigation has the following options:

- **Home** – Can create a new app and review documentation or apps.

- **Learn** – Displays help articles in the Microsoft documentation, especially getting started material.

- **Apps** – Displays a list of "Apps" and allows new ones to be created from this screen.

- **Data** – Adds to and views the data model for the Common Data Service and Dynamics 365 CE.

- **Flows** – Displays all the Flows in this environment without navigating to flow.microsoft.com, which is the specific Power Automate environment.

- **AI Builder** – Adds flows that are triggered from Power Apps here.

- **Solutions** – Only visible in Model-Driven mode; lists the solutions in the same way as the solutions are listed within Dynamics 365 CE. New solutions can be made and imported from here.

The main area of functionality is the "Data" option, which allows administrators and customizers to view and modify the schema of the Common Data Service and that of Dynamics 365 for Apps (Figure 1-5). When you click the "Data" option, more options become available, including the following:

- Entities

- Option sets

- DataFlows

- Export to DataLake

- Connections

- Custom connectors

- Gateways

Note that navigation does change on occasion, and this may be different based on latest updates from what you see at the time of reading.

Figure 1-5. *The left-hand pane option "Data" houses the data model for Dynamics 365 CE and the Common Data Service*

Under the "Data" heading, in the "Entities" section, a list of the entities found in the Common Data Service is available. The entity list is filtered for default entities and can be modified to include custom entities or all entities by selecting the dropdown list in the top-right corner next to the search bar, as shown in Figure 1-6. When navigating the CDS this way, it is important to remember this filter when searching for specific entities.

Entities such as the Case entity, included in the Dynamics 365 Customer Service App, are classified as "Custom" and will not appear when filtered to "Default." New entities can be created here by selecting "New Entity" and completing the right-hand-side pane that appears, ensuring "Save Entity" is selected at the bottom. (However, Solutions should always be used to create new entities; see Chapter 10 for starting from a Solution and to know why this is important.)

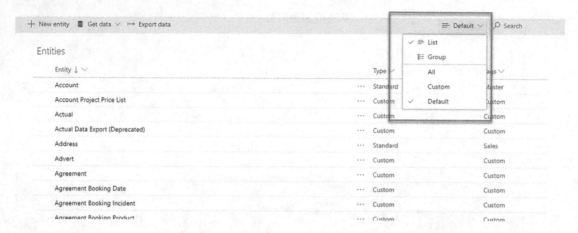

Figure 1-6. *The "Entities" list is pre-filtered to "Default." This can be changed in the filter options in the top-right corner*

Click an entity name to open the entity definition. The entity definition contains familiar items covered in this book, such as the fields, relationships, business rules, views, and data. In the "Data" tab on this view, the data from within the Common Data Service and Dynamics 365 CE can be displayed. Use the view selector in the top right, shown in Figure 1-7, to ensure the views match, to then see the data stored in the Common Data Service. This is the same data that users would see in Dynamics 365 CE. Again, changing the default view is essential as it can appear as if no data is visible in particular views as it is being filtered by default.

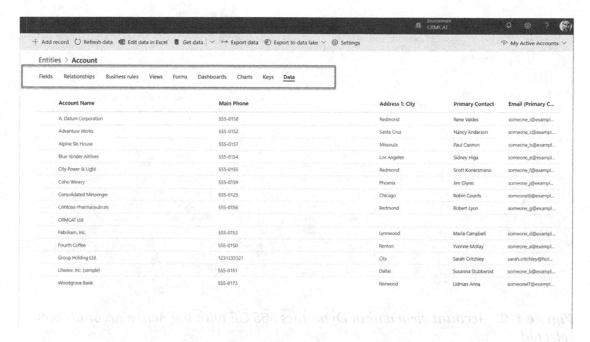

Figure 1-7. *The views can be changed when selecting the Data tab in the top right of the window*

In Figures 1-8 and 1-9, the same view of data for the Account entity is available in both the Common Data Service and Dynamics 365 CE using the view "All Accounts."

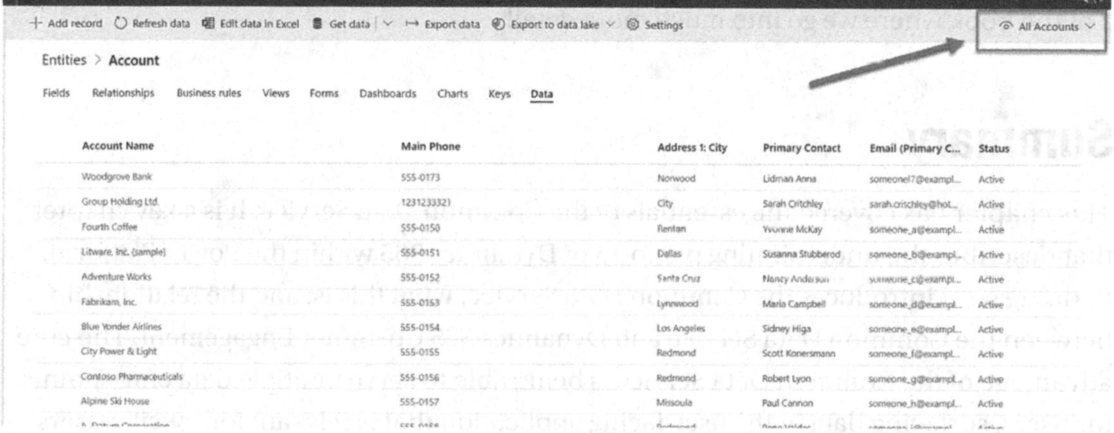

Figure 1-8. *Account view within the Common Data Service with the Active Accounts view selected*

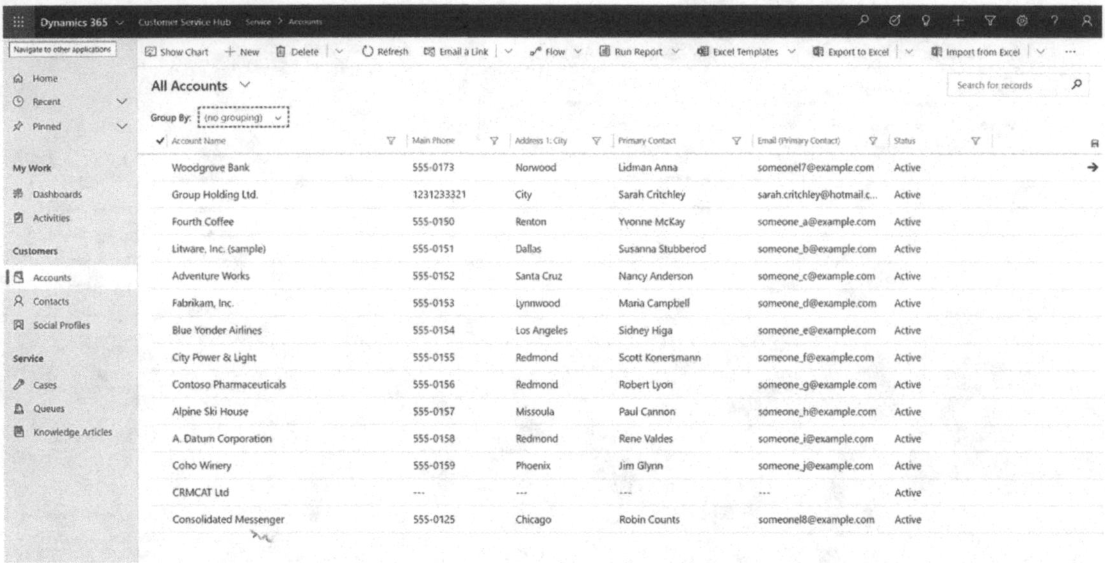

Figure 1-9. *Account view within Dynamics 365 CE with the Active Accounts view selected*

This further reinforces the point that the Common Data Service is a single database where data can be viewed and accessed from multiple places.

A lot more operations can be completed in this area, such as adding new fields under the "Fields" section of the entity, adding relationships and views, and creating new forms. Creation of this metadata for entities will be reviewed in later chapters in Section 2 of the book where we go into much more detail.

Summary

This chapter has covered the essentials of the Common Data Service. It is a key chapter that describes the underpinning platform of Dynamics 365 within the Power Platform. In doing so, it introduces the Common Data Service, what this is, and the relationship between the Common Data Service and Dynamics 365 Customer Engagement. The core advantage of the Common Data Service is being able to serve multiple data entry points for users, surfacing data in the user-facing application that is relevant for specific users using different types of apps.

There is a great deal of flexibility for organizations using the Common Data Service, especially following the upgrade to version 9 of Dynamics 365 CE. Organizations will utilize the Common Data Service through the Dynamics 365 Customer Engagement interface. Some users would likely never interact with the maker experience that you've seen in this chapter and only ever view the data through the relevant app (whether that is a Dynamics, Model-Driven, or Canvas application).

This chapter has covered how to get started using the Common Data Service, including familiarity with the interface and accessing entities and related data through views in the same way as Dynamics 365 Customer Engagement is structured for the user. New metadata can be added, such as fields, relationships, and option sets. Follow the chapter tasks at the end of this chapter to become familiar with this functionality and keep up to date on the latest releases of the Common Data Service, as with time the functionality will continue to grow and improve.

Chapter Tasks

Note: To complete these tasks, you will be required to create a free trial of Dynamics 365 Customer Engagement which can be found at trials.dynamics.com:

1. Navigate to make.powerapps.com and become familiar with the latest user interface.

2. Review the data model under the "Data" heading.

3. Navigate to the Account entity and filter the view under the "Data" heading to show "All" entities.

4. Navigate to the Dynamics 365 Customer Engagement Sales App, locate the accounts and the same view, and compare the data – it should be the same.

5. Change environments using the environment picker.

6. Navigate to "Apps" and create a "Model-Driven App" and then a "Canvas App." Note the differences between the two "creation" experiences.

Further Reading

Common Data Service (Microsoft, 2018). URL: https://docs.microsoft.com/en-us/powerapps/maker/common-data-service/data-platform-intro

Solutions in the Common Data Service (Microsoft, 2018). URL: https://docs.microsoft.com/en-us/powerapps/maker/common-data-service/solutions-overview

Restricted Entities (Microsoft, 2018). URL: https://docs.microsoft.com/en-us/powerapps/maker/common-data-service/data-platform-restricted-entities

Center of Excellence (Microsoft, 2019). URL: https://powerapps.microsoft.com/en-us/blog/introducing-the-powerapps-center-of-excellence-starter-kit/

Center of Excellence (GitHub, 2020). URL: https://github.com/microsoft/powerapps-tools/tree/master/Administration/CoEStarterKit

CHAPTER 2

Customer Management

This chapter will introduce the *Account* and *Contact* records and explain why these are so fundamental within Dynamics 365 Customer Engagement. This introduction will include key things to consider when using these records at the start of implementations and how such records can be customized to suit the needs of the business. It will then move on to email integration options, focusing on installing the latest App for Outlook before moving on to how activities can be utilized and how they are paramount for customer interaction and insight, timeline management, and customizing the timeline. This chapter will set you up with core knowledge about Dynamics 365 CE, allowing you to move forward with confidence into the next chapters.

Accounts and Contacts

Accounts and Contacts are two fundamental record types within Dynamics 365 CE. Record types are often referred to as *entities* within Dynamics 365 CE. Entities are used to categorize the *types* of a record and in database terms are the same as a table within a database. Users and processes create records of a type within the user interface or programmatically, creating rows within that table. Entities have related metadata linked to them, such as fields, views, and forms. *Fields* are columns within the database linked to the entity and are the descriptive information that is stored within the row. Dynamics 365 CE comes with many entities already pre-created and used within defined business processes, such as Accounts and Contacts. There is also the ability to create custom entities that can be used to support existing processes or, instead, to create entirely new processes.

Most interactions within the rest of the system center around these records. Because of this, they are often the most customized or renamed entities in the standard system. The name is often changed to "People" or "Organizations" to represent the terminology of a specific implementation. Changing the name of these entity types can often lead to

© Sarah Critchley 2020
S. Critchley, *Dynamics 365 Essentials*, https://doi.org/10.1007/978-1-4842-5911-5_2

more work than originally anticipated as a result of having to change any reference to the original names, such as in views and dashboards. In some areas, the original names cannot be changed, which then leads to further confusion as an organization has to be familiar with both terms.

To avoid renaming these fundamental entities, it helps to understand these records' potential within an organization and how they are represented. Despite changing the name of these entities within an implementation, people will often still find that the name is only representative of a department or a section of the company, while a different department would refer to them with another name. Understanding the potential of these records and looking at the different scenarios they are used in is so important for all projects and will lead to a greater appreciation of how they can fit within the organization using Dynamics 365 CE.

What Are Accounts and Contacts?

Accounts are fundamentally a collection of related records that are related to a specific engagement or business relationship. A contact represents how to contact a person. I have chosen my words very carefully here for good reason. Accounts often get used *specifically* as organizations or companies; however, using them in this way is fine only until you start getting into a few different scenarios. An example would be when using "Fourth Coffee" as the company:

- Is Fourth Coffee the legal entity, or is that a different company? Will that different company be its parent company?

- Is Fourth Coffee the one that invoices go to, or could another record deal with the invoices?

- Is Fourth Coffee a contractor that also is a contact and a company at the same time? What if a contractor utilizes subcontractors who belong to a different company?

Once these questions start to be asked, one might think they can be resolved by adding new fields to the entity, which becomes problematic. Data starts to become only important in specific scenarios, and these records become packed with fields that will not be relevant for all records.

Another consideration for the Account record is deciding where this would sit within the counterpart finance system structure. A Contact record would be linked to an Account record in CE, and other information would be held in the finance system. The front- and back-office systems often have different users, creating a requirement to "open up" the integration between the two systems so they display information from both systems. In finance and operations, a *Vendor* is a separate record type to that of an Account, which has a totally different meaning.

Returning to the definition of an account, as it is a collection of related records that are related to a specific engagement or business relationship, it's easy to see an account differently based on different perspectives. So, for those instances where you wish to add organization data or contractor data, an option would be to extend the Account record with custom entities specific to the type of data you're holding. This would abstract the data from the core record information.

The same challenges appear for contacts. Contacts often get described as "customers," but could refer to internal contractors and not necessarily an individual whom the business treats as a customer. The terms *individuals* and *people* are also a challenge, as these come with the assumption that only one of that record would exist, as only one exists within the world in which they do business. Within Dynamics 365 CE, uniqueness in relation to Outlook Integration (which will be discussed in a later chapter) is based on email address. This functionality underpins the creation of new contact functionality and links email activities to the contact. For this reason, it is then easier to approach the definition of a contact as being how to contact a person.

Ensure that your definitions of what an account and a contact are within a business system are clearly defined and are discussed early on in your project. This could help with enhancing the system through customizations if required and aid in resolving any problems created later with terminology misunderstandings.

Parent Accounts

Dynamics 365 CE provides the capability to associate one account with another account as its "parent." A *parent* can have many child accounts; this structure is easy to see in a visual format by clicking the Hierarchy icon on a view within the legacy Classic UI application. Figure 2-1 displays the field this is referencing within the form.

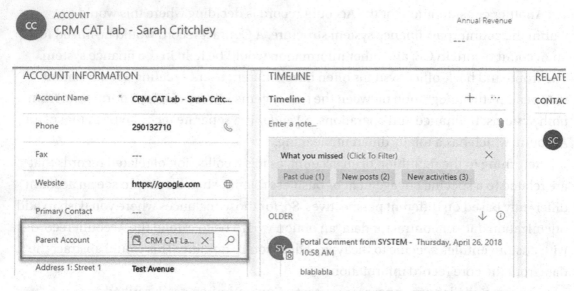

Figure 2-1. *An account with the Parent Account field set, making this a child account*

You can then visualize the hierarchy of accounts by clicking the Hierarchy button on the list view (next to its name). This is shown in Figure 2-2.

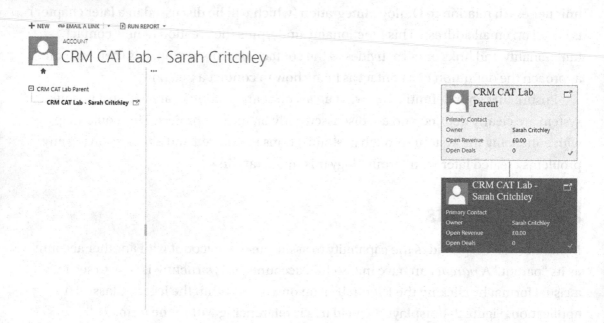

Figure 2-2. *Visual hierarchy view available in the Classic UI application version 9.02*

Associating an account as a child or a parent of another doesn't just give helpful reporting capabilities. It also automatically rolls up associated activities, such as appointments and emails, from the child account and makes them visible within the parent. This is especially helpful when a parent account has multiple child accounts, so that all activities will be visible at the parent level, without users having to individually find those activities within the children.

This relationship is especially useful when an account is responsible for invoices, as they can normally be associated with a parent account (which is the case for local authorities in the United Kingdom in a specific region; normally one is invoiceable). By associating these relationships, it means any further customizations done within this area to automate functions can be easily achieved.

Standard Features Associated with Accounts and Contacts

There is standard functionality available on the Account and Contact records that is useful to be aware of when using Dynamics 365 CE.

Like the account and parent account rollup functionality, activities from an associated contact automatically roll up to the contact's associated account. This is especially useful in instances of Outlook Integration where a user is using Outlook to communicate with a customer; for example, when investigating a case, those emails can be automatically tracked to the Case record within Dynamics 365 CE using the Outlook Integration feature. When that record is viewed within Dynamics 365, those email activities can be seen not only in the Contact record but also in the associated Account record, giving a single record within the system the ability to see all communication from all associated Contact records.

To use this feature, ensure the relationship between Contact and Account records is set using the Account Name field within the Contact record; the associated activities will automatically roll up.

In Figure 2-3, the phone call was scheduled on a Contact record.

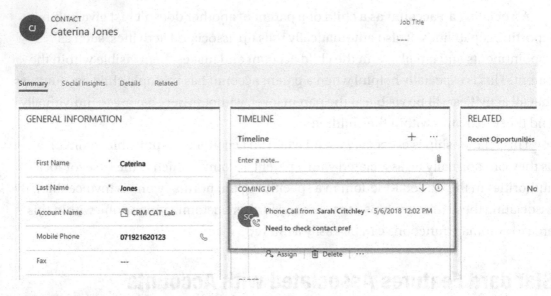

Figure 2-3. *A Contact record with an upcoming Phone Call activity*

The phone call can be seen within the Account record in Figure 2-4, as it has rolled up to the associated account.

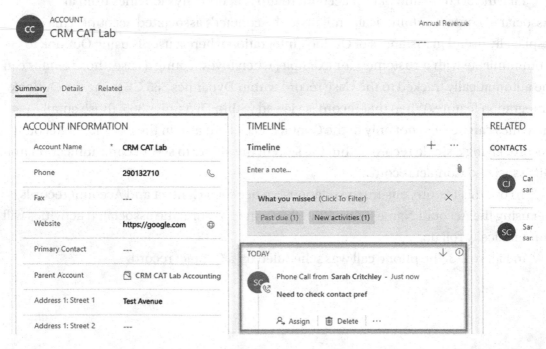

Figure 2-4. *The account associated with the Contact record, showing the Phone Call activity, despite it not being directly associated*

Within the Account and Contact records, there is a standard feature that allows users to control whether emails and bulk emails are to be sent from within Dynamics 365 CE to those contacts. This feature is particularly useful when automated emails are being sent from within the system and an organization needs to prevent these from being sent. It doesn't, however, prevent a user from sending a contact an email directly from within Outlook.

The fields that can restrict this process are included in the section called "Contact Preferences" within the Details tab, which can be seen in Figure 2-5. The "Email" field will prevent any email from being sent from within Dynamics 365 in both the context of an individual email activity and bulk emails. Emails are classified as "bulk email" when they are sent from quick campaigns, campaign activities, or customer journeys (using the Dynamics 365 Marketing) or are sent using the Send Direct Mail feature available on a Contact record. Individual emails are single email activities associated with individual records. The "Bulk Email" field will prevent emails from being sent out only when considered a bulk email.

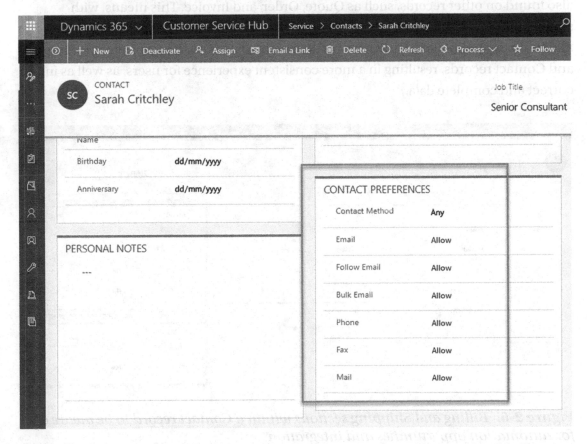

Figure 2-5. *The Contact Preferences section within a Contact record holds the "Email" and "Bulk Email" fields*

These fields are often utilized within marketing add-ons to the Dynamics 365 CE platform through marketing lists or segmentations. Subscription lists are a common feature underpinning how contacts are contacted to be able to tailor the marketing experiences they receive. A part of this is where a user can unsubscribe from a list so as to no longer receive messages using a specific channel, such as email. A contact can also ask an organization to not contact them again regarding any sort of message and to withdraw any sort of service from the contact. These examples are where Contact record preference fields hold a high value, as they then prevent automated messages from being sent and assist in segmentation within queries.

Lastly, there are some fields to be aware of before you begin any sort of customization that come as part of the native Dynamics 365 CE product. These include the fields within the Billing and Shipping sections of Account and Contact records, highlighted in Figure 2-6. These fields, while not holding any functionality, are often also found on other records, such as Quote, Order, and Invoice. This means, with some relative ease, by using relationship mapping, covered later in the book, you can automatically populate these fields with the default data from the associated Account and Contact records, resulting in a more consistent experience for users, as well as in correct and complete data.

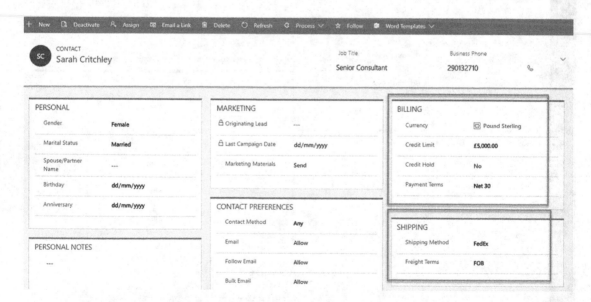

Figure 2-6. *Billing and Shipping sections within a Contact record to be aware of for automation opportunities and integration*

Be aware of the fields that are used within the form. There are many fields on an entity that come as part of the platform – which you can see within the Form Designer's field explorer – that hold standard features (Figure 2-7). These include Last Login, Modified On, SLA, and others that you may wish to review before customizing the system, as you may create similar fields. This will assist you in getting the most out of the standard platform. Customizing the user interface and the Form Designer is covered in Part II of this book.

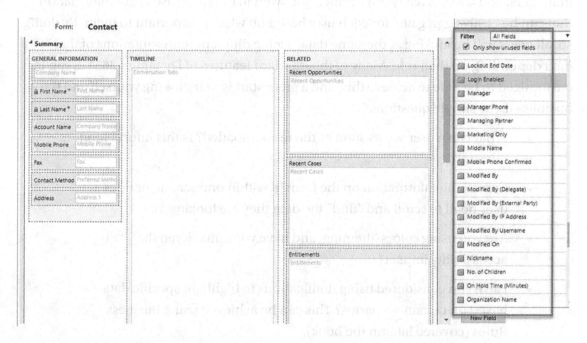

Figure 2-7. *Form Designer within Dynamics 365 CE with the field explorer highlighted, displaying fields not considered standard on the Contact form*

Address Entity

On Account and Contact records, the "Address" fields look like any standard field where you can enter lines of the address, the city and zip code, and save those details, report on them, and have them appear in views. These types of fields are often referred to as "composite" field controls and compress multiple fields. In addition to this, there is a separate Address entity that can be utilized within Account and Contact records and is used to store addresses linked to those records, ready for use in other processes. This Address entity can be added to Accounts, although not customized to include other relationship (lookup) type fields, and therefore has limitations for extensibility.

360-Degree View of the Customer

A common requirement for organizations is to be able to view an Account or Contact record and get a "360-degree view" of the customer. This view is different depending on not only the organization using Dynamics 365 CE but also the department that is using it, all the way down to the user and what information is *relevant* for them, at *that* specific time. Understanding what information is useful to the organization, department managers, and users is really important if you want to obtain a cascade of information that can be easily aggregated for each user based on what is important to them. By doing so, all users will be looking at the same data, seeing different representations of that data depending on their role. Many of the standard features of Dynamics 365 CE can be customized to be able to achieve this, and a great start is to try asking yourself and the business these simple questions:

- What can a user see as soon as the form is loaded? Is this information relevant?

- Can all the information on the form fit within one screen, or does a user need to scroll and "find" the data they are looking for?

- Are you using colors/theming, and have you considered the accessibility impact?

- Have you considered using notifications to highlight specific data based on certain scenarios? This can be achieved using Business Rules (covered later in the book).

- How many entities are included in the related tab? Are all of them relevant?

- Do all the entities have appropriate icons and views set up for them? Views within sub-grids should display key data.

- Are the views editable where they need to be, allowing users to quickly add data when required without having to navigate away?

- Have main views been configured to give users a 360 view of all relevant data for multiple records at any one time? This can even remove the need to click into a form.

- Have Quick View forms been utilized? Quick View forms allow users to see a small set of information for related records without having to navigate into them.

Answering these questions will help you design views and forms for users who make use of standard features and provides a realistic 360-degree view of the customer for most users. Run user experience workshops and create material to show users how to obtain the information they need and how to obtain feedback and modify the view as appropriate. UI customizations are covered in Second Section of this book, which looks at how to customize views and forms and create dashboards.

Email (Outlook) Integration for Dynamics 365 CE Online

Dynamics 365 CE allows for native Microsoft Outlook Integration so that a user's current day-to-day activities within Outlook can be kept within the Outlook application and integrate in the background using Dynamics CE. A user's day-to-day tasks might not look like Microsoft Outlook and can include other email providers, such as Gmail. Integration capabilities are still there for other providers using POP3 or SMTP email protocols; however, some functionality is limited (such as manual tracking). The intention in this section is not to provide a full list of current capabilities and versioning, as this can easily be obtained by reviewing the official Microsoft Doc page, linked in the "Further Reading" section at the end of this chapter. Instead, this chapter will look at how to set up the latest connector, the different options available when setting up email integration, challenges, and possible mitigations.

Being aware of the capabilities of Outlook Integration is important as it has a direct effect on the way users interact with contacts and accounts within their day-to-day activities. Email is utilized regularly across multiple devices, where multiple users are interacting with those records regularly. Integration within Dynamics 365 is often an expected and required function in order for businesses to operate seamlessly between Microsoft Outlook and Dynamics 365 CE.

Microsoft Outlook Integration is the preferred option for integrating with Dynamics 365, providing most functionality and often what can be described as "native" integration. There are two ways to integrate Dynamics 365 CE with Microsoft Outlook, as follows:

- The Dynamics 365 full add-in is often referred to as the Outlook Add-In Client, or even Dynamics 365 for Outlook. This is installed locally on the user's machine by downloading the .exe file and installing it. This has since been scheduled for deprecation by Microsoft.

- The Dynamics 365 App for Outlook is the latest version of Outlook Integration and was rebuilt using HTML. It can be deployed via Dynamics 365 without the need to install anything on the users' machines. This also appears in Outlook Web Access (OWA) for those users. This is currently a preview feature for 9.0 that has been made GA in the 9.02 release in April 2018. You *must* use server-side synchronization integration, described later in this chapter, to utilize this version.

Using both add-ins at the same time is unsupported, so an organization must choose one version of the Outlook client. Microsoft has communicated within its documentation, found in the "Further Reading" section at the end of this chapter, that the preferred way is to utilize server-side synchronization with the Dynamics 365 App for Outlook. The following includes steps to set up the app using server-side sync, allowing access to the features from the Web, desktop, and mobile.

This section will look at the steps to set up the mailbox before you configure the Dynamics 365 App for Outlook. If you navigate to the "App for Outlook" area within Dynamics 365 CE and don't see any users, this is normally caused by the fact that you do not have an approved and running mailbox. A mailbox within Dynamics 365, as seen in Figure 2-8, represents the link between a user's mailbox on the exchange server (that stores its email messages) and Dynamics 365. The options configured within this record in Dynamics 365 CE are created per user and govern how the email synchronization is managed between the two systems. Within "System Settings," users can configure default mailbox settings for each user, so there will be no requirement to configure the following steps separately as new users are added. This is particularly useful when there are hundreds or even thousands of users:

1. Navigate to Settings; click "Email Configuration" and then "Mailboxes."

2. You will see a Mailbox record created for each user you have in the system, but they are not going to be activated and running by default.

3. Set the fields within the Synchronization Method tab to "Server-Side Synchronization" (Email Router is an older option of integration that provided a separate service, or "route," by which to send the messages between an exchange server and Dynamics 365, but required Outlook to be running to synchronize).

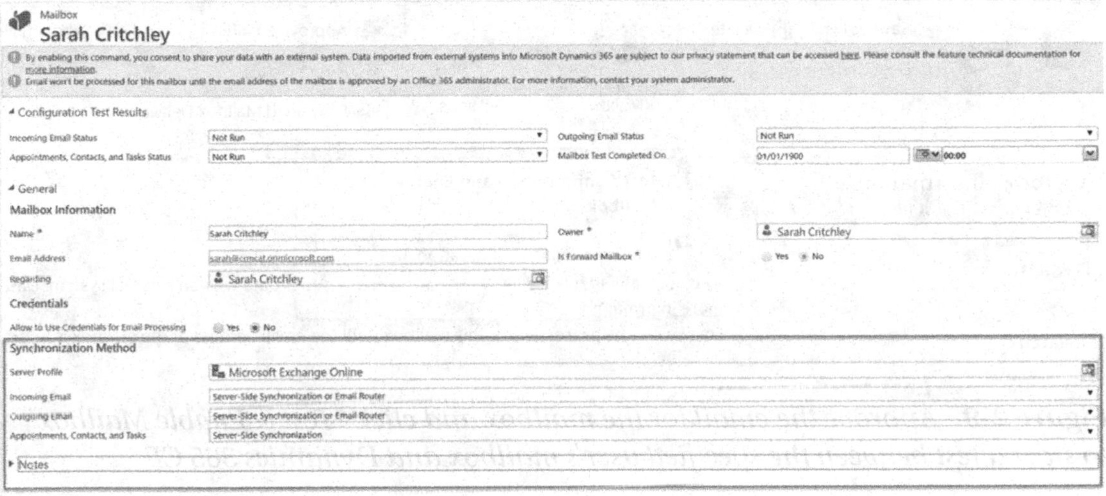

Figure 2-8. *Dynamics 365 CE Mailbox record with the synchronization method being configured for server-side sync*

Server-side synchronization is the term used to specify which type of synchronization this specific mailbox is using. It allows for Dynamics 365 CE to communicate directly with the exchange server without having the middleware of an email router. As each mailbox is a separate record, each can be different for different users. Specifying server-side synchronization has the advantage of being able to track emails, contacts, tasks, and appointments dynamically and automatically, at a minimum frequency of every five minutes, without the need to have the Outlook application open. This frequency can happen quicker, depending on the mailbox, but because each mailbox is different (the rate of emails being sent and received is rarely the same for individuals), this can be shorter or longer.

The next steps to activate this mailbox are as follows:

1. Ensure the email for the user is approved to send emails by clicking "Approve Email," as seen in Figure 2-9.

2. Click "Test & Enable Mailbox"; there will be a test message sent using the options you configured. The outcome of this test can be seen in the fields in the mailbox itself.

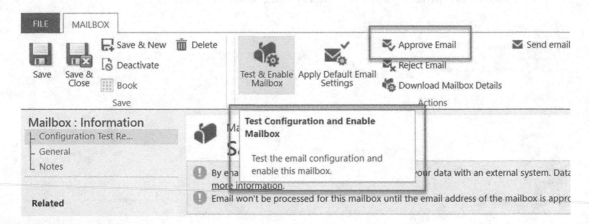

Figure 2-9. *Approve the email for the mailbox and click "Test & Enable Mailbox" to start a test between the specified user's mailbox and Dynamics 365 CE*

Once activated, the user who is associated with this mailbox should receive an email, as seen in Figure 2-10, confirming the activation.

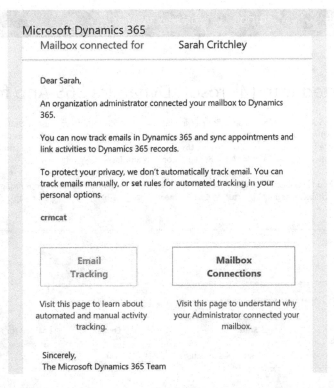

Figure 2-10. *Confirmation email after Dynamics 365 and Outlook have been successfully linked*

Once a mailbox is active and running for a user, App for Outlook can be installed. The app offers functionality across the Web (through Outlook Web Access), mobile (Microsoft Outlook App), and desktop (Microsoft Outlook, also available on Mac). Dynamics 365 provides the capability to push this app automatically to the accounts of users via Office 365 so there is no direct install required for users. Within the "Settings" area, you can also automatically push the app directly to those who have an eligible mailbox, as follows:

1. Navigate to Settings ➤ Dynamics 365 App for Outlook.

2. Select the user(s) you wish to push the app to and click "Add App for All Eligible Users" as shown in Figure 2-11.

3. After doing so, you will see the status of those users as "Pending."

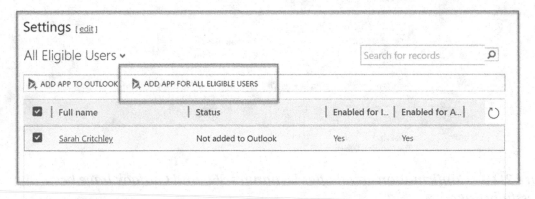

Figure 2-11. *Installing the Dynamics 365 App for Outlook for eligible users*

Once the app is installing, within the "All Eligible Users" view, you can see the status of the app and when it is pending or installed successfully, as seen in Figure 2-12.

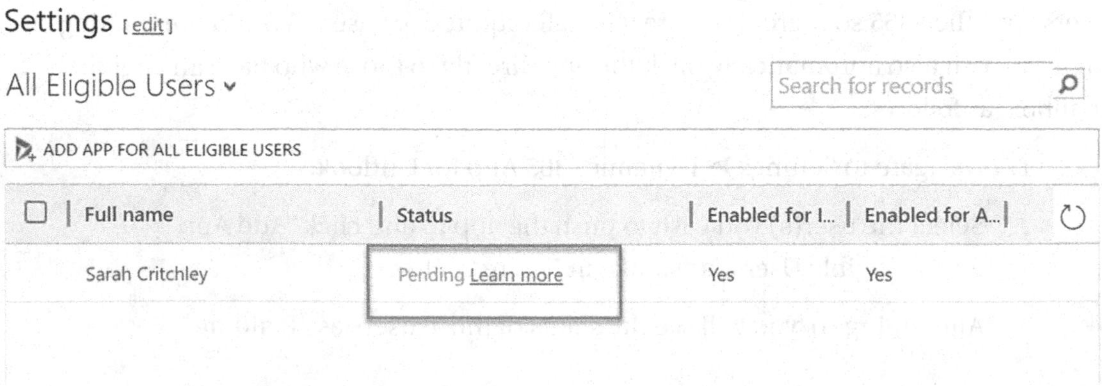

Settings [edit]

All Eligible Users ❯

Full name	Status	Enabled for I...	Enabled for A...	
Sarah Critchley	Pending Learn more	Yes	Yes	

Figure 2-12. *Once added, the status will be updated. Once completed, it will say "Completed," and refresh to display "Added in Outlook"*

Once the app has completed installation, which can take up to 15 minutes, the Dynamics 365 button will be visible within the clients. When accessing the Dynamics 365 App for Outlook across clients, there is still a familiar interface and loading screens across all of them. These can be seen in Figures 2-13, 2-14, and 2-15.

Inbox - sarah@crmcat.onmicrosoft.com - Outlook
To Manager
Done
Steps
Move
Rules
OneNote
Move
Assign Policy
Unread/ Read
Categorize
Follow Up
Tags
New Group
Browse Groups
Groups
Search People
Address Book
Filter Email
Find
Read Aloud
Speech
Store
Add-ins
Customer Manager
Dynamics 365
Sarah Critchley
Sarah Critchley
15:31
Your mailbox is now connected to Dynamics 365
This message was sent with Low importance.
Microsoft Dynamics 365
Mailbox connected for
Sarah Critchley
Dear Sarah,

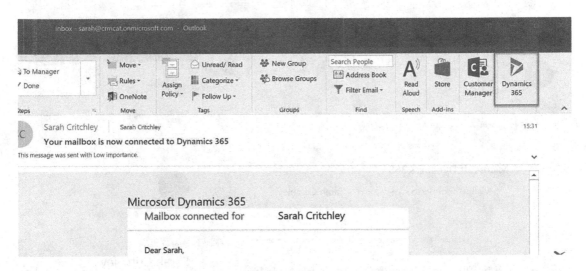

***Figure 2-13.** Desktop client with the Dynamics 365 button available in the ribbon*

The Dynamics 365 button can be seen near the "Reply All" dropdown in Outlook Web Access (OWA), as seen in Figure 2-14.

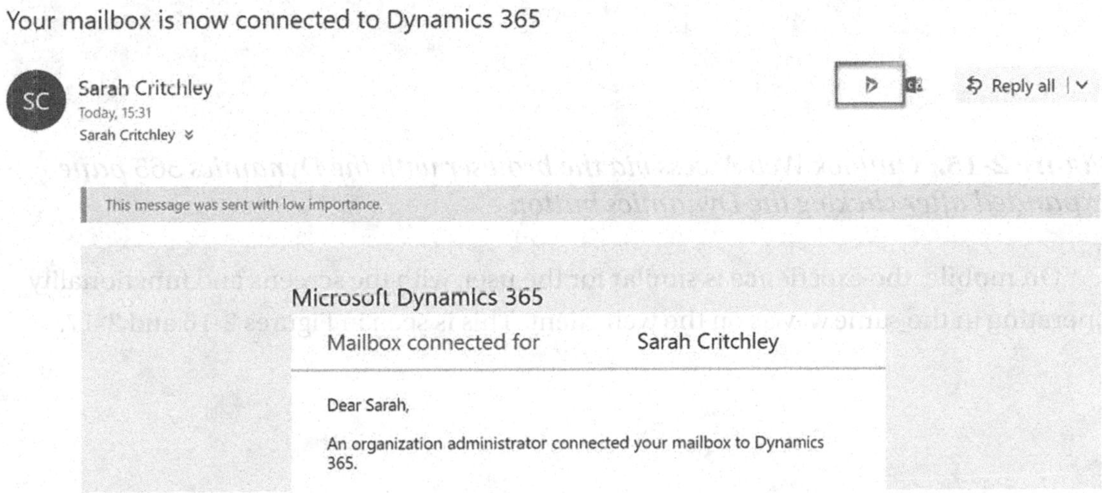

Your mailbox is now connected to Dynamics 365
SC
Sarah Critchley
Today, 15:31
Sarah Critchley
Reply all
This message was sent with low importance.
Microsoft Dynamics 365
Mailbox connected for
Sarah Critchley
Dear Sarah,
An organization administrator connected your mailbox to Dynamics 365.

***Figure 2-14.** Outlook Web Access via the browser with the Dynamics logo visible in the toolbar*

When you click the Dynamics button within OWA, the Dynamics 365 pane expands on the right-hand side to give contextual information about the recipient of the email (Figure 2-15).

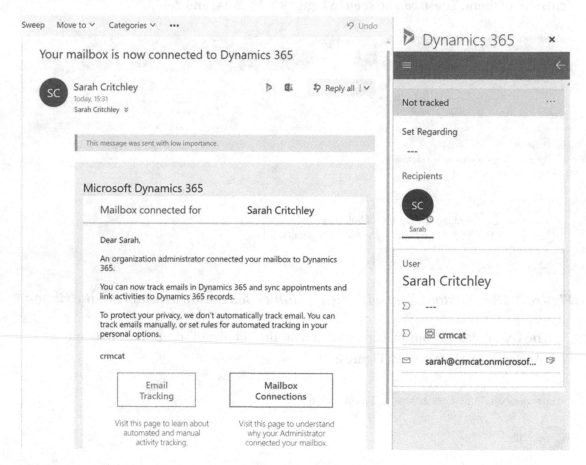

Figure 2-15. *Outlook Web Access via the browser with the Dynamics 365 pane expanded after clicking the Dynamics button*

On mobile, the experience is similar for the user, with the screens and functionality operating in the same way as on the web client. This is seen in Figures 2-16 and 2-17.

Figure 2-16. *Opening the Dynamics 365 Add In*

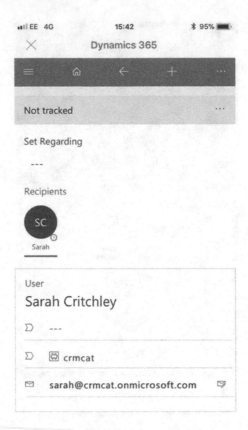

Figure 2-17. *Microsoft Outlook for iOS with the Dynamics 365 option and pane open*

The contextual information still appears on mobile at the bottom of the screen when setting the reference "Set Regarding" field within the record of the activity (Figure 2-17).

Once the app is installed, emails and activities can begin being tracked. Users will see similarities between all different clients, such as when a "Set Regarding" field is set to an email and a notification then appears to let you know this was successfully tracked, displaying the quick view information of the record within the pane (Figure 2-18). A "Regarding" field is a link to an associated record from an activity. For those who are not familiar with the "Regarding" field, this is covered in the "What Are Activities?" section.

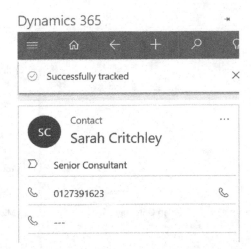

Figure 2-18. *Successfully tracking an item within the Outlook app*

Within the Dynamics 365 App for Outlook pane, users can also click the action menu ("...") and choose to either associate the record with a different regarding, remove the link altogether, or view the record within Dynamics 365.

It is the same experience when creating appointments and tasks within Outlook. Users can click the Dynamics 365 button and choose the regarding record with which to associate the activity. Setting the regarding record will queue the activity record to be created within Dynamics 365 CE and then to be linked together, creating a copy of that activity within the Dynamics 365 CE application and also tracking it for changes. This is especially useful where a user is managing their day-to-day activities within Outlook on any device and their colleagues can see the latest updates from within Dynamics 365.

One of the major differences between the App for Outlook and the older "full" add-in is that manual tracking is not possible within the app and this is instead performed in the background; however, tracking is very close to immediate within the application.

Users can also add activities (tasks, phone calls, and appointments) to records from within Outlook. This can be done by clicking the action menu button and then "Add Activity." A user can select the type of activity and complete the form to save this in Dynamics 365 CE (Figure 2-19). This is especially useful in scenarios of task management, as the ownership of the task or activity can often change, and thus you might need to create and synchronize a task or other activities for a different user directly from Outlook.

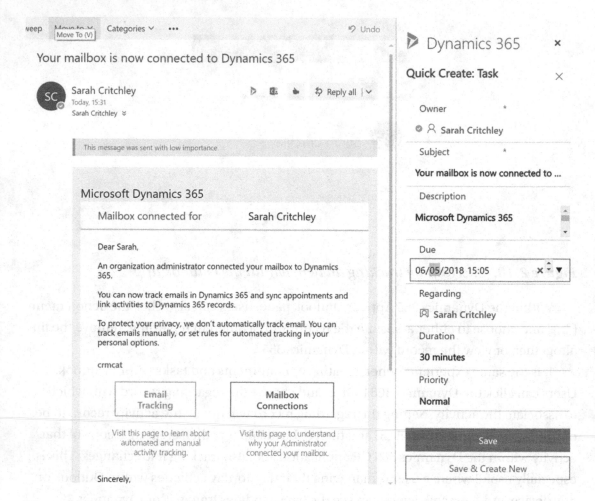

Figure 2-19. *Creating a task within Outlook and setting the owner of that task will display it within that user's dashboard*

Creating and synchronizing activities directly within Outlook means you can remain within the Outlook app while creating tasks and appointments, knowing they are being synchronized in the background (Figure 2-20).

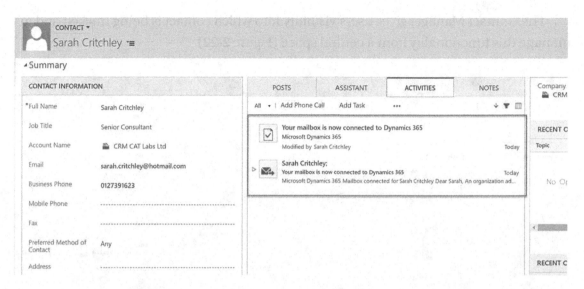

Figure 2-20. *The email message and task synchronized to the contact in Dynamics 365 from within Outlook*

Managing the synchronization between contacts can be easily set up by tracking contacts directly from Outlook. Open the Contact Manager Add-In by clicking "Add-ins" and then "Dynamics 365," as shown in Figure 2-21. This will open a view of the Outlook contacts, and the Dynamics 365 contacts will also be visible (because the Outlook application creates and manages a Contacts list as Dynamics 365 CE does). Click the Contact and click "Track." The "Link" button will associate it with the account you select and also track it, automatically tracking any associated email messages linked to this contact.

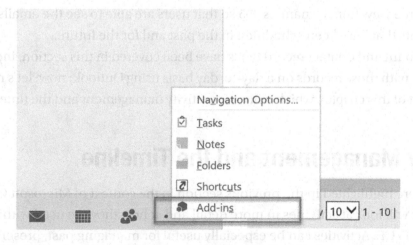

Figure 2-21. *Selecting the add-in from within the Outlook application*

The Contact Manager gives users visibility into which contact is being tracked and to manage this functionality from a central space (Figure 2-22).

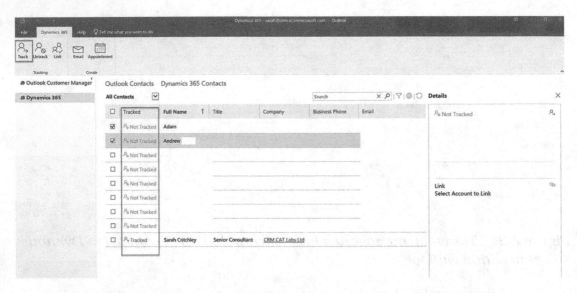

Figure 2-22. *Review which contacts are being tracked from the Contact Manager*

In summary, setting up the App for Outlook should be discussed within organizations at the start of implementations to ensure the functionality meets their needs. The app allows users to keep their often normal, day-to-day operations within Microsoft Outlook and to benefit from the background synchronization achieved using the native integration functionality. The contact users have with customers then creates the 360-degree view from Dynamics 365 so that users are able to see the emails and appointments that have been scheduled in the past and for the future.

The Account and Contact record types have been covered in this section, including how to work with those records on a day-to-day basis using Outlook; now, let's move on to the final part of this chapter, which will cover activity management and the timeline view.

Activity Management and the Timeline

Activities were highlighted in the previous section in the context of Microsoft Outlook. This section will look at activities in more detail and at how they are used within Dynamics 365 CE. Activities can be especially useful for managing past, present, and future customer engagements. They can be read and interpreted using the timeline interface, underpinning reporting and customer engagement across the entire system.

What Are Activities?

Activities are a special type of record within Dynamics 365 CE that can be associated with any other record type within the system enabled for activities. Examples of standard activities include phone calls, tasks, appointments, and emails. With specific apps within Dynamics 365 CE, such as Field Service or Portals, more activities become available, expanding the types of activities available within the system. They are best considered as supporting records that add extra dimensions and information for users, giving them visibility into every record from the timeline view. Because of this, the data within these records can be easily filtered and sorted depending on the need. Activities are often considered to be "schedulable" as they all have a start and end date by default. The reason this happens is that all activities are child entities associated with a parent Activity Pointer entity (Figure 2-23).

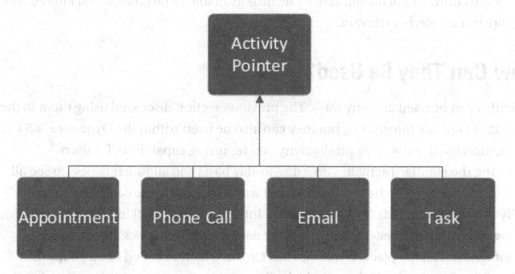

Figure 2-23. *Activities roll up to the Activity Pointer entity*

The Activity Pointer is a non-customizable entity within the system that provides Activity records with a base set of field information so that any record type defined as an activity will have the same set of fields at a minimum, in addition to specific ones for that type. When a new activity record is made by a user, a new Activity Pointer record is also created that holds base fields such as start and end times, due date, and duration. The Activity Pointer records can be seen under the Activities entity within Advanced Find, available on the main navigation bar allowing users to search for and query records within the system.

Dynamics 365 CE hides the fact that two entities are created from the user interface (for the most part) and only the specific record – for example, a phone call – is visible within the system so the user can focus on the record type based on their needs at the time.

Making a new entity an activity-type entity can be done when creating the record within the entity definition itself. Consideration needs to be given when creating a custom activity because that activity is going to be available to be created on any other type of record and will be available within the timeline for those records. If the record type is only going to be appropriate in one entity, it may be best to simply create a normal entity and not make it an activity. This is a critical point and an important design decision. Creating a full entity and then creating a relationship between that and the related entity allows the child records to be visible via a sub-grid component. This design avoids the confusion of having activity records available to be created and filtered where they are not needed or relevant.

How Can They Be Used?

Activities can be used in many ways. The previous section discussed using them in the context of Outlook Integration, but they can also be used within the Dynamics 365 CE application itself, enhancing productivity and reporting capabilities for users.

Using the standard activities on a day-to-day basis will allow a business to see all the contact points with their customers and will also provide the capability to more easily manage workloads. By using Outlook Integration and tracking, all email activities are logged within the system, and any other user within Dynamics 365 CE can see the integration taking place. Dynamics 365 CE has a feature called Phone Support in the Customer Service Hub app, which allows a new Case record to be created and automatically creates and opens a Phone Call activity at the same time. Creating phone calls for the future will allow a salesperson to plan their weekly calls and estimate how long they will take. Appointment activities can also be synchronized with Outlook Integration, allowing other users and colleagues to see availability and when interactions are taking place, such as when the last face-to-face meeting was.

Activities don't just have to be created manually and are often automatically created through workflows and other customization options set on specific actions being taken within a system. This gives the capability for dashboards of tasks and phone calls for the week to be created and to be visible as soon as a user logs into the system. While this seems like basic functionality, by using this feature, an organization gains access to the following information:

- Interaction with the customers (visible on the rollup from Contact to Account records)

- Length of support given to customers

- Appointments and meetings taking place

- Email engagement and conversations with customers

- Missed opportunities (where activities are *not* taking place)

- Scheduled workload (by using the duration of all planned activities)

This information is not only easily obtainable from activities but is also what is used in the latest "Relationship Assistant" functionality in Dynamics 365 CE. Relationship Assistant gives the user informed recommendations about their next best action based on real activity data.

Relationship Assistant can be selected within the navigation bar in Dynamics 365 via the lightbulb icon (Figure 2-24). When clicked, it displays action cards that give recommendations based on those activities within the system. It would suggest if you have not contacted somebody for a while, upcoming appointments, and even actions based on email messages that have not been responded to.

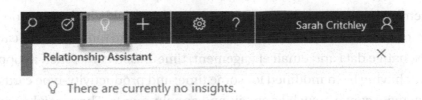

Figure 2-24. *Relationship Assistant button on the navigation within Dynamics 365 CE*

Relationship Assistant can also be added as a form component so as to be seen by users as soon as they open a record. This is configured as standard on the Opportunity form, as seen in Figure 2-25.

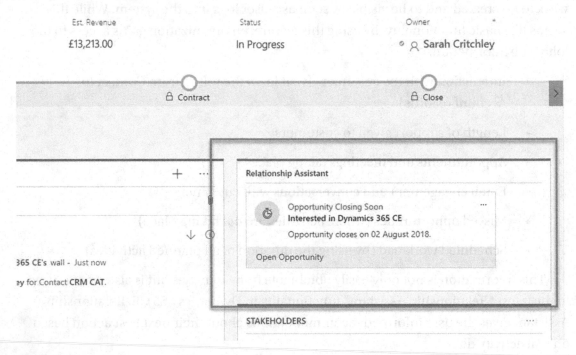

Figure 2-25. *An example of a card generated by the Relationship Assistant*

The Relationship Assistant can be used from the icon on the header, from within dashboards, and as embedded into forms. There is a variety of cards available, with the main being "base cards." These often refer to upcoming activities that are due today or appear when things have been missed (e.g., activities past their due date with no action taken on them). These cards are the only type of cards available in the Relationship Assistant for on-premises Dynamics CE customers. There are more-tailored cards that use email exchange data and email engagement; time-based cards, such as opportunity closing or not having been modified for some time; and productivity-type cards based on specific activity content, such as emails and appointments. These can be configured via the Options icon on a card itself or within the personal options of a user under the General tab. Click "Manage personal relationship assistant settings" to configure, as shown in Figure 2-26.

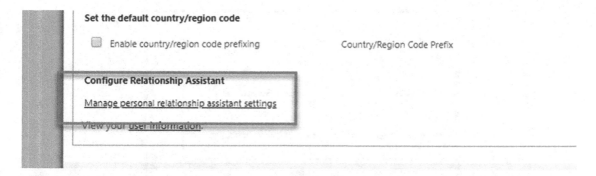

Figure 2-26. *Managing Relationship Assistant settings*

Taking full advantage of activities and using them within Outlook and Dynamics 365 CE also allows the Relationship Assistant feature to give a more-tailored experience to users. It gives them next-best-action recommendations on specific records with the aim to remind them and allow them to be more productive.

Activities are also used within out-of-the-box features, such as closing opportunities and cases (e.g., an "Opportunity Closing" record). These activities are created when a user attempts to close a record, such as an Opportunity. If activities are still in an "open" state, the closure activity won't be able to be applied. If an activity is in an open state, it normally means it is scheduled for the future or has not been completed; hence, the system assumes there is still some action to do. This would normally generate a warning to notify the user that the record cannot be closed until all activities are completed. The Case entity has a similar feature and also has notable functionality related to its "Total Time" field. Upon case resolution, the "Duration" field is rolled up on all associated activities (as this comes from the Activity Pointer), displaying this within the "Total Time" field, as seen in Figure 2-27, and then copying it to the "Billable Time" field – but leaving this editable. This field is also especially important for entitlements, where they are configured to decrement on minutes.

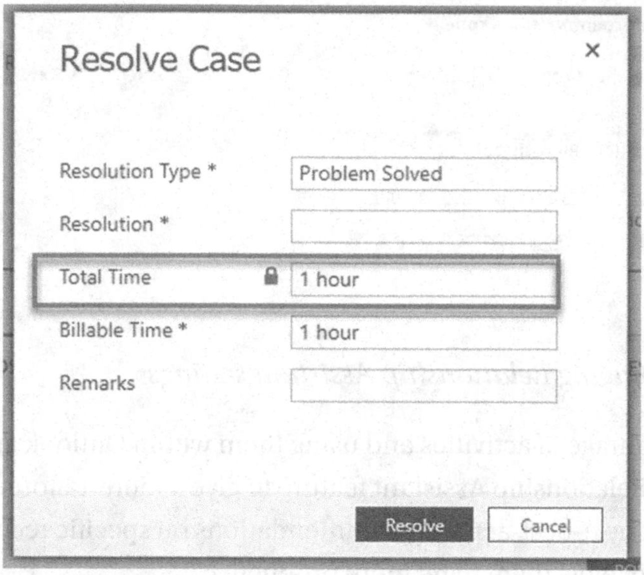

Figure 2-27. *Case Resolution form with the rollup of associated activities from their "Duration" field*

The Timeline

The timeline was introduced in the latest version, at the time of writing, of Dynamics 365 (9.0) and displayed a combination of all activities and notes within a single view. It replaces the old Activities tab, where activities, posts, and notes were all in separate tabs that a user had to select to view. The timeline feature allows a user to perform filtering and sorting to find anything specific they are looking for within that single view. It also provides notifications, such as new activities or activities that are overdue, straight away to users as they load the form.

The timeline can be found on standard records at the center of the screen, highlighted in Figure 2-28. It forms a central space for activities to be used and communication to be easily visible to give a clear view of what the latest information is regarding this record.

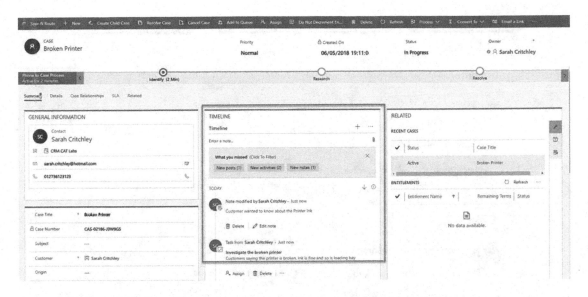

Figure 2-28. *Timeline form component displays activities, posts, and notes in a single view*

The timeline has the capability to track the new activities the user has not seen and flag them to the user when they load a record, as seen in Figure 2-29.

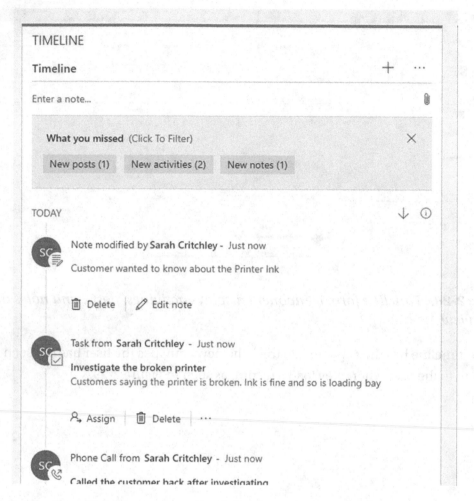

Figure 2-29. *Timeline form component displaying items missed*

As the timeline can potentially have a lot of information within a small area of the form, there are a lot of configuration options to ensure this is set up to get the best out of the functionality of each record type. This is especially important to allow activities to be used easily.

In the Activities tab, there are a number of customization options:

- Display all activities within the system or select specific activities to display. (Note: As is standard, this means *display only,* not necessarily create.)

- Sort fields to sort the timeline. Note that these are only fields on the Activity Pointer record, not specific record types (so you cannot filter on "Call To," e.g., but you *can* filter on "Sort Date" because this is an Activity Pointer field).

- How the fields are displayed on the form, including creating activities using Quick Create or main forms.

One special point to make is the sorting of the timeline. Dynamics 365 CE provides a field called "Sort Date" on the Activity Pointer entity. This field is blank by default until it is populated by custom business logic, for example, automation can be used to sort on the timeline in ascending or descending order. The feature of this field is that it can be populated based on the information specifically related to the requirement or business. A phone call sort order can be one date and an email another. But that date would be held within the same field name, providing a user with the ability to see those activities sorted within the timeline and sorted in a single space, despite their being different record types.

Filtering is achieved by clicking the action menu button within the timeline and selecting "Open Filter Pane." This opens the filter options, which allow you to sort by record type, status, and date. Especially useful is the ability to see the number of activities as an aggregate and see the activities immediately in an open state, as this would also indicate they have a pending action, as seen in Figure 2-30.

Figure 2-30. *Timeline filter*

Summary

This chapter has covered the core introduction of Dynamics 365 CE with accounts, contacts, activities, and timeline management. In addition to that, it introduces the Microsoft Outlook Integration capabilities and options. These areas are fundamental to understanding how to utilize some of the key features within the platform. Accounts, contacts, and activities are used in almost every record, especially standard out-of-the-box record types. This chapter covered getting started with the timeline and the configuration options available so that readers can set up the timeline as is best suited for the record types in question.

Chapter Tasks

1. Review the account and contact relationship by creating new records and associating contacts with the account.

2. Create a hierarchy of a parent account with child account records and view them within the hierarchy.

3. Create an activity within a Contact record of type Email, Phone Call, Appointment, and Task.

4. Check the activity rollup feature from a child account to a parent account.

5. Set up the Dynamics 365 App for Outlook by following the walk-through within this chapter.

6. Create activities that are due soon so that they appear within the Relationship Assistant. See them within the Relationship Assistant and become familiar with the cards.

7. Close an Opportunity record (by clicking "Close as Won") and see the activity within the timeline called Opportunity Close.

8. Review the timeline and perform filters and sorting.

Further Reading

Dynamics 365 CE Outlook Integration Versioning and Information (Microsoft, 2018). URL: https://docs.microsoft.com/en-us/dynamics365/customer-engagement/outlook-app/v8/deploy-dynamics-365-app-for-outlook

Dynamics 365 CE Outlook Integration Frequency Information (Microsoft, 2018). URL: https://docs.microsoft.com/en-us/dynamics365/customer-engagement/admin/server-side-synchronization#server-side-synchronization-frequency

Dynamics 365 CE Outlook Supported Apps (Microsoft, 2018). URL: https://docs.microsoft.com/en-us/dynamics365/customer-engagement/outlook-app/v8/deploy-dynamics-365-app-for-outlook#supported-operating-systems-for-outlook-on-the-desktop

CHAPTER 3

Customer Service

Dynamics 365 CE includes a Customer Service app that has a range of functionality designed to give you the core capability to deliver an omni-channel customer service experience. Omni-channel experiences have progressed from the ability to simply deliver multichannel experiences, which allow organizations to deliver their messages across more than one channel, such as social media and their website. Omni-channel customer service allows organizations to retain the context of the customer's inquiry when a customer switches channel and gives the capability to be able to transfer that from one channel to another seamlessly.

An example of an omni-channel customer service experience would be an individual tweeting the organization about a defective product. This tweet automatically creates a case within Dynamics 365 CE, as it was picked up by the keyword search and negative sentiment rule within Microsoft Social Engagement. The customer's details and history are available because the social profile is synchronized with Dynamics 365 CE. The case is automatically put in the account manager's queue, and they tweet back, suggesting moving the conversation to private message so they can discuss more personal information. A private link is given so as to transition easily. The account manager organizes a phone call, as it would be easier to resolve the issue and have a conversation. The conversation ends, and the account manager logs it against the account. An email is then sent out to confirm the resolution. A response is received, and the account manager closes the case.

There are many examples like this one: the ability to transition between different channels within a single inquiry is something that is required of customer service departments within organizations. This chapter will explain how to set up the functionality provided within Dynamics 365 CE that allows departments to achieve this.

S. Critchley, *Dynamics 365 Essentials*, https://doi.org/10.1007/978-1-4842-5911-5_3

What Are Cases and How Are They Used?

At the center of any customer service management system is the ability to log the details of a customer's incident. The record that holds this information in Dynamics 365 CE is the *Case* entity. Cases can manage both support tickets and inquiry records. They are built to be generic so they can guide a user through solving a problem. Their generic nature is a core advantage: cases are a common place to see customizations within the system, tailoring them for a specific organization. This allows any industry to make minor customizations to the entity so it becomes specific to their requirements, should they need it to be.

Cases can integrate with extensions, such as CTI (computer telephony integration), service-level agreement (SLA) functionality, and entitlement contract management. The Case entity is the central record within Dynamics 365 CE that these extensions operate from, allowing self-service channels like portals and chat bots to provide an omni-channel experience that gives customers the ability to choose the channel best suited for them and allowing users within the system to use a single space to facilitate customer engagement.

Having the ability to use the context of the customer is one of the important capabilities of the Case record type as discussed in the previous section. Once a customer is associated with a case, a user can see contextual information about that customer instantly, including contact details, entitlement details and SLAs, and all the associated history for the customer. If a case is created from Twitter or another social profile using Dynamics 365 Social Engagement integration, the details of the profile would also be visible from the case record. This information is available as soon as the record is created by users, allowing them to act instantly. Service-level agreements are time-based expectations, and every second is important to be able to provide a timely resolution, so having access to information about the customer when it's needed plays a huge part in meeting those agreements between the customer and the organization.

The Lifecycle and Functionality of a Case

Cases have a lifecycle that includes expectations of the user at specific places within it. The lifecycle begins with the identification of a customer. As a customer service agent, the user needs to know who is making the query or who has the issue. The agent would learn this by searching the system to find the customer, normally based first on the name of the company they are with and then on the name of the person, using their first and last names on the filtered list from the identification of the account.

Identifying the customer and setting the fields with links to those records populates the Quick View form with core information about the customer (Figure 3-1). The Quick View form gives the user the opportunity to verify that the customer's details are correct using the extended information, or they can use the form for a quick reference without having to open the full record and navigate away from the case at hand.

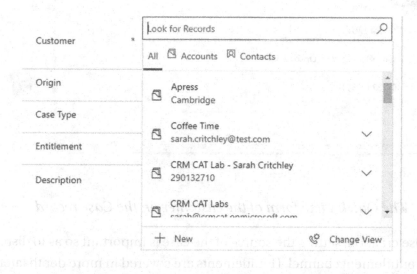

Figure 3-1. Adding an Account record within the "Customer" field

The Quick View form shows read-only information from a related record, which is the customer on the Case form, as seen in Figure 3-2. It allows the user to check information without having to navigate away from the case. Modifying Quick View forms is covered in the second section of this book.

The "Customer" field can include an Account record *or* a Contact record. It is a special type of field that allows for a dual lookup of these two types of records. As there is already a "Contact" field on the Case record (within the Details tab) and other functionality uses this as an "Account" field, it is normally best practice to use this for the Account record.

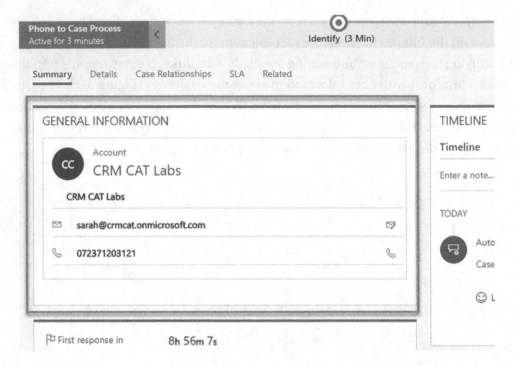

Figure 3-2. *The Quick View form of the customer on the Case record*

Upon case creation, setting the source of the case is important so as to distinguish any specific entitlement channel. (Entitlements are covered in more depth later in this chapter.) Products have a similar impact where they can be related to entitlements, so including them at case creation allows for the "Entitlement" field to be filtered by contact, origin, and product (the next chapter covers products and the product catalog in greater depth). Having these field values populated where relevant allows for the "Entitlement" field to filter on more data, reducing the number of matching records, thus helping the user make a quicker decision to associate the correct entitlement to the case.

Saving the record at this point associates these contractual details with the customer and triggers any SLAs associated with the entitlement contract, or organization as seen in Figure 3-3. The user does not need to know the details about the entitlement, because they are focusing on information related to the issue the customer is experiencing.

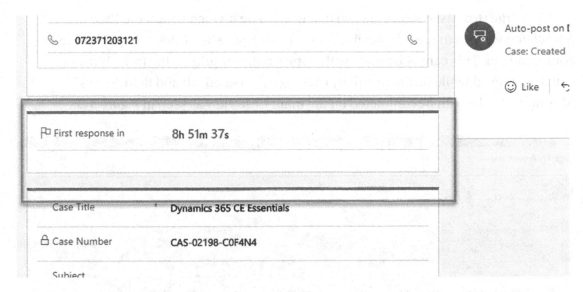

Figure 3-3. *A service-level agreement activating on the case, counting down*

Sub-grids become available after the creation of a record; in these, a user can see the existing case for the Account record selected. Related case visibility is especially important for a number of reasons, the most obvious of which is to see a case history, but there is more to it than just that. A user will also be able to use this information to see if there are any other cases open that are the same or similar and identify patterns that could indicate a different issue than the ones being reported.

If these scenarios occur, such as a duplicate case being created, there are some remedial actions the user can perform that are native functionality to Dynamics 365 CE. This includes merging the cases (the one the user just made and the duplicate). If they are not the same and instead linked, the user can create a parent/child relationship, linking the two (Figure 3-4).

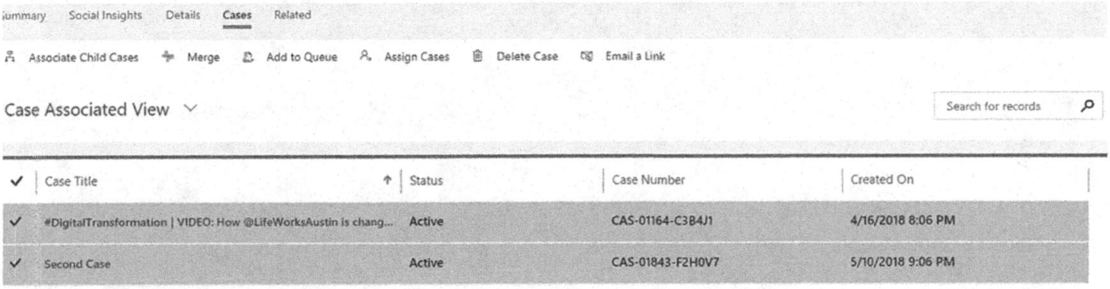

	Case Title	↑	Status		Case Number		Created On	
✓	#DigitalTransformation | VIDEO: How @LifeWorksAustin is chang...		Active		CAS-01164-C3B4J1		4/16/2018 8:06 PM	
✓	Second Case		Active		CAS-01843-F2H0V7		5/10/2018 9:06 PM	

Figure 3-4. *Selecting cases to merge them using the Merge button on the command bar*

To merge two cases, select the two that need to be merged within the Case Associated view so they are highlighted, as seen in Figure 3-4. Click "Merge" on the command bar. This cannot be done within the small sub-grid on the form, but can still be achieved while on the record by clicking the Related tab and then "Cases." Alternatively, this can be completed on the main Case view as seen in Figure 3-5.

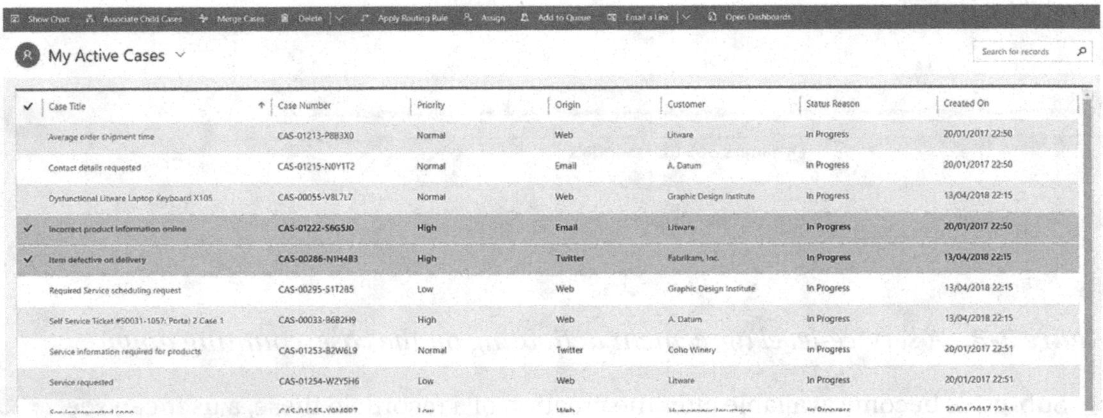

Figure 3-5. *Selecting cases to merge using the main My Active Cases view*

You can see the cases that have been merged into the current record by navigating to the Case Relationships tab on a Case record and reviewing the Merged Cases sub-grid. When a case is merged, it is not deleted; the status is simply changed, as shown in Figure 3-6, and some of the data from the merged record is then transferred to the main record.

When merging cases, Dynamics 365 CE displays a notification to choose the main case that the other case(s) will be merged into.

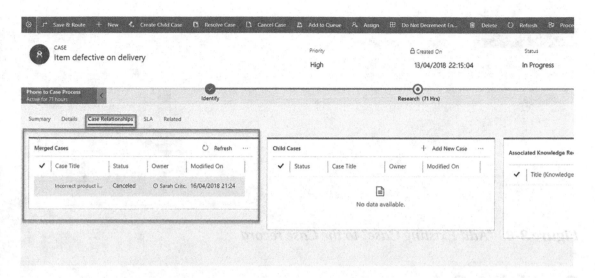

Figure 3-6. *Reviewing merged cases using the Merged Cases sub-grid*

From parent cases, users can create a new case directly from the current case. This would make the current case the parent and the new case the child. This is achieved by clicking the Create Child Case button on the Case record (Figure 3-7).

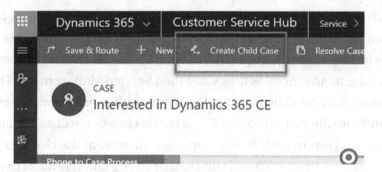

Figure 3-7. *Create Child Case button on the Case record*

If the child case is already created, you can navigate to the Case Relationships tab, go to the "Child Cases" section, click the action ("...") button, and select "Add Existing Case," choosing from the grid view (Figure 3-8). Adding a child case adds some restrictions on the case resolution of the parent case while the child case record remains open, which are highlighted in the next section.

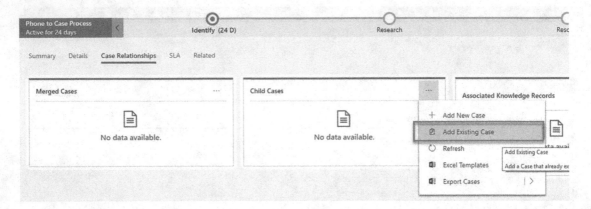

Figure 3-8. *"Add Existing Case" to the Case record*

Resolving Cases

When using the parent and child case relationship functionality, as described in the previous section, there are some key considerations in relation to case resolution. If a user attempts to resolve the parent case while any number of child cases are still open, there are three separate behaviors that Dynamics 365 CE can be configured for. If they are not configured and are left as "default," then the parent and child cases can be resolved without any conflict, and so if a parent is closed before a child, it is deemed as acceptable within the business operation. If not, these can be modified within the Classic UI. Navigate to Advanced Settings and then Service Management. There is a configuration area that allows users to configure two additional behavior settings.

You can configure the system so that if a parent is closed, it will automatically resolve all linked child cases (Figure 3-9). Another option is to prevent the closure of the parent if there are still active child cases. There is no right or wrong configuration in this instance, and both options are viable ones for organizations. Discuss the definition of what the organization would classify as a child case in the context of the services they provide and which behavior is acceptable. As a parent and child relationship naturally infers a dependency, a popular option is to apply the preventative functionality.

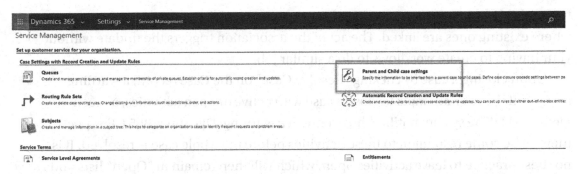

Figure 3-9. *Parent and child settings within the Classic Client under "Settings"*

Click "Parent and Child case settings," which opens a new screen. Select the attributes to move over to the child case and specify the closure preference from this screen in the available options, as seen in Figure 3-10.

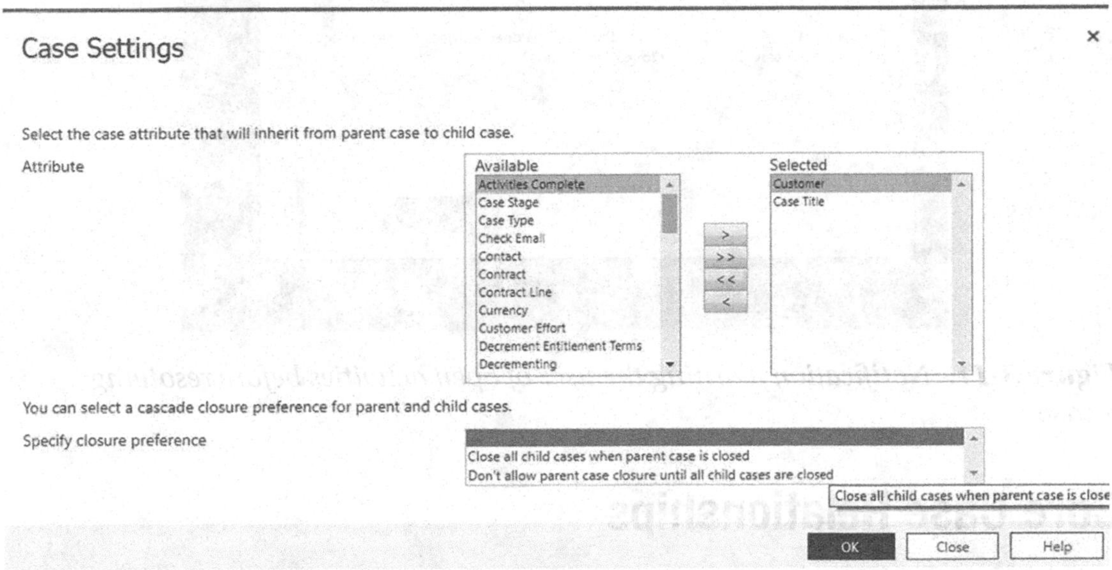

Figure 3-10. *Case settings for configuring parent/child case resolution settings*

There is also functionality when defining the parent/child relationship in order for the child to inherit specific values from the parent record. This inheriting behavior is very similar to relationship mapping, discussed in the second section of the book, where if a user creates a child record while on the record of its parent, the 1:N mapping allows certain fields to be auto-populated. However, this is normally only available for making *new* records; the case here is special. It allows a user to map attributes from the parent to the child not just for new cases made in the context of the parent record, but also even where existing ones are linked. The act of the association triggers the update without your having to create workflows to do a similar job.

Upon closing a case by clicking "Resolve Case" on the Case record, a warning appears if the user attempts to close a case with active or open activities, as seen in Figure 3-11. The system notifies the user with a warning. Dynamics 365 CE expects there to be some resolution to these activities before the whole case is resolved. It is not best practice to leave activities open, which will then remain in "Open" lists and dashboards; it often means these will be orphaned and never updated. For this reason, it's recommended to ensure all activities are closed before resolving a case.

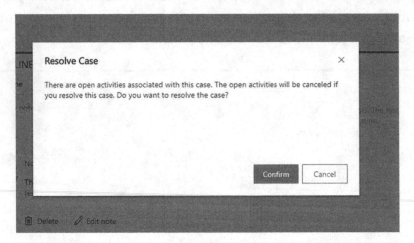

Figure 3-11. *Notification warning the user of open activities before resolving a case*

Core Case Relationships

There are a number of key relationships within a Case record that are important to be aware of. Some are only populated under certain conditions, and some have to be manually populated.

On the main Case form, the "Customer" lookup field normally refers to the account. It was discussed earlier in the chapter that you should use this as an account rather than a contact lookup, despite the option being there for both. There are also standard sub-grids on the form, such as Related Cases, which are linked to the account and not to a contact. There is also an Entitlements sub-grid displaying associated entitlements linked to the account.

A Knowledge Article sub-grid is available on the Case form. This is slightly different in how it operates compared with Related Cases and Entitlements. As opposed to being a link between other records and the case, it operates as a search tool to find articles that can assist the user in the resolution of the case, as seen in Figure 3-12.

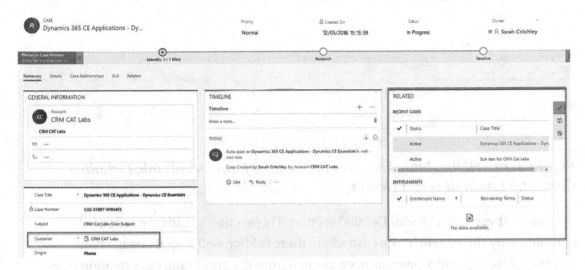

Figure 3-12. *The Related sub-grid on the Case form*

On a Case form, the Details tab includes more relationships. The "Contact" field, for example, will be filtered based on the account selected within the "Customer" field. This doesn't need to be populated; however, as cases are opened by being reported by an individual, it is normally the best practice to do so. In addition to this, Contact records have a direct relationship to the entitlements available, and by selecting this users can filter down to which entitlements are applicable in that instance.

Service-level agreements are a key relationship for cases. They can be found under the SLA tab within the Case form, as seen in Figure 3-13. This will be reviewed with entitlements and SLAs later in this chapter. The SLA tab links the SLAs that have met the activation condition(s) on the case. The most popular and standard SLA types are "First Response By" and "Resolve By." These are normally referred to as key performance indicators (KPIs) and provide deadlines for when a user must send the first response on case creation and when a case must be resolved.

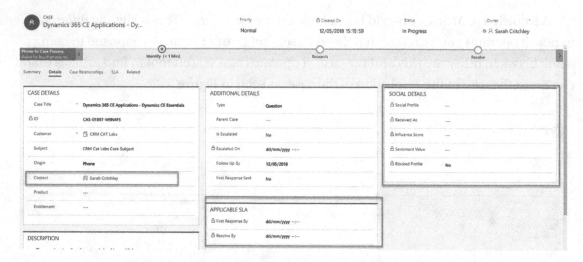

Figure 3-13. *Highlighting key areas on the Case form Details tab, including Contact, SLAs, and Social Details*

Lastly, there is the "Social Details" section. This section's fields are only ever completed by the system in the case where there is Microsoft Social Engagement integration set up and a case has been created from the automatic case creation rules within Dynamics 365, the setup of which will be covered in a later chapter. These fields are read-only and cannot be modified or manually entered, even to correct wrong information.

Phone Support, CTI, and Skype for Business

Functionality in Dynamics 365 CE that automatically detects who is calling is a common requirement in call center operations. This functionality can save a large amount of time as it reduces the time a user is searching for a record while the customer is waiting on the phone. In addition to that, it also helps customer service because it reduces overall call time and improves efficiency. Automatically detecting the contact from a phone call is often referred to as CTI – computer telephony integration.

CTI normally handles inbound and outbound calls to/from an organization, identifying the contact from the Dynamics 365 system. When the record is located, this is displayed to the user so they can begin the service call without ever needing to search. The elimination of searching is especially important as cases within Dynamics 365 can be directly linked with little or no effort. CTI is also relevant for outbound calls, where the connector provides a user interface that allows an agent to dial directly from the Contact record and gives them the ability to make a phone call without ever having to lift the phone. Dynamics 365 CE does not perform this feature as standard, and many connectors interface with Dynamics 365 CE and various phone systems.

There is also sometimes a requirement for IVR (interactive voice response) systems to be linked to the CTI functionality. IVR systems provide customers who dial a phone number a confirmation message stating whom they have called and often then give callers the opportunity to route themselves to the correct department based on their query. IVR functionality is most beneficial when it hands off to a CTI and completes the process as just described. This can often then be routed to queues and teams automatically.

Despite the requirements for CTI, Skype for Business and, more recently, Microsoft Teams are becoming popular tools for business-to-business relationships. Dynamics 365 version 9.0 provides the capability for seamless Skype for Business integration, giving users the ability for increased productivity without any setup or cost associated with it, provided the correct Office 365 version is in use. This was available in previous versions; however, now users can see the status straight from the record that the user is displayed in, that is, mainly "owner"-type fields. Hovering over the "Owner" field, for example, brings up their IM and call details so they can single-click IM or Call directly from Dynamics 365, opening Skype for Business from within the context of that user (Figure 3-14).

Even if an organization is not using any IVR or CTI, by navigating to the Case view, a user can click the Phone Support button instead of New, which automatically creates a new case and opens a blank Phone Call activity. While this seems a minor step compared to the functionality just described, it is great practice to allow users to utilize the activity communication that Dynamics 365 CE provides.

Figure 3-14. *Hovering over the "User" field displays the IM detail from Skype for Business*

Clicking the IM opens Skype for Business, allowing a call to be created and connected without having to dial a number, as seen in Figure 3-15.

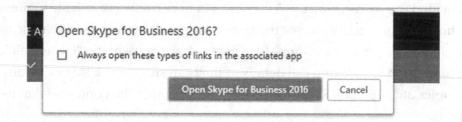

Figure 3-15. *Clicking the IM allows for Skype for Business to be directly opened from Dynamics 365 CE*

Unified Service Desk

The Unified Service Desk (USD) is a client application installed on users' machines, normally in a call center environment or where there is a large number of users. It is designed to offer a single unified interface for users to be able to access contact information quickly, often integrating with CTI solutions; it provides script capability for users to follow scripts dynamically with customers based on the user's need. The USD can be configured so that data from within the full Dynamics 365 CE environment can be aggregated and visible as a high-level overview for the contact desktop application.

It is designed to reduce load time of records and is specifically configurable to ensure organizations get the most out of and focus specifically on the customer experience.

USD utilizes the UII, Unified Interface Integration, which is a modular framework that allows these customizations to take place, often with limited code, and provides a faster to-business scenario. It ships with adapters and has the ability to connect with other applications and host the CTI framework. USD is on its own release cycle compared to the Dynamics 365 CE main application. It links with modern, omni-channel forms of communication and does an excellent job of holding context between them, such as starting from a web chat and moving easily into a phone call. Context transfer is engineered to allow call center agents to access the right data for the right call, handle multiple sessions, retain that context, and reduce the work required before and after a call, often handled with CTI and transcribing of calls.

This book does not cover functionality concerning Unified Service Desk; it is highlighted here as an available option for customer service and specifically high-volume call center scenarios. There is a great deal of information available from Microsoft and the Dynamics 365 community on getting started with USD, which can be found within the "Further Reading" section at the end of this chapter.

Queues and Routing

Dynamics 365 CE has long had queues as an integral part of service management functionality. Queues allow any record type, configured for queues, to be placed within a queue of items to be acted on by a user. There are some record types configured for queues as standard, such as Cases. Custom entities can be enabled for queues within the entity definition, described in the second section of this book. Any record type enabled for queues has the Add to Queue command bar button available. This can be operated manually or can be used within a workflow. Adding the item to a queue creates a queue item, which logs which queue it is in, who is working on it, and the time at which it entered the queue.

Users can navigate to queues by selecting them from the Customer Service Hub app. Once selected, "All queues you're a member of" will be the default queue selected. This view is a combination of all the items within all available queues you as a user are a member of. Users can filter and change that by selecting a different view. Queues have different views, for example, "Items available to work on" and "Items working on" within the same queue. Users can change the queue and have the same set of views available with which to change and filter the records, just like within other areas of the system.

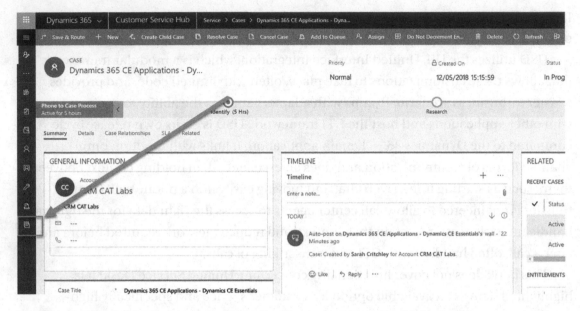

Figure 3-16. *Selecting queues from the Customer Service Hub sitemap*

Click the Queue button within the sitemap in the Customer Service Hub app, as shown in Figure 3-16. Select the different queues using the dropdown list that looks like an option set, and select the views by clicking the view name, as seen in Figure 3-17.

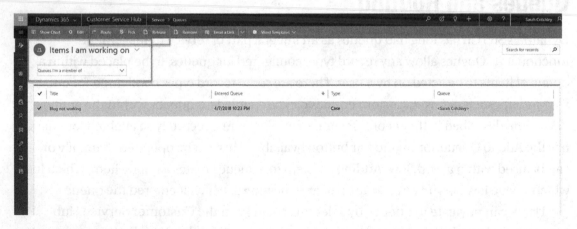

Figure 3-17. *Selecting the queue, view, route, pick, and release from the command bar*

The benefit of queues is that a user would be able to be part of a queue that is normally available to other users and can pick items from that shared list of "to-do" items. The action of "picking" logs who is working on that item, having picked it.

Queues are especially important for customer service scenarios. An item may not be completed within a single queue from start to finish. Instead, it could be routed from one queue to another either manually or automatically based on the data contained in the item. Queues are often used in escalation scenarios and when support teams escalate between the different support levels. Queues are designed to be able to move between teams seamlessly, using routing rules where possible.

Queues are created automatically for users and teams when the user or team record is created. They can also be created on their own and set as public or private depending on if an organization wishes to keep those queues open or only for a specific set of users. Queues created automatically are shown with "<" and ">" characters.

You can manually add to a queue by clicking "Add to Queue," as shown in Figure 3-18.

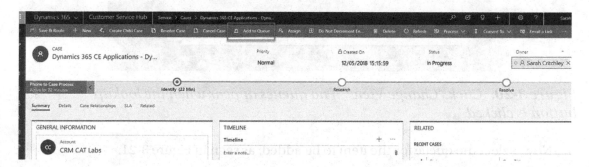

Figure 3-18. *Clicking "Add to Queue" from within a Case record*

Then, select from the available queues, as seen in Figure 3-19.

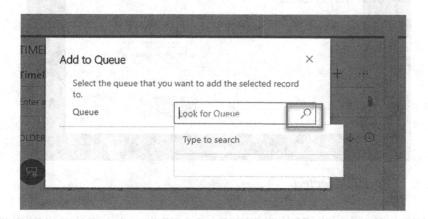

Figure 3-19. *The notification after clicking "Add to Queue"; a user must select the queue to add the record to*

To add a record to a queue (and create the link to a queue from the record – the queue item), click "Add to Queue" from the Case record (or other entity record activated for queues).

Select the queue from the lookup. Click "Change View" if required and select a different view where a user will be able to see queues, as shown in Figure 3-20.

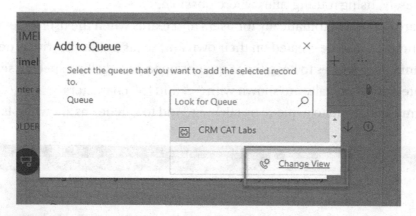

Figure 3-20. *Click "Change View" if no queues appear when the lookup button is clicked*

Now, select the queue for the item to be added, as seen in Figure 3-21.

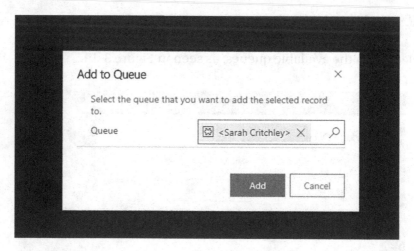

Figure 3-21. *A queue selected*

In a queue, you can click the Pick button. This function allows you to notify the queue that you are working on the item; this will populate the "Worked By" field within the queue item with your user record.

The Unified Interface, at the time of writing, does not display the queue item's detail; instead, this can be visible from the Classic UI. Navigate to a record in a queue (e.g., a case) and click "Queue Item Details," which will open a new window (Figure 3-22). Here, the queue item's detail is visible. The Queue Item record displays which record the item is related to as well as the field "Worked By," which is populated automatically when a user clicks "Pick." A significant amount of reporting can be achieved from this queue item detail, such as workload of teams, backlogs, or items not being worked on.

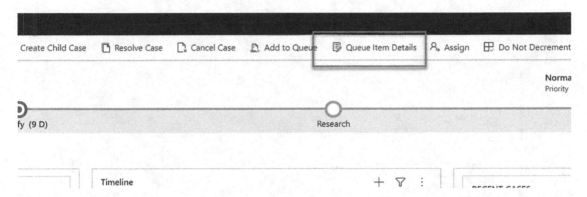

Figure 3-22. *In the Unified Interface, click "Queue Item Details" to open further information about the Queue record*

More details are available on the queue item, such as when the item entered the queue and when it was last modified; this is also useful information for reporting, seen in Figure 3-23.

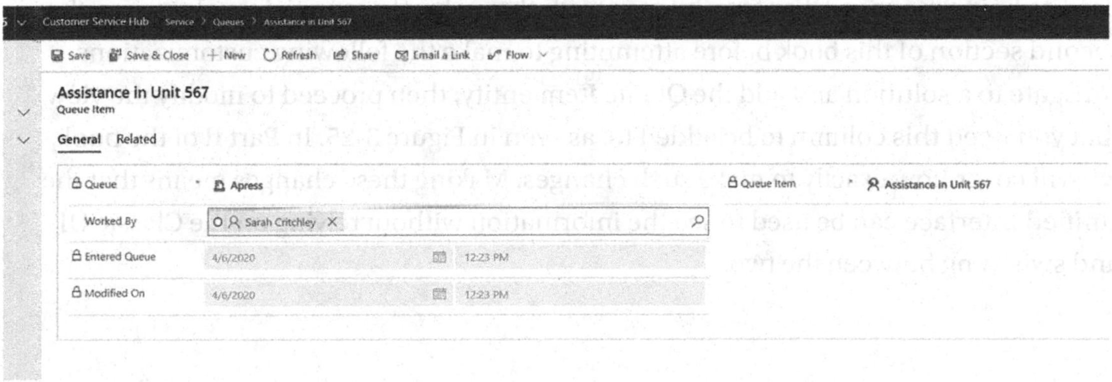

Figure 3-23. *Queue item record*

The queue itself can be viewed in the Unified Interface by clicking the queue name or by navigating to Queues on the sitemap. This view displays all the current queue items within that queue and who is working on them under the "Worked By" column (Figure 3-24).

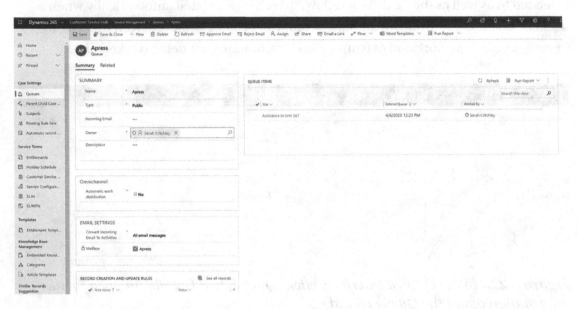

Figure 3-24. *Queue Item sub-grid within a Queue record displaying all the queue items within it*

The queue item views don't display the "Working On" attribute nor other important critical information that may be useful for reporting. They can be modified though, despite being managed. For step-by-step walk-throughs of customizing, please see the second section of this book before attempting to make the following customizations. Navigate to a solution and add the Queue Item entity; then proceed to modify the view that you need this column to be added to, as seen in Figure 3-25. In Part II of the book, we will cover how exactly to make such changes. Making these changes means that the Unified Interface can be used to see the information without relying on the Classic UI and switching between the two.

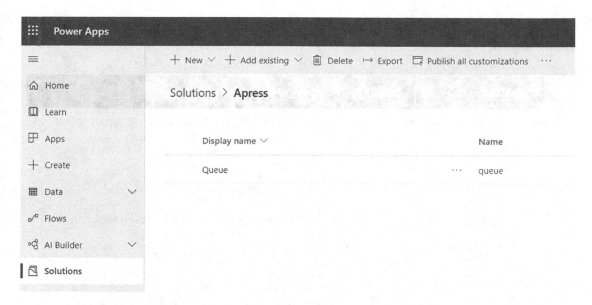

Figure 3-25. *Put the queue in a solution to see the view of the queues to add further information for users*

Creating and Configuring Queues

The configuration and creation of queues must be completed using the Classic UI, at the time of writing (Figure 3-26); however, this service management configuration is expected to be possible within the Customer Service Hub app coming in the October 2018 release of Dynamics 365 CE.

Task: Create a new queue.

Navigate to Settings (or Service Management for the Unified Interface) ➤ Queues.

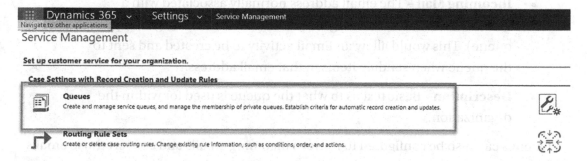

Figure 3-26. *Click "Queues" from the Classic UI to begin creating a new queue or modify existing ones*

Click "New" to create a new blank queue (Figure 3-27). This opens a new empty Queue record.

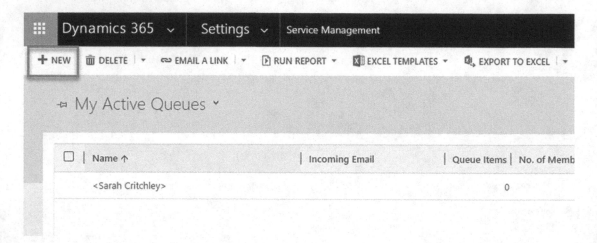

Figure 3-27. *Click the New button to create a new queue*

There are several configuration options available, as displayed in Figure 3-28. Let's review those options and what they mean:

- **Name –** The name of the queue.

- **Type –** Queues can be public or private. Public queues can be visible to all users. Private queues need to be added via the Customer Service Manager, System Customizer, or System Administrator roles, and members must be added to them to be able to see the queue and the queue items.

- **Incoming Mail –** The email address normally associated with a shared mailbox that is managed by a number of users (e.g., a support queue). This would allow an Email activity to be created and sent to the queue when sending items to that email address.

- **Description –** Basic text as to what the queue is used for within the organization.

Queues can also be configured to retrieve incoming emails and convert those emails to Email activities. Queues are set up with an email address that a customer can email and, based on the email settings within the queue, convert those received emails into Email activities and add them to the queue.

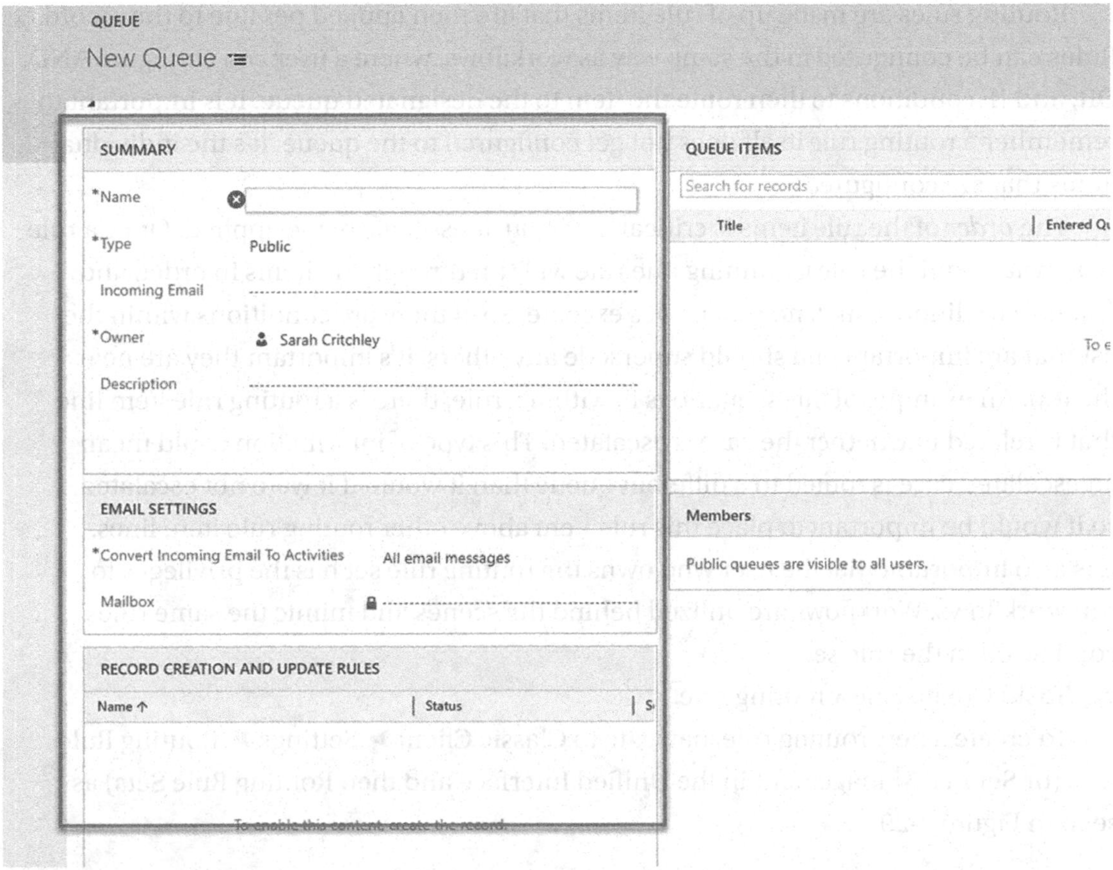

Figure 3-28. *Configurable queue options*

The "Record Creation and Update Rules" section allows for records to be automatically created and routed to specific queues. Records can be configured to be automatically routed to a queue after completing their creation/update logic. These will be discussed later in the chapter.

Routing Rules

Routing rules can be configured to allow cases to be routed automatically and dynamically based on the data within the record. Records that are created automatically get the rules applied to them automatically. They can also be manually applied to cases by clicking the Save & Route button. This functionality is also critical for those scenarios where items are passing between teams and queues.

Routing rules are made up of rule items that are then applied per line to the record. Rules can be configured in the same way as workflows, where a user can configure AND, OR, and IF conditions to then route the item to the designated queue. It is important to remember a routing rule itself does not get configured to the queue; it's the individual items that are configured.

The *order* of the rule items is critical to the business logic being applied. Once a rule is activated and the rule is running, the rule will run through the items in order, and when a condition is met, no other rules execute. So, if there are conditions within the list that are important and should supersede any others, it's important they are near the top. An example of this scenario is if, within a rule, there is a routing rule item line that is related to whether the case is escalated. This type of information could mean an escalated case is routed to a different queue than it would if it were not escalated, so it would be important to place this rule item above other routing rule item lines. It is also important that the user who owns the routing rule set has the privileges to run workflows. Workflows are utilized behind the scenes and mimic the same rules configured in the rule set.

Task: Create a new routing rule.

To create a new routing rule, navigate to Classic Client ➤ Settings ➤ Routing Rule Sets (or Service Management in the Unified Interface and then Routing Rule Sets) as seen in Figure 3-29.

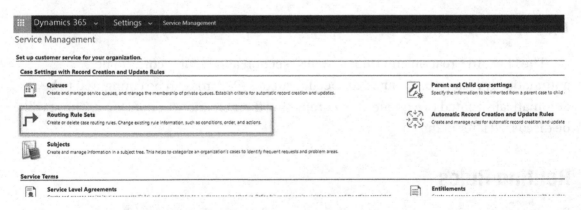

Figure 3-29. *Click "Routing Rule Sets" from the Classic UI*

Create a new rule item by entering text in the "Name" field; then save the record. Click the plus icon within the sub-grid, as seen in Figure 3-30, to begin creating rule items. Examples of rule items can be where subjects are specific or can indicate the products they are relevant for.

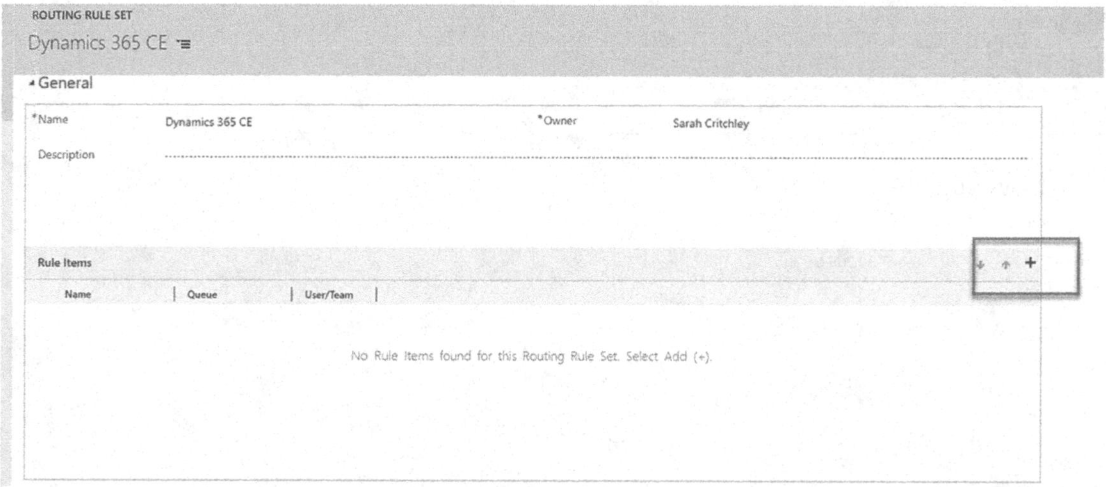

Figure 3-30. *Create a new Routing Rule Set record and click the "+" icon on the Rule Item sub-grid to create a new item*

Configuring a Rule Item

Upon clicking the plus icon from the sub-grid within a Routing Rule Set record, seen in Figure 3-30, a new window will open, which is an empty rule item (Figure 3-31). Enter a name and a description. Within the "Rule Criteria" section, define a simple rule item line by selecting a case as the entity type and the "Subject" as the field. This must equal a specific subject, such as the default subject, for example, purposes.

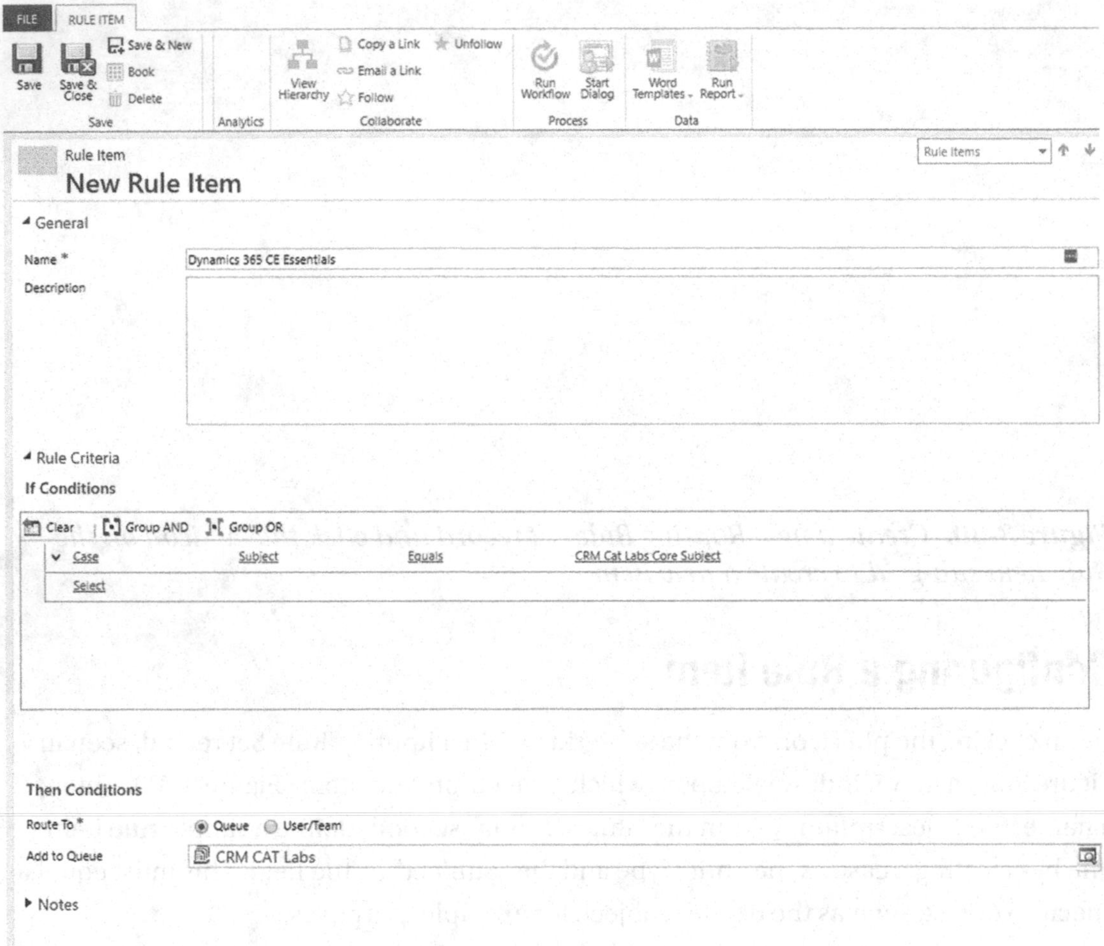

Figure 3-31. *Create a new rule item and rule criteria*

Save the rule item and activate the rule set, by clicking "Activate" on the command bar, as seen in Figure 3-32.

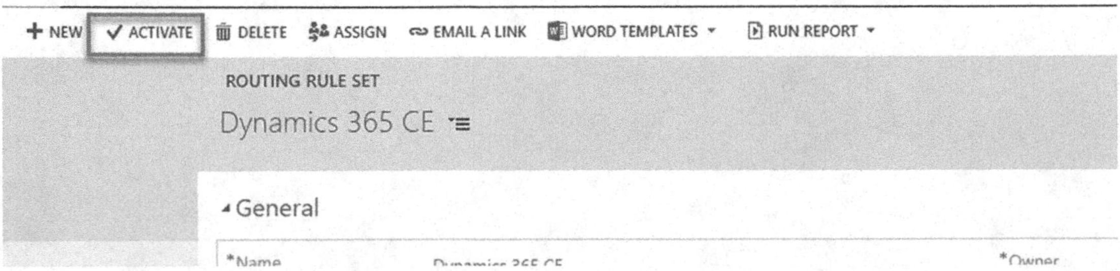

Figure 3-32. *Activating a routing rule set*

Once selected, a warning will appear that only one rule set can be activated at any one time, which can be seen in Figure 3-33. This is why it is really important to include all relevant items within the same rule set as individual rule items.

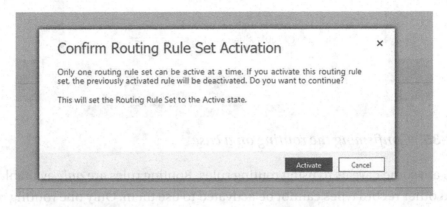

Figure 3-33. *Click "Activate" to begin using the routing rule set*

Click the Activate button on the warning message to deactivate any currently active rule sets and activate the one just created.

From now on, any cases automatically created within Dynamics 365 CE will have this routing rule set applied to them. For cases created manually, you have the option to save the case and click "Route" or to click "Save & Route," as seen in Figure 3-34.

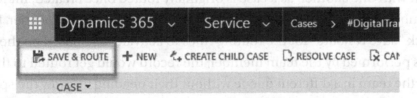

Figure 3-34. *Clicking "Save & Route" on a Case record*

When using the "Save & Route" button, you will need to click "Route" on the notification to confirm the routing rule set to be applied when a case is manually routed (Figure 3-35).

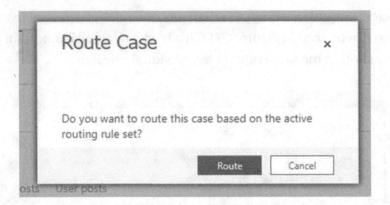

Figure 3-35. *Confirming the routing on a case*

There are some caveats to using routing rules. Routing rules are *only* available for cases, and other record types cannot be activated to use them. Only one routing rule set can be applied per organization, further adding to why the rules need to be applied within a single routing set.

Using Queues and Routing Rules to Manage Workloads

Queues and routing sets can be used to manage cases effectively and efficiently as they are owned and actioned by different members of the team. They can be used in conjunction with one another, as a case is originally routed once created, managed by a team member, and then needs to be handed over to another team member. Users need to click "Save & Route" for the routing rules to activate, and based on the data and the updates performed by the team member, the record would get routed to the next member of the team in a different queue without their needing to know the specific rules or teams they need to go to. This can then continue until the case is resolved, cutting down wait time resulting from members having to use dashboards or rely on automatic emails.

Now that you know what queues are and how to create new queues and routing rules, use this chapter to review the following items:

- Review your queues created automatically from users and teams – are they being used?

- Are any new queues required? Do you have any escalation processes?

- Have you trained your users how to use queues?

- Do you require any specific routing rules and conditions to be included to make use of escalation functionality?

Figures 3-36 and 3-37 display a suggested process for using queues and a routing rule set and how they can be used automatically and manually and be routed through multiple users.

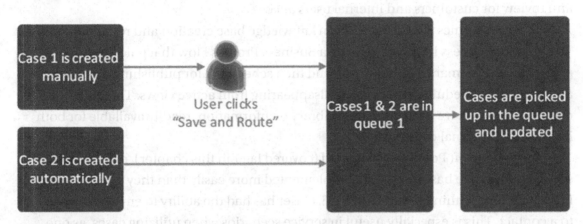

Figure 3-36. *A suggested implementation of queues and a routing rule set (part 1)*

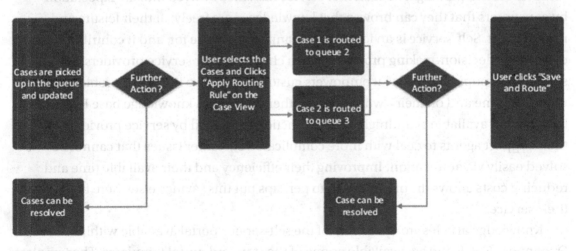

Figure 3-37. *A suggested implementation of queues and a routing rule set (part 2)*

Knowledge Base Implementation and Feedback

As part of the core customer service functionality, the *knowledge base* provides the ability for users of Dynamics 365 to create, store, and revise articles of information. That information can be anything from details about the service the organization provides and the products they create to internal training and how to use the system – the list is endless. This information is and should be readily available for consumption, feedback, and review for customers and internal users alike.

Within Dynamics 365 CE is a built-in knowledge base creation and revision process. The creation process is managed using a Business Process Flow that guides a user to create the article, mark it for approval, and then schedule it for publishing automatically, automatically scheduling it for expiry, disappearing from active views. This allows organizations to have a self-managing library of information, readily available for both internal and external consumption.

Since Microsoft Portals was released (covered later in this chapter), external self-service knowledge bases have been implemented more easily than they were previously. For a long time within Dynamics 365 CE, a user has had the ability to email an article to a contact. This is especially useful in service scenarios when utilizing cases, as one can find a useful article and email the contact a copy embedded within the email itself. The self-service paradigm of customer service has since evolved into an expectation by consumers that they can browse that knowledge more freely, at their leisure and requirement. Self-service is an ideal that organizations strive for, and it contributes to customers' decision-making processes when choosing their service providers. Self-service is so popular because it empowers customers to solve their own problems in their own time and on their own terms, whether that is via a knowledge base FAQ or a live chat bot available at midnight. These functions provided by service providers allow their support agents to deal with more complicated customer issues that cannot be solved easily via automation. Improving their efficiency and their available time and reducing costs allows the organization to perhaps put this savings elsewhere to improve their service.

Knowledge articles are at the core of the self-service portal available within Dynamics 365 CE and are available as one of the standard portal templates. The template allows articles to be visible externally, whether a user is authenticated or not. Articles can be highlighted as being external or internal, allowing an organization to configure which records appear on the portal for customers and which remain internal to the business.

With the recent releases of Dynamics 365 CE, it is essential to know there are currently two different types of knowledge articles within the system. It is not known how long they will remain visible within the platform before they are removed. *Articles* are the legacy type of knowledge base articles, with the entity name called *kbarticle*. The latest, updated version with improved functionality are called *knowledge articles*, with the entity name *knowledgearticle*. Knowledge articles are the only one in the latest UI, which is an effective way to differentiate the two. While knowledge articles can be viewed within the Classic UI (Figure 3-38), they are not editable, and the formatting is not correct, as they were not designed to be viewed using the Classic UI.

Figure 3-38. *Both types of articles visible within the Classic Client sitemap*

Knowledge articles have more enhanced functionality (Figure 3-39). This functionality includes a rich text editor and a familiar way to create content – one that is not defined on templates as it was previously. HTML can be used to create more visual content. In addition to that, users can preview the article on different form factors, allowing them to see how the article will look on the Web, in different dimensions, and on mobile. Customers are often using their phones to achieve their day-to-day activities and interact with their service providers. This often replaces desktop PCs while on the go, especially with data connectivity widely available for 4G and 3G networks. This is why it is so important for organizations to consider the mobile consumption of material. This book will look at mobile more in depth in a later chapter.

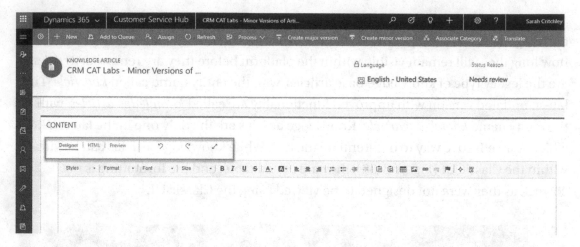

Figure 3-39. *The rich text editor, HTML, and preview capabilities of the new knowledge article*

Knowledge Article Lifecycle

Like cases, the knowledge article lifecycle is straightforward because it is guided through the process using a Business Process Flow. Business Process Flows give the user the ability to run through a process while being reminded of certain data to be entered at a specific point within the lifecycle (Figure 3-40). The fields within a stage are not visible until a user clicks the target icon for that stage. The user can keep the stage docked in a panel on the right-hand side of their screen by clicking the "pop-out" icon to keep the fields displayed. This can help with navigating records that utilize Business Process Flows.

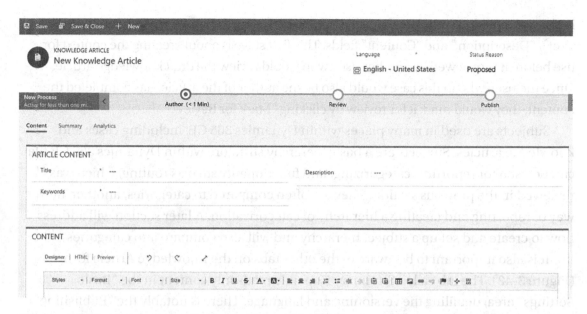

Figure 3-40. *A new knowledge article with the Business Process Flow stage minimized*

Figure 3-41 shows the "pop-out" icon available on a Business Process Flow stage.

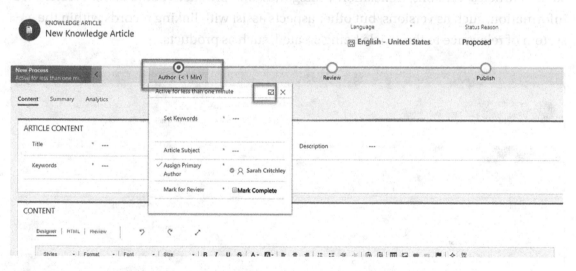

Figure 3-41. *The Business Process Flow fields visible on the stage and the "dock" button highlighted to dock the fields*

In the first stage of the Business Process Flow for a new knowledge article, a user is prompted to complete the keywords for the article. These keywords are the words a different user would search for when looking for a relevant article for their needs. The article creator is also prompted to complete the "Title," "Subject" (using the subject hierarchy, covered later), "Description," and "Content" fields. This first stage is about creating the context for use before it is reviewed by another user, who would review the draft knowledge article. Once the user, who in this case would also be the author of the article, has completed the content, they would mark it for review by clicking "Mark for Review."

Subjects are used in many places within Dynamics 365 CE, including cases and knowledge articles. Subjects are a basic hierarchy structure within Dynamics 365 CE that can be used for reporting, categorizing, and functionality such as routing, which was reviewed in the previous section. They are often compared to categories, another, newer way of reporting and creating a hierarchy of categorization. A later section will address how to create and set up a subject hierarchy and will also compare it to categories.

It is also important to be aware of the other tabs on the Knowledge Article form (Figure 3-42). The tab called Summary is mainly read-only content in the "Basic Settings" area, detailing the versioning and language. There is notably the "Publishing" area, which can be modified; however, this is completed near the end of the knowledge article creation lifecycle within the Business Process Flow. On the right-hand side of the form, there is a "Related Information" section. This area also manages related items, such as articles, versions, translations, categories, and products. Some of this is reference information, such as versions, but other aspects assist with linking records within the system of relevance to the article being created, such as products.

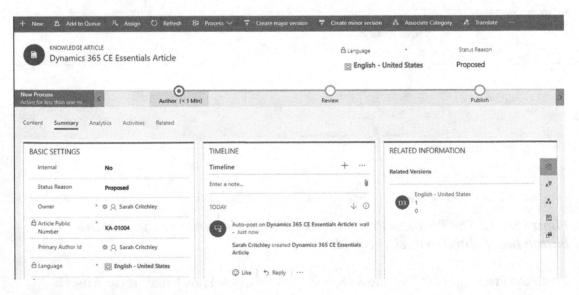

Figure 3-42. *Knowledge article Summary tab displaying "Basic Settings" and "Related Information" areas*

The third tab, Analytics, includes three sections, as seen in Figure 3-43. The first is a section that manages the views of the article. When a user or a portal user views the article, this is logged, and metrics can be seen in this area. The second section displays feedback for the article, managing where a user has scored the article and left feedback, aggregating the scores to an overall number. Lastly, where a case has utilized the article and linked it to the case, it is visible within the "Case" area, so a knowledge article manager can easily see the most used articles.

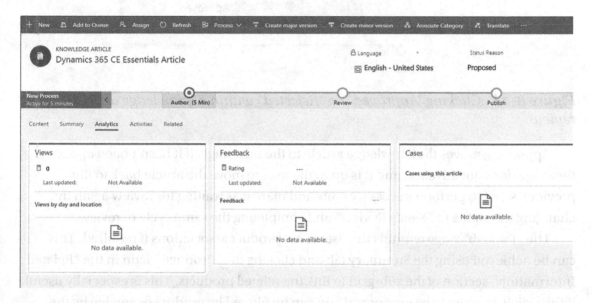

Figure 3-43. *Knowledge article Analytics tab*

Once the "Author" stage of the Business Process Flow has been completed and marked for review, the next step for the user would be to click "Add to Queue," adding it to a knowledge manager's (named user's) queue, before clicking "Next Stage" for the "Review" stage, knowing that it is within a queue to be reviewed as part of the internal organizational process. Knowledge articles are another record type configured for queues as standard, so no customization is needed. This queue can be for users who have the Knowledge Article Manager or Reviewer role, where they review the article or use the standard Knowledge Manager dashboard, identified with the "Needs Review" status and stream. Once the article has been reviewed, the reviewer clicks "Approved" or "Rejected" in the next stage of the Business Process Flow, as seen in Figure 3-44. This action updates the status of the record to either "Approved" or "Rejected" automatically. A user also can click "Approve" from the command bar to perform the same functionality.

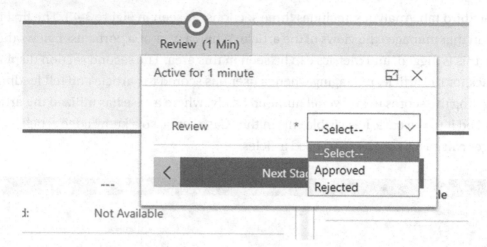

Figure 3-44. *Clicking "Approved" or "Rejected" within a knowledge article review*

Approving moves the knowledge article to the next stage. If it hasn't been approved, the stage does not advance, and it is up to the user to move the article back to the previous stage to perform necessary edits and mark it as waiting for review again by changing the status to "Needs Review" and completing the same cycle of review.

The "Publish" stage reminds the user to set product associations if required. This can be achieved using the Summary tab and clicking the "Products" icon in the "Related Information" section of the sub-grid to link the related products. This is especially useful if the article is going to be on a portal and can be filtered by product or service by the user. Once completed, or if not required, check the box and then set the expiration date for the article, as seen in Figure 3-45. The article will automatically expire once this date is reached, and no user interaction is required. It's a clear process where a user writes content, reviews it, publishes it, and uses the standard knowledge dashboards to manage expiring articles and update them.

Figure 3-45. *Setting the expiration of an article*

Now that the Business Process Flow is completed, the user needs to publish the article (finishing the Business Process Flow doesn't automatically publish it). This can be done by clicking "Publish" on the command bar (Figure 3-46).

Figure 3-46. *Clicking "Publish" to complete knowledge article creation*

A panel will appear on the right-hand side of the screen, as seen in Figure 3-47, where a user can configure any extra details, such as when to publish (which can also be completed earlier on the Summary tab) and the expiration status; this is the status and status reason to be set once the expiration date is reached. "Publish" is clicked on the pane once all the information is correct.

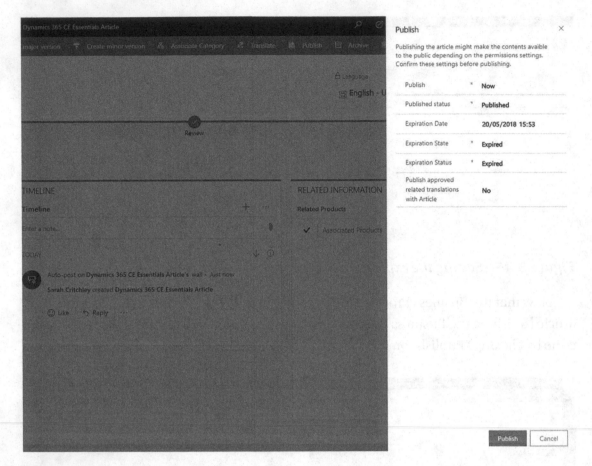

Figure 3-47. Completing the final details for the article before it is published

Once the knowledge article is published, the status changes to "Published," and the Major Version Number will be incremented to 1 (Figure 3-48).

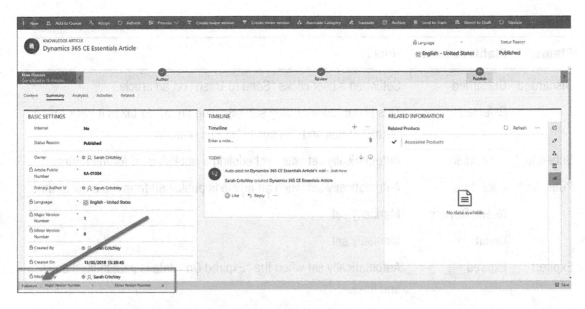

Figure 3-48. *Published knowledge article*

Knowledge Article Statuses

There are various statuses of the knowledge article. Use Table 3-1 to become familiar
with how they are set, as some are set automatically following certain user actions.

Table 3-1. *Knowledge Article Statuses*

Status	Status Reason	Notes
Draft	Draft	An article begins in this state, but the status reason "Draft" is manually set.
	Proposed	An article normally begins in this state. Even restoring an article will be in "Draft" status with a "Proposed" status reason.
	Needs Review	Manually set.
	In Review	Manually set.
Approved	Approved	Updated to this status once "Approved" is selected on the command bar.

(continued)

Table 3-1. (*continued*)

Status	Status Reason	Notes
Discarded	Discarded	Set when a user clicks "Send to Trash" on an article.
	Rejected	This is not automatically set; rejecting an article takes it back to "Draft" status and "Proposed" status reason.
Scheduled	Scheduled	Automatically set when scheduling a publish date for the future.
Published	Published	Automatically set when an article is published from the present time.
	Needs Review	Manually set.
	Updating	Manually set.
Expired	Expired	Automatically set when the "Expired On" date is past today's date and time.
	Rejected	This is not automatically set; rejecting an article takes it back to "Draft" status and "Proposed" status reason.
Archived	Archived	Set when a user clicks "Archive."

To archive a knowledge article normally means the knowledge article is no longer relevant or important for an organization, but the organization wishes to retain it. Click the Archive button, shown in Figure 3-49, to change the status to "Archived."

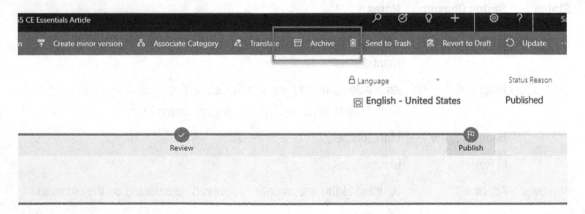

Figure 3-49. *Click the Archive button on the command bar to change the status to "Archived"*

Knowledge articles can also be discarded by clicking the Send to Trash button, as seen in Figure 3-50. This is like sending a document to the recycle bin, where it is no longer needed and will most likely be removed from the system.

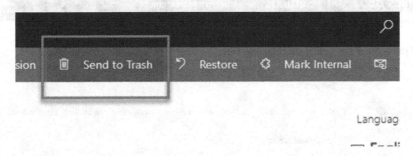

Figure 3-50. *Sending an article to trash updates the status to "Discarded"*

Knowledge articles that have been sent to the trash can be restored, again like a recycle bin on a computer. This is often done if the user reviewing the knowledge article confirms that it should be retained within the system and that a status of "Archived" might be more appropriate. Knowledge articles can be restored by clicking the Restore button, as seen in Figure 3-51, when an article is in a "Discarded" state.

Figure 3-51. *Users can restore articles previously set as "Discarded"*

Subjects and Categories

Subjects are a special type of hierarchal field allowing a user to set a value that is associated with that record. They are configured within the Classic UI, soon to be available in the UCI Client under the Customer Service Hub app in the Service Management module, expected in October 2018. When configuring subjects, a user can add a new subject and child subjects, creating a topical hierarchy.

Task: Set up subjects. To set up the subject tree, navigate to Service Management from the "Settings" area in the Classic UI and select "Subjects" (Figure 3-52).

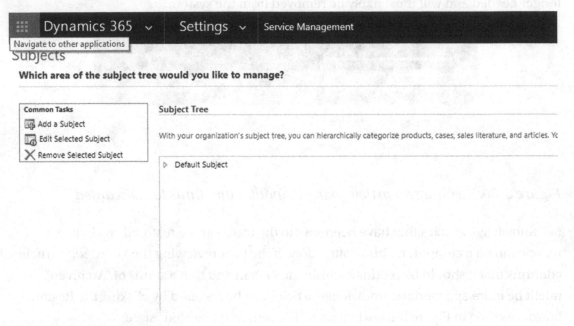

Figure 3-52. Subjects within the Classic UI

Click "Add a Subject." You will be asked to name the subject within the "Title" field. Populating the "Parent Subject" field means this will be underneath that parent subject; if left blank it will be classified as a parent itself. Click the Add button to confirm this item is to be added to the subject hierarchy (Figure 3-53).

Figure 3-53. Defining a new subject

In contrast, *Categories*, released in the later versions of Dynamics 365 CE, are a record type linked to knowledge articles as standard. Categories can also be configured to be linked to other entities through customization. Categories have very similar functionality to subjects, but with an improved interface, and can be added to knowledge articles in two ways. First is by using the Related Information sub-grid and clicking "Relate Category," as seen in Figure 3-54. You will then be prompted to add the category. The key difference from subjects is that more than one category can be linked to a record, while only a single subject can be linked.

Categories, when created, have a category number assigned by the standard auto-numbering functionality within Dynamics 365 CE. This can be configured within the Classic UI in the "Administration" area.

The second way to associate a category with a knowledge article is to click "Associate Category" on the command bar while in the Knowledge Article form. This is a convenient way of doing so: once selected, you simply select the category and click Save. You can repeat the process however many times necessary to add multiple categories.

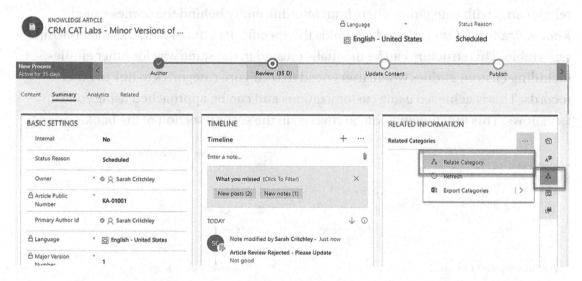

Figure 3-54. *Relating a category to a knowledge article using the sub-grid*

Task: Associate a category with an existing knowledge article.

Navigate to an article and click the "Categories" icon in the Related Information sub-grid on the Summary tab. Click the action button ("...") and "Relate Category," as seen in Figure 3-55. Select the category from the lookup record.

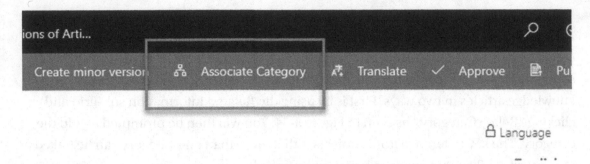

Figure 3-55. *Associating a category with a knowledge article using the command bar button*

One of the benefits of using categories rather than subjects is being able to link multiple categories to a record. This allows views to be created and embedded into dashboards using the Advanced Find feature in the Classic Client or the "Customization" area (Figure 3-56).

Behind the scenes for knowledge articles, there is a many-to-many (N:N) relationship with categories. There is an interlink entity behind the scenes called *KnowledgeArticleCategories*, which holds the specific data that makes this relationship reportable. This structure can be manually created in the same way for other entities, including custom entities where users need to configure categories to link to other records. This is achieved using customizations and can be approached using code or workflows. This functionality will be covered in the second section of the book.

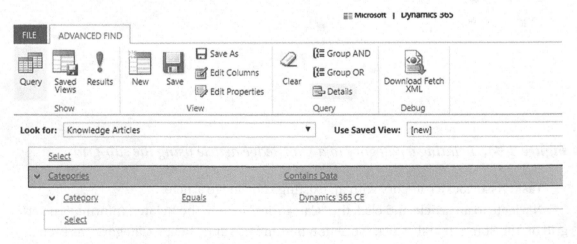

Figure 3-56. *Using Advanced Find to report on categories*

Feedback

Dynamics 365 CE provides users with the ability to give feedback on knowledge articles. Feedback is also configurable for other entities (by selecting "Feedback" within the entity configuration). Feedback gives internal and external consumers of the knowledge article the opportunity to rate the article and provide comments. Authors and organizations then have the chance to revise and update the article.

On the Analytics tab of a knowledge article, there is a section labeled "Feedback." This gives users an aggregate of the normalized ratings of all associated feedback entries (Figure 3-57). This field updates regularly but not in real time. It will not display the updated rating aggregate straight away, despite there being associated feedback records.

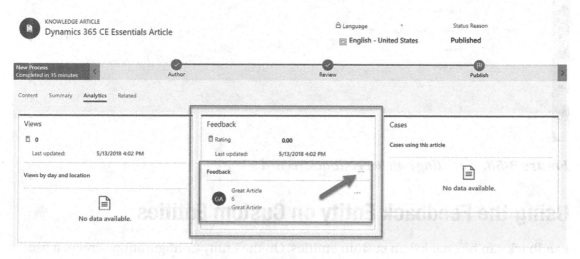

Figure 3-57. *"Feedback" section within knowledge articles*

Clicking the action button ("...") and clicking "Create Feedback" opens a new blank Feedback record (Figure 3-58). A user then needs to complete the fields, including the "Regarding" field. Note: The system does not auto-populate as standard because the field is a special "regardingobjectid" field, like that of activities. At the time of writing, this doesn't auto-populate when created in the context of its parent record, as activities do.

The fields "Minimum Rating," "Maximum Rating," and the actual "Rating" get completed by the user. This is an important part of how the feedback aggregates, because all users and organizations can be different in how they rate something. Therefore, the minimum and maximum ratings can be entered by a user manually. Equally, it can also be auto-populated through customization by organizations to enforce it. Regardless, the

"Rating" is entered, which must be between the min and max, and then it is normalized into a rating that can be aggregated based on a percentage of the given min and max. The normalization formula is (Rating – Minimum Rating)/(Maximum Rating – Minimum Rating).

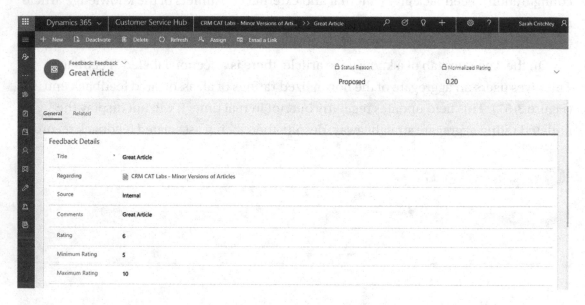

Figure 3-58. *Creating a new Feedback record*

Using the Feedback Entity on Custom Entities

Feedback can be enabled on custom entities. On the Entity Configuration screen, a user selects "Feedback" within the entity definition, as seen in Figure 3-59. It is important to know that once selected and saved, this option cannot be undone, as it creates fields within the background system.

Once activated, users have access to the same functionality available within the knowledge article. For the Classic UI, this will already be available using the associated relationships, and the ability to create feedback is already there. For adding the custom entity within the Unified Interface, a new sub-grid will need to be created, similar to that available on the knowledge articles, as this is not automatically created.

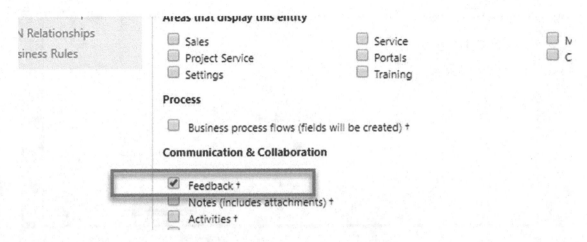

Figure 3-59. Configuring feedback on other record types

SLAs and Entitlements

Service-level agreements (SLAs) are not a new concept to the service industry. They are an agreement between a provider and a customer on a specific commitment in relation to the service they receive. This commitment is normally based on time, which is how it is represented within Dynamics 365 CE. Within Dynamics CE, SLAs are configured for a number of standard record types, including Cases and Leads, and can be configured for custom record types as well. SLAs give the ability to embed the timer visualization within those record forms.

Creating SLAs is currently achieved in the Classic UI; however, it is expected that in the October 2018 release, it will be possible to create SLAs within the UI Client in the Customer Service Hub app.

Task: Create a new SLA.

1. To create a new SLA, in the Classic Client, navigate to Settings ➤ Service Management ➤ Service-Level Agreements.

2. Click "New," and a prompt will appear to name the SLA and select the entity (Figure 360). The dropdown list is populated by all record types enabled for SLAs, which is configured in the entity configuration area in the relevant or default solution, in the same way as feedback.

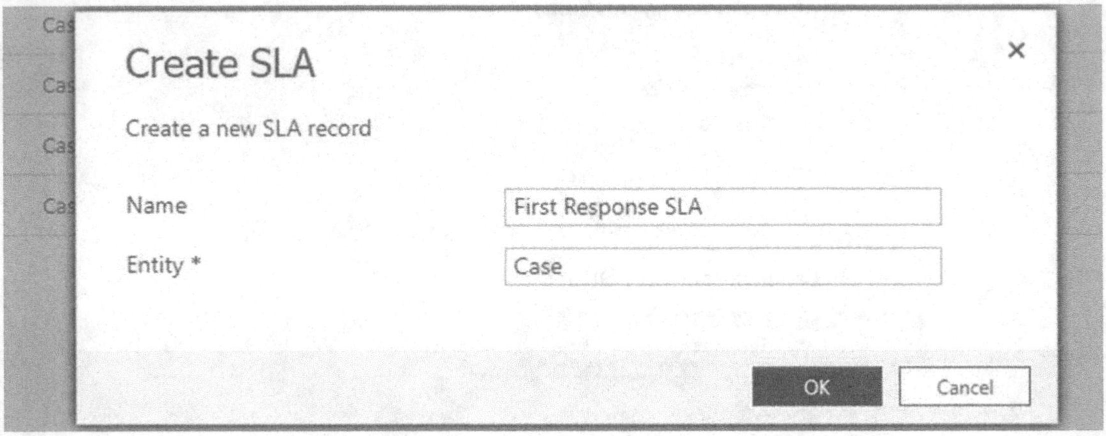

Figure 3-60. *Navigating to service-level agreements within the Classic Client*

The next section will walk you through how to add SLA detail items and the details related to the SLA record.

Creating a New SLA for the Case Record

SLAs are made up of core SLA information, such as the type, date it is applicable from, and SLA items (Figure 3-61). The SLA items manage the conditions and actions that should take place under certain conditions. The core SLA information includes when the SLA is applicable *from*, which can be any datetime field on the selected record type. For "First Response"-type SLAs, this is often a "Created On" field. Business hours can be set if this area of Dynamics 365 CE is being utilized. This area manages the hours agents are available and can be set up in the same area.

The "SLA Type" field gives two options: simple and enhanced. The timer isn't available for simple SLAs, nor are pausing and resuming; however, Microsoft has announced that simple SLAs will be deprecated, so for now select "Enhanced." Keep "Pause and Resume" set to "Allow," which will be discussed shortly as far as how this is managed in system settings using the different statuses.

Once the base information on the SLA is set up, save the record and click the plus icon in the sub-grid to create an SLA detail item.

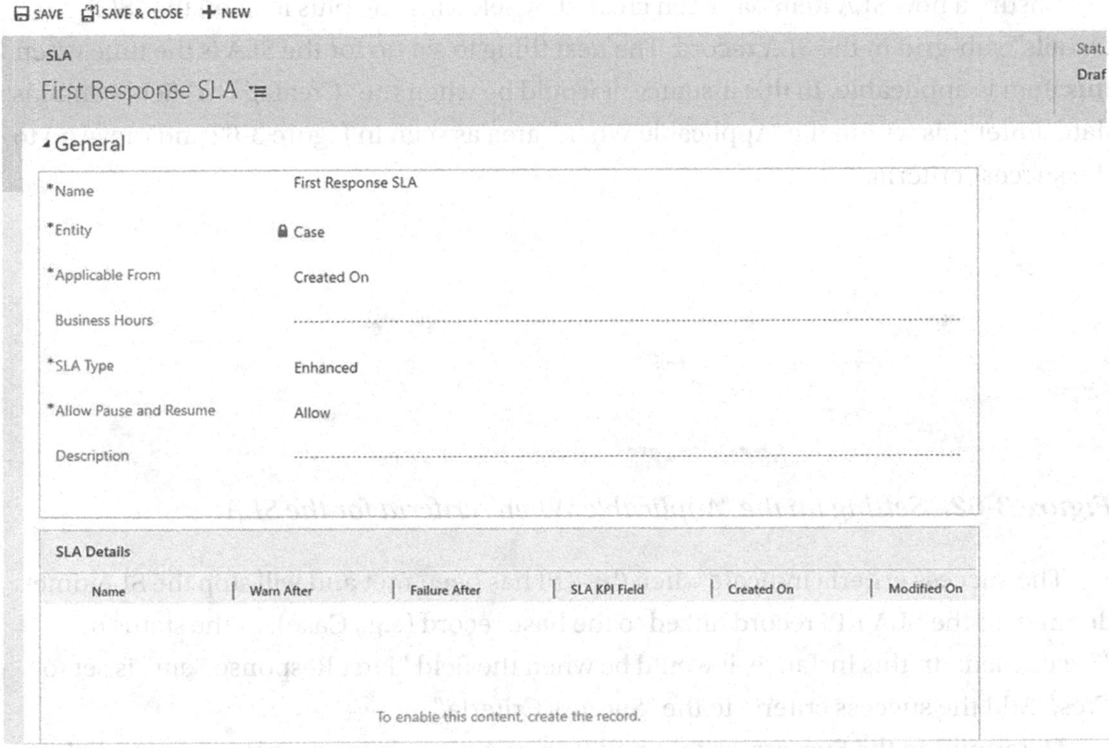

🖫 SAVE   🖫 SAVE & CLOSE   ✚ NEW

SLA	Statu
First Response SLA ☰	Draf

▲ General

*Name	First Response SLA
*Entity	🔒 Case
*Applicable From	Created On
Business Hours	....
*SLA Type	Enhanced
*Allow Pause and Resume	Allow
Description	....

SLA Details

Name	Warn After	Failure After	SLA KPI Field	Created On	Modified On

To enable this content, create the record.

Figure 3-61. *Creating a new SLA and configuring the base configuration information*

Each SLA detail line associated with an SLA record is what is known and seen in the system as an *SLA KPI*. If the conditions are met, a new SLA KPI Instance record is created – for example, in the context of a case – and a timer begins for that specific item. This gives organizations the capability to manage multiple SLA indicators and monitor them within the case, including their pass and fail metrics, helping to identify areas of improvement within an organization.

The two KPI instances set up for a case by default are the First Response and Resolve By KPIs, which are very common in the service industry. They can be configured without any customizations. To expand this to different KPIs, a customizer will need to navigate to the entity, for example, a case, and create a new lookup field to the SLA KPI Instance entity. The name of the lookup field will then be available in the "SLA KPI" field dropdown list when configuring the item.

This example will continue to go through the setup of an SLA KPI called "First Response by KPI."

Ensure a new SLA item has been created by selecting the plus icon on the "SLA Details" sub-grid in the SLA record. The next thing to set up for the SLA is the time when this item is applicable. In this instance, it would be when the "Created On" field contains data. Enter this within the "Applicable When" area as seen in Figure 3-62 and move on to the success criteria.

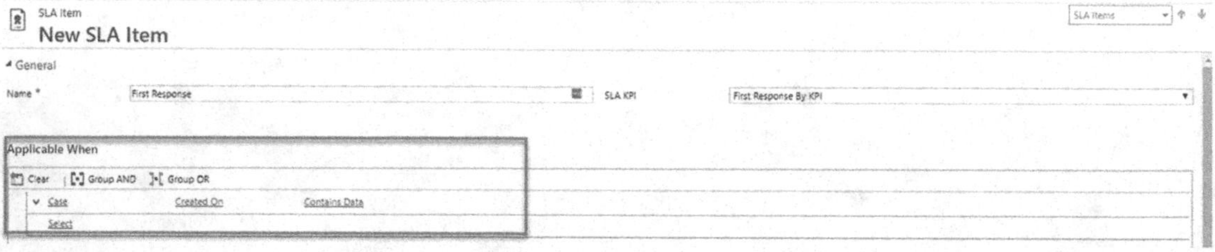

Figure 3-62. *Setting up the "Applicable When" criteria for the SLA*

The success criteria indicate when the KPI has been met and will stop the SLA timer defined on the SLA KPI record linked to the base record (e.g., Case), as the status of "Succeeded." In this instance, it would be when the field "First Response Sent" is set to "Yes." Add the success criteria to the "Success Criteria."

Determining the Success Actions and Failure Actions is the next step to completing the item. The failure criteria specify the conditions for failure of the SLA and are indicated by time. The "Failure After" field is a dropdown field, but a user can enter any time frame they require, even if it's not displayed, in hours, as seen in Figure 3-63.

Figure 3-63. *"Failure After" field can be manually entered and not just selected from the dropdown list*

Failure Actions can be set up, such as sending an email to the owner of the Case record. This is very similar to some actions available in workflows. We will cover those in more depth in Part II of the book.

Warning times can indicate to the owner of the record that the time is approaching when the SLA will be considered as failed. It is also normal to notify the owner of the record by creating a new email or a new activity, which they would see within a dashboard. Success Actions can also be set up, as seen in Figure 3-64, once the SLA's configured Success Criteria are met in the same way. Success and Failure Actions are not necessarily required; however, they can assist in the awareness and management of the SLA to improve the chances of their being met.

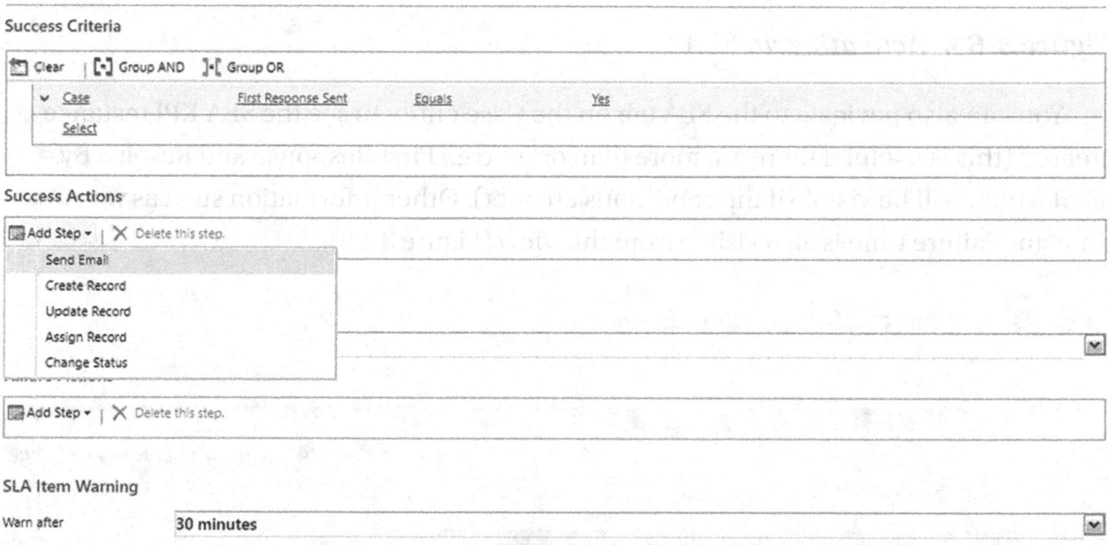

Figure 3-64.   *Setting the Success Criteria and Actions*

Setting Up Success Actions in the SLA Detail Record

Once the SLA detail item is completed, click "Save and Close" and then activate the SLA by clicking "Activate" on the command bar. This updates it to a read-only status. Once the SLA is activated, the SLA can also be set as the default SLA. Across the Dynamics 365 CE instance, the SLA can be applied to all cases (or other entities) by default without being linked to an entitlement. Only one default SLA can be set per organization. For the purposes of the next task, choose "Set as Default" on the SLA record.

Task: Test the SLA.

Navigate to a case and create a new case. With the SLA set as default, an entitlement won't need to be set. Once saved, the First Response KPI SLA begins; and a timer automatically starts counting down, as seen in Figure 3-65.

101

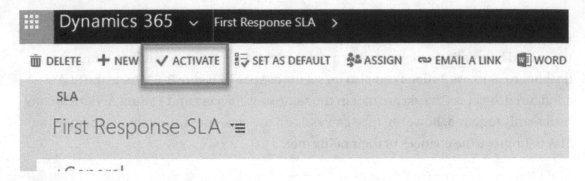

Figure 3-65. Activating an SLA

You can also navigate to the SLA tab on the Case entity to see the SLA KPI instance created (this is useful if there are more than one – e.g., First Response and Resolve By – all of which will be visible if the conditions are met). Other information such as warning time and failure time is also visible from this view (Figure 3-66).

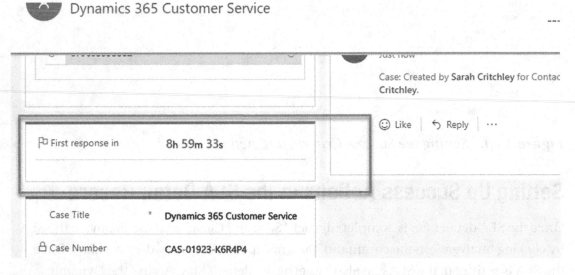

Figure 3-66. The timer counting down based on the SLA item detail

The SLA tab gives more contextual detail about the SLAs, as seen in Figure 3-67, and can be reviewed, especially if a timer isn't available for all applicable SLA KPI instances.

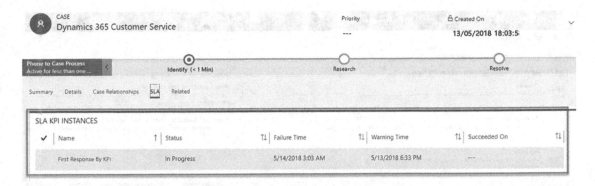

Figure 3-67. *SLA KPI instances available to view from the SLA tab on the Case record*

SLAs are fantastic on their own when not linked to accounts or entitlements directly, but their limitation is that only one can be applied per organization. This is a great opportunity to define a base level of expectation for service staff. It does not, however, give customers a personalized experience. SLAs are normally linked to entitlements, which will be covered in the next section. Normally, the service level is agreed upon within a contract and terms and conditions, and SLAs provide an extension for entitlements to fulfill that as part of the contract.

Entitlements

Entitlements are an improvement upon the legacy Contract entity found in Dynamics 365 CE (Figure 3-68). Contracts have been announced as being deprecated, and therefore entitlements are a natural progression for contract-based functionality. Entitlements give organizations the capability to manage contractual commitments for the accounts they hold and provide a level-of-service commitment to them.

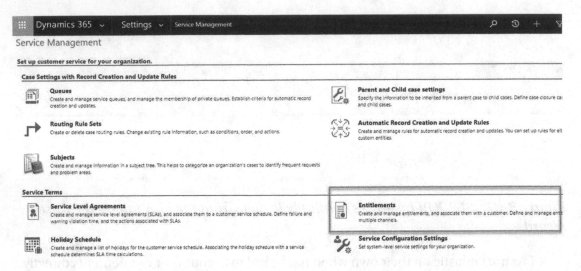

Figure 3-68. *Navigate to Service Management and click "Entitlements"*

Entitlements allow organizations to manage the start and end dates of these commitments automatically. Users can set an entitlement to start in the future, putting it in a "Waiting" state. A future date when the entitlement should expire will also be set, at which point the record will become inactive automatically, no longer able to be utilized with cases.

Entitlements hold an allocation of the number of either cases or hours an account can have within a set period of time. These terms are then logged and automatically decremented based on either case resolution or case creation.

Organizations can further limit when the entitlements can be used by specifying the following:

- **Channels** – This is linked to the origin of the case (e.g., phone, Web, etc.) and specifies a certain number of allocations per channel.

- **Products** – The entitlement is valid for.

- **Contacts** – The entitlement is valid for.

If an entitlement is set to restrict the creation or resolution of cases based on the terms, it means it could prevent cases from being created or resolved when there are no more terms left. This could be argued as being the whole point of entitlements; however, it can get tricky when multiple agreements are linked, as entitlement terms cannot go into negative numbers. In this scenario, using the standard case functionality of "Do not decrement entitlement terms," available on the "..." action button, can come in handy. This is also useful for when something should be completed free of charge and not be decremented.

Entitlements are simple to set up. Before beginning this next step, deactivate and reactivate the SLA from the previous step if this was followed, so it is no longer set as the default.

Figure 3-69. *Entitlement record within Dynamics 365 CE*

Creating a New Entitlement

Like SLAs, entitlements currently can only be created within the Classic UI. This is expected to change in the October 2018 release, when they will become able to be created from the UI Client within the Customer Service Hub app.

Task: Create an entitlement. Navigate to Settings ➤ Entitlements in the Classic Client and click "New."

1. Complete the basic details for the entitlement, such as the "Name," "Primary Customer" (the account this should be linked to), "Start Date," and "End Date" fields (Figure 3-69).

2. Use the Entitlement Channel sub-grid to set the "Origin" field to "Phone."

3. Link the SLA made in the previous step by searching for it in the lookup field. This is how SLAs are designed to work together with entitlements. Together, they operate a contractual service-level agreement framework, which is available to users without any customization.

Channel is important to note for restrictions, as some of the "Origin" options are set as standard on the Case entity, which is useful to be aware of. They are as follows:

- **Phone Support** – The origin is set to "Phone."

- **Social Activity** – The origin is set to "Twitter" when linked via Social Engagement automatically.

- **Web** – Through Customer Service Portals, this is set to "Web" automatically.

Activate the entitlement using the Activate button on the command bar and confirm activation, as seen in Figure 3-70.

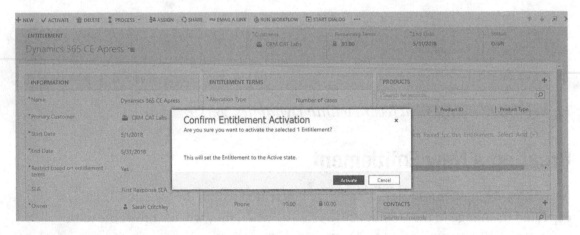

Figure 3-70. *Entitlement record within Dynamics 365 CE*

Activating the Entitlement on a Case

Let's see the entitlement in action on a Case record:

1. Within the Customer Service Hub app, create a new Case record for the account specified within the entitlement.

2. Ensure the Origin field is set to the one specified in the Channel Filter ("Phone") if the example was followed, from the previous section if this was used.

3. The new entitlement will be available within the dropdown as shown in Figure 3-71. Select it and save the record.

The SLA will have been activated without it being set as the default, and as seen in Figure 3-71, the entitlement terms have been decremented, as has the channel, since it matched the channel specified within the Case record.

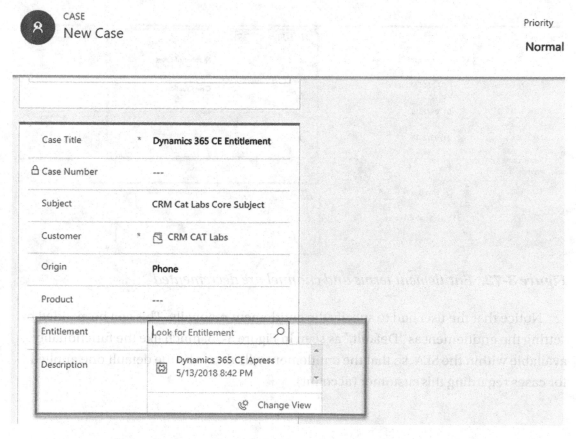

Figure 3-71. Selecting the new entitlement in a Case record

When an entitlement is linked to a case, the terms are automatically decremented, and if the origin matches the origin specified within the Case record, that too is decremented (Figure 3-72). Entitlement channels are a useful way of logging how often a customer raises cases in specific ways, offering the potential for organizations to drive them toward using self-service routes such as portals.

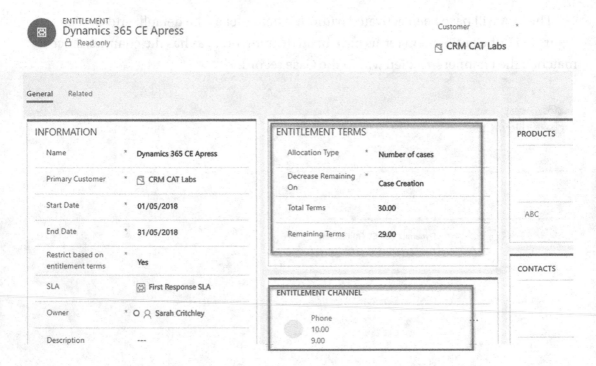

Figure 3-72.   *Entitlement terms and channel are decremented*

Notice that the user had to specify the entitlement manually. This can be avoided by setting the entitlement as "Default," as seen in Figure 3-73, much like the functionality available within the SLA, so that the entitlement will always be the default one applied for cases regarding this customer (account).

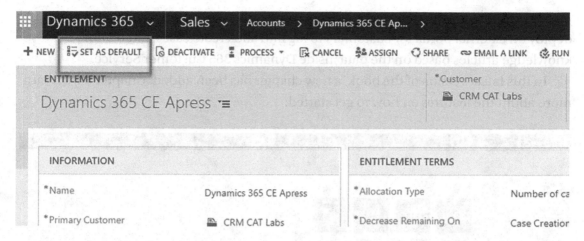

Figure 3-73. *Click "Set as Default" to automatically apply this entitlement for the specified customer*

Entitlements are a useful way to manage contractual and service-level agreements without doing any customization within the system. A small amount of configuration sets an organization up to effectively manage terms and conditions and also to manage customer service departments and a core set of principles regarding the service they provide.

Microsoft Portals (Power Apps Portals) Configuration for Self-Service

Microsoft Portals is based on the framework from ADX Studios. Microsoft acquired ADX Studios in 2015 and developed its portal product further to create Microsoft Portals. Microsoft Portals for Dynamics 365 allows a user to achieve a configuration-focused approach to creating an external or internal portal environment connected to Dynamics 365 CE data as opposed to going through extensive development.

Licencing requirements are fluid in nature, and at the time of writing, Microsoft Portals is available to Dynamics 365 users to allow them to utilize the premade templates such as Customer Service Portals. These templates are not available for Power Apps Portals which are base portals expected for customized content via the designer and portal management application. Templates use standard out-of-the-box entities to provide a framework so organizations can get started straight away and customize going forward depending on requirements.

The Customer Service Portals allow for organizations to be able to automatically deploy an external portal for customers to log into and create cases and review knowledge articles based on the data inside Dynamics 365 Customer Service.

In this latest version of the book, a new chapter has been added, Chapter 14, to learn more about the features on how to get started.

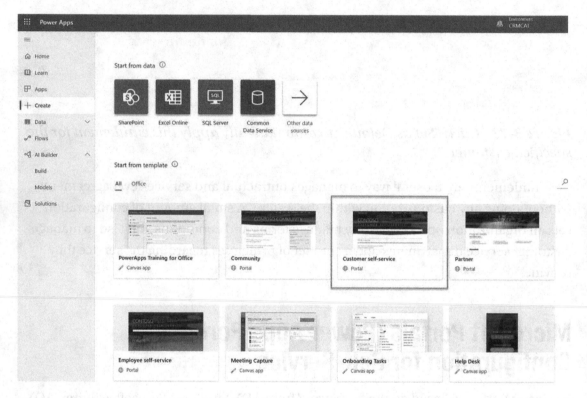

Figure 3-74. *Access the Dynamics 365 portal templates from the maker experience*

Navigate to the maker experience and select "Create." This screen displays templates for apps. If the environment is configured for Dynamics 365, the portal templates related to Dynamics 365 functionality, for example, Customer Service, will be available, as shown in Figure 3-74.

Figure 3-75. *The standard layout of a template for Customer Service*

There is a large amount of functionality available in the standard Customer Service Portal template which does not require any further customizations, which includes the following:

- Visibility of published knowledge articles

- Authentication through portal contacts, invitation functionalities, and portal user management

- Forums and the ability for signed-in users to create new posts

- Case management – Signed-in users to view related cases

- Case management – Signed-in users to make new cases

- Case management – Signed-in users to edit existing cases (Close and Cancel)

- Account management from the portal

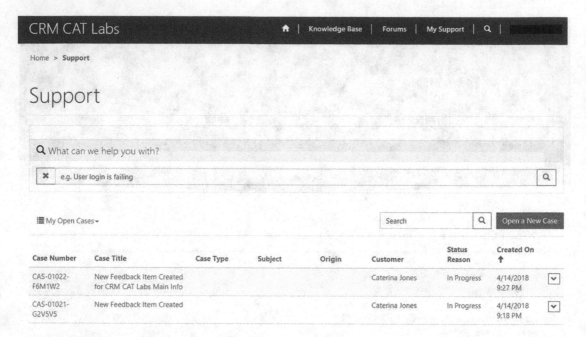

Figure 3-76. *Creating a case from the portal creates a Case record within*
Dynamics 365

Organizations can use the Customer Self-Service Template, modifying the branding
to get started on using the capabilities of the portal, to enhance their customer
engagement. Details on how to modify branding and other options within Microsoft
Portals are included in the "Further Reading" section at the end of this chapter.

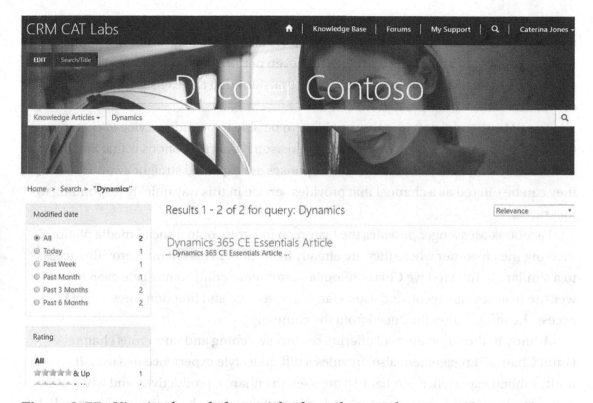

Figure 3-77. Viewing knowledge articles from the portal

Omni Channel Engagement

Omni Channel Engagement is one of the latest applications to be added to Dynamics 365 Customer Service. It provides the capability to manage multiple inbound channels, retaining the context of the customer's data and queries while agents switch channels. This allows them to still be able to have access to the same conversation and information as in the previous channel. This is often referred to as "omni-channel" capabilities.

Omni Channel Engagement is an add-on and requires the base Customer Service licence for Dynamics 365. Through the release cycle, more channels are released, and at the time of writing, the channels that are available are Live Chat, SMS (via a third party, TeleSign), and Facebook Messenger.

The Live Chat channel of Omni Channel Engagement uses technology from Microsoft Teams to provide a live chat experience which can be started from websites, for example. This experience can connect a customer, or potential customer, directly to a real customer service agent so they can ask questions based on their needs.

The Live Chat experience can be enhanced with the Power Virtual Agents technology, covered in later chapters. This allows for a bot to be present in the chat instead, capable of answering questions and even performing actions based on the customer's needs. Then the customer can be transferred to a live customer agent based on their needs.

The SMS channel provides the capability to be able to provide service to customers using TeleSign services asynchronously. The reason it's asynchronous is that SMS isn't traditionally a real-time channel where responses are expected straight away. However, they can be offered as a channel that provides service in this way quickly responding to messages.

Facebook Messenger provides the feature to integrate onto a social media platform, meeting the customer where they are already likely to be. This channel provides access to a similar channel to Live Chat, without a customer needing to navigate even to the website to access an agent, and uses a familiar interface and function (messenger) to access the information they need from the company.

Adding to the capabilities of offering context switching and numerous channels, Omni Channel Engagement also provides a different style experience to a user. It gives a multi-tabbed experience, similar to a browser, to enhance productivity and where they may need to research the customer's issues in real time (e.g., by accessing the knowledge base). It also allows agents to specify which channels they can accept messages from and what their capacity is. This is similar to Field Service (see Chapter 5) where users (agents, in this scenario) won't receive notifications from queue routing if their current queue is at capacity based on their current allocations.

There is some setting up to do for Omni Channel, and the next section briefly covers how to set up Omni Channel Engagement for Live Chat.

Omni Channel Engagement Setup

There are two apps relating to Omni Channel Engagement. These are Administration and Omni Channel for Customer Service. These can be seen in Figure 3-78.

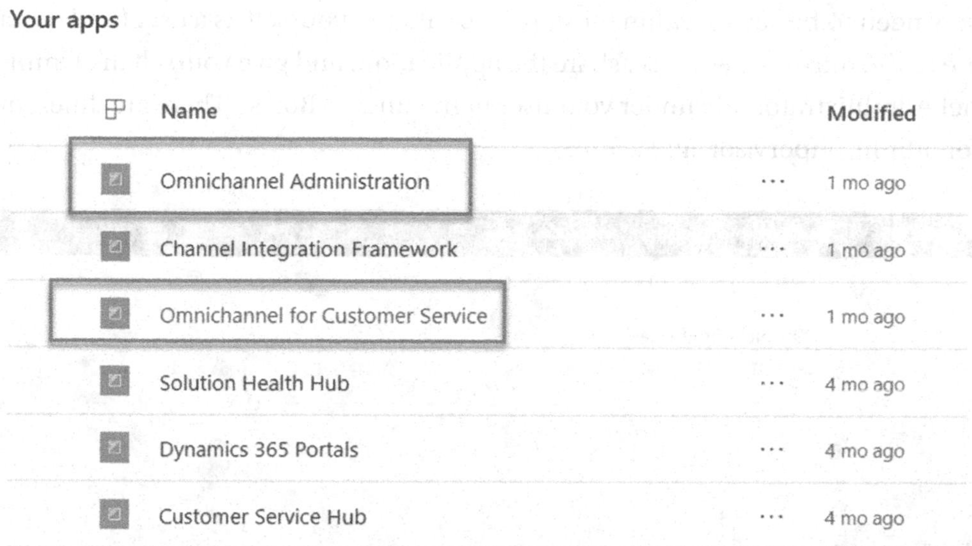

Your apps

	Name		Modified
	Omnichannel Administration	...	1 mo ago
	Channel Integration Framework	...	1 mo ago
	Omnichannel for Customer Service	...	1 mo ago
	Solution Health Hub	...	4 mo ago
	Dynamics 365 Portals	...	4 mo ago
	Customer Service Hub	...	4 mo ago

Figure 3-78. *Two Omni Channel Apps in the maker experience*

The Omni Channel Administration App is used for configuring channels and the setup of the omni-channel experience and also for supervisors.

The Omni Channel for Customer Service is the app which the agents will utilize to take oncoming messages via a number of different channels. This can be seen in Figure 3-79 where there is a different experience from other apps. There is a more "tabbed" experience which can be seen where a user can have more than one item open at once from within a single screen.

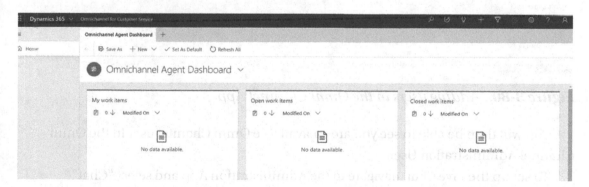

Figure 3-79. *The agent experience of the Omni Channel Engagement App*

Users need to be set up within the app. To configure yourself as a user (and others), navigate to the maker experience, share the application, and give yourself the Omni Channel Administrator role under your user name under "Roles." There are different roles for admin, supervisor, and agent.

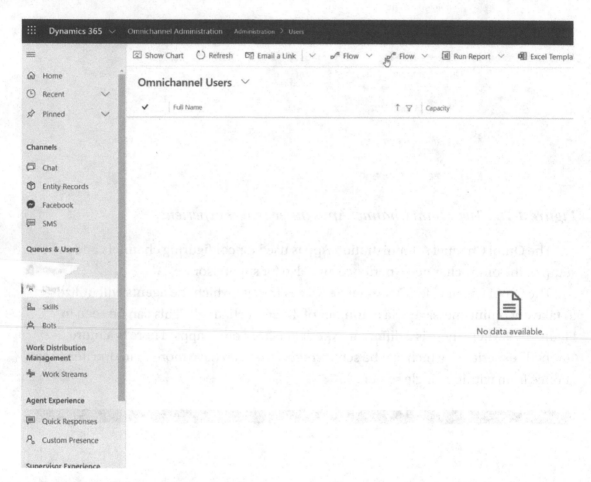

Figure 3-80. *Adding users in the Omni Channel App*

You will then be able to see you are an available Omni Channel user in the Omni Channel Administration User.

To set up the Live Chat, navigate to the Administration App and select "Chat" and "New." This creates a new Widget; go ahead and name the application and save the record. This generates a code snippet which you can use on an external website (including a Power Portal). This appears as a "Let's Chat" icon on the website.

When someone interacts with the Chat Widget from the website, users on the Omni Channel for Customer Service App would be able to see an incoming stream from the Chat which creates a new "Conversation" entity. On a single screen, the customer and agent can discuss their issue on the left-hand side of the screen, associate an Account or Contact, and also create a case directly from a conversation.

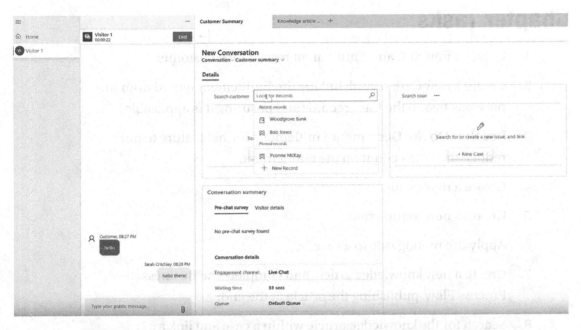

Figure 3-81. *The Conversation activity available in Omni Channel Engagement*

Summary

This chapter has covered an extensive amount of information on how to get started with the standard customer service capabilities that Dynamics 365 CE has to offer. It has covered how important it is to engage customers socially using the Microsoft Social Engagement platform, which together with the Case record is at the core of logging, managing, and solving customer queries and problems. Managing those engagements contractually and in a timely manner using entitlements and SLAs allows organizations to offer their service to customers and tailor the type of service they can offer while maintaining a core expectation of when they should be responded to and resolved by. Using Microsoft Portals to offer a self-service feature to customers empowers customers to solve their own problems using knowledge articles and submit their own support tickets, taking the incoming service inquiries down from other channels such as the phone. It then finally covered getting started with one of the latest Customer Service apps, the Omni Channel Engagement experience. By using these features together, organizations will be able to provide a high level of customer service and offer enhanced levels of capability compared to their competitors.

Chapter Tasks

1. Create a new SLA and Entitlement record for a customer.

2. Create a new Case record, linking the Entitlement record from the previous task to the Case record (and ensuring it is applicable).

3. Use the "Do Not Decrement Entitlement Terms" feature to not reduce the terms count on the entitlement.

4. Create a new queue.

5. Create a new routing rule.

6. Apply the routing rule to a case.

7. Create a new knowledge article and complete the Business Process Flow, publishing the article at the end.

8. Search for the knowledge article within a case and link a knowledge article to the case.

9. Set up the Customer Service template for Microsoft Portals and search for the knowledge article within the portal and log a case while logged in.

10. Set up an Omni Channel Engagement App trial and configure the minimum requirements for enabling Live Chat on an external website

Further Reading

Unified Service Desk and Dynamics 365 CE (Microsoft, 2018). URL: `https://docs.microsoft.com/en-us/dynamics365/customer-engagement/unified-service-desk/unified-service-desk`

Microsoft Portals (Microsoft, 2018). URL: `https://docs.microsoft.com/en-us/dynamics365/customer-engagement/portals/configure-portal`

Introduction to Omni Channel for Customer Service (Microsoft, 2019). URL: `https://docs.microsoft.com/en-us/dynamics365/omnichannel/introduction-omnichannel`

CHAPTER 4

Sales

Managing a sales pipeline can be challenging for organizations. Often, salespeople need to have the latest information regarding their customers' interactions readily available. They need to be able to easily update the system and advance opportunities to the next stage of development, as well as provide accurate quotes and correct product estimates. This is done while providing a great service to potential customers and collaboratively working with their sales team and company to get what they need at the right time in the lifecycle. Sales is not about just pipeline management, but also the setup behind the scenes. The sales lifecycle is enhanced by the setup and use of the product catalog, which allows organizations to manage the products they sell from the front-line sales team and provide an integration point to back-office systems. This chapter will cover a deep dive into the sales lifecycle, what the product catalog is in Dynamics 365 CE, and how to set it up.

Product Catalog Setup and Management

Dynamics 365 CE has a sales cycle that is underpinned by opportunities, quotes, and invoices. Products are an optional feature of Dynamics 365 CE, and the sales lifecycle can be utilized without defining specific products and relationships. That said, being aware of products and related functionality can assist organizations in knowing how best to implement the product catalog within Dynamics 365 CE and to keep it maintained with little effort while still providing enhancements to their sales lifecycle. As the sales cycle progresses through to an opportunity and then to a quote, order, and invoice, the products related to these records are retained throughout the lifecycle, providing reporting capabilities and suggestion features that are aimed at helping a salesperson in their day-to-day role. Products are not the only thing within the catalog. It is made up of a framework that creates a structure allowing products to be available at different prices and price formulas, linking together with recommendations for cross-selling, up-sell opportunities, managing different units of sale, and discount availability.

121

© Sarah Critchley 2020
S. Critchley, *Dynamics 365 Essentials*, https://doi.org/10.1007/978-1-4842-5911-5_4

The product catalog within Dynamics 365 CE does not formulate an actual warehousing solution, something Dynamics Finance and Operations would be more suited for. It would, however, be a great starting point for integration between a back-office system that is better suited for warehousing and inventory management and Dynamics 365 CE, thus adding value.

A product is defined as an item which is sold; this can be an actual physical item or a service, for example. A Product record in Dynamics 365 CE can be seen as the "Product Definition." Instances of the products are associated on "price lists" as price list items. Hierarchal family relationships can be created with products, which have a lineage of related properties that are inherited down across the children of the parent products, becoming uneditable and eliminating the possibility of more properties being added at each stage. They can, if required, be overridden. Properties can normally be attributes that need to be displayed on the Product record at the sales stage. Examples could be "Color" or "Number of Rooms," often determining characteristics that could assist in the picking and selling of the item.

A product is always associated with a *unit* and a *unit group*. Units manage the quantity and sizes of the product that ships. Unit groups always start out with a singular unit. In the following examples, the custom unit group "Crate" was created and has a unit quantity of 1. A second unit was associated with the unit group "Large Crate," which has a base unit of "Crate" with a quantity of 2. Units can be easily built up to ensure the quantity of the product being sold is correct. Another example is fruit. A singular fruit can be sold, but it can also be sold as a six-pack or a twelve-pack, often seen in supermarkets. This example is shown in Figure 4-1.

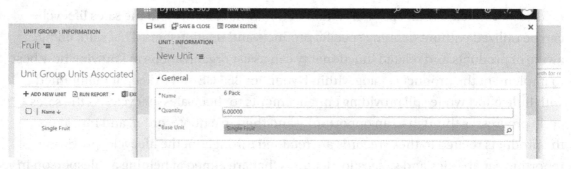

Figure 4-1. *Units and unit groups – using the base unit*

The diagram in Figure 4-2 is a basic entity relationship diagram (ERD) that displays how the unit groups, units, product families, products, and other related record types fit together to be available on a price list. To summarize

- A product instance is referred to as a *price list item*.

- A price list item is a specific instance of the product with a set cost.

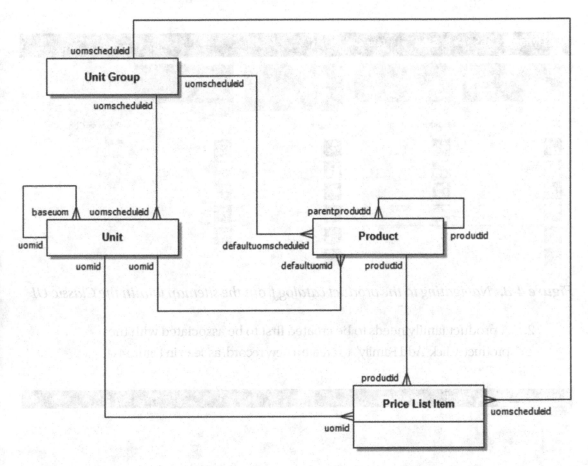

Figure 4-2. *Overview of the entity relationship diagram of the product and unit structure*

When a user creates an *opportunity*, a *price list* is specified. A price list item is linked to a specific price list. The user can then use all of the products available from the price list as *opportunity products* to sell as part of the sale. The next section will walk you through how to set up an example product catalog using all of these configurations.

123

Creating a Family Hierarchy and Properties

This section will walk you through how to get started with products and create family hierarchies with properties.

Task: Create a family hierarchy.

1. Navigate to Classic UI ➤ Settings ➤ Product Catalog (Figure 4-3).

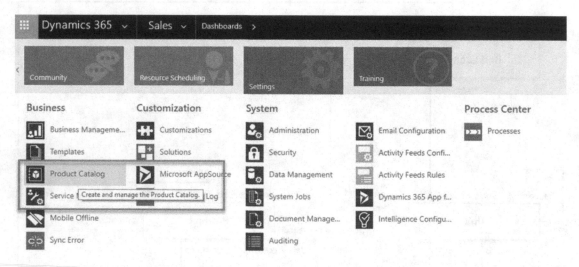

Figure 4-3. *Navigating to the product catalog from the sitemap within the Classic UI*

2. A product family needs to be created first to be associated with the product. Click "Add Family" to create a new record, as seen in Figure 4-4.

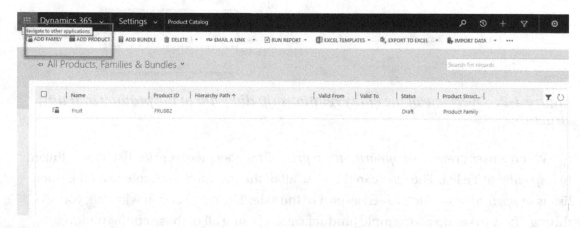

Figure 4-4. *Click "Add Family" to create a blank Family record*

3. Type "Fruit" as the name, type a product ID (which must be unique), and save the record (Figure 4-5). (You can set expiry for the family if you wish so it can no longer be used for new products, but we won't use that for now!) You should then be taken back to the product list.

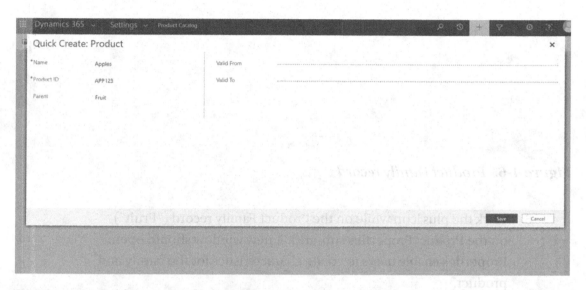

Figure 4-5. *Adding a new product family*

4. Repeat these steps to create a second family, but instead call this "Apples," and in the "Parent" lookup select the family created in the previous step: "Fruit." Save the record and then open it from the view by double-clicking or selecting its name.

5. Publish the family by clicking the Publish button dropdown icon and then choosing "Publish Family," as shown in Figure 4-6.

    Opening a product family could be confusing as it appears the same as a Product record. A family can be distinguished by its name, which has been appended with "Product Family:" at the beginning. Having a blank "Product Details" section is normal for a product family as a lot of the fields are relevant for only products.

Figure 4-6. *Product Family record*

6. Click the plus icon while on the Product Family record ("Fruit") on the Product Properties sub-grid. A new window should open. Properties enable users to create characteristics for the family and product.

7. Type the name of the property: "Color."

8. Leave the remaining configuration options as they are; however, it is important to understand what they do, which is summarized in the following:

    - **Read Only** – This means the property will not be editable within the product grid in the opportunity, quote, order, or invoice.

    - **Required** – It will be required for the user to complete the product grid in the opportunity, quote, order, or invoice.

    - **Hidden** – It will not show up within the product property editor when adding product line items in the opportunity, quote, order, or invoice.

9. Set the "Data Type" field to "Option Set." These field options relate to the types of fields this property is referring to and would need to be completed when adding the product line items on an opportunity, quote, order, or invoice.

10. Save the record, which will enable the sub-grid to add option-set items for the "Color" field. Add a small number of options, for example, "Yellow," "Red," and "Blue."

11. Once completed, save and close the record. See Figure 4-7.

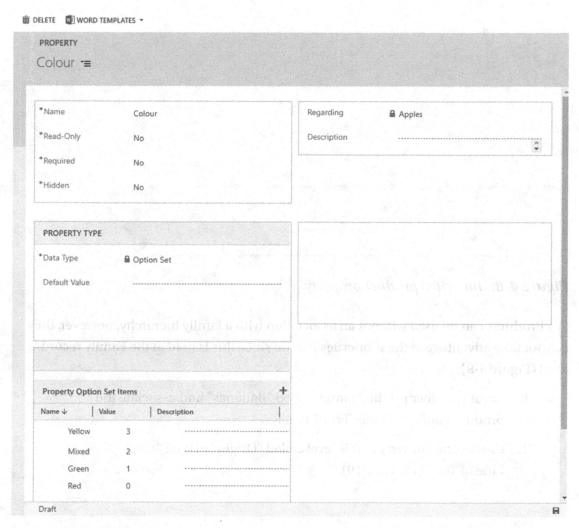

Figure 4-7. *The product Property form*

In the current example, the "Fruit" family now has a product property. This property will be inherited by the Apples family, which is visible when you navigate to the Apples Product Family record, as shown in Figure 4-8. It will be marked as an inherited property, and, while it cannot be deleted, it can be overwritten or hidden.

127

All products associated with the level of hierarchy will inherit those properties when they are associated with the family, and users will be prompted to complete those properties when associating product line items within an Opportunity, Quote, Order, or Invoice record. Properties must be created at the family level and cannot be created at the product level.

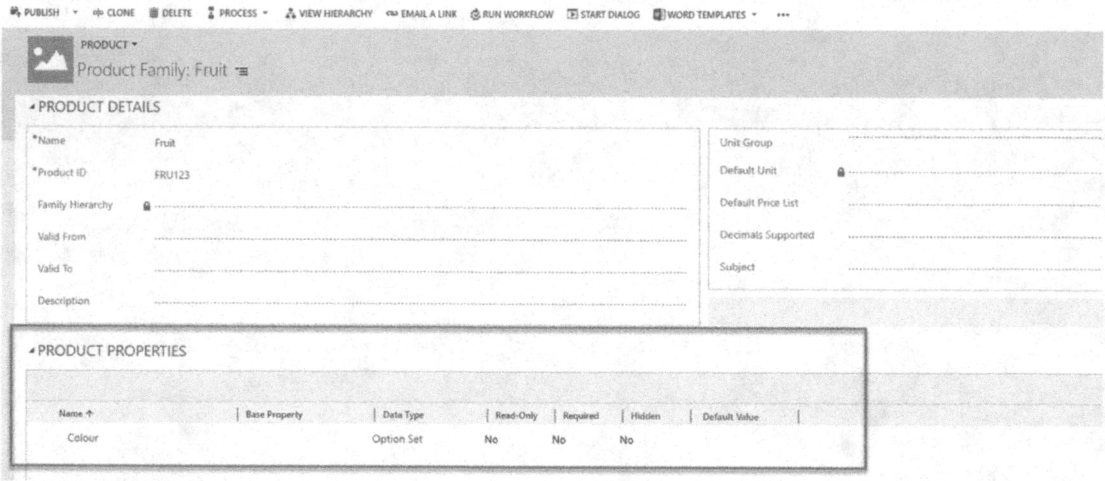

Figure 4-8. *Inherited product property*

Products can be used without an association with a family hierarchy; however, they cannot take advantage of the Properties feature since this is held at the Family record level (Figure 4-9):

1. Create another product family called "Bananas" and associate the product family with the "Fruit" family.

2. Create one property at this level called "Origin" of type "Single Line of Text" (Figure 4-10).

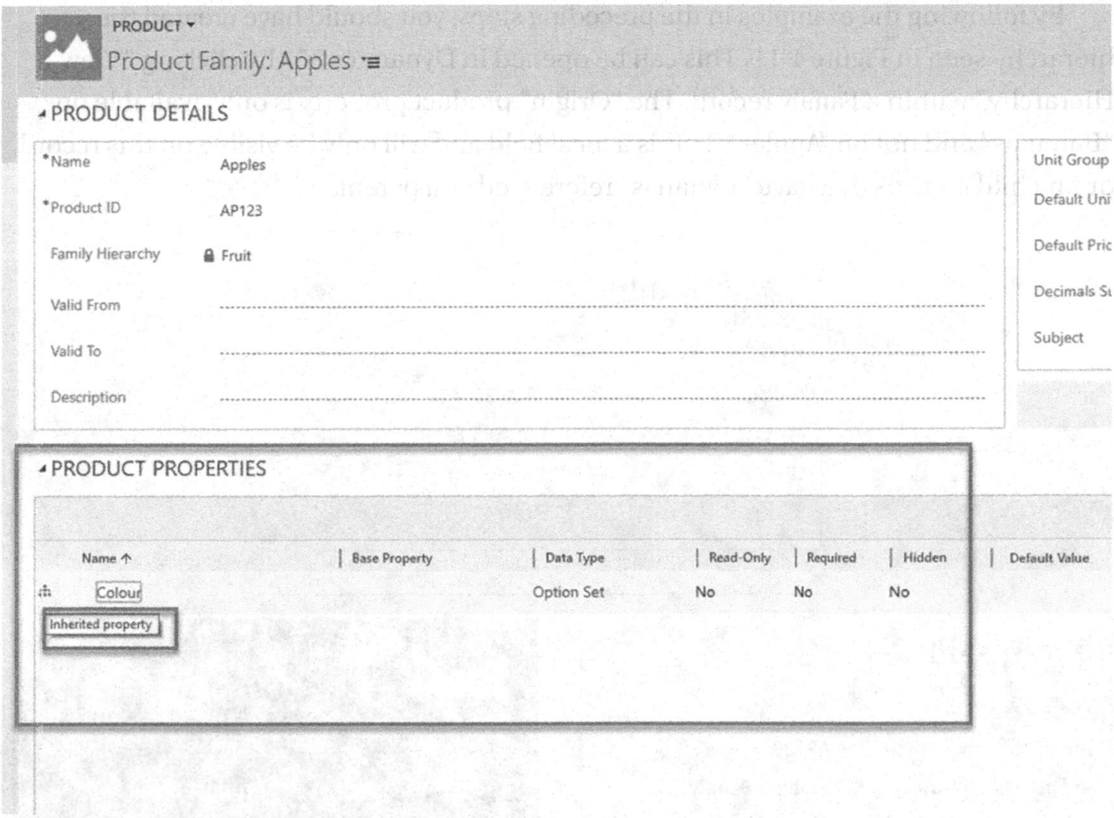

Figure 4-9. *Inherited property on the family level*

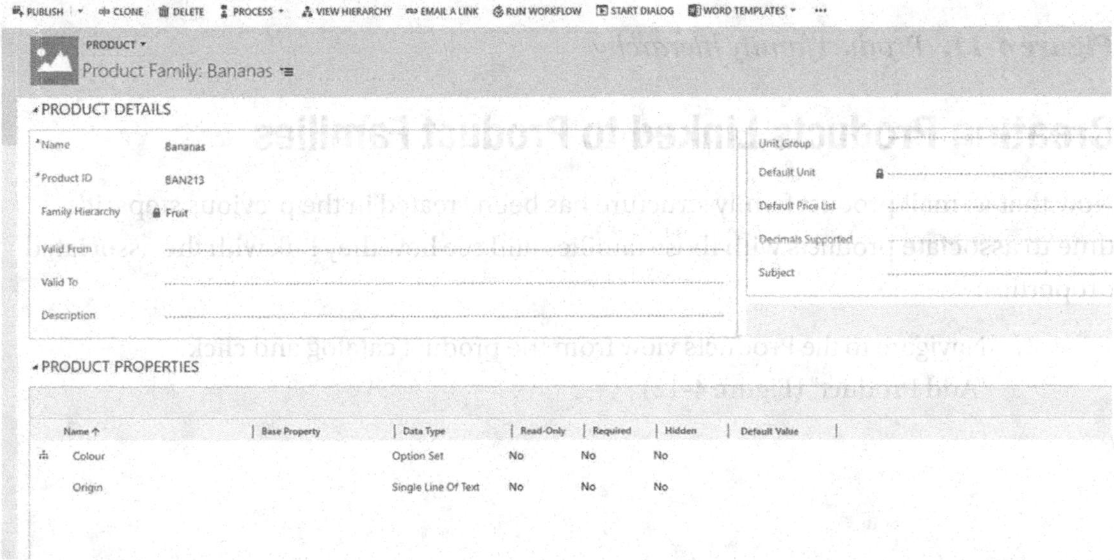

Figure 4-10. *New product family with one inherited property*

By following the examples in the preceding steps, you should have created the hierarchy seen in Figure 4-11. This can be opened in Dynamics 365 by clicking "View Hierarchy" within a Family record. The "Origin" product property is only available on "Bananas" and not on "Apples." This is a local field and will only be visible on this record, or on child records that have "Bananas" referenced as a parent.

Figure 4-11. *Product family hierarchy*

Creating Products Linked to Product Families

Now that a small product family structure has been created in the previous steps, it's time to associate products with those families and see how they link with the associated properties:

1. Navigate to the Products view from the product catalog and click "Add Product" (Figure 4-12).

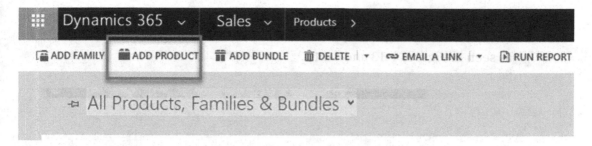

Figure 4-12. *Adding a new product*

2. Complete the details within the form. In the "Product" lookup, ensure "Banana" is selected as the family to associate this with as seen in the "Parent" field. Like product families, products can expire; enter start and end dates to set up the scheduling and expiry engine automatically so that it cannot be used when it is no longer valid in the business.

3. Click "New" on the lookup for "Unit Group." Create the unit group and group as described here:

    - **Unit Group** – Name: Fruit

    - **Unit Group Base Unit** – Name: Single Fruit

    This creates a unit group called "Fruit" and a unit called "Single Fruit" that has the quantity of 1. This is the base unit and the lowest amount of units this product is sold by.

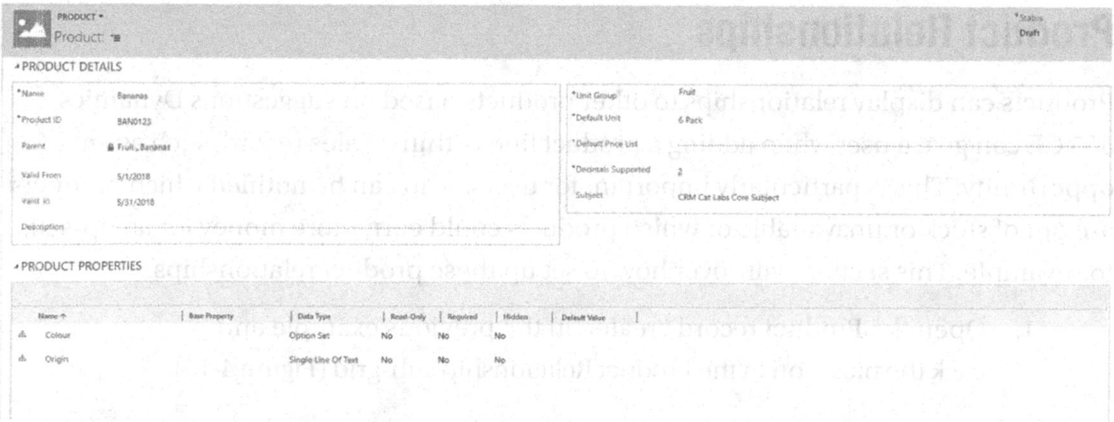

Figure 4-13. *Adding a new product*

4. Create a second unit associated with the unit group "Fruit" called "6 Pack" and enter quantity as "6" and base unit as "Single Fruit," as seen in Figures 4-13 and 4-14.

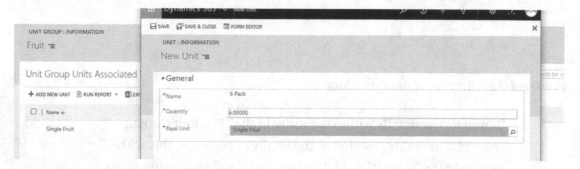

Figure 4-14. *Creating a unit group and units*

5. Complete the Product record by setting the decimals in the "Decimals Supported" field (normally 2) and the subject if required (as discussed in an earlier chapter).

6. Save the record.

Upon saving the record, the Product Properties sub-grid will be populated with the two properties set up in the earlier steps. This demonstrates the inheritance the product has obtained from being associated with the linked product family. Following the previous steps, create another two products, "Oranges" and "Pears," in the same way to use in the next steps.

Product Relationships

Products can display relationships to other products based on suggestions Dynamics 365 CE can give a user when adding a product line within a Sales record, such as an opportunity. This is particularly important for users, who can be notified which products are out of stock or unavailable or which products could earn more money for an up-sell, for example. This section will cover how to set up these product relationships:

1. Open the Product record created in the previous example and click the plus icon in the Product Relationship sub-grid (Figure 4-15).

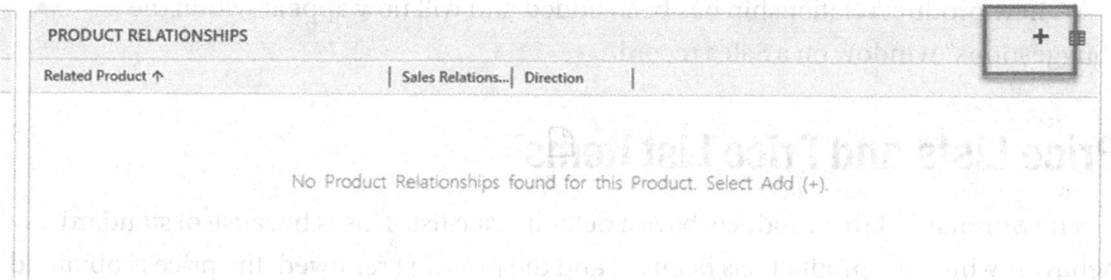

PRODUCT RELATIONSHIPS

| Related Product ↑ | | Sales Relations... | Direction | |

No Product Relationships found for this Product. Select Add (+).

Figure 4-15. *Creating a product relationship*

2. A new window opens for you to create a new product relationship. This form is referred to as the Quick Create form and is shown in Figure 4-16.

3. Select another product to relate it to, which can be any of the products made in the previous examples.

4. Select "Cross-Sell" in the "Sales Relationship Type."

5. Select the direction as "Bi-Directional." *This is how it differs from unidirectional:* If "Pears" was selected by a user on the Product sub-grid in a Sales record, such as an opportunity, and if the relationship was unidirectional only, only the Banana record would be visible this way. If a user does the same on the Banana record, Pears wouldn't be offered as a cross-sell item, as the relationship is one-directional. Bidirectional means it would appear in both scenarios as a cross-sell relationship suggestion.

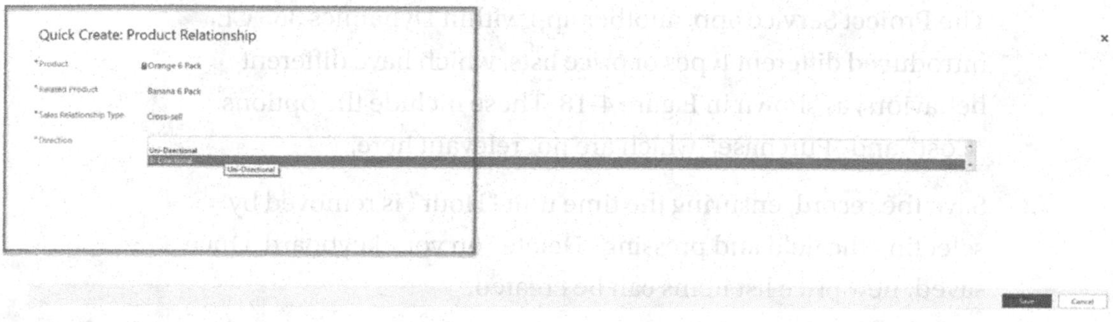

Quick Create: Product Relationship

*Product	Orange 6 Pack
*Related Product	Banana 6 Pack
*Sales Relationship Type	Cross-sell
*Direction	Uni-Directional / Bi-Directional

Figure 4-16. *Adding a product relationship*

A new product relationship has been added and will now appear within the "Suggestions" window on a Sales record.

Price Lists and Price List Items

It is recommended that products have a default price list. This is because of standard behavior where if a product has been set and the price list removed, the price is obtained from the default price list set on the product. A price list is a list of products that can be selected from within an opportunity. Only one price list can be associated with a record. *Price list item* is the name given to the specific instance of a product on a price list at a particular cost or calculated cost. The next steps will guide you through creating a new price list:

1. Navigate to the Classic UI; then go to Settings ➤ Price Lists ➤ New (Figure 4-17).

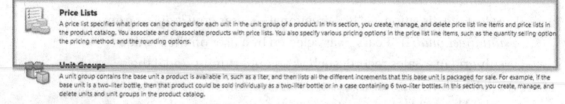

Price Lists
A price list specifies what prices can be charged for each unit in the unit group of a product. In this section, you create, manage, and delete price list line items and price lists in the product catalog. You associate and disassociate products with price lists. You also specify various pricing options in the price list line items, such as the quantity selling option, the pricing method, and the rounding options.

Unit Groups
A unit group contains the base unit a product is available in, such as a liter, and then lists all the different increments that this base unit is packaged for sale. For example, if the base unit is a two-liter bottle, then that product could be sold individually as a two-liter bottle or in a case containing 6 two-liter bottles. In this section, you create, manage, and delete units and unit groups in the product catalog.

Figure 4-17. *Adding a price list*

2. In the new blank Price List record, select the "Sales" option for the field "Context."

   The Project Service app, another app within Dynamics 365 CE, introduced different types of price lists, which have different behaviors, as shown in Figure 4-18. These include the options "Cost" and "Purchase," which are not relevant here.

3. Save the record, ensuring the time unit "Hour" is removed by selecting the field and pressing "Delete" on your keyboard. Once saved, new price list items can be created.

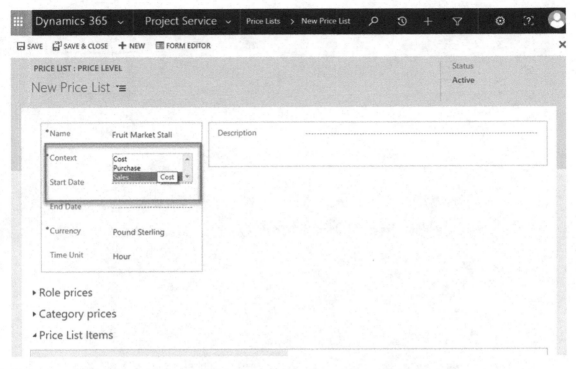

Figure 4-18. *Price list context, added for Project Service Automation customizations*

> 4.   Expand the Price List Item tab in the Price List form, and click the plus icon on the sub-grid to create a new price list item (Figure 4-19).

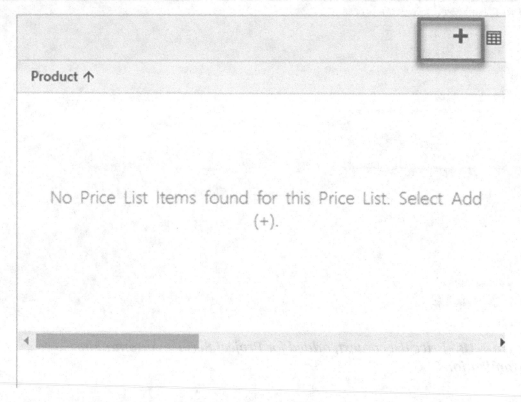

Figure 4-19. *Click the plus icon in the sub-grid to start creating price list items*

The price list item is the link between the Product record and the specific instance of it on a price list. A product can have multiple prices and so would have different Price List Item records on different price lists, all relating back to a single Product record. The Product record stores core information about a product that does not change often and is generic for the organization.

5. Complete the initial record details for the price list item, as shown in Figure 4-20, including the "Product" and "Unit" lookup fields. There are some specific fields on this record that require some explanation:

- **Quantity Selling Option** – Allows the user to split the quantities, for example, decimals and halves.

- *Price Method* – This is specifically regarding how the amount/ price of this instance of a product is calculated. This will be covered in more depth shortly.

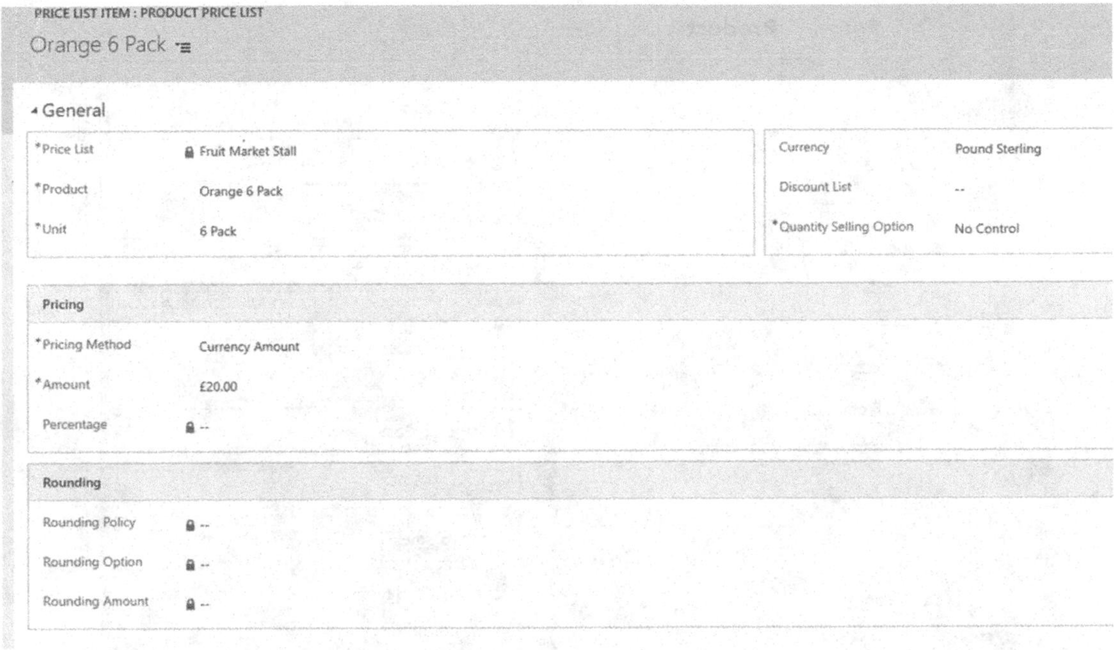

PRICE LIST ITEM : PRODUCT PRICE LIST

Orange 6 Pack ⩸

⊿ General

*Price List	🔒 Fruit Market Stall	Currency	Pound Sterling
*Product	Orange 6 Pack	Discount List	--
*Unit	6 Pack	*Quantity Selling Option	No Control

Pricing

*Pricing Method	Currency Amount
*Amount	£20.00
Percentage	🔒 --

Rounding

Rounding Policy	🔒 --
Rounding Option	🔒 --
Rounding Amount	🔒 --

Figure 4-20. *Price list item being created using the pricing method "Current Amount"*

Some fields need to be added to the Product entity to make it more relevant as these have been removed by default in previous updates of Dynamics 365 CE. Skip ahead to Setup to learn how to add fields or get a customizer to add hidden existing fields onto the Product form, shown in Figure 4-21. Once the changes have been made, ensure the customizations have been saved and published so you can see them on the Product record:

- List Price (required)
- Current Cost (required)
- Standard Cost (required)

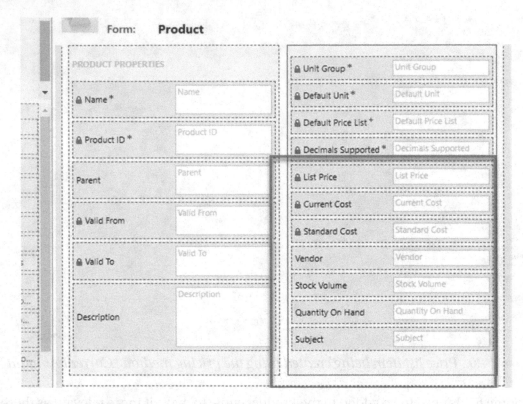

Figure 4-21.   *Adding standard fields not visible on the form*

Figures 4-20 and 4-21 display how the fields can be dragged over from the Field Designer onto the Product form, how it looks in the Form Designer, and how that translates to a real Product form for a user.

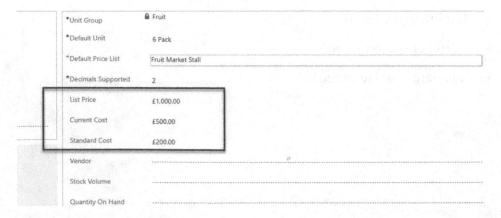

Figure 4-22.   *Pricing values critical to understanding the different pricing methods on the price list item*

Figure 4-23 shows the different pricing options available for a price list item based on the data of what is on the Product record it is related to – all except "Currency Amount," which is based on a simple value amount set on the price list item itself.

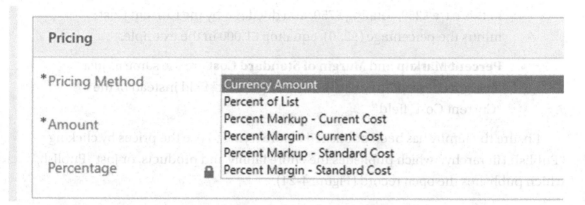

Figure 4-23. *The different pricing methods available on the price list item*

There are several different options available for managing the price of a product on a price list. There is no correct or incorrect way of pricing products; it is based on what and how the organization sells their products:

- **Currency Amount** – It displays an "Amount" field, and you enter a value – the most straightforward of the options.

- **Percent of List** – A user specifies a percentage – for example, 50% – and a rounding option (e.g., none, up, or down), which is calculated from the field *List Price* on the related product. In the example, this would be £500. 50% of that is £250.

- **Percent Markup of Current Cost** – Takes a percentage – for example, 50% – and a rounding option (e.g., none, up, or down) and calculates the percentage of the "Current Cost" field, in this case £500, and adds that amount ONTO the amount displayed in the "Current Cost," marking the value up by this percentage. In the example, this would be £250 + £500 = £750.

- **Percent Margin of the Current Cost** – Takes a percentage – for example, 50% – and a rounding option (e.g., none, up, or down) and calculates the percentage of the "Current Cost" field, in this case £500, and adds the Current Cost PLUS the amount of the percentage, in this case £250, totaling £750, and divides it by the Current Cost minus the percentage (£250), equaling £1,000 in the example.

- **Percent Markup** and **Margin of Standard Cost** are the same as just described, except they use the "Standard Cost" field instead of the "Current Cost" field.

Ensure the family has been published before trying to use the prices by clicking "Publish Hierarchy," which publishes the entire family and products, or just "Publish," which publishes the open record (Figure 4-24).

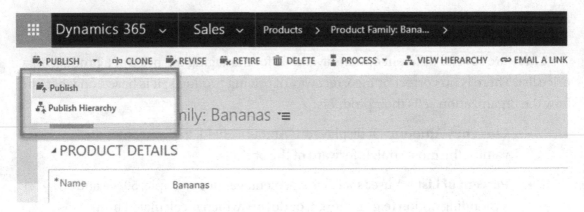

Figure 4-24. *Publish Hierarchy allows for the full family hierarchy to be made available and published for use*

Task: Create three price list items for all the products, trying different pricing methods to see how they work. Once set up, ensure you open an Opportunity record, select the price list, and add your items to see the real amounts based on the options you configured in the earlier steps (Figure 4-25).

Figure 4-25. Examples of the pricing based on the preceding definitions

Discount Lists

Discount lists are linked to price list items, where a specific volume has been purchased within a product line item (Figure 4-26). They can be associated with a price list item and allow for the discount to be applied should the product line item quantity be between the Begin and End amounts set on the associated Discount List record.

Figure 4-26. Adding a new discount list

Task: Create a new discount list. Navigate to Settings ➤ Product Catalog ➤ Discount List.

1. Click "New" and create a new discount list.

2. Set the "Type" option as "Amount."

141

Discounts can be set to be based on an amount or on a percentage. *Amount* means a set value amount to be discounted, whereas *Percentage* means a percentage of the cost of the item (Figure 4-27). The Percentage option is much more fluid because the overall discount then depends on the pricing option of the related price list item (Figure 4-28).

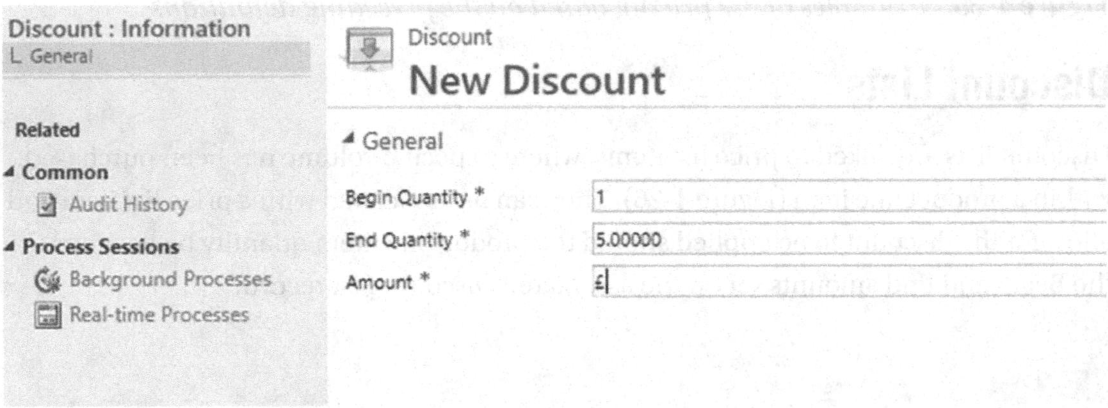

Figure 4-27. *Setting the Begin and End quantities in the fields "Begin Quantity" and "End Quantity" for the volume discount*

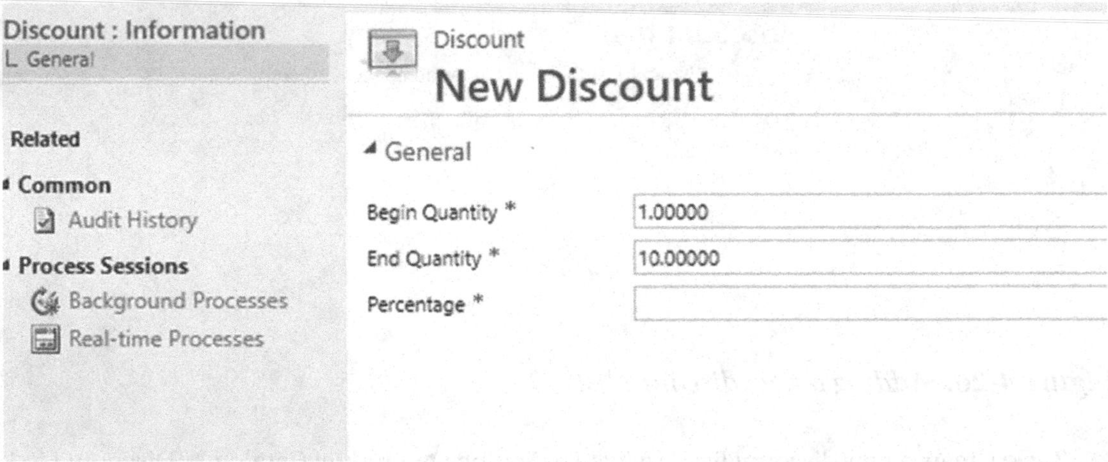

Figure 4-28. *Setting the Begin and End quantities for the volume discount; type is Percentage*

Once the discount list has been created, it is then associated with a price list item within the "Discount List" lookup (Figure 4-29). Only one discount list can be active at any one time for a price list item.

3. Associate the discount list with a price list item by opening the Price List Item and adding the record made in the previous step to the "Discount List" field.

4. Navigate to an Opportunity record and add a product line item, incrementing the quantity to be within the Begin and End quantities listed as set in the Discount List form in the earlier step. There should be a discount applied as specified within the associated discount list.

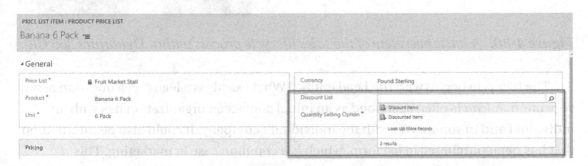

Figure 4-29. *Associating the discount list on the price list item*

Leads-to-Invoice Sales Lifecycle with Product Catalog Integration

Dynamics 365 CE has a full sales lifecycle that reaches across five core entities, with other areas and functionality supporting those areas throughout the process. The product catalog is one of those supporting features.

The sales lifecycle begins with a lead and ends with an invoice. The two core areas of this lifecycle are the initial creation of a lead and the transition to an opportunity. Quotes supplement the opportunity, and once it has been won, orders and invoices act as reference records with the same detail going forward (Figure 4-30). These records are often integrated with another system or used by entirely separate departments owing to their similarity in nature to each other.

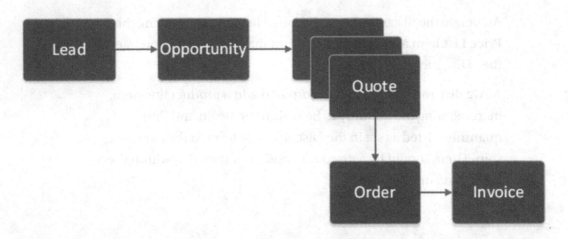

Figure 4-30. *A basic overview of the sales lifecycle process within Dynamics 365 CE*

The lifecycle begins with the Lead entity. "What exactly is a lead?" is a question asked very often. A *lead* is often described as an initial contact an organization has with an individual and in some cases with the individual's company. It could also be information that has been purchased in list form, which is a common case in marketing. This information is considered low quality and minimal. Leads can also be records created from marketing automation tools, where they have been scored, graded, and assigned to a member of the sales team to move forward.

The information captured at the lead level is the name, company, and notes of their initial interaction. As with most records within Dynamics 365 CE, activities can be utilized, such as logging when phone calls happened and tracking email conversations. Leads combine the information associated with the contact, account, and opportunity, and once the lead is qualified, those records branch out within Dynamics 365. This branching process creates more "permanent" records within the system, such as Contact and Account records, with the sales process moving forward as a qualified opportunity (Figure 4-31).

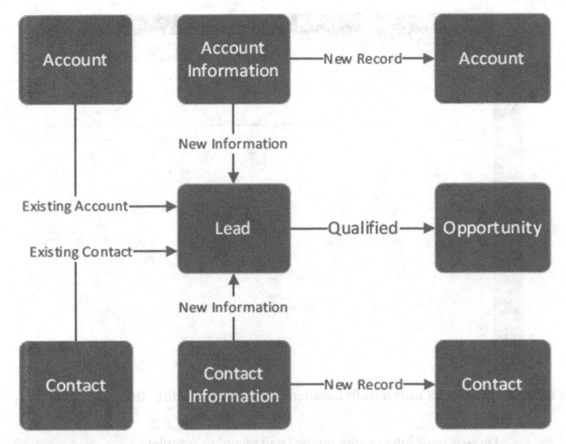

Figure 4-31. *The qualification process of a lead creates new Account and Contact records where none were specified*

When qualifying a Lead record, if an existing Contact and/or Account record was associated with the Lead record, it would take the information and use it to create new records within Dynamics 365 CE, such as Contact and Account records, taking the initiative to assume existing records were not associated with it and so it would create them for you. It would then take the information regarding those records and data contained within the Lead record, close the Lead, and create a new Opportunity record, associating the new Contact and Account records with the new Opportunity.

Task: Create a new Lead. Open the Sales Hub App within the Unified Interface and click "Leads" on the sitemap (Figure 4-32).

1. Click "New," which opens a blank Lead record.

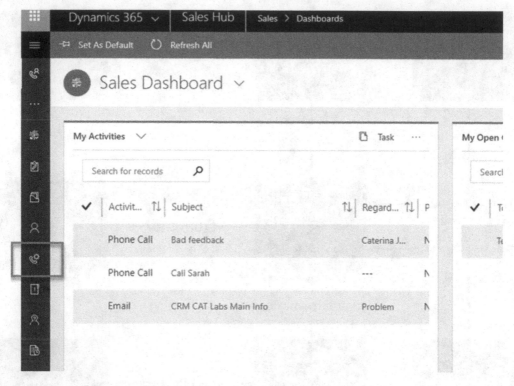

Figure 4-32. *Click Leads within the sitemap in the Sales Hub App*

There is basic information on the Lead record to complete,
including the topic, which is normally a highlight of the
interaction and some detail of the requirement or context in
which they are created. Also the name and company details of the
person are needed. Standard Dynamics 365 CE assumes this is a
sales engagement, and so it includes connection grids specifically
designed to include your stakeholders and competitors so as to
identify key individuals and organizations your organization is
running in competition with.

2. Complete the initial details of a lead, including the topic, contact
    information, and company information. Once completed, save the
    record (Figure 4-33).

Figure 4-33. *Creating a new lead within the Sales Hub*

The lead-to-opportunity process is guided by the lead-to-opportunity Business Process Flow (Figure 4-34). The Qualify stage is singular and references the Lead record only. The fields in this stage reference existing Contact and Account records and prompt the user if they already exist within the system to associate them now. If they do exist, users can utilize the "Existing Account" and "Existing Contact" fields to identify them. Leads can be linked to existing records, especially in the context of returning business.

Figure 4-34. *The Business Process Flow from lead to opportunity*

3. Complete the rest of the fields within the Lead form, including budget-related fields.

Leads can exist for a period during which they are gaining additional score points if lead-scoring functionality is being used (as an extension to the platform or by utilizing the Dynamics 365 for Marketing app, covered later in the book). Leads can be marketed to, and once they meet qualification criteria, they can be converted into opportunities. Leads are not designed to stay active, but rather are meant to last for a limited time. The fundamental point is that qualification and disqualification criteria are internal decisions, not ones made by Dynamics 365 CE. The user decides based on their interactions with the individual whether they have met enough criteria to warrant qualification (Figure 4-35).

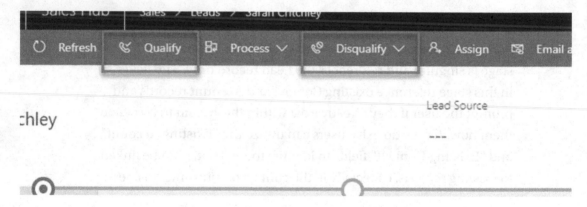

Figure 4-35. *Qualify and Disqualify buttons on the lead*

Disqualifying a lead would close it, making it read-only and giving it a specific status reason, for example, "Lost" or "Cannot Be Contacted."

Qualification will close the lead as "Won," automatically creating an Opportunity record and Account and Contact records if existing records were not selected. It would maintain the link from the Lead record to the Opportunity record in the fields "Originating Lead" and "Qualifying Opportunity" for any marketing playback of reporting, especially to determine return on investment (ROI).

4. Click the Qualify button on the command bar of the Lead record to qualify the lead, ensuring no data is entered in the "Existing Account" and "Existing Contact" fields. It will automatically close and then open a new, linked Opportunity record, creating the Contact and associated Account records (Figure 4-36).

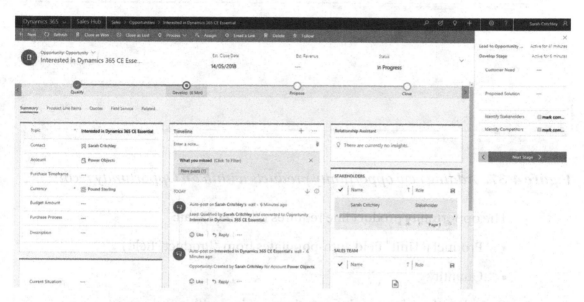

Figure 4-36. *Qualifying a lead creates a new Opportunity record with fields auto-populated from the information entered at the lead stage*

The opportunity's creation prompts you to gather more detailed information about the opportunity than that required at the lead stage. Gathering more information will take time as you nurture and develop relationships, moving the sales cycle toward a conclusion. The Business Process Flow prompts for information at each stage, with some data being mandatory before the stages can be advanced. For example, as time goes on, estimated closure dates, more accurate budgets, and products will be discussed, which can be captured within the Opportunity record.

Adding the associated products is managed using the Product Line Items tab within the Sales Hub application. A price list must be entered, and then you add a product line item per product by clicking "Add New Opportunity Products" within the sub-grid (Figure 4-37).

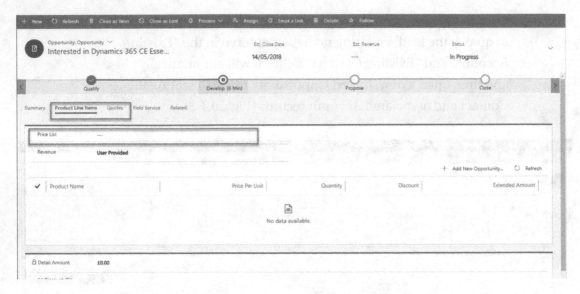

Figure 4-37. *Adding new opportunity products within an Opportunity record*

The opportunity product line requires minimal detail:

- Product ("Unit" field auto-populates from "Product" field)

- Quantity

5. Complete the minimum information required within the "Develop" stage of the Business Process Flow on the Opportunity record.

6. Move to the "Propose" stage by clicking "Next Stage" in the Business Process Flow.

7. In the Product Line Items tab, add a Price List record with active price list items from the task earlier in the chapter. Click "Add Opportunity Product" in the sub-grid of the Opportunity and create two new lines, adding them to the Opportunity record, as shown in Figure 4-38. Minimal detail is entered as the pricing will be configured on the product. Enter the "quantity" and ensure the product is selected via the lookup.

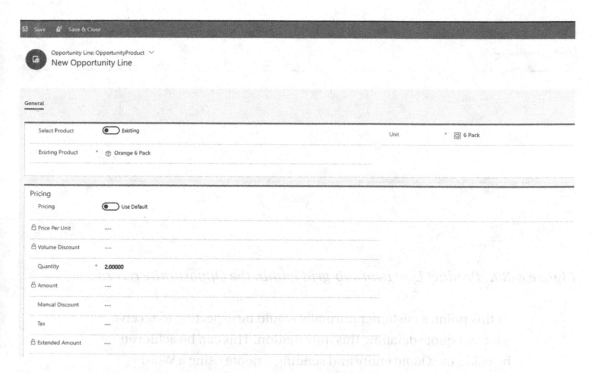

Figure 4-38. *Creating a new opportunity product line*

8. Once finished, click "Save and Close" on the product line item.

    Specific information is automatically populated by the details
    set up within the product catalog, including the amount. This
    is also where you can add a discount per line if required, either
    automatically, per any associated discount list, or manually. You
    can also add any relevant tax.

    Users can, if the security permission "Override Opportunity
    Pricing within their security role" is selected, override the
    pricing and manually enter any amount they wish by clicking the
    "Override Pricing" button.

    Once completed, the Product sub-grid will show the correct price,
    quantity, and total for the information just entered. Users can add
    as many lines as they require (Figure 4-39).

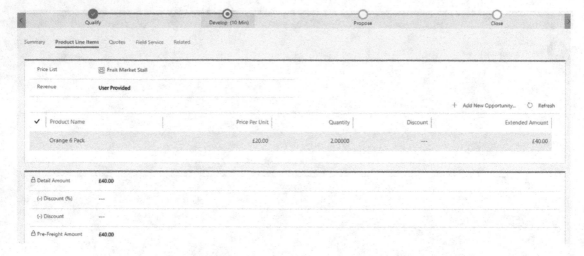

Figure 4-39. *Product Line Item sub-grid within the Opportunity record*

At this point, a customer normally would be expecting to receive a formal quote detailing this information. This can be achieved by using the Quote entity and sending a quote using a Word template, which is provided as standard within Dynamics 365 CE.

9. Navigate to the Quotes tab and click "Add New Quote." This is shown in Figure 4-40.

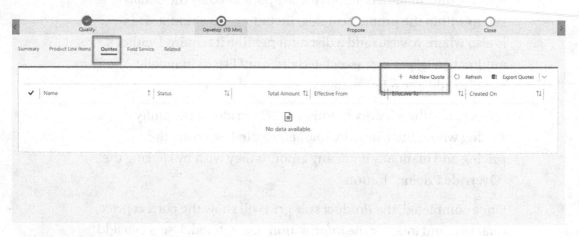

Figure 4-40. *Navigate to the Quotes tab and click "Add New Quote"*

A new Quote record will appear in the sub-grid and then automatically open. Dynamics 365 CE prepopulates most of the information, including quote lines. This is copied from the originating Opportunity record (Figure 4-41).

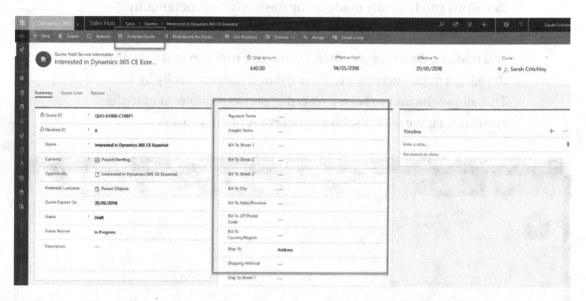

Figure 4-41. *Completing the payment terms and activating the quote*

The quote contains information about who is responsible for payment and the location to where the item should be shipped. Dynamics 365 CE does assume this is a physical item or that there is a physical place to go, as there is a "Shipment Address" field. The quote needs to be activated once it is no longer a draft and is ready to be sent to the customer. This is done by clicking "Activate Quote" on the command bar. An active quote is read-only, so it can be viewed. An active quote is one that is the most recent, up-to-date quote and is awaiting a customer decision (and therefore shouldn't be modified).

10. Complete the blank information within the quote where appropriate.

11. Click "Activate Quote."

More than one quote can exist at any one time. "Add Quote" from the Opportunity record can be used as many times as required. The quote itself has a lifecycle, as it is expected to be updated and changed based on customer feedback and requirements. Revisions can be easily made using the Revision functionality.

Clicking "Revise" on an activated quote closes the current quote and makes a direct copy in draft format so a user can make changes. Revising a quote increments the revision ID automatically by 1. This allows the user to keep a record of previous quotes sent to the customer. Figure 4-42 displays an overview of this process.

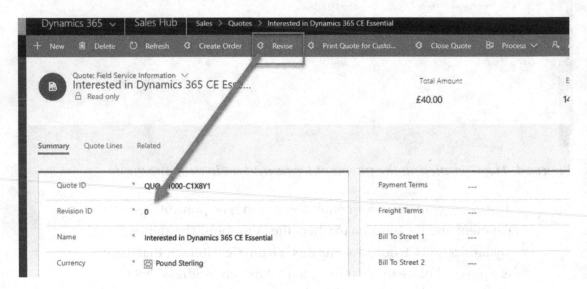

Figure 4-42. *The revision ID being incremented when the quote is revised*

12. Click "Revise" on the activated quote from the previous step. Notice this has now copied the previous quote and incremented the revision ID by 1 (Figure 4-43).

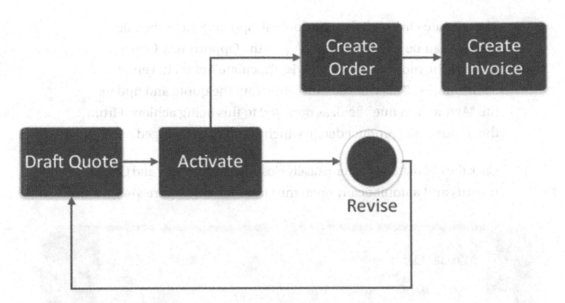

Figure 4-43. *The revision ID is incremented when the quote is revised*

When a customer has agreed on a quote, it is time to close the Opportunity and Quote records. This will create a new Order record. Creating an Order record and closing the Opportunity and Quote records at the same time can be achieved with a single click.

13. Navigate to the quote agreed upon and click "Create Order," as shown in Figure 4-44.

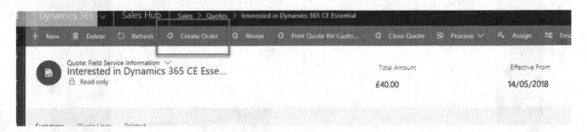

Figure 4-44. *Use the Create Order command bar button on the activated quote to create a new order*

Note   If there is more than one active quote associated with an Opportunity, a different notification will appear asking the user to close the quotes.

The "Create Order" dialog window will appear, where specific options can be selected that roll up to the Opportunity Close record. The most important one is "Calculate Actual Revenue from Quotes." This will take the value from the quote and update the "Actual Revenue" field, as opposed to this being achieved from the opportunity product detail, which could have changed.

14. Click the OK button to automatically close the Opportunity and Quote records and automatically open the Order record (Figure 4-45).

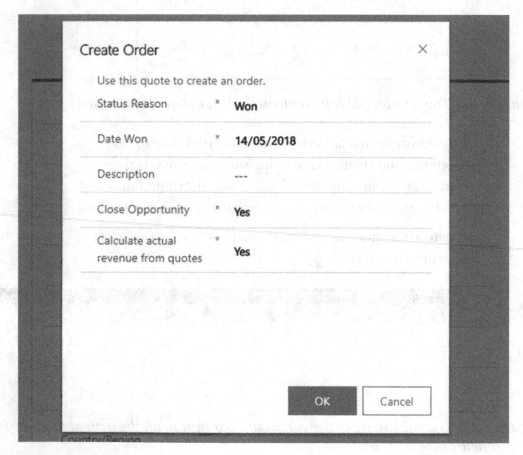

Figure 4-45. *"Create Order" Dialog*

An Order record in Dynamics 365 represents a confirmed order (Figure 4-46). This can normally mean that a formal confirmation of work has been agreed upon and signed, such as a contract.

It could indicate to a warehouse the need to obtain the items and complete the order, shipping any physical items to the shipping address provided. It could also represent a record of shipment. These examples demonstrate how flexible this record is and what it can represent in an organization's sales process.

Figure 4-46. *Order record*

The Order record has notable functionality. The Create Invoice button on the command bar does not close the order and instead creates a new invoice and associates it with the order. An order represents a contractual commitment to provide a service, and so it is assumed this would remain open and active within the system until that is delivered or provided. Keeping an order open means more than one invoice can be associated in instances of payment plans and paying in part, not just the scenario of a single payment.

The order itself could be shipped in more than one part, allowing a user to select "Partial" as the status reason, which closes an order when set to "Fulfilled." Orders can also be cancelled, and selecting "Cancel Order" updates the status and makes the Order record read-only (Figure 4-47).

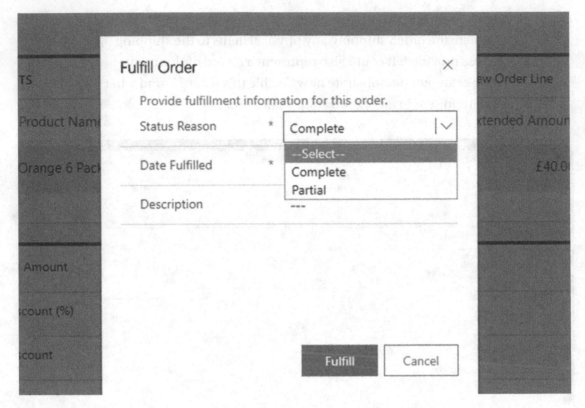

Figure 4-47. *Fulfilling an order and selecting "Complete" or "Partial"*

15. Click "Create Invoice" on the Order record. This should open a new Invoice record (Figure 4-48).

16. Navigate back to the Order record (easily by clicking the "Order" lookup field from the invoice) and select "Fulfill Order," selecting "Complete" as the status reason.

Figure 4-48. *Selecting "Create Invoice" from an Order record creates a new Invoice record, auto-populating data from the Order record*

The Invoice record, like the Order record, has notable functionality:

- The Confirm Invoice button confirms the invoice has been billed; invoices can be generated but not necessarily sent, which is where this differentiation is important and useful.

- Invoices can be cancelled – when they have been made in error, for example.

- The same as an order, invoices can be marked as paid, but also can be paid partially. To make new invoices for scenarios of partial payment or payment plans, click "Create Invoice" from the Order record as many times as required, manually editing the products and the cost to suit the invoices being paid.

17. Open the Invoice record and select "Invoice Paid" from the command bar, selecting "Complete" as the status reason (Figure 4-49).

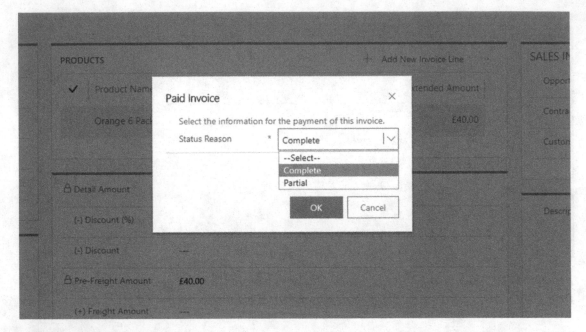

Figure 4-49. Confirming the invoice has been paid is similar functionality to the fulfillment of an order

Supporting Sales Functionality

There are several different record types that support the sales lifecycle discussed in the previous section. These records can enhance the sales lifecycle by providing more information that can be optionally used by users.

Competitors

Within the Sales Hub application, there are some extensions to the standard sales process that can be utilized to enhance the features and user experience.

The Competitor record is available on the UI Client sitemap and is a simple concept: a Competitor record holds details of a competitor for an organization. These records are often linked to Opportunity records, allowing the sales team to see whom they are up against for the competition of a contract. Information available in the Competitor record includes contact information, revenue, and strengths and weaknesses.

The Opportunities tab on the Competitor record provides users with the ability to see straight away which opportunities the competition is linked to (Figure 4-50). This functionality can be extended to reports or rollup fields to see how many opportunities the sales team has won instead of the competitor so as to create rankings of the largest competitors in the business. In Part II, some of these extensions will be explored.

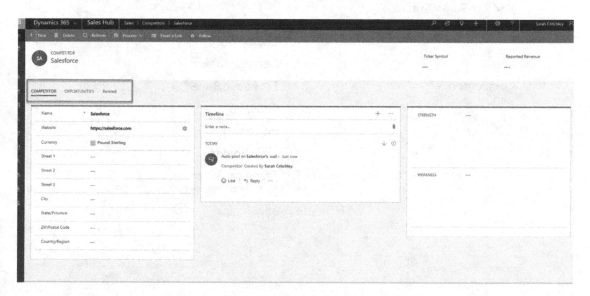

Figure 4-50. *Competitor record available in the UCI and linked to an Opportunity record*

Connections

Connections within Dynamics 365 CE allow a user to connect any record type to another record type. Examples include connecting an Account to an Account or a Contact to a Work Order. A "role" is specified when creating the link; this is the reason for connecting record A to record B. The specified role can include a reciprocating role from B to A. A simple example here is a real-life parent and child relationship. A to B could have the role Parent. B to A would be Child. These are managed by "connection roles." There are a large number of connection roles as standard, but new custom connection roles can be created via Classic UI at the time of writing by navigating to Settings ➤ Business Management and clicking "Connection Roles."

Connections, while simple, can prove to be useful in sub-grids. They allow users to see relationships to other records. It empowers users to link associated records without having to make customizations for basic relationships and information. Leads and opportunities use these sub-grids as standard in the Stakeholders grid by using the Stakeholder connection role (Figure 4-51).

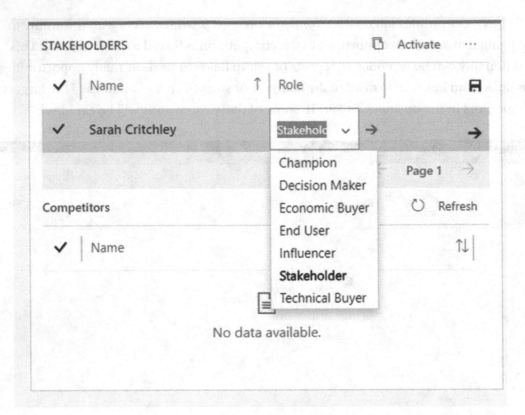

Figure 4-51. *Connections being used in standard sales functionality under the "Stakeholders" role*

The query used by the Stakeholders grid is shown in Figure 4-52. The query has the "type" conditioned to "Contact" and the "to" role as a stakeholder, creating the filtered view. This can easily be achieved for any other standard or custom connection roles to provide a tailored experience using standard features.

Edit Filter Criteria   ×

Define the filter and search criteria for this view to use.

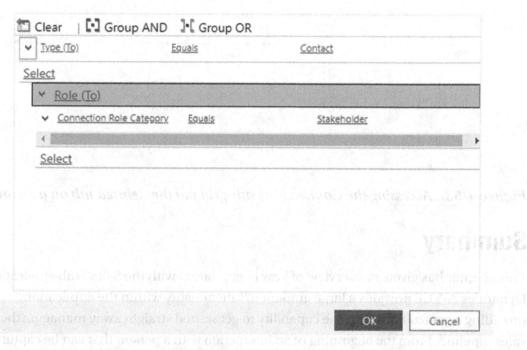

Figure 4-52. Standard query used for the Stakeholders Sub-Grid

The Connections sub-grid can be accessed from the Related tab on all records (Figure 4-53). From there you can add connections. Connections can be used for more than sales within other areas of Dynamics 365 CE, such as customer service.

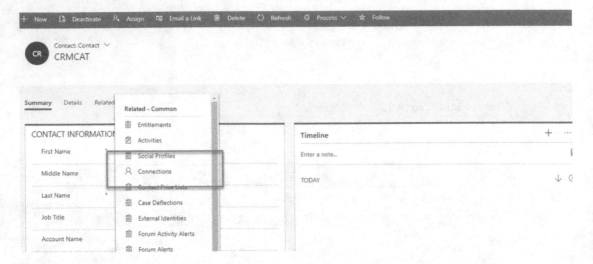

Figure 4-53. *Accessing the Connections sub-grid via the Related tab on a record*

Summary

This chapter has given an overview of how to get started with the Sales Hub application. Dynamics 365 CE provides a large amount of functionality within the application, providing organizations with the capability to get started straight away managing their sales pipeline. From the beginning of an interaction with a person that can be captured within a Lead entity all the way through to managing the generation of invoices, the lifecycle not only supports salespeople in obtaining the sale through easy collaboration and availability of the most useful data but also helps other staff through the creation of order and invoice information, which can provide useful integration points to back-office systems.

The customer engagement involved in a sales interaction can be managed through the records in the process, providing support to users through the features of the whole platform. This includes relationship insights, suggestion cards, and reminders about activities. Microsoft Outlook Integration gives users a seamless way to communicate with potential customers within a sales cycle while focusing on the interaction; the data is automatically synchronized to the Dynamics 365 CE platform. Finally, supporting records such as connections, covered within the last section of the chapter, can give relationship insights to other data held within the organization. Together, these features support users in their use of the app within their organization's sales lifecycle.

Chapter Tasks

1. Create a product family hierarchy larger than three levels with associated product properties at each level.

2. Create new products related to the product families.

3. Create product relationships on the products created in the previous step.

4. Create a new price list and associate the products as price list items.

5. Create a new lead, associating new contact and account information. Disqualify the lead.

6. Create a new lead and qualify the lead.

7. Add more data into the Opportunity record and add product line items.

8. Create a connection from the opportunity to another record in the system using the standard connection roles.

9. Create a quote, revising it several times.

10. Create a new order from the quote made in the previous step.

Further Reading

Troubleshooting the Sales Hub Application (Microsoft, 2018). URL: `https://docs.microsoft.com/en-us/dynamics365/customer-engagement/sales-enterprise/troubleshooting-admin`

Troubleshooting for Sales People in Dynamics 365 (Microsoft, 2018). URL: `https://docs.microsoft.com/en-us/dynamics365/customer-engagement/sales-enterprise/troubleshooting`

Lead to Qualification Overview (Microsoft, 2018). URL: `https://docs.microsoft.com/en-us/dynamics365/customer-engagement/sales-enterprise/nurture-sales-from-lead-order-sales`

CHAPTER 5

Field Service and Resource Scheduling

Dynamics 365 CE includes an extensive Field Service application that gives organizations the ability to create work orders and schedule resources for those work orders to be completed on-site. The Field Service app provides the capability for asset management, inventory adjustment and management, and scheduling the resources using a detailed, easy-to-use scheduling board. It shares a component, Universal Scheduling, with the Project Service Automation application, also available within Dynamics 365 CE. Universal Scheduling is available to any organization, provided at least one of these apps is licensed, and gives the capability for anything to be scheduled, including custom entities. This increases the available scope within organizations, allowing them to create more specific workflows around custom components.

The Field Service app provides offline capability through the support of Resco.net built-in features that give engineers peace of mind that they do not have to rely on connectivity to complete work within the app. The app is also capable of managing stocks and products so that an organization can manage the full end-to-end lifecycle of an engineer's needed parts to use and bill for on-site.

This chapter will focus on the essentials of Field Service (Figure 5-1). These essentials are how to get started, create work orders and bookings, and use the scheduling board. The chapter will then take a deep dive into the mobile application and how an on-site staff member would set up and complete an assigned job. The end of the chapter will cover some specific functionality that supplements the basic lifecycle of a work order. This chapter will give you enough essential knowledge to be confident in the theory and practicality of getting started with the Dynamics 365 Field Service app so other resources can be investigated for specific use cases and configuration.

167

© Sarah Critchley 2020
S. Critchley, *Dynamics 365 Essentials*, https://doi.org/10.1007/978-1-4842-5911-5_5

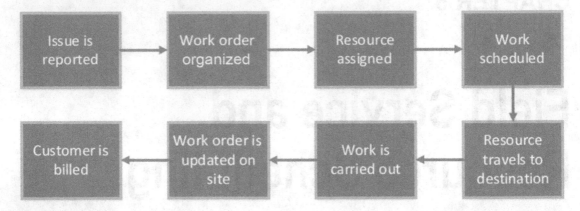

Figure 5-1. *An overview of the core process within the Field Service application*

Roles Within Field Service

Field Service functionality assumes there are distinct roles during the lifecycle of a work order. Beginning from the origin of the work order, which could be a case or an opportunity or even result from another work order, the role of the user creating the work order can be different. It could be support staff, a salesperson, or another field engineer. Once a work order has been created with basic information, it is then up to the user in the role of the *dispatcher* to complete any missing information and schedule resources to complete the work required. The dispatcher is essential to the scheduling of bookings based on the current workload of the available resources and is also the final say as to what is being booked. There are automated engines to suggest the most appropriate times and display these in priority order. The booking itself is completed by the dispatcher and managed from the schedule board. One of the primary reasons for this is because booking a work order is not the only scenario that requires management; there is also reorganizing and changing the work orders and providing field support to the engineer on-site should they require it. Dispatchers also manage the completed work order, passing the record over to back-end staff, for example, inventory or finance management, to bill the customer.

Organizations often have conflicting requirements for the dispatcher role, as they often want to omit this role and offer appointments externally to customers to book. Also, organizations want to be able to automatically optimize the scheduling regularly. There are two challenges with these requirements that are worth briefly discussing.

The challenge with offering appointments externally is that it removes the ability to optimize the resource based on both preference and utilization. The functionality would be best approached by adding custom statuses for resource bookings, but this still would require customization to find and locate a resource to see if the appointment is still available and book them in. It would also provide conflict if the resource booked were to reject the order.

Another issue as far as being able to optimize is concerned is that the scheduling engine considers many pieces of data about the related work order and customer, including their preferences. It also includes location optimization by not suggesting people outside of a set radius, as well as by suggesting a particular resource that matches the skills the work order requires and has the availability. Meeting customer preferences may not result in also meeting optimization targets for users nor take into account their previous location before that appointment. Organizations need to be able to prioritize what is the most important element within the scenario, which further demonstrates the helpfulness of having a user in the dispatcher role, as they can make those decisions based on the resources suggested by the system. More details on the roles within the Field Service application can be found within the "Further Reading" section at the end of this chapter.

In summary, the dispatcher is a prominent role within the Field Service app for use with the schedule boardIf this is functionality or a role that doesn't fit with the requirements or model of a company, there will likely be extra customization involved. That said, automatic scheduling is possible without the dispatcher. However, it does not come with the Field Service app as standard and is an extra, licensed solution. It provides the ability to schedule open work orders automatically based on the arguments referenced in the previous paragraph. It is not covered in this book; however, details can be found within the "Further Reading" section at the end of this chapter.

Setting Up Resources

Resources are what is referred to within Dynamics 365 CE as a bookable resource. The terminology is careful in relation to what this resource can be referring to, as it does not necessarily mean it is a human being. A bookable resource is *often* referred to as a field engineer, but this could mean any sort of human being who is bookable for any task and doesn't have to be one with parts or the standard "engineer in a van." It can also refer to a drone or a piece of automated equipment that can be booked and scheduled.

A Resource record is where administrative information about the resource is set, such as defining the starting point of the resource for jobs, if time-off requests should be approved, and if they should be displayed on the schedule board and included in availability searches. This information is set per individual resource and can be different per bookable resource.

Resource roles are associated with a resource and are roles that will be required in order for a work order to be completed. These roles are something specific that a bookable resource will have proficiency at based on their skills and the skills defined within the expected role.

Task: Create a new resource role.

1. Navigate to the "Resource Scheduling" section of the Classic UI, select "Resources," and click "New" (Figure 5-2).

Figure 5-2. *Navigate to "Resource Scheduling" and click "Resources"*

2. Set the Resource Type to "User" or "Contact," not entering any other information, and use the default "Main" warehouse and an hourly rate of an arbitrary value, such as $100 (Figure 5-3).

3. Enter a target utilization based on the metrics (e.g., 80% billable time out of 100% they are working) so performance can be measured, as well as the specific billing type of this role (e.g., is it a free role or a chargeable role?).

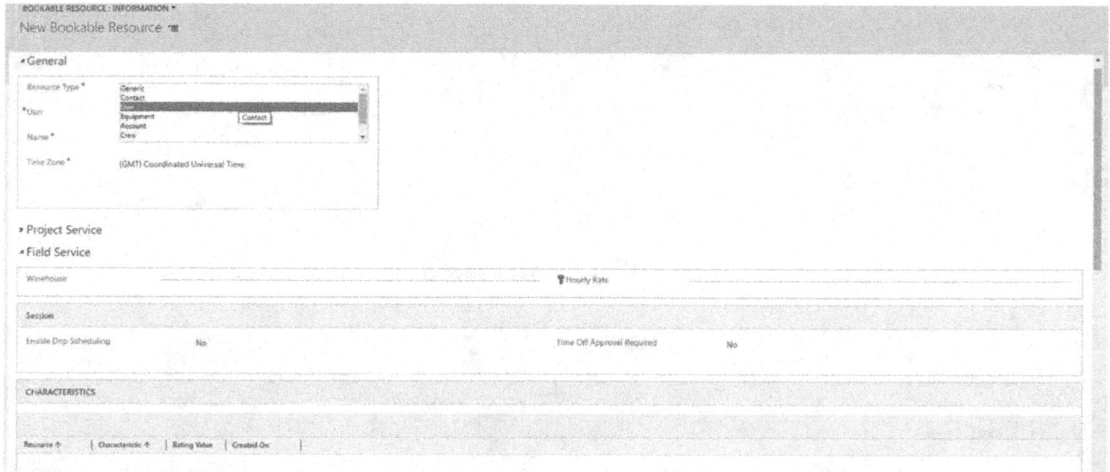

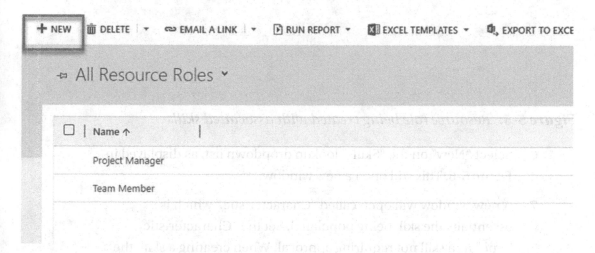

Figure 5-3. *Set the Resource Type to "User" or "Contact"*

4. Save the record.

5. Navigate to "Resource Roles" and add some skills to the role using the plus button in the sub-grid, shown in Figure 5-4.

Figure 5-4. *Adding a new resource role*

If this is your first time in the Field Service app, there will be no skills set up. This is an appropriate time to create new skills and get used to the process (Figure 5-5). Alternatively, test data can be imported, which is highlighted at the end of the chapter. While the sub-grid refers to skills, they are based on the Role Competency Requirement, which references a separate Skill record and what level this skill must be for this role.

171

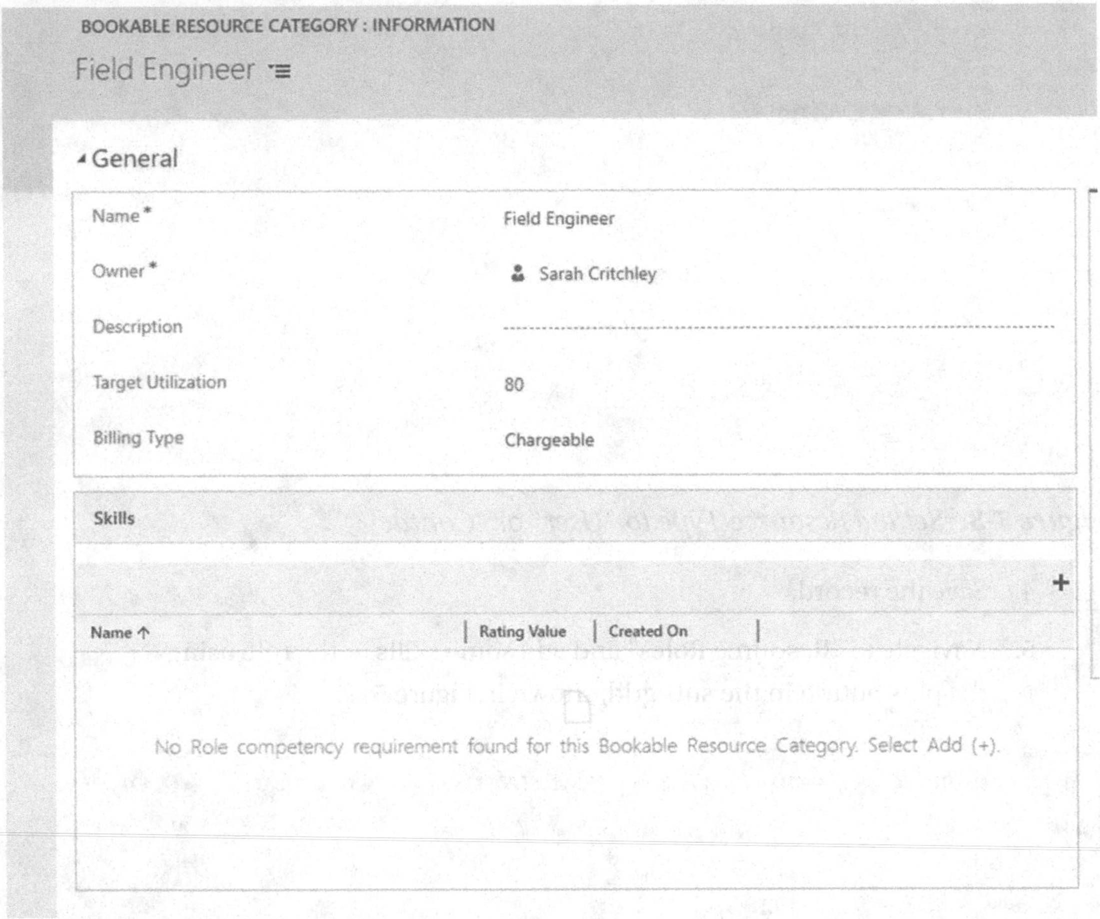

BOOKABLE RESOURCE CATEGORY : INFORMATION

Field Engineer ⁃≡

▲ General

Name *	Field Engineer
Owner *	👤 Sarah Critchley
Description	
Target Utilization	80
Billing Type	Chargeable

Skills

Name ↑	Rating Value	Created On	

No Role competency requirement found for this Bookable Resource Category. Select Add (+).

Figure 5-5. *Resource role being created with associated skills*

6.   Select "New" on the "Skills" lookup dropdown list, as displayed in
     Figure 5-6. This will open a new window.

7.   A new window will open called "Characteristic," which is
     essentially the skill being populated. Set the "Characteristic
     Type" as a skill not requiring approval. When creating a skill, the
     proficiency ratings are already created. These can be removed,
     and a specific (custom) proficiency rating can be used for the
     organization if required. For this chapter, we will be using the
     standard proficiency system.

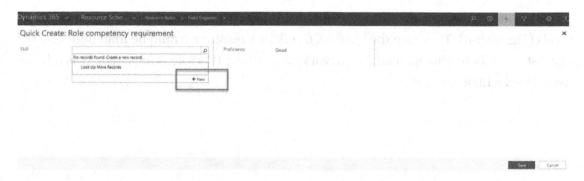

Figure 5-6. *Using the Quick Create form to create a new skill*

8. Save the record.

9. Select this as a skill for the resource role on the Quick Create form, which should still be open from the previous step, as shown in Figure 5-7.

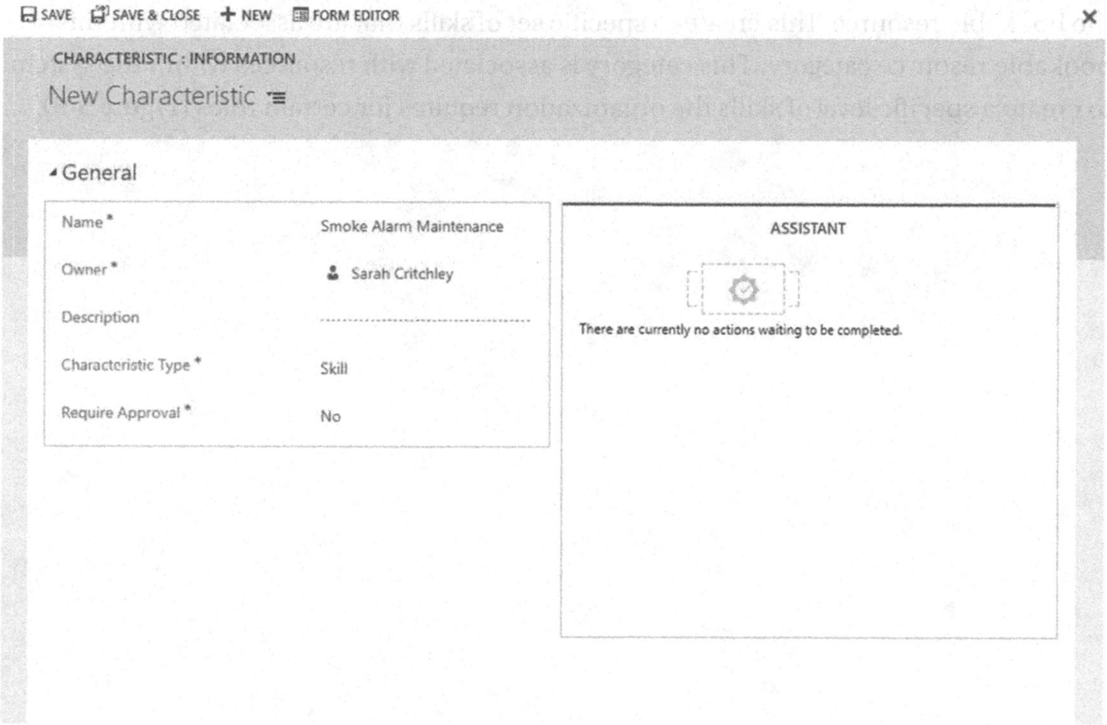

Figure 5-7. *Creating a new Characteristic record (skill)*

A resource role has now been created that has some skills at specific proficiency levels (Figure 5-8). These are the levels of the skills a resource would be matched against when being mapped against a work order where this role is required. This role is associated with a resource.

Figure 5-8. *Setting the proficiency for the skill required*

You can repeat the steps starting from Step 6 to create another skill associated with the bookable resource. This creates a specific set of skills that are associated with this bookable resource category. This category is associated with resources within the system to create a specific level of skills the organization requires for certain roles (Figure 5-9).

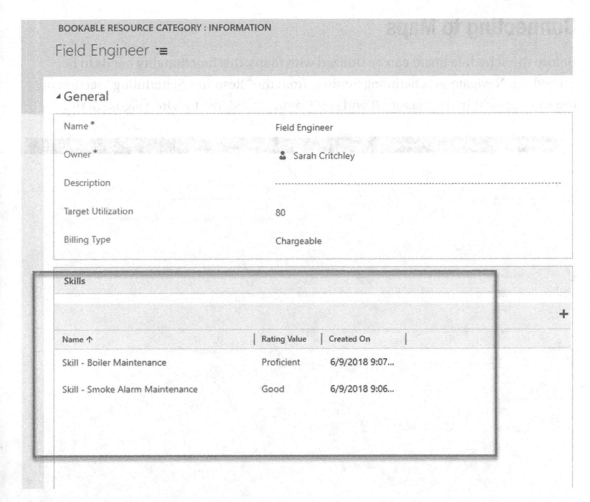

Figure 5-9. *A resource role with two associated skills of different proficiency levels*

Schedule Board

The schedule board is at the center of the Field Service app. The schedule board allows users to see unscheduled items (including work items or requests for work); schedule those items; see the resource list, resource times, and current schedule; check out distances on maps; and filter the data extensively. This section will cover how to get started using the schedule board.

Connecting to Maps

Before the schedule board can be utilized with maps, this functionality needs to be turned on. Navigate to Scheduling Settings from the "Resource Scheduling" section of the sitemap within the Classic UI and set "Connect to Maps" to "On" (Figure 5-10).

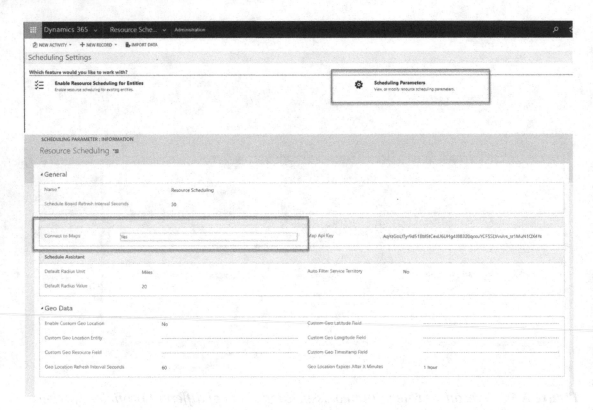

Figure 5-10. *Connecting the schedule board to maps within Dynamics 365*

Schedule Board Functionality

Let's get started setting up the schedule board:

1. Navigate to the schedule board via the Classic UI and select "Schedule Board." The board is going to look blank at this stage, but on the left-hand panel, the resource created in the previous steps should be visible (Figure 5-11).

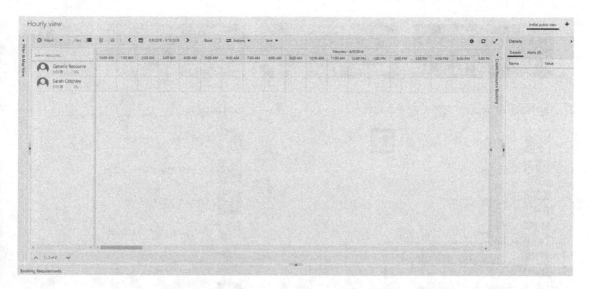

Figure 5-11. *Schedule board in the Field Service app with no scheduled items*

A resource can get booked under the following conditions:

- There is a resource requirement created that is open.

- An unscheduled work order exists.

- A project exists (this is not covered in this section and is related to the
  Project Service Automation App).

A *resource requirement* is a generic piece of work that is covered under the "Resource
Scheduling" section of the sitemap within the Classic UI and is a way for a requirement
to be made within the system and then have a resource booked against it (Figure 5-12).

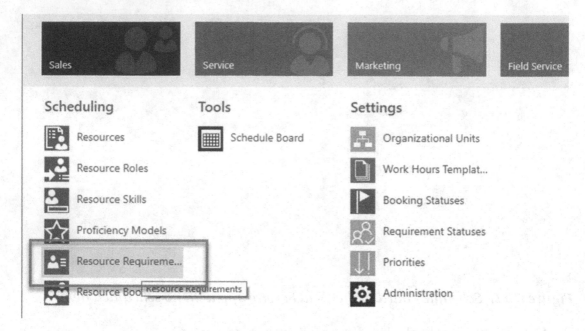

Figure 5-12.   *Creating a new resource requirement*

Resource requirements can be linked to work orders from a field service perspective, but there is not a requirement to – keeping a generic resource scheduling element that allows users to schedule a piece of work without a work order. Specific linked items can be associated with a resource requirement, including skills and roles required to fulfil that requirement. Inclusive of this are preferences and also specific organization units. These links are used within the resource scheduling engine to suggest the most available resource with the required skills (Figure 5-13).

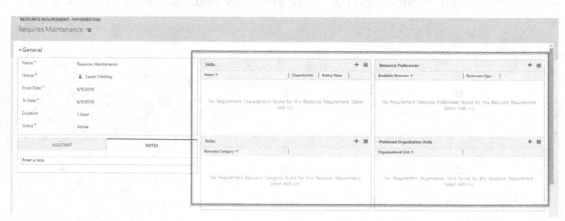

Figure 5-13.   *A resource requirement and the associated items required that would influence scheduling resources*

Task: Create a new resource requirement.

1. Select the "Resource Requirement" item from the sitemap and click "New."

2. Name the requirement and select "From" and "To" dates inclusive of today's date.

3. Once the duration is set, save the record.

4. Associate the skills that were created in the previous section so that the resource requirement is set up. This is shown in Figure 5-14.

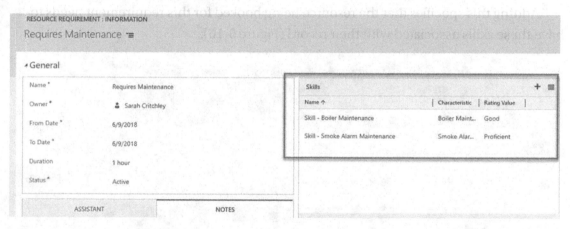

Figure 5-14. *A resource requirement with associated skills*

5. Navigate back to the original resource requirement and go to the Characteristic sub-grid.

6. Click "New" on "Add New Bookable Resource Characteristic" that also matches these skills which are part of the resource requirement (Figure 5-15).

Figure 5-15. *Link a new bookable resource requirement*

Adding this specifies that the resource being booked for this requirement needs to have these skills associated with their record (Figure 5-16).

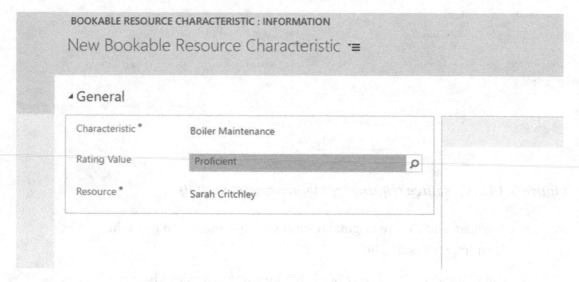

Figure 5-16. *Associating an existing skill and proficiency to the Resource Characteristic record*

Navigate back to the schedule board; there are two changes to the board. The section "Open Requirements" now has the requirement made in the previous step which is waiting to be scheduled, as shown in Figure 5-17.

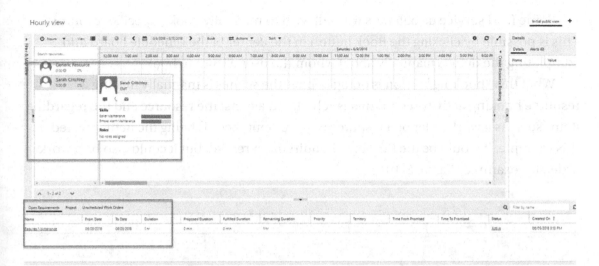

Figure 5-17. *In the "Open Requirements" heading, the new Resource Requirement record can be seen*

Clicking the "Requires Maintenance" resource requirement highlighted in Figure 5-18 opens the details regarding that record on the right-hand side. Again, this is particularly useful so that the user, in this case the field service dispatcher, doesn't have to click to open a record and then navigate back to the schedule board. They can perform the tasks from one screen.

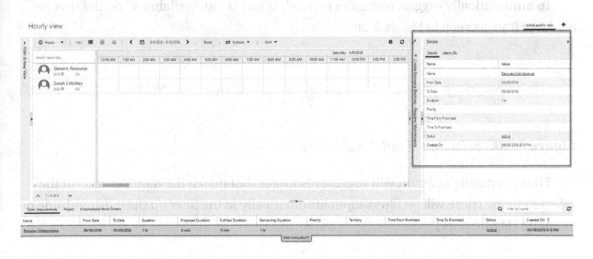

Figure 5-18. *Resource requirement specification can be seen from the schedule board*

Some field service dispatchers will still wish to manually book a specific resource. This is possible by clicking the Book button in the center of the schedule board and completing the details manually about whom the user wishes to book.

What this "booking" action is doing behind the scenes is manually making a resource booking activity record that is scheduled against the resource and the regarding item (such as a work order or a resource requirement record) being the item selected. In this example, it would be the Resource Requirement record, but it could also be a work order, for example (Figure 5-19).

Figure 5-19. *Manually creating a resource booking activity*

To automatically suggest resources instead, select "Find Availability" on the specific resource line, as seen in Figure 5-20.

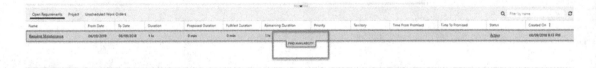

Figure 5-20. *Selecting "Find Availability"*

The scheduling assistant will suggest resources that match the requirements of the selected item. There will be filters input automatically in the filter on the left-hand side of the pane (Figure 5-21).

Figure 5-21. *The result of the system's suggesting potential resources from "Find Availability"*

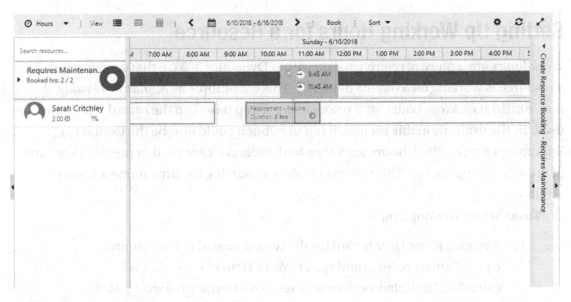

Figure 5-22. *The requirement can be dragged into the schedule board at the specific time to book*

The scheduling engine will highlight the unbooked time window in the resource calendar, and the user can click the Book button to create a new resource booking. This can be selected and dragged to another area if required (the system will suggest the first available unbooked time), as shown in Figure 5-22.

So far, this chapter has not discussed setting up working hours for the resource or the time available for the resource. This will be done in the next section. It is, however, important to realize that scheduling can be achieved at its most basic level by setting up the following steps:

- Have a resource.

- The resource has a role.

- The role has skills.

- The requirement has a time frame.

- The requirement has a specific role requirement.

Setting Up Working Hours for a Resource

Work hours are a piece of reference data within Dynamics 365 CE that specify when a resource is working on a day-to-day basis. This is as simple as *Monday to Friday, 9 a.m. until 5 p.m.* Work hours for a resource are set up based on the record type being used. In the example in this section, it is a user, but it could also be the Contact or Equipment record. Work hours are a standard, older concept used in previous versions of the scheduling engine. This process involves specifying the time frame a resource is available.

Task: Set up working hours.

1. Navigate to the User record (or the record related to the resource, e.g., a Contact record) and select "Work Hours," which loads a calendar. The default calendar is set so that a resource works 24/7. This is not sustainable or realistic for resources, so it is important this be modified.

2. Select "Set Up" and select "New Weekly Schedule," as shown in Figure 5-23.

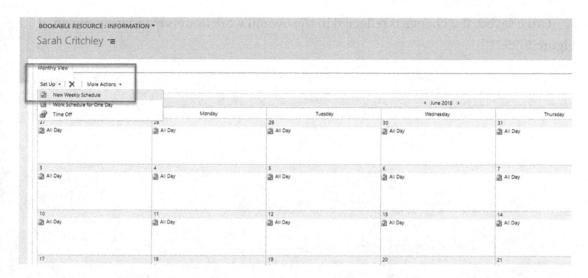

Figure 5-23. *Selecting "New Weekly Schedule" when creating work hours for a resource*

3. Select "Set Up Work Hours," and a new screen will open that displays the days of the week. Selecting "Set Work Times" opens a second popup screen, where a user can set a configurable time frame a resource works daily. This can be seen in Figure 5-24.

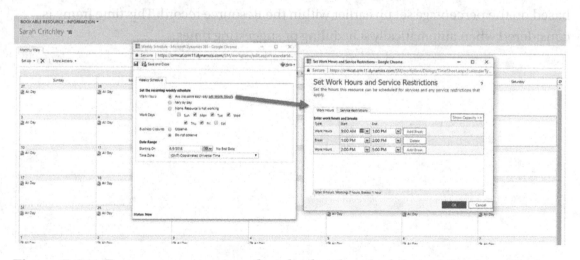

Figure 5-24. *Two new screens open that display the schedule and then specific times*

4. Change the schedule to 9 a.m. until 5:30 p.m., Monday to Friday, and click the OK button.

Once saved, the change is reflected in the overall work hours calendar, as shown in Figure 5-25.

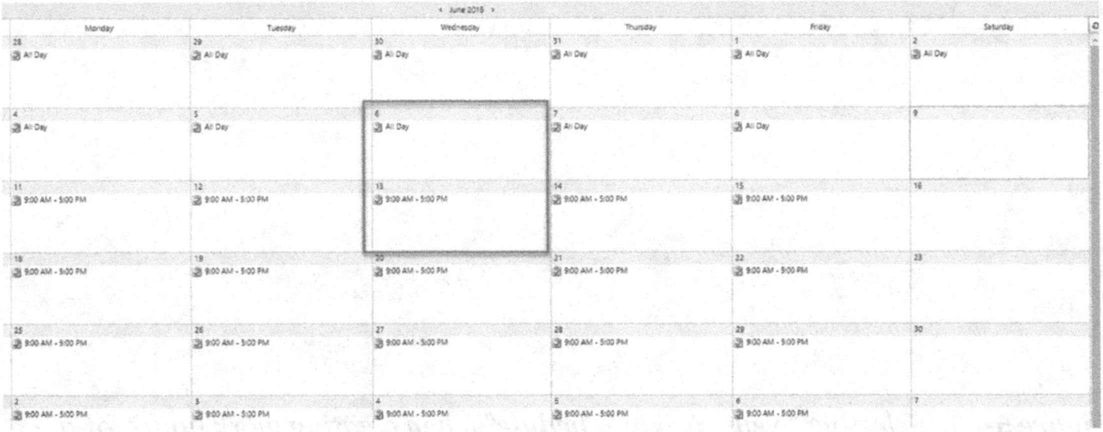

Figure 5-25. *Changes reflected in the main calendar*

Work hours are important as they affect scheduling and the schedule board. Navigate back to the schedule board and the resource that was configured in the previous step. The working hours are visible by the hours that are *not* grayed out (Figure 5-26). The utilization is also affected by the amount of time considered to be working hours and is based on the percentage set up earlier within the Resource record. This time frame is considered when automatically scheduling or suggesting times.

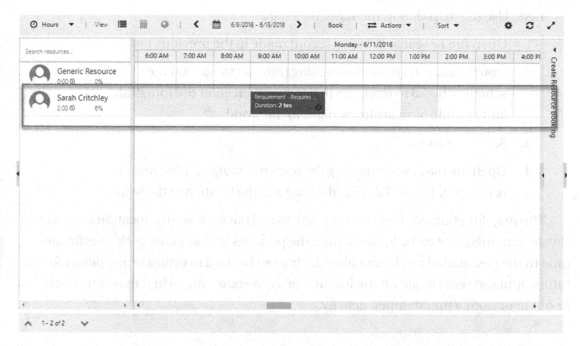

Figure 5-26. *Grayed-out times on the schedule board indicate unbookable times*

Map View on the Schedule Board

The map view is a particularly useful piece of functionality as it allows a dispatcher to see exactly where a resource is and their destination point for a booking on a map (Figure 5-27).

Figure 5-27. *Map view within the schedule board*

Task: Use the map view in the schedule board.

1. Open the Resource Booking record made in the previous task.

2. Double-click the resource booking (blue rectangle) on the schedule board to open the record and then enter the longitude and latitude of an arbitrary place in the world.

3. Save the record.

4. Open the map view, ensuring the resource booking (blue rectangle) is selected. This will display the map and the location of the work.

The map functionality begins to become useful once a resource location is known (by default, this is set to the location from the previous job) as items such as estimated time to the destination can be calculated. This can be used to estimate any delays for future appointments based on the location of the resource and when they last checked in or out to or from a timestamped activity.

Work Order Setup

Work orders are at the core of the business process within the Field Service app. Work orders define a piece of work that needs to be done and scheduled. It can often link to a Case entity that has been identified by the customer. The work order would take the place of the Resource Requirement entity created in the previous step, except this time the work order holds much more detail and context within the lifecycle associated with field service. The Resource Requirement entity is a more generic bookable item compared to the work order. This can be seen in Figure 5-28.

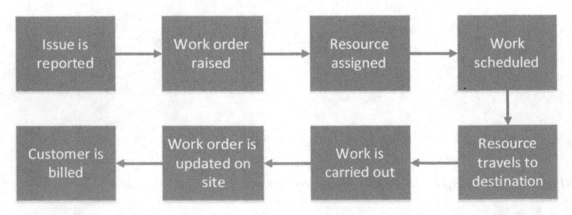

Figure 5-28. *Basic lifecycle of a work order within the Field Service application*

Where an issue is reported, a case will be created from within the Customer Service Hub app and be then converted to a work order. At the time of writing, within the Unified Interface Client, converting to a work order from a case is not possible without customizations. However, while this capability is expected to be updated as part of upcoming releases, it is still possible within the Classic UI. This can be seen in Figure 5-29.

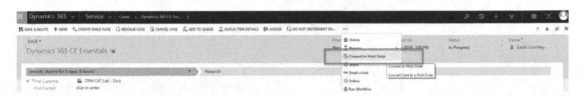

Figure 5-29. *Converting a case to a work order available via the Overflow button on the Case record*

It is important to set up important configuration records before creating a work order. This includes the service task types. Service task types describe tasks that need to be completed on-site by the resource and can be seen as a way of creating an action list of tasks included as part of the work order.

Task: Set up service task types.

1. Navigate to "Field Service" within the Classic UI ➤ "Administration" ➤ "Service Task Types" and click "New."

2. Fill in the "Name," "Estimated Duration," and "Description" fields (Figure 5-30).

3. Repeat these steps several times, creating different service task types until you have an assortment of different records.

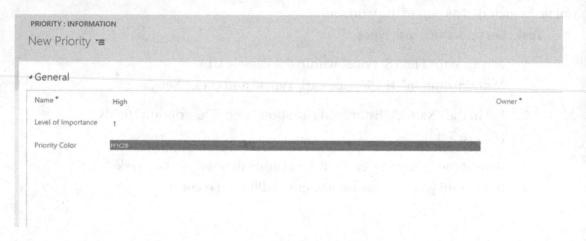

SERVICE TASK TYPE : INFORMATION

Fix Boiler ⁼☰

◢ General

Name *	Fix Boiler	Owner *	👤 Sarah Critchley
Estimated Duration	2 hours		
Description	Fix the Boiler at the Location		

▸ Notes

Figure 5-30. *Create a new service task type*

Task: Set up priorities.

Priorities color-code the schedule board based on the priority set. Priorities will also be taken into account within the scheduling engine (Figure 5-31).

PRIORITY : INFORMATION

New Priority ⁼☰

◢ General

Name *	High		Owner *
Level of Importance	1		
Priority Color	FF1C2B		

Figure 5-31. *Create a new priority with color-coding*

1. Navigate to "Field Service" within the Classic UI ➤ "Administration" ➤ "Priorities" and click "New."

2. Fill in the "Name" and "Level of Importance" fields and set the color by selecting one in the "Priority Color" field.

3. Save the record.

4. Repeat these steps, creating at least two other priorities with different colors.

The final piece of information that is required is the Work Order Type record. A work order type is a category that the work order is linked to. The Work Order Type record specifies rules, such as whether there should be a case linked and the associated price list.

Task: Set up work order types (Figure 5-32).

1. While still within the Administration area, navigate to "Work Order Type" and click "New."

2. Populate the "Name" field.

3. Specify if a case is going to be required as part of the work order.

4. Add a related price list (see Chapter 2).

5. Specify if it is taxable (set to "No").

It's important to highlight that a Work Order record will not always be associated with or created from a Case record. It could be created from a sales opportunity or from a recurring agreement or schedule. If so, the work order type cannot be set to a type that requires a case (incident) in the configuration.

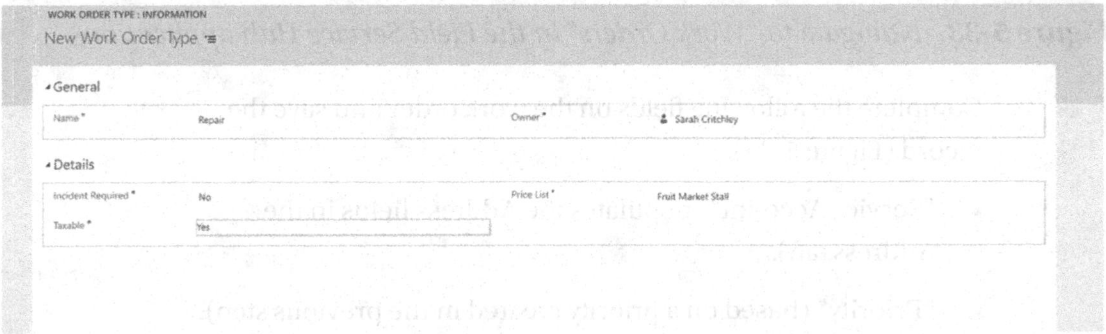

Figure 5-32. *Creating a new work order type*

Creating a Work Order

Now that the configuration records have been set up, it's time to create a work order.

Task: Create a new work order.

1. Navigate to the Field Service Hub application and then "Work Orders" and click "New," as shown in Figure 5-33.

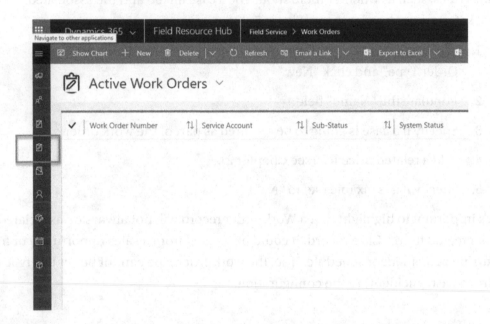

Figure 5-33. *Navigate to "Work Orders" in the Field Service Hub application*

2. Complete the following fields on the work order and save the record (Figure 5-34):

   - "Service Account" (populates the Address fields in the Address tab).

   - "Priority" (based on a priority created in the previous step).

   - "Instructions."

   - "Work Order Type" (based on a type created in the previous step).

   - Change "Taxable" to "No."

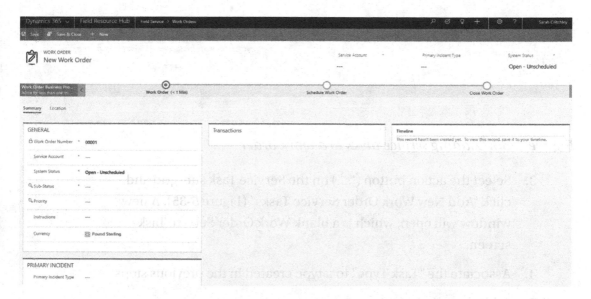

Figure 5-34. *Creating a new work order within the Unified Interface*

The next action goes through adding the service tasks configured in the previous step. Setting these on the work order will define the tasks that need to be completed by the resource selected for completing the work.

Note   The "Service Account" field appears to be mandatory; however, this can be changed to optional in the configuration area of Dynamics 365 CE. It does mean the address details will not be copied through from the service account, and this must be entered manually or through customization in other areas of the system. This is particularly useful, as the address where the work is carried out may not always be the address on the Service Account record.

Service tasks will be visible within the sub-grid that will become available on the initial save action of the Work Order record. Products can also be associated at this point, as can services.

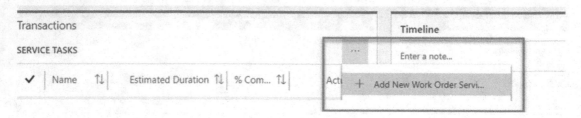

Figure 5-35. *Adding service tasks to a work order*

3. Select the action button ("..") on the Service Task sub-grid and click "Add New Work Order Service Tasks" (Figure 5-35). A new window will open, which is a blank Work Order Service Task screen.

4. Associate the "Task Type" to a type created in the previous steps.

5. Add a description.

6. Confirm the "Estimated Duration" field is correct.

7. Click "Save and Close." The previous work order should now be visible, with the new work order service task added in the sub-grid, as shown in Figure 5-36.

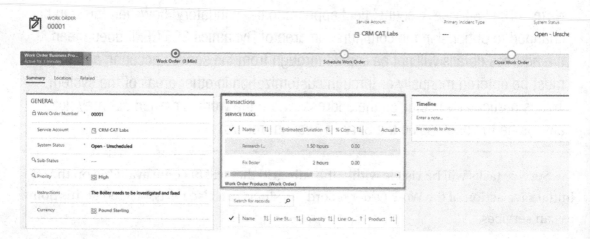

Figure 5-36. *Service tasks are displayed within a work order*

8. Open the Business Process Flow on the Work Order record by clicking the "Work Order" stage. Review the steps and confirm all required steps have been completed. Move the record onto the next stage, "Schedule Work Order," by selecting "Next Stage."

Using the Business Process Flow is good practice so as to know which steps need to be completed and the lifecycle of a work order.

In the previous section, we reviewed scheduling a generic Resource Requirement record. Now, let's look at scheduling a work order.

9. Navigate to the Classic UI and select "Schedule Board."

10. Click the "Unscheduled Work Orders" list; it should have the work order created from the previous step within the list (Figure 5-37).

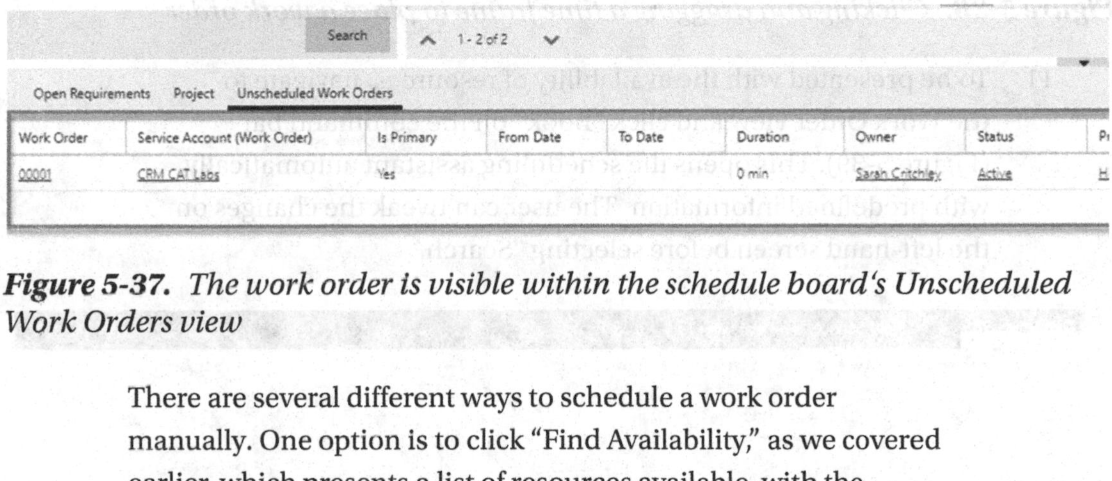

Work Order	Service Account (Work Order)	Is Primary	From Date	To Date	Duration	Owner	Status	Pr
00001	CRM CAT Labs	Yes			0 min	Sarah Critchley	Active	H

Figure 5-37. The work order is visible within the schedule board's Unscheduled Work Orders view

There are several different ways to schedule a work order manually. One option is to click "Find Availability," as we covered earlier, which presents a list of resources available, with the specific skillset required displayed in a list to the user. A user could also drag the work order onto the board from the view itself, or they could click and drag a time frame onto a resource (Figure 5-38).

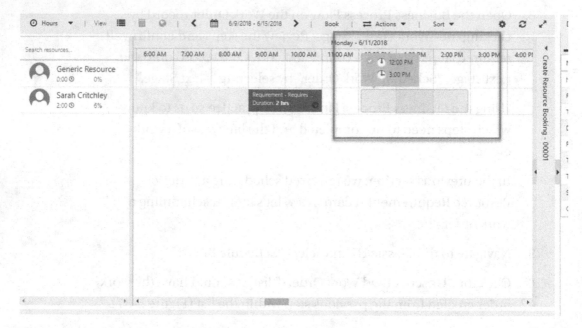

Figure 5-38. *Clicking and dragging a time frame to place a work order*

11. To be presented with the availability of resources, navigate to
the Work Order view and click "Book" on the command bar
(Figure 5-39). This opens the scheduling assistant automatically
with predefined information. The user can tweak the changes on
the left-hand screen before selecting "Search."

Figure 5-39. *Select "Book" on a selected work order to open the scheduling
assistant*

Scheduling in these examples is simply suggesting the available resources that match the skill level of the requirements. This is the initial stage of scheduling. There is also the option to optimize the route from the resources' set start location to the resources' end location.

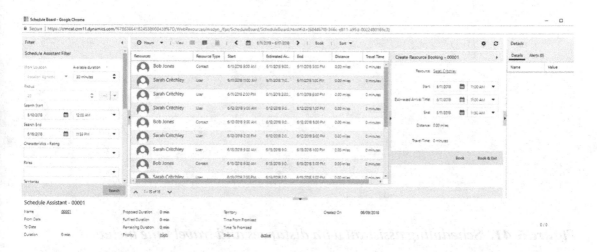

Figure 5-40. *Being presented with resource options in the scheduling assistant*

At the moment, the example shown in Figure 5-40 does not include location data within the scheduling engine or the records. Scheduling in these examples is suggesting the available resources that match the skill level of the requirements.

Important! This is where it is critical to set the work location on the work order, as well as the resources' work locations in the same space (Figure 5-41). Should a resource and requirement (whether it is a resource requirement or a work order) not match their work location, the scheduling engine will not suggest their availability. This was highlighted in a previous release note for Field Service, which can be found within the "Further Reading" section at the end of this chapter in the February 2017 Release Notes.

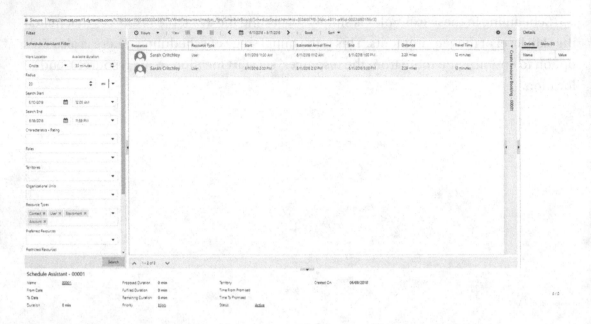

Figure 5-41. *Scheduling assistant with distances and travel time included*

Once the work location matches, the directions and miles will be visible from the maps and the resource schedule, as seen in Figure 5-42.

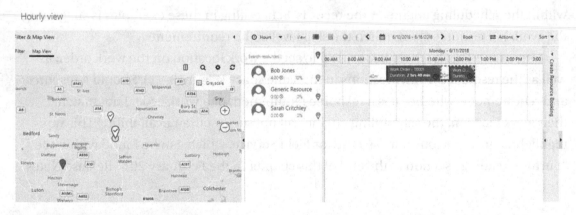

Figure 5-42. *Using the maps within the schedule board to see the different pins of work orders*

The radius in the scheduling assistant defaults to 20, which can be modified within the Resource Scheduling administration settings, shown in Figure 5-43.

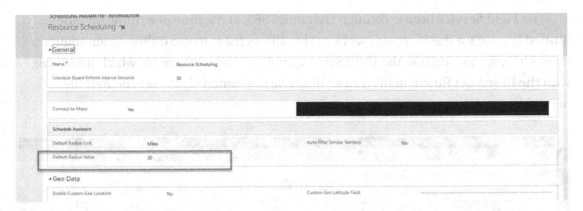

Figure 5-43. *Setting the default "radius" value in the Resource Scheduling settings*

The radius specifies how close the resource must be to the location specified within the requirement (Figure 5-44). If they are outside of that radius at the time, they won't be suggested to complete this work order.

Figure 5-44. *Changing the "radius" setting within the search information on the scheduling assistant*

From a field engineer's perspective, now that there are some bookings in the diary for jobs with specific locations, the engineer, user, or contact can see the visibility of these through the Field Resource Hub or through the Field Service app, which is linked to the Resco.net service (Figure 5-45).

199

The Field Service license through Dynamics 365, at the time of writing, includes a limited license for the Resco.net service. This allows users to use offline functionality through Resco.net and use the Field Service application by Microsoft, which interfaces with the Resco.net functionality, rather than use the standard offline functionality offered by the Dynamics 365 CE app.

Figure 5-45. *Resource booking visibility available in the Field Service app*

The Field Service app would be downloaded to the user's device and configured for the user (Figure 5-46). This enables them to select those bookings that relate to the resource bookings booked in by the dispatcher role through scheduling, as seen in the previous sections. Before this app can be properly used, there needs to be some configuration set up, which has been documented and can be referred to in the "Further Reading" section at the end of this chapter for more details than covered in this chapter.

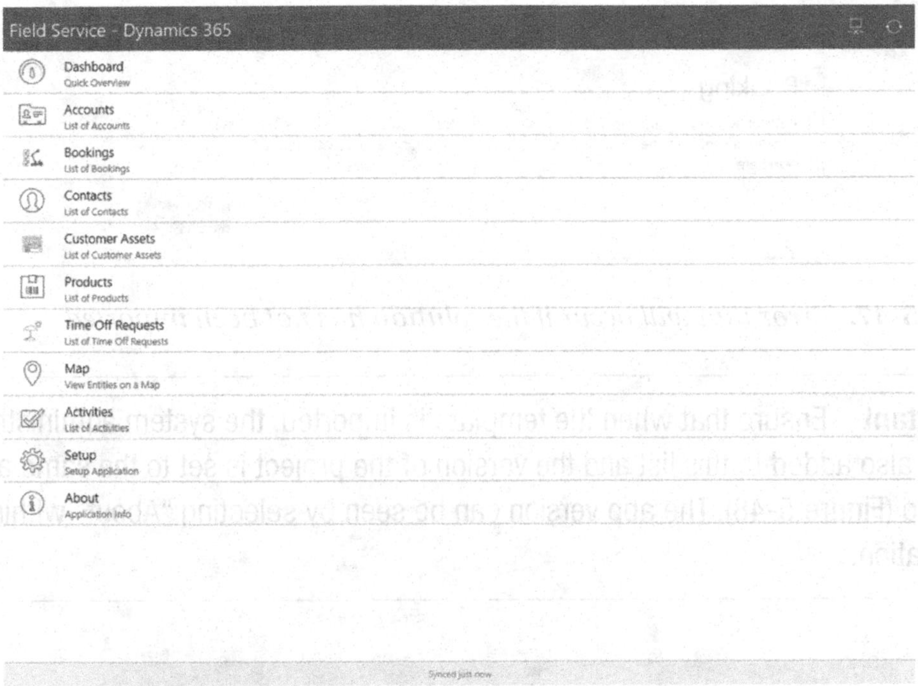

Figure 5-46. *Resco.net Field Service app*

Task: Configure the mobile Field Service app.

It is important to note that there are no customizations being applied to the Field Service application at this stage; we are simply installing and configuring it. For that, the "Woodford" solution needs to be installed and a minor setup completed. The "Setting up the Mobile Field Service App" link within the "Further Reading" section contains the template that needs to be imported into Dynamics 365 CE by an administrator to continue to use the mobile Field Service application.

If the templates are not installed and published, an error will occur, stating that the solution has not been imported and the functionality will not be accessible (Figure 5-47). Ensure the steps have been completed as referenced in the documentation found in the "Further Reading" section.

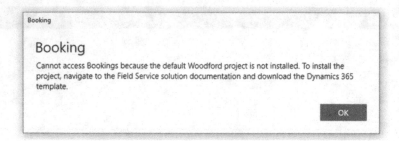

Figure 5-47. *Error that will occur if the solution has not been imported*

Important   Ensure that when the template is imported, the system administrator role is also added to this list and the version of the project is set to the same as in the app (Figure 5-48). The app version can be seen by selecting "About" within the application.

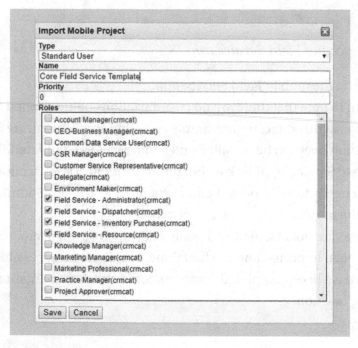

Figure 5-48. *When the Woodford solution is open, select the roles for the application to be accessible to*

To synchronize the changes made within the solution setup, click the Refresh button on the application to pull the changes (Figure 5-49).

Figure 5-49. *Setting up the instance to the application – use the Refresh button to connect*

The Resco.net mobile Field Service app interface is designed to be an easy-to-use interface for people using the app on a phone or tablet device.

Once the template has synchronized, there is a clear change in how the app looks, as you can now browse bookings via the day, week, or month, as shown in Figure 5-50. Inclusive of this, you can see an agenda, which displays the current work for that day. This is the same for both tablet and mobile.

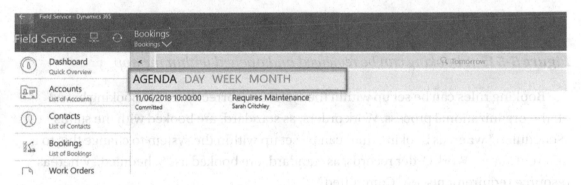

Figure 5-50. *The Resco.net Field Service app, once configured, can display the agenda and schedule for the users*

Within the mobile Field Service application, you can open a booking from the agenda and review its status (Figure 5-51).

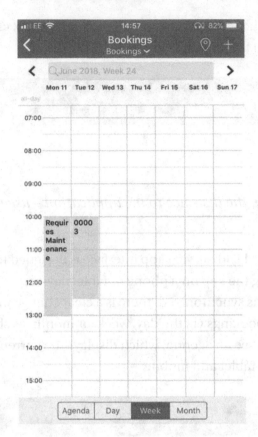

Figure 5-51. *A booking can be reviewed and opened within the app*

Booking rules can be set up within the system to correctly set the booking based on the organizational process. Work orders, as standard, are booked with the status "Scheduled," whereas booking rules can be set up within the system to change this to a different status. Work Order records, as standard, are booked as "Scheduled," whereas resource requirements are "Committed."

Users can use a filter and see different views based on these statuses. This is where an approval gateway can be created so that bookings are not automatically scheduled and are based on the prior approval of the engineer. An external customer message can be used by the customer service agent or the external portal when the time is being confirmed, even something as simple as "Awaiting Confirmation." Sending automated emails or notifications to the customer about the resource's arrival is also an effective way to use status changes to improve customer service and give on-site resources a degree of autonomy.

This is often seen in applications where a user would be texted or emailed to notify them when their delivery was on the way. This can be customized through Dynamics 365 using workflows and add-on solutions that allow for SMS features. The second section of the book details how to make more custom solutions.

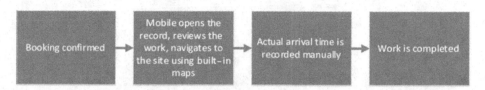

Figure 5-52. *Process flow of a confirmed booking and the next steps to be completed by the user*

Once an engineer has arrived at their destination, the application does not automatically log that they have arrived. This needs to be manually entered by the on-site resource if the information is required or expected by the business (Figure 5-52). (Note: This would be another good customization point.)

Once arrived, the user can review what work needs to be completed using the service tasks from the associated work order. The service tasks are useful here as they assist the engineer in knowing what they need to do; they also provide a link back to the original case, if it was created from a Case record, so the engineer will know the issue raised by the customer and gain visibility into the reported issue.

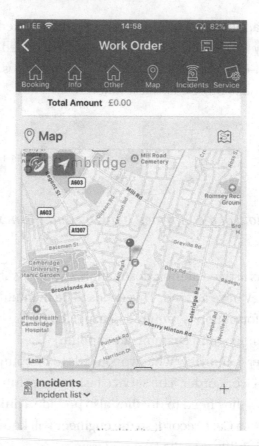

Figure 5-53.   *Using the navigational capabilities of the Field Service app and related map apps on the phone to achieve this*

Users can use the map application on their device as a navigation tool to get to and from bookings. This is shown in Figures 5-53 and 5-54.

Figure 5-54. *Using a map application on the device to travel to and from bookings*

Once a service task has been completed, the engineer can enter the percentage completed against each task, as shown in Figure 5-55, but this is unlikely to happen in real life. The time and effort required for a user to navigate to and find the record and then enter the information can be cumbersome. This can be customized within the application to make this process easier if required.

Figure 5-55. *Service tasks visible on the application for the user to complete*

Once the work has been completed, the application allows a signature to be obtained from within the app as standard and for videos and photos to be taken as evidence of the completed work (Figure 5-56).

Figure 5-56. *Using the application to capture signatures*

As things do not always go to plan, it may be that there are problems or issues preventing the work from being completed. Photos and videos would be helpful in this scenario. In addition to that, you can create a follow-up work order to the current one, which can be achieved directly from within the app (Figure 5-57). The work order is auto-populated with basic details for the dispatcher to then complete and schedule.

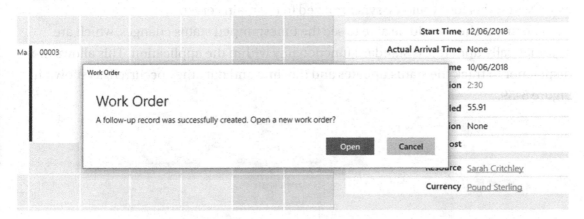

Figure 5-57. *Creating a follow-up work order from an existing work order*

Once a work order has been completed, the user updates the status from within the application to "Completed," and the end time is captured. This is so it can be reported how long the actual job has taken and metrics can be tracked (Figure 5-58).

As far as the user who is the on-site resource is concerned, at this point the job has been completed, and they can leave the site, loading up their agenda, selecting the next job, and then traveling to the destination as before.

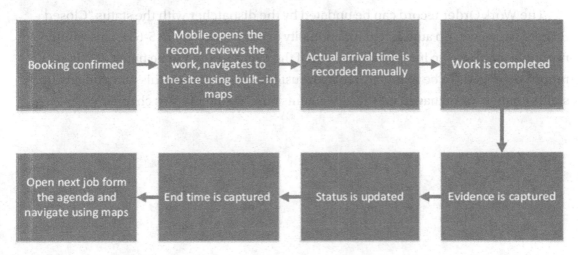

Figure 5-58. *Field Service basic process flow*

The mobile application will synchronize the data from the local machine (e.g., the smartphone) to the Dynamics 365 server once a connection has been established on the device (if the connection was originally lost). It will update the resource booking and the work order with the fact that the booking has been completed and will include the related notes and pictures. If a follow-up work order has been created because there were issues, this too would be synchronized to the main server.

The dispatcher would be able to see the timestamped status changes, which are automatically updated as standard functionality within the application. This allows the dispatcher to track the status updates and the time and date they occurred, as shown in Figure 5-59.

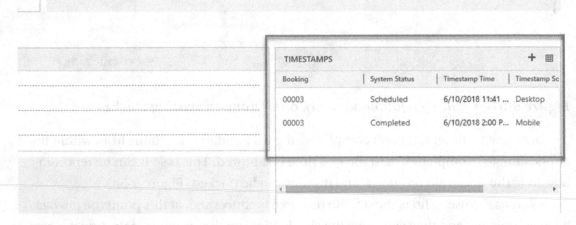

Figure 5-59. *Timestamped status updates by the user visible in the work order*

The Work Order record can be updated by the dispatcher with the status "Closed – Posted"; however, no automated functionality occurs here (Figure 5-60). This would normally be where an invoice was created if the client needed to be billed. If this is required, it needs to be manually created, customized to provide this functionality upon status change, or managed via the agreements covered later in this chapter.

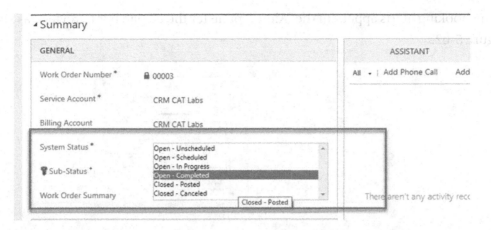

Figure 5-60. *Updating the work order status to Posted/Completed*

Booking Alerts

A booking alert is a new activity introduced within Dynamics 365 CE Field Service. It can be related to any activity type record; however, they are normally used as a way to notify a user of a booking and appear on the scheduling board. They are also often used to provide a notification to the dispatcher.

Task: Create a booking alert.

1. Navigate to the Resource Scheduling board and select "Actions."

2. Select "New Booking Alert," as shown in Figure 5-61.

3. Complete the fields within the new record, including the "Subject" and "Assignees" fields, and click "Save and Close."

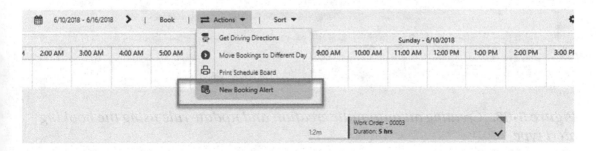

Figure 5-61. *Creating a new booking alert*

The booking alerts appear in the "Alerts" pane for the dispatcher to review, as shown in Figure 5-62.

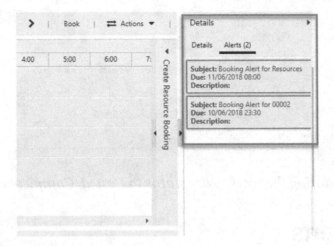

Figure 5-62. *Alerts pane within the schedule board*

Booking alerts can also be created via a workflow. Automatic creation and update rules, seen in Figure 5-63, can be used to create a subsequent action upon the creation of a new booking alert, which can be used to create related records and more complex business logic.

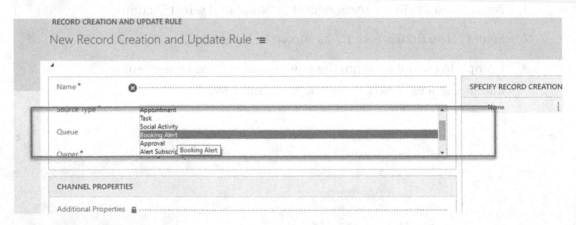

Figure 5-63. *Creating an automatic creation and update rule using the booking alert type*

Time-Off Requests

Work hours specify the everyday schedule of the resources. It is important to have a way to utilize holiday and time off, which can be scheduled on late notice or in a more ad hoc way. Time-off requests are part of the Dynamics 365 CE Field Service solution, which handles these types of events. Within the Resource record at the very start of this chapter, when creating a resource, one of the configuration fields was whether the resource required approval for time-off requests.

Task: Set up time-off requests.

1. Create a new request by navigating to the Field Service App ➤ Time Off Requests and clicking "New." This can be done via the Classic UI, the Unified Interface, and the mobile application.

2. Set start and end times for when the time-off request is for (Figure 5-64).

3. Click "Save and Close."

The request has been created and will now be visible within the "Time Off Requests" section of the sitemap, where it can be approved.

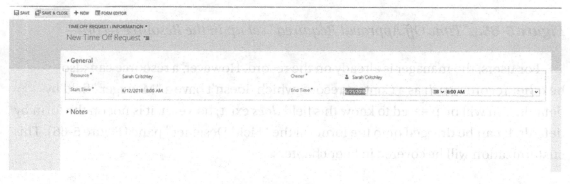

Figure 5-64. *Creating a time-off request*

If a resource does not require approval (set in their Resource record), the request will be automatically deactivated (and set to an inactive status), and the time off will be approved. The time specified will be grayed out in the resource calendar, and the scheduling engine will not incorporate this into suggested times.

As highlighted, approval requirements are configured in the Resource record shown in Figure 5-65. Should the request require approval, the defined manager within Dynamics 365 CE will need to approve it.

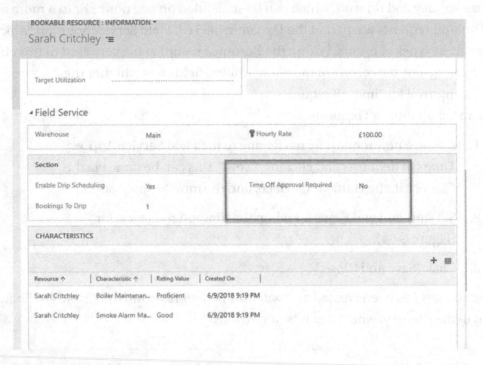

Figure 5-65. *"Time Off Approval Required" set up in the Resource record*

For users, the manager is already on the record. However, a resource can also be other records, such as a Contact record, which doesn't have a "Manager" field by default. You will be pleased to know this field *does* exist; however, it is not on the form by default. It can be dragged onto the form via the "Field Designer" pane (Figure 5-66). This customization will be covered in later chapters.

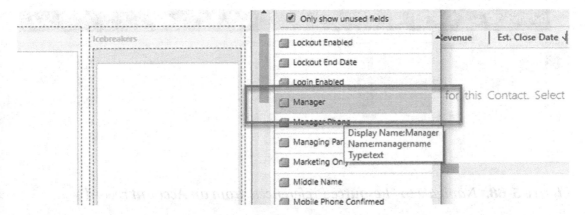

Figure 5-66. *The "Manager" field on the other types of resources can be moved onto the form and set*

Unapproved time-off approval records will remain within the Active view until approved (Figure 5-67). All approved time-off requests are deactivated, changing to an inactive status.

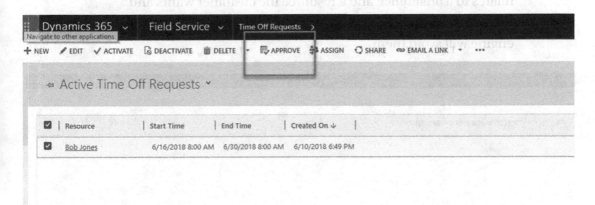

Figure 5-67. *Approve time-off request by clicking "Approve" on the selected request*

Customer Preferences

It has been highlighted a few times within this chapter that the Dynamics 365 CE Field Service scheduling engine has the capability to take into consideration customer preferences. Where these preferences are hard to find, as in a previous version of Dynamics 365 CE, they were specific fields. This has been updated in later versions, where preferences are set up within a new entity called Resource Preferences that is available on all resource-type records (Figure 5-68).

Figure 5-68. *Navigate to "Resource Preferences" from an Account record*

Task: Set up customer preferences.

1. Navigate to a Customer record and select "Resource Preferences."

2. Create a new resource, as shown in Figure 5-69.

3. Set whether this should be "Preferred" or "Restricted." *Preferred* relates to a preference and a resource the customer wants and *Restricted* to a resource they do not want, and thus the scheduling engine will avoid them.

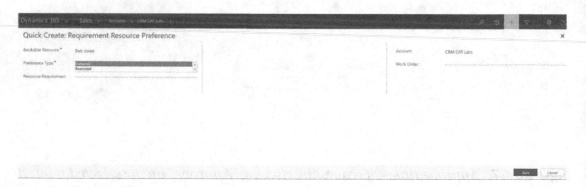

Figure 5-69. *Creating a new Customer Preference record*

4. Once this is set up within the Account ("Service Account" field and record associated with work orders), create a new work order.

The resource preference set up at the Account record level cascades to the work order and the resource requirement, which is automatically created behind the scenes (this is what is scheduled). This process is shown in Figure 5-70.

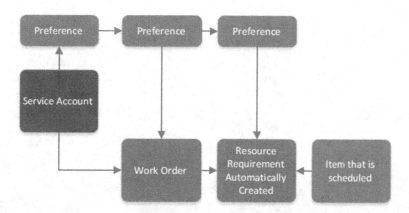

Figure 5-70. *Preference record cascading to related work orders and resource requirements*

This preference is added automatically into the scheduling engine when it searches. Figure 5-71 shows the resource preference for the resource "Bob Jones" being automatically added and changes the results of the search.

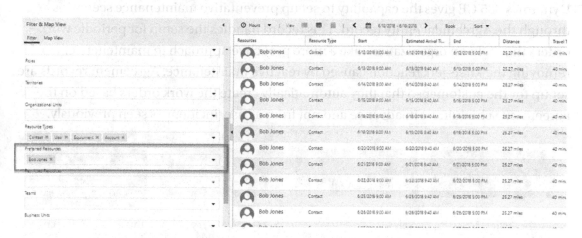

Figure 5-71. *Preferred resources set automatically within the service schedule configuration. Bob's record is the only record displayed in the search results*

Figure 5-72 shows the results of a search with the preferences removed. The differences are that the suggested resources are focused around providing the resource specified within the preference.

Should there be multiple preferences at the service account level, more than one resource would be named within the "Preferred Resource" field. The functionality for "Restricted Resources" works by removing those resources referenced in this field from the search result.

Hourly view

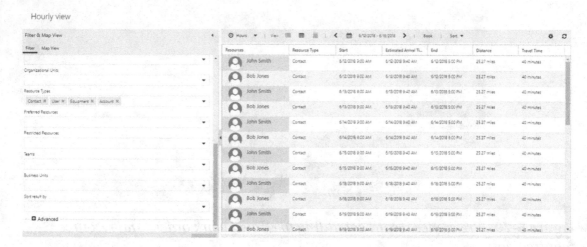

Figure 5-72. *No preferred resources selected*

Schedule Multiple Bookings/Recurring Bookings

Dynamics 365 CE gives the capability to set up preventative maintenance scenarios through the Agreement entity record. This record handles the setup for periodic work orders that help an organization take a more proactive approach to maintenance, removing the knee-jerk reaction caused by reactive maintenance. Agreement records are set up for the customer so that they automatically create the work orders based on the agreement schedule set in advance and not from a case/incident as seen previously.

Figure 5-73. *Navigate to "Agreements" within the Classic UI*

Task: Create an Agreement record.

1. Navigate to the "Agreements" area in the sitemap within the Classic UI and select "New" (Figure 5-73).

2. Complete all the mandatory fields (Figure 5-74).

3. A price list with active products is not required to create a financial element here; this is related to the invoice setup, which is also performed periodically, despite this chapter not focusing on this area. In Chapter 3, products were covered extensively, and you can use the same price list for this example exercise.

4. Complete the start date and end date, ensuring they include today in the time frame so it works straight away when testing it.

5. Save the record.

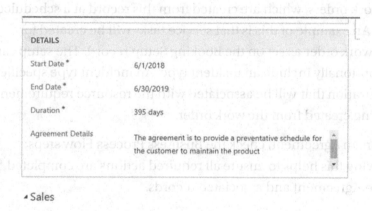

Figure 5-74. *Setting up the agreement details*

6. Once created, on the right-hand side, click the plus icon on the Booking Setup sub-grid as shown in Figure 5-75.

7. This creates an Agreement Booking Setup record, which is the definition for all the work orders automatically generated through this record.

8. Complete all the fields for this record and save it.

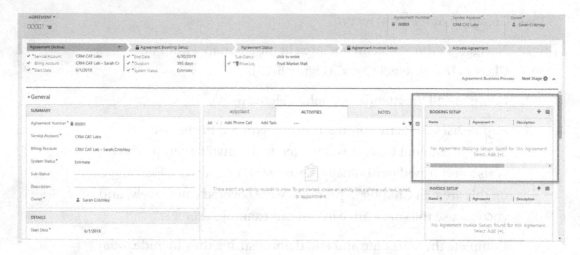

Figure 5-75.   *Creating Booking Setup records*

Much of this information on the Agreement record will cascade to
the work orders, which are created from this record at a scheduled
time. An example of this is that service tasks will be created for
each work order as set on the Booking Setup record. The setup can
also optionally include an incident type. An incident type specifies
the duration that will be associated with the resource requirement
booking created from the work order.

Within an Agreement, check the Business Process Flow steps;
following this helps to ensure all required actions are completed
on the Agreement and associated records.

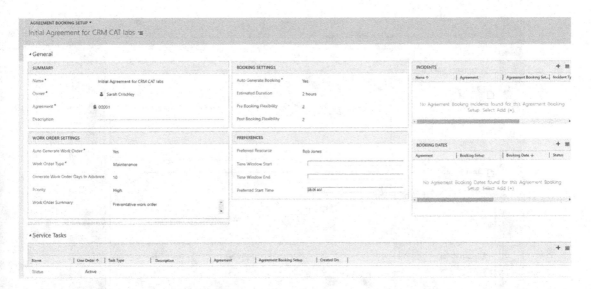

Figure 5-76. *Setting up the agreement schedule ("Booking Setup")*

9. Select the Booking Maintenance button on the ribbon to now schedule the recurrence. The recurrence setup is very similar to the experience in Microsoft Outlook when setting recurring meetings. This is shown in Figure 5-77.

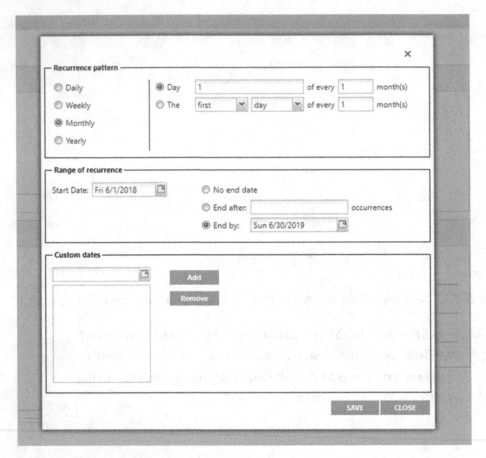

Figure 5-77. *Setting up the booking recurrence*

10. Specify the settings and click the Save button. You also have the option to add custom dates based on the requirement.

11. Once completed, update the status to "Active," as shown in Figure 5-78, either on the Business Process Flow or within the form.

Once activated, a background workflow is triggered for the system that will generate all booking dates based on the recurring schedule which can be seen in the "Booking Dates" sub-grid.

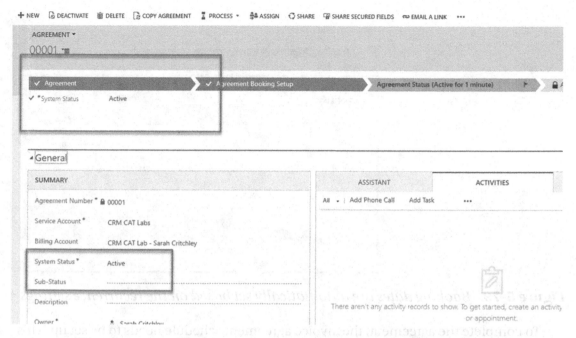

Figure 5-78. *Updating the status to "Active" triggers the background process to create the Booking records*

When the "booking dates," shown in Figure 5-79, are reached, a work order is generated automatically, which also generates a resource requirement, allowing the order to be scheduled (as opposed to having to wait for manual intervention).

A user could alternatively manually generate a work order, if required, from an agreement booking. This can be done by selecting the Generate Work Order button while on the record. This can be useful, for example, if work needed to be scheduled before the date had been reached.

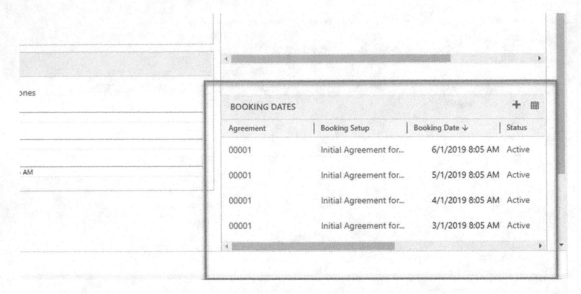

Figure 5-79. *Booking dates are automatically set based on the recurrence settings*

To complete the agreement, the invoice agreement schedule needs to be set up. This is a similar process to the generation of work orders from the bookings; it automatically generates invoices related to the work being prescheduled. The Invoice records are quite limited in what a user can bill for – the related products cannot be dynamic and instead need to be a set product, for example, a maintenance fee, set within the Agreement record. These invoices are not set up to be dynamic, and, instead, if an organization wants to bill based on the situation while the engineer is on-site doing the work, they would need to raise another invoice manually and associate the specific product to this invoice instead.

Task: Set up the invoice agreement schedule.

1. Navigate to the Agreement record created in the previous step.

2. Within the Invoice Setup sub-grid, shown in Figure 5-80, select "New."

3. Complete the basic information and add a field service product (by selecting this in the Field Service tab when creating the product; remember to publish any products used).

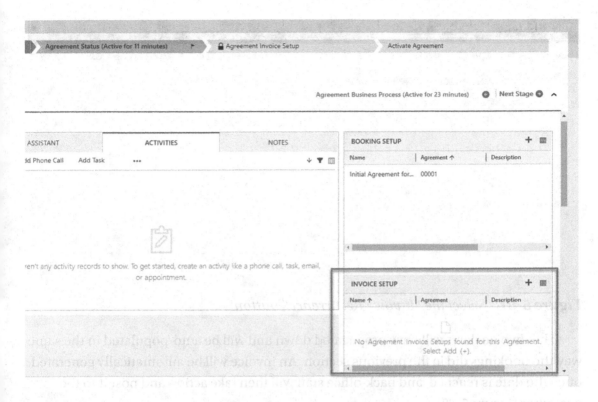

Figure 5-80. *Invoice Setup grid on the Agreement record*

4. Once completed, click "Invoice Recurrence" on the ribbon bar, shown in Figure 5-81. Set the recurrence schedule up in the same way as in the previous "Booking Recurrence" functionality.

5. Save the record.

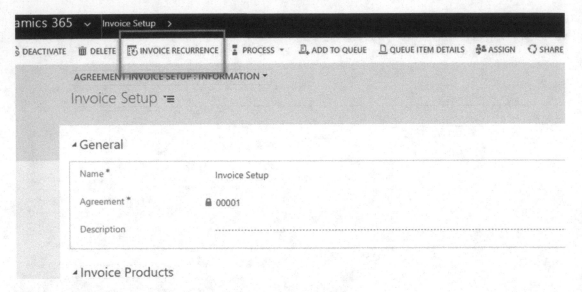

Figure 5-81. *Select the "Invoice Recurrence" button*

The invoice dates will have propagated down and will be auto-populated in the same way the bookings did in the previous section. An invoice will be automatically generated once the date is reached, and back-office staff will then take action and post it to the customer (Figure 5-82).

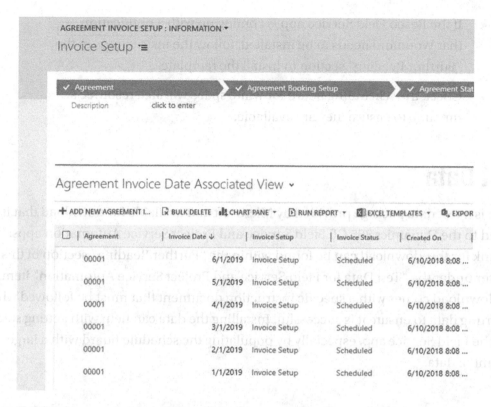

Figure 5-82. *Agreement invoices created automatically*

Common Issues Experienced with the Resource Scheduler

There are some common issues that can occur when using the Dynamics 365 CE Field Service application that may lead users to believe things are not properly working, especially with the resource scheduler.

Here is a list of common troubleshooting tasks to complete when the scheduler is showing that no resources are available:

- If the radius on the default map in the Field Service settings is set to a low amount, try increasing this in the scheduling pane to find out if this is the problem. Configure this within Field Service settings if required.

- Have the required skills been added to the resource?

- If the Resco Field Service app is coming up with an error, try synchronizing.

- If the Resco Field Service app is coming up with a notification that Woodford needs to be installed, follow the instructions in the "Further Reading" section to install the template.

- Check the scheduling board for white space within a resource's timeline to ensure they are available.

Test Data

There is a test data package provided by Microsoft and available for download that is related to the Dynamics 365 CE Field Service and Project Service Automation apps. The link for this download can be found within the "Further Reading" section of this chapter under the "Test Data for Field Service and Project Service Automation" item. The download comes with a specific instruction document that must be followed when importing data to ensure it is successful. Installing the data can help with getting started with the Field Service app, especially by populating the schedule board with a large amount of data.

Summary

This chapter has been an introduction into the "essentials" of the Field Service application within Dynamics 365 CE. There are still many additional ways to set up and customize the application to suit specific needs. This includes sending notifications and automatically creating records through workflows, as well as the resource scheduling automation available as an extension of Field Service.

What is commonly discussed when talking about Field Service for business applications is the ability to perform different types of maintenance. These include reactive, preventative, and predictive types. Reactive maintenance is what has been possible for some time. This includes creating a case when a customer notices a problem, which is then reported and reacted upon. Work orders are scheduled, and an engineer can be booked. The organization is reacting to something happening, normally the customer's notifying them of the issue.

Following that, preventative maintenance occurs through scheduling work orders for future dates based on a custom time frame to prevent the customer service incident from ever happening. This is similar to yearly car maintenance, where there doesn't have to be anything necessarily wrong. However, the action is carried out to prevent issues from occurring and is used to reduce risk.

This chapter has covered both of these types of field service through the creation of work orders (in some instances, from cases) and scheduling these using the schedule board. Agreements and the automatic scheduling of work orders for future dates are examples of the functionality provided for preventative scheduling within an organization. The additional solution, Resource Schedule Optimization, which is a licensed add-on for Dynamics 365, automates this functionality even more.

The final type of maintenance is predictive maintenance. This is achieved using artificial intelligence (AI) applications such as machine-learning models to create a predictive model for customer assets, the history of the product, and how often they are likely going to require an on-site visit. This can be achieved by extending Dynamics 365 to use machine-learning models, such as Azure ML Services Web APIs.

In between these types, IoT (Internet of Things) technology can be used for both preventative and predictive maintenance scenarios that would allow organizations to obtain real-time data from the asset (e.g., a boiler) through a sensor. This information could include the temperature or movement. Alerts could be created based on certain set threshold values. From these values, actions can be triggered within Dynamics 365 CE, such as the automatic creation of a Work Order record, creating a more preventative model and an increased level of customer service. The data can also be used from the devices to create more accurate predictive models.

In summary, Dynamics 365 CE provides a vast amount of capability for organizations to leverage multiple field service frameworks, from the most simple to a more complex model, based on the focus of the organization.

Chapter Tasks

1. Set up a resource role and associated resource skills.

2. Create a resource requirement and access it via the schedule board.

3. Spend time becoming familiar with all the components of the schedule board.

4. Attempt to schedule the resource requirement.

5. Convert a case to a new work order.

6. Schedule the work order.

7. Set up the mobile Field Service application.

8. Complete a work order from the mobile Field Service application.

9. Create a new Agreement record, setting it up for recurring bookings and invoices.

10. Create a new time-off request.

Further Reading

Test Data for Field Service and Project Service Automation (Microsoft, 2018). URL: www.microsoft.com/en-us/download/details.aspx?id=56050

Universal Resource Scheduling (Microsoft, 2018). URL: https://docs.microsoft.com/en-us/dynamics365/customer-engagement/common-scheduler/schedule-anything-with-universal-resource-scheduling

Dispatcher Role Within Field Service Scenarios (Microsoft, 2018). URL: https://docs.microsoft.com/en-us/dynamics365/customer-engagement/field-service/create-work-order

Resource Optimization (Microsoft, 2018). URL: https://docs.microsoft.com/en-us/dynamics365/customer-engagement/common-scheduler/resource-scheduling-optimization

Release Notes for Field Service Feb 2017 (Microsoft, 2018). URL: https://blogs.msdn.microsoft.com/crm/2017/05/19/dynamics-366-for-field-service-and-project-services-automation-february-2017-updates/

Setting up the Mobile Field Service App (Microsoft, 2018). URL: https://docs.microsoft.com/en-us/dynamics365/customer-engagement/field-service/install-the-mobile-app

CHAPTER 6

Dynamics 365 for Marketing

The standard marketing capability found in previous versions of Dynamics 365 CE could have been considered the least functional area of the platform. It allowed organizations to create marketing lists; create campaigns, including campaign activities; and send bulk emails through quick campaigns. This functionality might have been able to serve businesses' marketing requirements a long time ago, but in society today, where marketing has become increasingly digital, requirements have evolved way beyond this functionality to the point that the old marketing features of Dynamics 365 struggle to meet those requirements.

For this reason, the marketing area of Dynamics 365 CE has become a popular place for ISVs (independent solution vendors) to create their own managed solutions. These solutions either are embedded into the application, like ClickDimensions and PowerObjects marketing add-ons, or act as "connectors" to other marketing applications, such as DotMailer. This has allowed the platform to functionally meet the changing needs of marketing in a more digital and omni-channel space.

In the past year, Microsoft has redesigned the standard marketing features of the Dynamics 365 CE application and introduced the Dynamics 365 for Marketing application. This application is licensed separately, like the other Dynamics 365 CE first-party apps, and has been created by Microsoft to introduce marketing departments to the latest Microsoft technology and Dynamics 365 CE capabilities. It includes the capability to create segments, design simple to complex emails, create behavior-driven customer journeys, score leads, and use an extensive Event Management module. The event management feature allows organizations to create an external portal for events and manage pages for events for the organization, from speaker sessions to event registrations. This chapter aims to be an essential guide to this functionality within the Dynamics 365 CE for Marketing application and to allow you to get started.

© Sarah Critchley 2020
S. Critchley, *Dynamics 365 Essentials*, https://doi.org/10.1007/978-1-4842-5911-5_6

Leads in Dynamics 365 Marketing

Leads can be used in segments within Dynamics 365 for Marketing. However, leads must include a linked Contact record.

There has been an understanding that a Lead record is separate from a Contact record. The lead is seen as an unqualified contact and has historically allowed an organization to keep unqualified contacts away from the main data store of the Contact table. This is done until they reach a qualified state, at which point a Contact record is created as part of the qualification process. Following that, qualified contacts would then be able to have leads created and associated under the "Existing Contact" field (or "Parent Contact for Lead" field), which represents existing or continuing business. The way Dynamics 365 for Marketing utilizes leads is as an *expression of interest* and means a contact must exist for both new business and existing business, should they wish to be marketed to. It introduces a marketing-managed process for leads and a period of time when a lead is "owned" by marketing before it is classified as a sales-ready lead. This gives organizations some distinct advantages, as follows:

- Being able to produce a lead lifecycle report through a contact.

- It does not reach the sales team until it is scored or already prequalified for specific reasons.

- Clear definitions between ownership of marketing and sales.

- A single place to manage consent if contact should unsubscribe or change their preferences; this is managed in a specific area of the segmentation and would automatically drop out.

- The rare occasion of having two or more leads at one time is possible and can be managed.

- Providing organizations with extensibility options should the preceding hold no distinct advantages. If the Lead record does not add any value to sales, the transition to sales ready could be automatically qualified through customizations, creating an opportunity, and instead full ownership of a lead can lie within marketing and be used to manage the topic or product marketing.

Organizations have, in the past, purchased leads that they often wish to keep separate from the main Contact table, as referred to earlier. If this is the case, it would mean that they would need to mark imported contacts as not sales ready and create a contact that has been set as "Marketing Only."

The Contact record holds the details for consent and whether the individual can be contacted and how, which is linked to data protection regulations. The Contact record is a single point of change for this data. It also allows organizations to keep their marketing consistent to a single contact.

It can be argued that this approach to leads is going directly against the core Dynamics 365 CE platform. Dynamics 365 CE has, however, always had an "Existing Contact" record lookup field on the Lead form, and the change of moving toward creating contacts together with a Lead record (initially) would affect the organizations that are using a strict lead management process (e.g., not creating contacts before creating a lead and qualifying).

The marketing-to-sales process needs to be defined when implementing these features. The ownership of the records, what and where exactly the transition point is from the marketing team, and where the transition happens to the sales team need to be addressed. Obtaining this distinction and being able to attribute sales back to a specific campaign or customer journey is a challenging task for organizations and a core requirement of marketing to ensure they can measure the effectiveness of their strategy, even if it's not just by revenue made, but by influence in the number of interested parties and contacts gained from it. Lead-scoring functionality can help in this area. A lead, which is linked to a contact, can be automatically updated to "sales ready" when it reaches a score. At this point, any amount of automation can happen using configuration such as workflows. This can include the owner being changed (which would drop it out from marketing views and into sales views), or it could automatically qualify the lead to an opportunity, and more. Once sales owns the lead, they can see the Contact 360 in more depth, so they can have direct access to all the interactions associated with the lead and what has led to that score. They would be able to take the best route based on the information contained within that data to take the opportunity forward in the sales lifecycle.

Getting Set Up with the App

At the time of writing, Dynamics 365 for Marketing is available in a trial form, in the same way as the other Dynamics 365 CE apps, for example, Customer Service and Sales. It can also be added into existing subscriptions and licensed separately. Dynamics 365 for Marketing uses the Unified Interface and is not available within the Classic Client. When setting up the application for the first time, users must ensure the home URL is set for the event portal functionality and agree to consent about the marketing data and how it is processed. Once this is set, it takes a moment, and the instance is ready to use (Figure 6-1).

Dynamics 365 for Marketing has its own email servers that it sends the marketing emails from, and all sender IPs by Microsoft are shared with other organizations using the app. This means a portion of the delivering of emails is managed by Microsoft, and by having a shared IP, the deliverability of the emails is improved compared with a new IP, which must gain the trust of email providers and build up a positive reputation score. There is the possibility that organizations can use a dedicated IP, which is discussed in the "Further Reading" section at the end of the chapter.

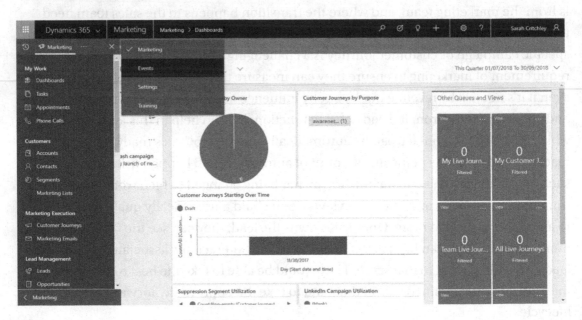

Figure 6-1. *Dynamics 365 for Marketing*

Dynamics 365 for Marketing utilizes a small number of configuration records set up behind the scenes. These are the Default Content Settings, Default Marketing Page, and Default Marketing Settings records. These records are used to manage litmus integration (a marketing preview and testing feature), the address and core details of the organization, and the main Subscription Center that is linked to these settings. Subscription Centers are a way to manage subscription lists within the Dynamics 365 for Marketing application and are covered in more depth in the "Segmentation" section of this chapter. Subscription lists are based on the legacy Marketing List entity as a static list and are used to manage the subscribes and unsubscribes of customers. These lists are associated with a customer journey, which, when it sends a marketing email, sends the subscription link details along with it for several reasons, one being a legal requirement to provide a way for a customer to unsubscribe.

Core entities are set up for marketing as standard, which include the Contact, Lead, and Account records. Any entity, including custom entities, can be set up for use within the Dynamics 365 for Marketing application; however, it must be turned on to synchronize with the Customer Insights Service, which manages the segmentations. Despite any entity being able to be utilized in the query, the query must still end in the associated Contact record and in the linked relationship being defined from that query. Once an entity has been set up to be synchronized, it cannot be unsynchronized.

Task: Update the marketing settings to configure the app for additional entities.

1. Open the Dynamics 365 for Marketing app.

2. Navigate to Settings ➤ Advanced Settings ➤ Marketing Settings ➤ Customer Insights Sync to open a page that looks like Figure 6-2 and contains a list of the entities within the system.

3. Select the entity checkbox that needs to be set up and synchronized.

4. Select "Publish Changes" and wait for the confirmation at the top of the screen.

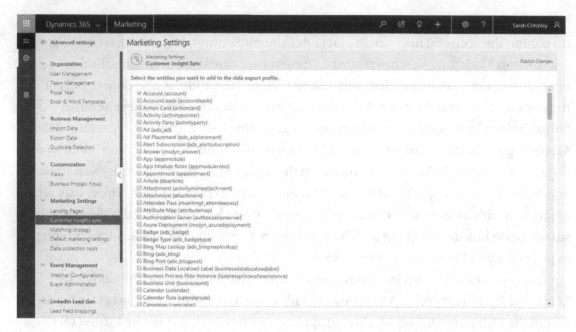

Figure 6-2. Advanced Settings in Dynamics 365 for Marketing

Segmentation

Segments are groups or lists of contacts within Dynamics 365 CE. Segmentation is a way to separate contacts into logical lists that have defining qualities about them relevant to the organization and their marketing strategies. By targeting specific segments of contacts, customer journeys can be tailored to be more relevant and better suited to a customer's needs. This can lead to a more positive interaction from within the journey, contributing to lead scores and more leads that can be passed over to the sales team. An example is where contacts are in a specific geographical location or if they have purchased a specific product.

As referenced in an earlier section, marketing lists are used to manage subscription lists, which can also be targeted through segments that will be referenced within a customer journey.

To create a new subscription list and use it within a customer journey, a new marketing list needs to be created and associated with a marketing form. The marketing form is then associated with a marketing page to create a new Subscription Center, which is referenced within a Content Settings record. This Content Settings record is associated with a customer journey. This allows tailored subscription links to be referenced within the email for the customer to unsubscribe from or subscribe to a specific subscription list.

You can also utilize this list to send marketing materials to the contacts as a segment. When adding a new segment, set the "Segment Source" field to be the marketing list that references the subscription list you wish to use. Marketing lists, where they are of a subscription type, are only ever static marketing lists. This means when a user unsubscribes or subscribes, essentially what they are doing is manually adding or removing themselves from this list.

For steps on how to complete these tasks, review the "Further Reading" section at the end of the chapter under "Subscription Center Management."

Segments have three different types, as follows:

- **Static segments** – Similar to a static marketing list, these are lists of contacts that are manually added to the list.

- **Dynamic segments** – A list of contacts that is based on one or more logical queries from a direct or indirect relationship.

- **Compound segments** – A combination of other segments that are published.

There are different routes by which to create Dynamics segments. They can be created by using the Designer, Flow, and Query methods. The Designer and Flow methods provide an additional function to "explore" a relationship, which shows a live map of the entities and their relationships to other entities, allowing a user to build a segment with extra visualization options. This is shown in Figure 6-3.

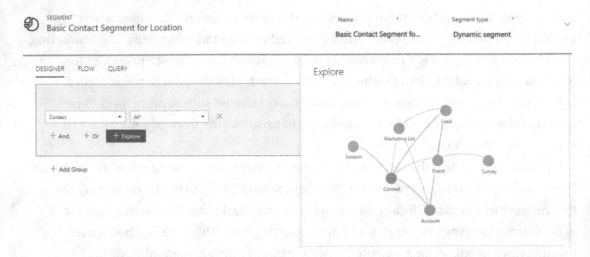

Figure 6-3. *Using the Designer method to create a segment with the Explore visualization*

The Designer method allows a query to be created by using lines of statements and operators that all need to evaluate as "true" for a contact to be included within the segment. Many more operators are being shipped in the October 2018 release of Dynamics 365 for Marketing, allowing greater control of the segmentation functionality (Figure 6-4).

Figure 6-4. *Creating a segment using the Designer method*

Using the Flow method, you can easily create a more dynamic experience as it allows greater control when using groupings such as Union, Intersect, and Exclude within queries (Figure 6-5):

- **Union** – Allows you to add another query group to the existing segment.

- **Exclude** – Allows you to define a query of contacts to remove from the total segment.

- **Intersect** – Targets a specific query of contacts. Those matching this query will be taken forward only to the next segment, and the remaining contacts that do not will be removed.

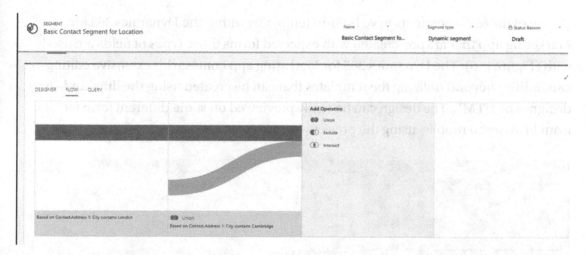

Figure 6-5. *Creating a segment using the Flow method*

Segments need to be published and in a "live" state before being used. Once in a live state, the segment cannot be changed until it is stopped and changed back to a "draft" state. Live segments are ready to be used within customer journeys.

Creating Marketing Forms, Pages, and Emails

Dynamics 365 for Marketing has three core components that are used to send emails and associated content messaging such as landing pages to customers:

- **Marketing forms** – Reusable form components used in marketing pages. These reference fields and data within the contact database. The form is intended to be filled in by a customer.

- **Marketing pages** – Marketing pages have three core types: Forward to a Field, Subscription Center, and a landing page. These can be sent as a separate block within a customer journey and do not have to be associated with an email. They will be sent as an email, and the page will form the "email" design.

- **Marketing emails** – Marketing emails are specific emails that are sent to a customer and can contain a marketing page, survey, or event and normally form a larger piece within a specific marketing strategy.

All of these components have built-in templates within the Dynamics 365 for Marketing app that are pre-created with expected forms those types of fields are used with (Figure 6-6). The Dynamics 365 for Marketing app comes with extensive editing capabilities beyond utilizing the templates that can be created using the drag-and-drop designer or HTML. The design can be easily previewed on some different form factors, from browser to mobile, using the preview feature.

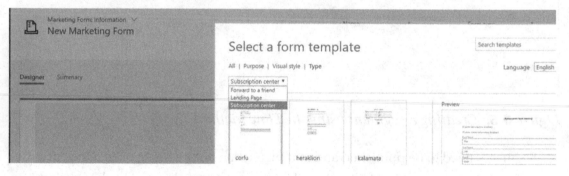

Figure 6-6. *Using templates within Dynamics 365 for Marketing*

Marketing forms have content and lead-matching strategies. Depending on the purpose of the form, it will be specified to create a contact or lead or create a new record based on the matching strategy. The matching strategy specifies which field or fields this matching should be based on. As a default, the strategy is based on the email address. These can be changed within the "Advanced Settings" area of the app (Figure 6-7).

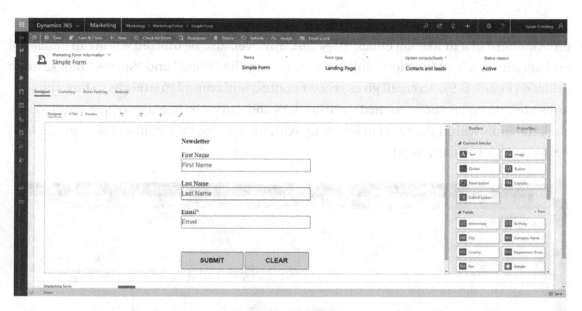

Figure 6-7. *Dynamics 365 for Marketing form*

Once a form is created, a new marketing page is also created. The "Form" block can be dragged over to the designer and configured using the Properties tab within the toolbox (Figure 6-8).

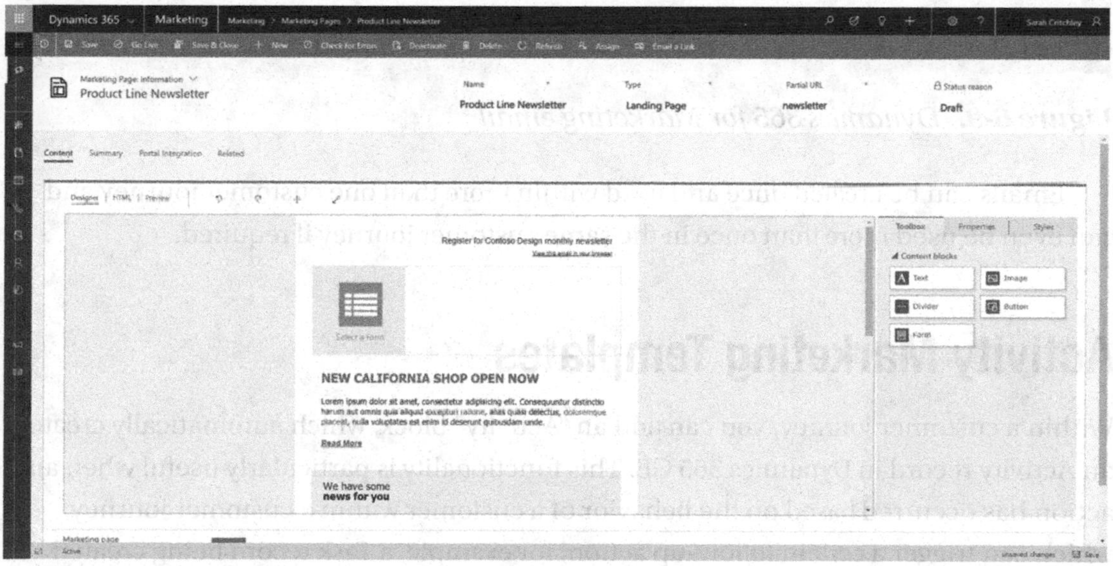

Figure 6-8. *Dynamics 365 for Marketing page*

Marketing pages can be utilized within a customer journey as a separate block, independent of a marketing email. They can, however, also be utilized within an email and appear as a "call to action" link in the same way the "Event" and "Survey" blocks are utilized (Figure 6-9). An email gives greater context and control to users as to how the links are portrayed and presented to customers and can assist in encouraging them to click the links within the email to follow up with the specific information (as opposed to being an independent page).

Figure 6-9. *Dynamics 365 for Marketing email*

Emails can be created once and used within more than one customer journey and can even be used more than once in the same customer journey if required.

Activity Marketing Templates

Within a customer journey, you can add an "Activity" block, which automatically creates an Activity record in Dynamics 365 CE. This functionality is particularly useful when an action has occurred based on the behavior of a customer within a customer journey, which can trigger a certain follow-up action, for example, a Task record being created and assigned to a member of the sales team.

To create activities in this way, an activity marketing template needs to be created that specifies a subject, priority, duration, and specific schedule type for the activity being created as part of that customer journey. When this block is used, the template is then referenced within the customer journey. The template can be set to be a fixed date, or it can be set to be delayed by a specific number of days, saving the time and effort of users having to complete specific details each time (Figure 6-10).

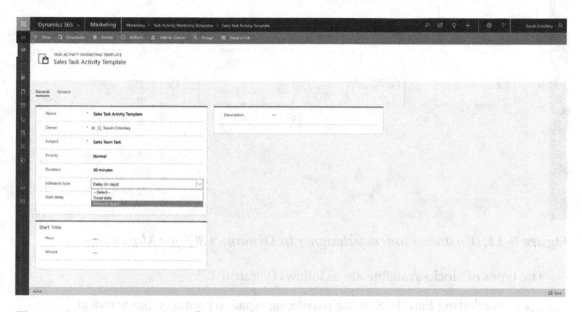

Figure 6-10. *Activity templates within Dynamics 365*

Customer Journeys

Customer journeys are behavior-driven journeys that are based on customer segments. Users can build customer journeys by using a series of blocks that reference an action, such as sending a marketing email, or reference a trigger, such as waiting for a set amount of time or after an email is opened. Customer journeys are driven based on the subsequent behavior of the customer (Contact record) in each block. Based on their behavior, they move throughout the journey, triggering actions within that.

Customer journeys use the same process designer as seen in earlier chapters and originally covered in Chapter 12, meaning the learning curve to get started with creating customer journeys is even smaller (Figure 6-11). Simple to more complex email marketing campaigns can be sent using customer journeys and other types of marketing, such as being sent "call to action"–style landing pages, newsletters based on subscription lists, event marketing, and follow-up surveys from a customer experience using the voice of the customer.

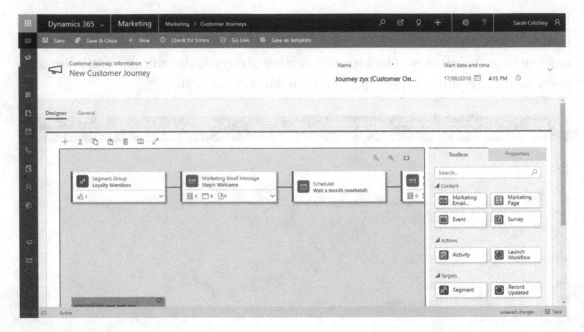

Figure 6-11. *Customer journey designer in Dynamics 365 for Marketing*

The types of blocks available are as follows (Figure 6-12):

- **Marketing Email** – Sends a marketing email to contacts that arrive at this block.

- **Marketing Page** – Sends a Call to Action button that links to the page or can be embedded within a "Marketing Email" block as a child block. Landing pages generate new leads or update existing leads based on the matching rules.

- **Event** – Similar to pages, are linked as child blocks within an email.

- **Survey** – Similar to events, are linked as child blocks within an email.

- **Activity** – Generates a new Activity record in Dynamics 365 CE.

- **Launch Workflow** – Launches a workflow process as part of the customer journey.

- **Segment** – A selection of people to target.

- **Record Update** – Used to add Contact records at a stage in the journey.

- **Scheduler** – Waits for a particular time before continuing.

- **Trigger** – Added after emails, pages, and events that are referenced in the properties and the specific trigger selected. Trigger actions change depending on what they are referencing.

- **Splitter** – Sends a random amount of contacts down a path.

- **Splitter Branch** – Used with splitter tiles to create branches in the customer journey.

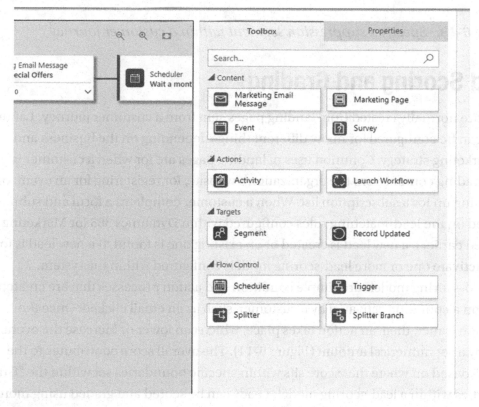

Figure 6-12. *Available customer journey blocks*

Customer journeys are linked to a Content Settings record that references the subscription list that manages new customers subscribing to that list and those existing ones unsubscribing. A suppression segment can be added so that a journey can reference a segment of contacts who should not be sent any of the content from this journey, even if they exist within the specified segments (Figure 6-13).

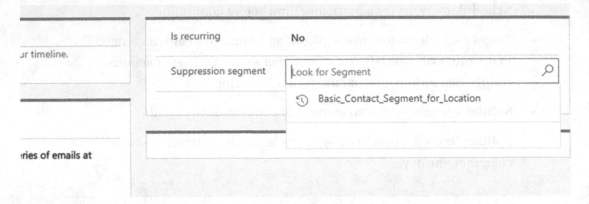

Figure 6-13. *Specify a suppression segment within a customer journey*

Lead Scoring and Grading

Leads are normally created from landing pages sent from a customer journey. Landing pages can be configured for many different things depending on the business and the marketing strategy. Common uses of landing pages are for when a customer is downloading content from the organization's website, for registering for an event, or for signing up for a subscription list. When a customer completes a form and submits it, based on the lead-matching rules configured within Dynamics 365 for Marketing (covered earlier), a new lead is created or an existing one is found. If a new lead is found, it can activate one or more lead-scoring models configured within the system.

Lead-scoring models are simple condition and action processes that are created based on a condition activated by a customer, such as an email clicked. Once the condition is met, then, an action takes place, which can lower or increase the overall score by a set numerical amount (Figure 6-14). The overall score contributes to the "grade" based on where that score sits within specific boundaries set within the "Grades" properties within a lead-scoring model. Leads can be scored and graded using more than one model when they appear on a sub-grid within the Lead record.

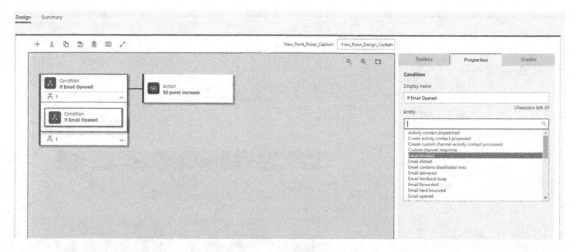

Figure 6-14. *Lead-scoring condition and action process design*

Lead models also have a specific "sales-ready" score set. The sales-ready score is the score a lead needs to reach (from any model) for the "Sales Ready" (yes/no) field on the Lead to be automatically updated to "Sales Ready" (Figure 6-15). Based on this action, any number of specific customizations can be completed, as discussed in the beginning of this chapter, in the lead qualification process of your organization.

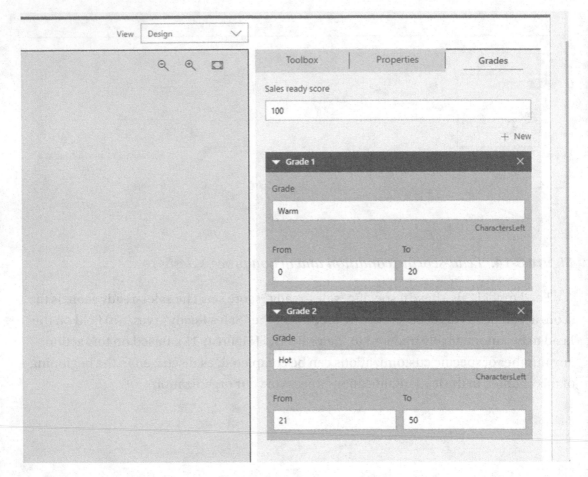

Figure 6-15. *Specifying the lead grades and sales-ready score*

Event Portal Overview and Setup

The Dynamics 365 for Marketing app has an extensive Event Management module that allows you to create an event management portal as part of Dynamics 365 CE using Microsoft Portals. The portal hosts all the published events, giving them each a separate homepage with display details of the event, sponsor advertisements, speaker information, session details, breakdown by the hour, pass information, and the ability for people to register for the event.

One of the things it does not include is integration with a payment gateway. By default, it includes a demo gateway, which can be removed, or a custom component can be added with some configuration.

The Event Management module is particularly useful for both internal and external events and gives the capability to manage logistics such as hotels and even the granular details of the rooms and financial details (Figure 6-16). The portal can be customized based on the Microsoft Portals capabilities and tailored to the styling and branding of your organization.

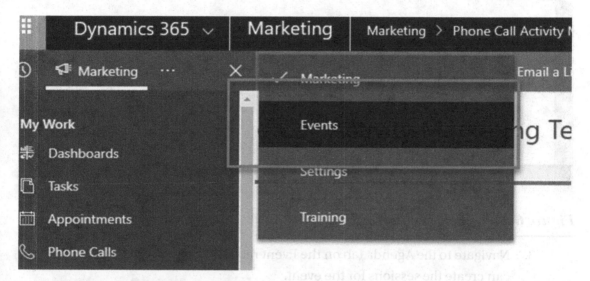

Figure 6-16. *Events section of the Dynamics 365 for Marketing application*

Events can be in-person and require a "Venue" field entry (which can also be managed via the app), or they can be webinars and take significantly less setup time.

Getting started with the Event Management module requires a small number of steps.

Task: Create a new Event record and publish it to the portal.

1. Navigate to the Event Management module and click "Events" and "New."

2. Fill in the "Event Name," "Format," "Start Date," "End Date," "Event Type," and "Venue" fields, saving the record as shown in

   Figure 6-17.

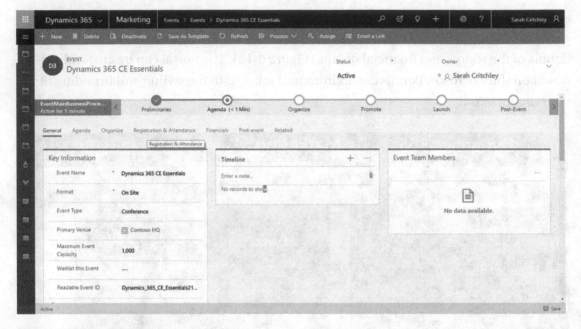

Figure 6-17.   A new Event record

3. Navigate to the Agenda tab on the Event record. This is where you can create the sessions for the event.

4. Click "Add New Session."

5. Fill in the "Session Title," "Start Time," and "End Time" fields, saving the record (ensuring the start and end dates are within the same date range set for the event itself).

6. Create another three sessions by repeating steps 4 and 5.

7. In the Agenda tab under the Speaker Engagements sub-grid, click "Add New Speaker Engagement," as shown in Figure 6-18. A panel should appear on the right-hand side of the screen.

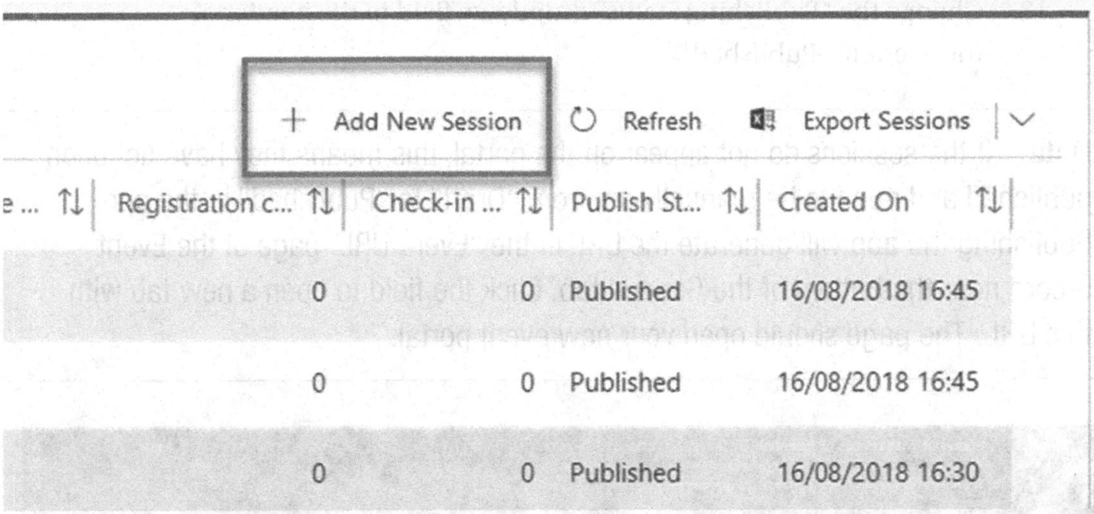

e ... ⇅	Registration c... ⇅	Check-in ... ⇅	Publish St... ⇅	Created On ⇅
	0	0	Published	16/08/2018 16:45
	0	0	Published	16/08/2018 16:45
	0	0	Published	16/08/2018 16:30

Figure 6-18. *A new Event record*

8. Fill in the "Name" and "Speaker" (Contact) fields and link the "Session" the speaker is linked to; then save the record.

9. Repeat steps 7 and 8 to create three more Speaker Engagement records.

10. Click the Registration and Attendance tab within the Event record.

11. In the Passes sub-grid, click "Add New Pass."

12. Enter the name of the pass, for example, Developer Summit; the number of passes allocated, which would be 0; and pass price, which can be any currency amount. (The "No. of Passes Allocated" field increments when a customer registers for this pass.) Save the record.

The core detail for the event has now been set up. There is a great deal of supporting information that can be added, such as sponsor records, more passes, tracks for the sessions, more session-descriptive information, and venue details, to name a few. These can be explored using the "Further Reading" section at the end of this chapter.

The next step is to publish the event so that a portal is created for it and customers can register.

13. Change the "Publishing Status" dropdown field in the header of
     the event to "Published."

Note   If the sessions do not appear on the portal, this means they have not been
published and need to be manually set from "Draft" to "Published" in the app.
Publishing the app will generate the URL in the "Event URL" page of the Event
record near the bottom of the General tab. Click the field to open a new tab with
this URL. The page should open your new event portal.

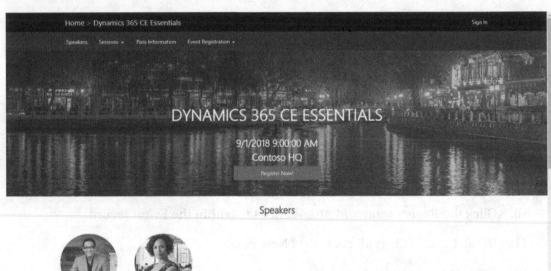

Figure 6-19. *A new event portal with a custom event*

A customer can navigate to the portal and click "Sessions" to see the different
sessions and specific times of the sessions in an easy-to-use timetable view (Figure 6-19).
They can filter on the speakers for the sessions, and if tracks have been set up, these can
be filtered in the "Tracks" dropdown (Figure 6-20). Tracks are a way of grouping sessions
into a specific category, for example, Administration, Development, or "No Code"
session types. If the event is across more than one day, the days appear as tabs across the
timetable view.

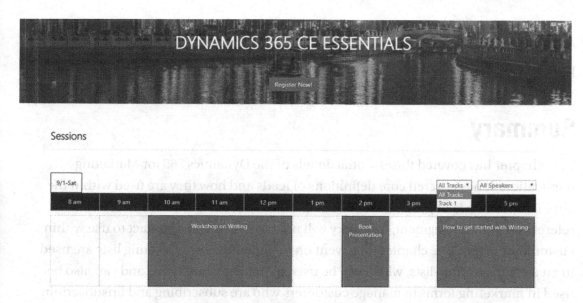

Figure 6-20. *Using the timetable within the portal to view sessions*

Users can register for the event by navigating to "Event Registration" on the portal and completing the registration details. This action creates a new Event Registration record within Dynamics 365 for Marketing and is associated with the event. It also generates a QR code that can be used for the attendee's registration (Figure 6-21).

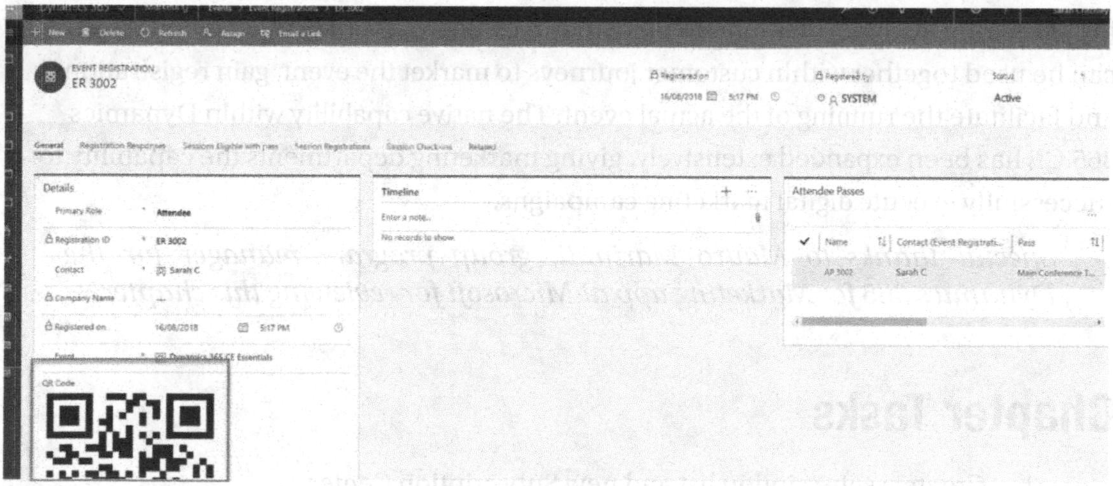

Figure 6-21. *Event registrations within Dynamics 365 CE*

Following the event creation, the event can be used in customer journeys using the "Event" block and is normally used within marketing emails to generate interest and prompt customers to register for the event.

Summary

This chapter has covered the essential details of the Dynamics 365 for Marketing application. It has covered core definitions of leads and how they are used within the app. This section is important, as without a Contact record associated with an entity referenced within a segment, the query will not be able to find a contact to use within a customer journey. The chapter then went on to highlight how marketing lists are used to create subscription lists, which can be used to market to segments and can also be used in marketing forms to manage customers who are subscribing and unsubscribing. Segments are a critical part of the marketing application as they represent whom the organization is going to be marketing to as part of their overall marketing strategy. The application allows these to be created in numerous ways and to be used in customer journeys to conduct behavior-driven marketing campaigns. Customer journeys often create leads and actions, which include triggers such as opening an email or clicking links. These actions can trigger lead scoring, affect lead scores and grades, and influence the accumulation of points for the "sales-ready" score to be triggered. Dynamics 365 for Marketing also provides functionality to run extensive event management, which can be used together within customer journeys to market the event, gain registrations, and facilitate the running of the actual event. The native capability within Dynamics 365 CE has been expanded extensively, giving marketing departments the capability to successfully execute digital marketing campaigns.

Special thanks to Mauro Marinilli, group program manager for the Dynamics 365 for Marketing app at Microsoft for reviewing this chapter.

Chapter Tasks

1. Create a subscription list and new Subscription Center.

2. Use the subscription list in a customer journey.

3. Create static, dynamic, and compound segments.

4. Create a marketing form and page.

5. Create a marketing email.

6. Create a customer journey that uses triggers and schedules.

7. Set up a lead-scoring model.

8. Create a new Event record and associated sessions.

Further Reading

Subscription Center Management (Microsoft, 2018). URL: `https://docs.microsoft.com/en-gb/dynamics365/customer-engagement/marketing/set-up-subscription-center`

Creating Segments (Microsoft, 2018). URL: `https://docs.microsoft.com/en-gb/dynamics365/customer-engagement/marketing/segmentation-lists-subscriptions`

Customer Journeys (Microsoft, 2018). URL: `https://docs.microsoft.com/en-gb/dynamics365/customer-engagement/marketing/create-simple-customer-journey`

Event Management in Dynamics 365 for Marketing (Microsoft 2018). URL: `https://docs.microsoft.com/en-gb/dynamics365/customer-engagement/marketing/event-management`

Customer Journey Tiles (Microsoft 2018). URL: `https://docs.microsoft.com/en-gb/dynamics365/customer-engagement/marketing/customer-journey-tiles-reference`

Lead Scoring (Microsoft 2018). URL: `https://docs.microsoft.com/en-gb/dynamics365/customer-engagement/marketing/qualify-leads-section`

Marketing Deliverability and IP Addresses (Microsoft, 2018). URL: `https://docs.microsoft.com/en-gb/dynamics365/customer-engagement/marketing/get-ready-email-marketing`

CHAPTER 7

Security Model

Dynamics 365 CE has a native security model that is based on users having various degrees of layered access to the application. This access is governed primarily using security roles assigned to users that refer to an access level with specific privileges. These privileges specify what a user can do on records normally relative to the owner of those records and can be influenced by the corresponding business unit they are part of.

Dynamics 365 has evolved with the Power Platform and now has Azure AD providing group-level security which can be managed via an organization's linked Azure tenant. This kind of security can manage a user's access to environments and app access. This chapter doesn't go into detail about this level of security and covers Common Data Service (CDS)–level security only. For more information on security at AD level, see "Further Reading."

Often, security within the Dynamics 365 CE application is summarized as having role, record, and field access. This is a good summary of the levels of access, and these types of access are achieved in many different ways, which this chapter will review. Role-based security is one of the primary ways to secure access to Dynamics 365 CE. This approach is also used per app module ("app"), and roles are applied to the app itself, so those users who have the security role linked to the app will have access to the app; however, they still will be restricted as to what the privileges are in their assigned security roles.

Given the application of the General Data Protection Regulation (GDPR) in addition to the Data Protection Act of 1991, organizations have begun looking more closely at their security within business applications. The GDPR looks at specifically embedding security as a company-wide policy and not something that is an augmentation of a business application system. Security within Dynamics 365 CE is as much about the capabilities of the platform as it is about the process an organization puts in place for specific data policy management and governance. Who has access to and can modify the data is part of not just data protection but also procedures, for example, when an employee leaves the organization and the effect this has on their data and the responsibilities they once had.

257

The end goal of an organization is to have a security model that is consistent, easy to understand, and reflective of the organizational policies. Dynamics 365 CE is just one part of the application and security within other applications, such as Azure, Power BI, and Office 365, where security within those applications also needs to be easily understood and documented within the overarching data policy of an organization. Provided that security has been configured for the corresponding data policy of an organization, users should be able to complete their role within the system with no hindrances or error messages preventing them from completing a task pertinent to their role. They would not have access to any records they do not need.

Security needs to be designed such that it makes sense to give access to an organization-level record such as an Account, Contact, and related data. It makes no sense to hide these types of records, as duplicate records would be created in their stead, leading to more data governance issues. Also, conflicting child records, such as leads and quotes, create multiple incorrect records. This example is the result of a poorly designed security model. Achieving a balance of giving enough information without providing too little or too much is the principal goal of security model design within Dynamics 365 CE.

Designing a security model can be started in several ways. A discussion of what distinct roles within an organization can do and should be able to do can help define the security roles within the organization. This can then be documented by an organization using Microsoft Excel or even Visio with a simple table or diagram of privileges and access levels, each sheet denoting a business unit. This can be created together with the implementing organization's key stakeholders and begins the design of the system with the "Privacy by Design" paradigm that is one of the main goals of data protection and the GDPR.

The following sections will review the constructs available within Dynamics 365 CE that will give organizations the capability to create a robust, privacy-led design that allows users to complete their tasks and gives users the data they need, when they need it.

Where to Configure CDS Security

Following the changes in the underlying platform for Dynamics (the Power Platform), there have been changes in how security is configured within the Common Data Service. It has moved from being managed in the Advanced Settings (where it can still be configured under "Security"; see Figure 7-2) to being managed directly in the Common Data Service. That isn't all. "Apps" themselves now need to be secured using Security Roles under the Apps page as seen in the following. This section aims to cover briefly the core areas where Common Data Security can be configured. It is expected some of these areas will change in future releases.

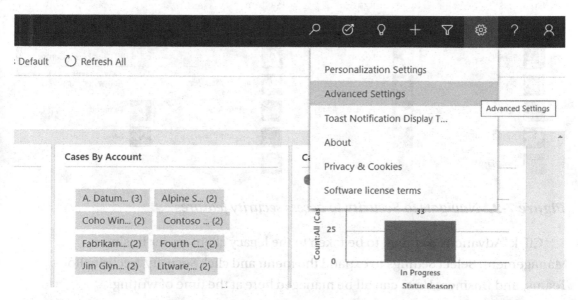

Figure 7-1. *In any Model-Driven App, including Dynamics, access Advanced Settings*

Within any Model-Driven App, including Dynamics 365, users can access the Advanced Settings using the "Cog" icon as shown in Figure 7-1.

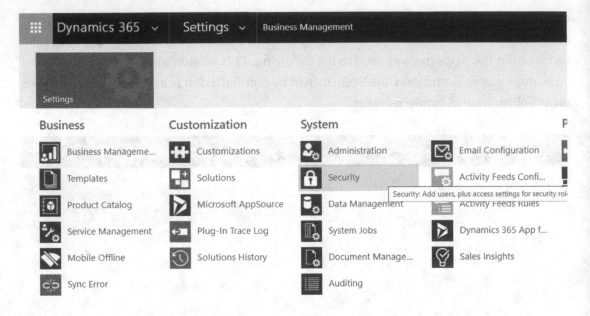

Figure 7-2. *Navigate to Security to access security features*

Click "Advanced Settings" to be taken to the legacy client under Business Management. Select Settings to expand the menu and click Security. Security Roles, Teams, and Business Units can all be managed here at the time of writing.

This is an older way to access the security within the Common Data Service. There are new ways to be able to configure which are being built within the Power Platform. Navigate to admin.powerplatform.com when you are signed into your Office 365 account, and to continue, you need to be a global administrator to have full access to all administrative actions, such as creating an environment or environment admin to be able to act on and change settings within an environment.

Select "Environment" and click Settings. This opens the screen as shown in Figure 7-3 where users can configure "Users and Permissions."

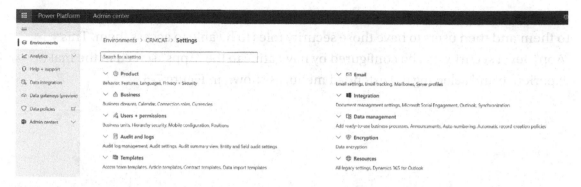

Figure 7-3. *Security configuration within the admin area of the Power Platform*

When this is expanded, you can access different areas such as Business Units, Hierarchy Security, and Security Roles, which are discussed in this chapter.

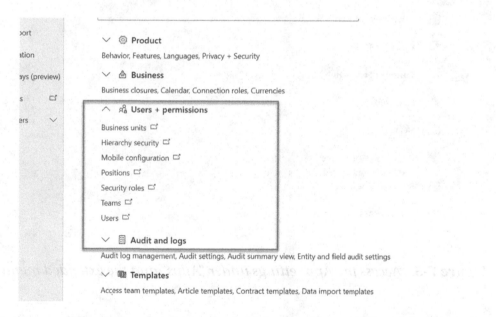

Figure 7-4. *Access different areas of security within the Common Data Service*

As you read this chapter, try and use the modern experience of accessing the environment first from admin.powerplatform.com and clicking the specific area of security you wish to configure. This would get you using the latest experience rather than relying on legacy experiences which are subject to change in later updates.

Apps, including Dynamics 365 Apps, require at least one security role to be applied to them and then users to have those security roles to be able to access them. This "App"-level security can be configured by navigating to the "Apps" screen in the maker experience and selecting the extended menu, as shown in Figure 7-5.

Apps

Apps   Component Libraries

	Name		Modified	Owner
	Omnichannel Administration	···	1 mo ago	Sarah Critchley
	Channel Integration Framework	···	1 mo ago	Sarah Critchley
	Omnichannel for Customer Service	···	1 mo ago	Sarah Critchley
	Solution Health Hub	···	4 mo ago	Sarah Critchley
	Dynamics 365 Portals	···	4 mo ago	Sarah Critchley
✓	**Customer Service Hub**	···	4 mo ago	Sarah Critchley
	Sales Hub			Sarah Critchley
	Field Service			Sarah Critchley
	Connected Field Service			Sarah Critchley
	Resource Scheduling			Sarah Critchley
	Dynamics 365 App for Outlook	···	5 mo ago	SYSTEM

> ✎ Edit
> ▷ Play
> ↷ Share
> 🗑 Delete
> ⚙ Settings

Figure 7-5. *Access the App settings under "Apps" and the extended menu*

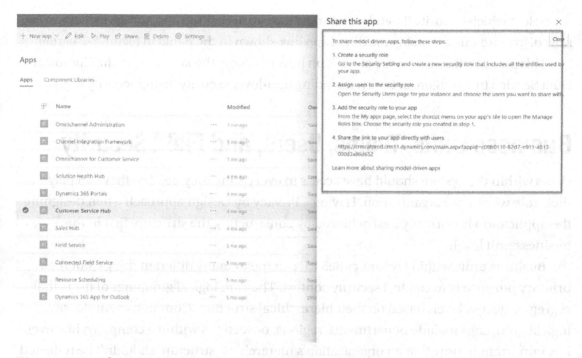

Figure 7-6. Share an App using Security Roles in the CDS

This opens a panel on the right-hand side of the screen shown in Figure 7-6. This panel gives you directions on how to share this app and directs you to the "My Apps" page which is seen in Figure 7-7. This screen summarizes all of your available applications. Select the Model-Driven App, including a Dynamics App, and select "Manage Roles." This opens another panel on the right-hand side of the screen.

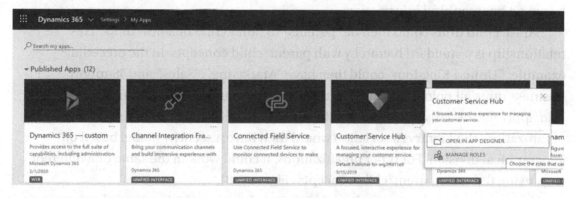

Figure 7-7. Manage App Roles for users accessing the App

Select which Security Role(s) a user must have to access the app and save this. You can now distribute this app using the direct app link shown in the panel in Figure 7-5 earlier.

This summarizes a number of ways on how to access the key areas in the Common Data Service to configure security, including app-level security, using security roles.

Business Units, Teams, Users, and Field Security

Users within the system should have access to everything they need so they can play their role within the organization. Having a Privacy by Design approach when designing the application is normally best achieved by constructing the structure first in the business unit level.

Business units within Dynamics 365 CE can mean many different things, but their primary purpose is to create a security context. They are logical groupings of users that segregate access levels based on their hierarchical structure. Common examples of logical groupings include departments, regions, or sections within a company; however, it is important to note that an organization's hierarchical structure shouldn't be reflected in the business unit structure as standard, and the security design and access to users and their roles should be considered first.

All organizations have a root business unit. This is created when a Dynamics 365 CE organization is created, and it cannot be deleted. A new layer of "child" business units can be created, which would have their "parent" defined as the root business unit. An example would be "Library Association" as the root and then divisions underneath as "United Kingdom," "Australia," and "United States." In this example, the divisions are based on geographical information.

Those child units could then be "parents" to other child business units. This relationship is a standard hierarchy with parent/child concepts. In the preceding example, "United Kingdom" could then have "Marketing," "Sales," and "Support" business units all pointing to the "United Kingdom" parent. A similar structure could also apply for the "Australia" and "United States" business units. For this fictional organization, the Library Association would then have a security model based on geographical division. For other organizations, it could work in the same or a different way, using the same parent/child concepts (Figure 7-8).

Users are assigned a specific business unit and can only be in a single business unit. This causes challenges when allowing access to records outside of their business unit, which is often overcome with teams, covered later in this chapter. An example would be user John Smith, who is based in the UK marketing department. John is placed within the "Marketing" business unit, which is a child business unit to the "United Kingdom." Ava Jones, sitting in the UK office, is a CEO and would instead sit at the United Kingdom business unit level, as she requires oversight of all divisions of the UK office.

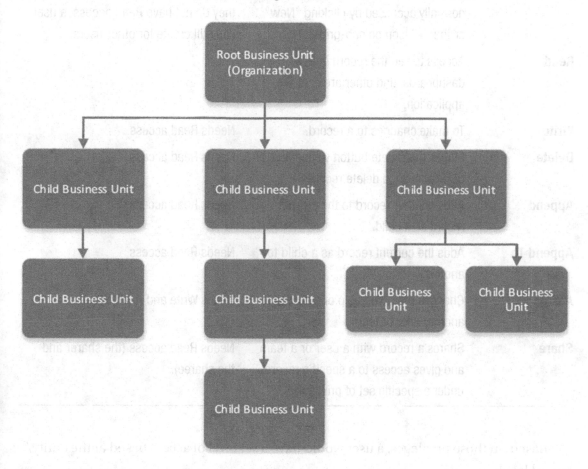

Figure 7-8. *Business unit parent/child structure within Dynamics 365 CE*

Security Roles

Security roles are a specific set of privileges and levels of access. Dynamics 365 CE comes with a list of predefined roles, for example, "CSR Manager" and "Marketing Manager," which can be found in the "Further Reading" section at the end of this chapter.

Privileges are an action a user can perform on the record. These are summarized in Table 7-1.

265

Table 7-1. *A List of the Diverse Types of Privileges Within Dynamics 365 CE*

Privilege Name	Description	Dependencies
Create	A user can create a new record, normally accessed by clicking "New" or the "+" icon on sub-grids.	Needs to have Read access. Note: If they do not have Read access, a user can still create for other users.
Read	Access to see the record in lists, dashboards, and other areas of the application.	
Write	To make changes to a record.	Needs Read access.
Delete	Makes the Delete button visible and gives access to delete records.	Needs Read access.
Append	Adds another record to the current record as a child.	Needs Read access.
Append To	Adds the current record as a child to another.	Needs Read access.
Assign	Changes the ownership of a record to another user or team.	Needs Write and Read access.
Share	Shares a record with a user or a team and gives access to a specific record under a specific set of privileges.	Needs Read access (the sharer and the sharee).

Based on these privileges, a user would have a set level of access based at the entity/record level.

Those access levels are summarized in Table 7-2.

Table 7-2. *Access Level Summary*

Access Level	Description
Basic or User	User level only; the user only has access to records they own.
Local or Business Unit	A user can see the records within their business unit only.
Deep or Parent: Child	A user can see the record within the business unit AND in the child business unit.
Global or Organization	Gives access to all records and ignores the business unit hierarchy.

More information on privileges and access levels can be found in the "Further Reading" section at the end of this chapter.

Security roles can be granted to users and teams. A user can have many security roles, and the same applies to a team. Security roles, however, are only available for users and teams specified within the business unit local to the user or team. If a user is at the "United Kingdom" level, and a security role is made at the business unit level, the "Australia" business unit will not be able to apply for the same security role. Upon security role creation, a security role is copied to all child business units of the business unit that the role was originally created at. This means, in this example, the role would be available at all child business units of "United Kingdom," which are "Marketing," "Sales," and "Support." These are referred to as *inherited roles* and cannot be modified.

The same functionality applies to teams. Only security roles available at the applied business unit directly linked to the team can be applied. Teams, however, have the additional functionality of allowing team members from *other* business units to join. Teams will be covered in the next section.

It would be useful to review a standard security role that Dynamics 365 CE comes with upon creating an organization. This is a good task to complete in a trial environment yourself as a reader, reviewing the same screens while reviewing the section.

Task: Review a standard security role within Dynamics 365 CE. Open the CSR Manager role within the "Security" area of the Classic Client or via the admin area of the Common Data Service (Figure 7-9).

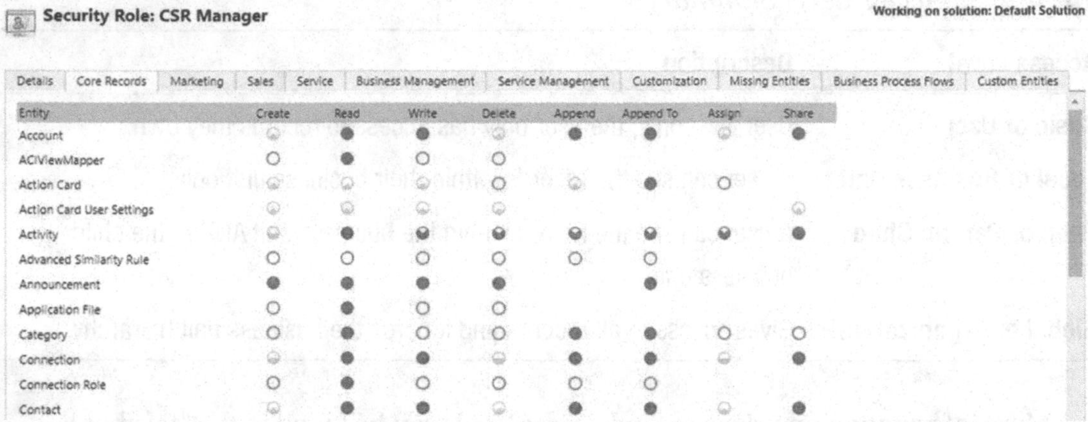

Figure 7-9. *CSR Manager security role, which comes standard with Dynamics 365 CE*

The role displays the privileges at the top of the table, which are denoted by the icons. The more progressively complete the circles are, the more access they have:

- Users with only this security role will be able to see all Account records within the organization (shown by the full green circle, showing organization-level privileges regardless of business unit).

- The user can only create Account records under their user (as opposed to creating an Account record owned by another user). They can also only assign records they own.

- In the Service tab owned by the Case entity, the user can create a Case record under the user of anyone within their business unit. They also can delete a Case owned by any user within their current business unit and any child business units (Figure 7-10).

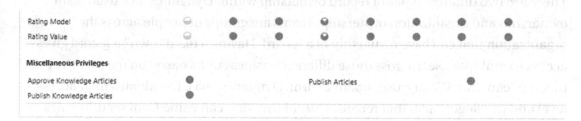

Entity	Create	Read	Write	Delete	Append	Append To	Assign	Share
Article	●	●	●	●	●	●	●	●
Article Template	●	●	●	●				
Bookable Resource	◔	●	●	◔	●	●	●	●
Bookable Resource Booking	◔	●	●	◔	●	●	●	●
Bookable Resource Booking Header	◔	●	●	◔	●	●	●	●
Bookable Resource Category	◔	●	●	◔	●	●	●	●
Bookable Resource Category Assn	◔	●	●	◔	●	●	●	●
Bookable Resource Characteristic	◔	●	●	◔	●	●	●	●
Bookable Resource Group	◔	●	●	◔	●	●	●	●
Booking Status	◔	●	●	◔	●	●	●	●
Case	◔	●	●	◔	●	●	●	●
Characteristic	◔	●	●	●	●	●	●	●
Contract	●	●	●	○	◔	◔	◔	●
Contract Template	●	●	○	○				
Knowledge Article	◔	●	◔	◔	●	●	●	●
Knowledge Article Views	●	●	◔	◔	●	●	●	●

Figure 7-10. *CSR Manager privileges, which come standard with Dynamics 365 CE*

Every record type within the system is defined as having a privilege, normally under the access conditions just specified. There are some special types of privileges that are covered under specific sections of the security role. These normally have only two levels of access: Organization or None. An example of this is within the Service tab in the CSR Manager role under "Miscellaneous Privileges" (Figure 7-11).

Rating Model	◔	●	◔	◔	●	●	●
Rating Value	◔	●	●	◔	●	●	●
Miscellaneous Privileges							
Approve Knowledge Articles	●		Publish Articles			●	
Publish Knowledge Articles	●						

Figure 7-11. *CSR Manager security role special privileges, which come standard with Dynamics 365 CE*

Creating a brand-new security role can be complicated, but it is the most secure way of ensuring an organization has enabled all privileges at the correct access levels. Many organizations will copy a similar type of role that has basic access and modify it to enable an easier transition. This is a great exercise for practice; however, if used in production environments, the roles must be thoroughly tested for their permission set.

Testing Security Roles

Regardless of how the security role is created, within the implementation it is imperative that the role be tested based on the original documented security diagram and model. Simple user stories and acceptance criteria can be created for each privilege upon each entity in each role. They can then be grouped by role and by entity to perform the test cases in a singular session.

It is important that testing is performed per security role so that any potential error or flaw in the security can be found immediately and be isolated. Then, testing can occur for combinations of roles, where they will be utilized within the initial implementation as a "real user." Testing this extra step can find any flaws in the security model design at the user level and not role level. Security roles are additive; roles will never *remove* privileges, but only add to them.

When testing a security role (singular) or security roles for a user, ensure you are not a system administrator and that you have multiple user accounts set up within the tenant to allow for switching between system admin roles (to change other users' privileges) and the roles you are testing.

Teams and Ownership

There are two different types of record ownership within Dynamics 365: user/team ownership and organization ownership. Teams are groups of people across the organization that can have ownership of a record. Having a team "own" a record gives access to multiple users across those different business units based on the security roles that the team has. When a user opens a form, Dynamics 365 CE evaluates their access level and privileges upon that record. This information can come from security roles directly from the user, a team, record sharing, or access teams. The evaluation of these then concludes in the totality of what a user has access to within the application. This information is cached locally in the browser and is made invalid every time a user record is updated or their roles change to reduce loading times (Figure 7-12).

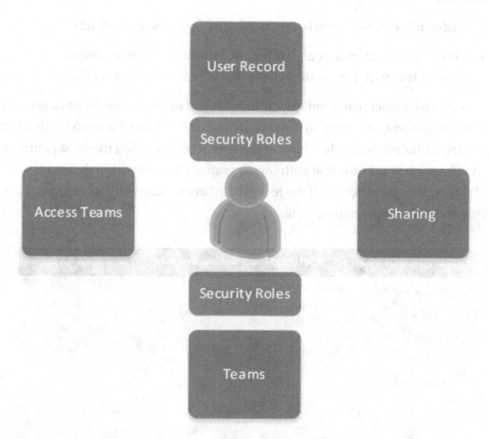

Figure 7-12. *Where security roles are used within Dynamics 365 CE*

Teams are assigned to a business unit. They can, however, contain users who exist across multiple business units. An example includes a "Conference 2018 Team" that has been created in Dynamics 365 for the Library Association organization. Both Ava and John can be a part of this team, which is assigned the root business unit level, even though Ava and John are users in different business units.

System teams are created per business unit and are a special type of team that cannot be modified and automatically log who is in a specific business unit at any one time. Teams can be created by navigating to "Security" settings via your chosen route (as highlighted at the beginning of the chapter) and then navigating to "Teams." Clicking "New" brings up a blank Team record. The following fields can be completed (Figure 7-13):

- **Team Name** – The name of your team.

- **Business Unit** – The business unit of your team; governs security roles available to apply to the team level.

- **Administrator** – Named user that can be accessed in workflows.

- **Team Type** – Owner or access teams. This section is referring to owner teams. Access teams will be discussed in the next section.

Once created, owner teams can "own" records just as users own records, giving the specific privileges from the team to those users included within the team for that record, on top of any other privileges they have at the user level (meaning the least restrictive layer). It is important to know that with owner teams, all users within that team are granted the same level of access. If the team members require a different level of access, access teams will be more appropriate.

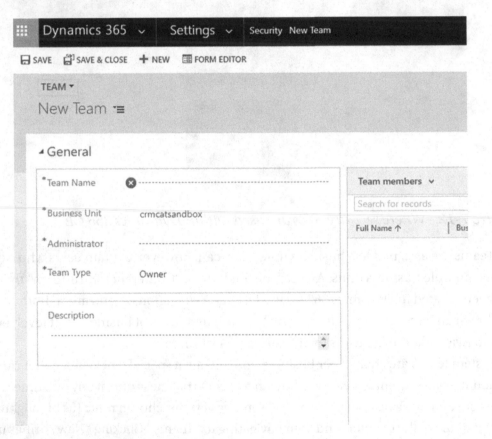

Figure 7-13. *Creating a new team in Dynamics 365 CE*

Select "Manage Roles" on a team to change the security roles of the team that are applied to all the members within that team. The members can be reviewed in the Team members sub-grid, as shown in Figure 7-14.

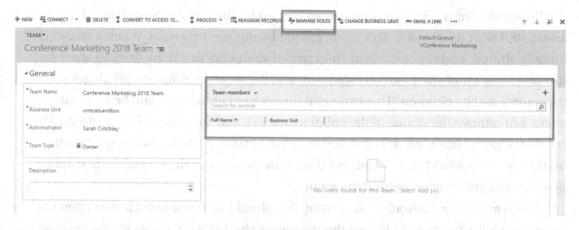

Figure 7-14. *Team record within Dynamics 365 CE*

Testing Teams

It is important to test security roles within team structures. Team structures are designed to give users an extra level of privileges they do not normally have at the user level. It will take more effort to design such tests as you must specifically give the testing user an original role with limited access so you can verify that the access granted by the teams is being applied correctly in all scenarios relevant to the organization and the security model.

As mentioned in the previous section, using teams gives users the capability to access records that are owned by a different user in a different business unit. This is one of the most useful aspects of a team; however, teams also can impact the security design. It is an important aspect of testing.

Sharing

Sharing is a privilege available to users so they can share the record specifically with another user or a team. Depending upon the access levels, users can share records they own, the business unit owns, the business unit and their children own, or any record within the system. Sharing should be used with caution as it allows users to get around the designed security model. For this reason, it must be ensured that sharing privileges are set to a minimum, if at all. Sharing is an access right given per entity; to restrict this, set this to "None."

When sharing a record, a share is also created for the child records behind the scenes associated with that parent. This could cause obvious security risks. When a record is initially shared, and the cascade of child record shares occurs, if the original share is modified, the child shares are *not* updated, and there can be different privileges set on the parent and its children. This can naturally get hard to manage and be confusing for users. (To remove the shares of the children, the original share must be removed.) This result of sharing has been documented to cause notable performance degradations on the Dynamics 365 CE environment due to the increase in the size of the SQL table holding this information behind the scenes.

There are many alternatives to sharing that should be considered before allowing users the ability to share. This includes managing sharing with access teams, covered in the next section. Access teams, for example, allow for a more flexible level of sharing that can be managed more easily and is visible to administrators. One can also reduce sharing with individual users and instead share on the team level.

***Figure 7-15.** Sharing within Dynamics 365 CE*

To share a record, if the user has permissions, navigate to the record and select "Share" (Figure 7-15). This is normally found on the action menu of a record. The user will then see a popup giving them the ability to share with a user or a team. They then select the privileges they wish to grant. A user who is sharing cannot grant another user or a team higher access levels or privileges than they already have. Once a record is shared, those who have received their share will be granted any additional privileges to the record they did not previously have (Figure 7-16).

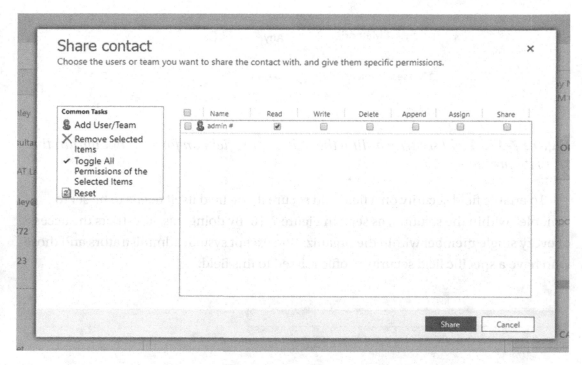

Figure 7-16. Specific sharing privileges within Dynamics 365 CE

Field Security

Sometimes a user needs to have Read access to a record, but certain aspects of that field should be restricted further as they should not have access to everything held at that level. Field-level security can be useful here and can be built into the security model. Field security requirements can be easily identified as a column within the documentation of the model's metadata definition when designing the entities and can also be added to the security model. Field security adds an extra dimension to a security model that can manage specific cases of sensitive data that doesn't include the whole record.

Field security within Dynamics 365 allows an organization to restrict the Read, Update, and Create privileges for a specific field on a record type using field security profiles. Users are applied to these profiles, allowing for granular access to these fields in combination with their security role unionization (Figure 7-17).

At the time of writing, field-level security in the Common Data Service can only be accessed via the Classic Client.

275

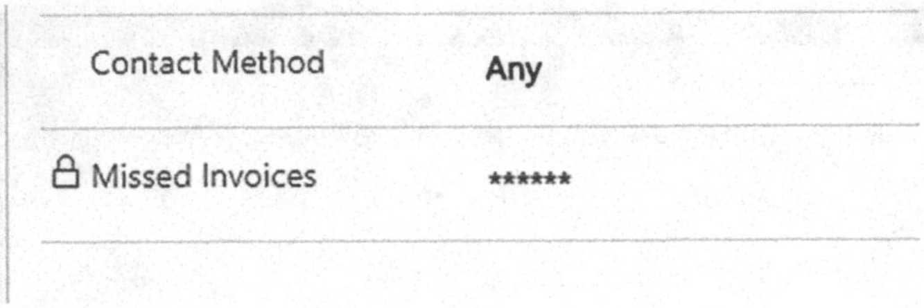

Contact Method	Any
🔒 Missed Invoices	******

Figure 7-17. *Field security hiding the value of the field on forms if not within the security profile*

To enable field security on a field and secure it, the field itself needs to be set to "Enable" within the solution, as seen in Figure 7-18. By doing this, it restricts the access of every single member within the organization except system administrators and those who have a specific field security profile related to this field.

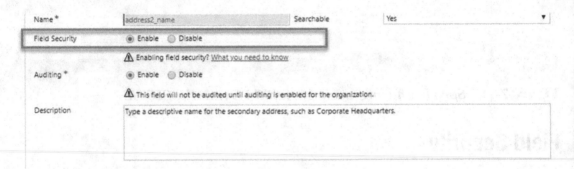

Figure 7-18. *Field Security option on the field definition*

Task: Create a field security profile.

1. Navigate to the Classic UI ➤ Settings ➤ Security.

2. Select "Field Security Profiles" and then select "New." Name your profile (Figure 7-19).

File
Save and Close
Actions
Field Security Profile: Campaign Restriction
General
Field Security Profile : Inf...
General
Related
Members:
Teams
Users
Common
Field Permissions
Audit History
General
Name *
Campaign Restriction
Description

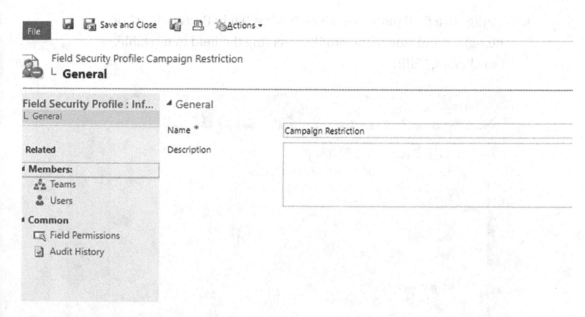

Figure 7-19. *Field security profile*

In the profile, there is a section called "Members." These are the teams and users granted the permissions within the system to have specific access (Read, Update, or Create) to the secure field.

3. Add a user to the new profile.

   Under the Field Permissions tab, all the fields with "Field Security" enabled are displayed. Selecting the field allows a user to specify what permissions they want users within this profile to have upon the secure field. The field permissions can be seen in Figures 7-20 and 7-21.

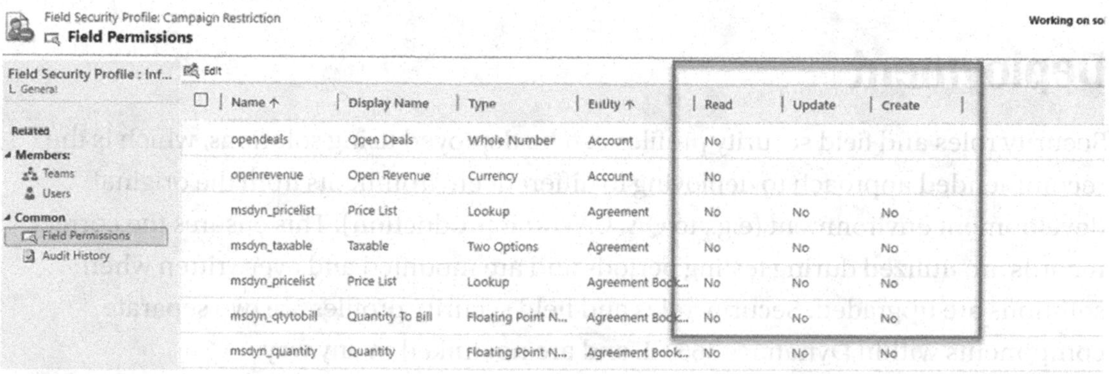

Field Security Profile: Campaign Restriction
Field Permissions
Working on so
Field Security Profile : Inf...
General
Edit
Related
Members:
Teams
Users
Common
Field Permissions
Audit History
Name
Display Name
Type
Entity
Read
Update
Create
opendeals Open Deals Whole Number Account No
openrevenue Open Revenue Currency Account No
msdyn_pricelist Price List Lookup Agreement No No No
msdyn_taxable Taxable Two Options Agreement No No No
msdyn_pricelist Price List Lookup Agreement Bo... No No No
msdyn_qtytobill Quantity To Bill Floating Point N... Agreement Bo... No No No
msdyn_quantity Quantity Floating Point N... Agreement Book... No No No

Figure 7-20. *Field security permissions*

4. Configure a field permission by selecting "Field Permissions" on the right-hand side of the profile, selecting the field in the table, and clicking "Edit."

Figure 7-21. *Field security privileges*

Organizations can view and review their metadata and modify their security easily by using the Entity Metadata Browser from the xrmtoolbox link within the "Further Reading" section at the end of the chapter.

Deployment

Security roles and field security profiles can be deployed using solutions, which is the recommended approach to deploying to different environments from the original development environment (e.g., to QA, UAT, and production). This ensures the correct records are utilized during testing periods and are modified and overwritten when solutions are upgraded. Security roles and field security profiles are two separate components within Dynamics 365 CE and are not linked in any way.

Access Teams

With owner teams, which obtain their security clearance from the roles assigned to them and from a team owning a record, the "basic" level of access gives team members the capability to perform anything on the record just as if they owned it. Access teams, however, do not own records; instead, they are very similar to sharing, where individual records are shared with a team, giving specific access that can be reported on and revoked.

Access teams are particularly useful if record-level access needs to be given that cannot be planned (again, very similar to the use case for sharing). Access teams allow a user to specify the privileges, and multiple teams can have different structured permissions, allowing a "not one size fits all" approach.

An important note, however, is that access teams do not give the capability for ownership of a record. This means views or reporting that is configured to allow the record to appear in views based on the value in the "Owner" field will not apply to access teams. This would need to be configured, which we will look at shortly.

To create an access team manually, often referred to as a *user-created access team*, complete the same steps as for an owner team, except set the "Team Type" field to "Access" as opposed to "Owner" (Figure 7-22).

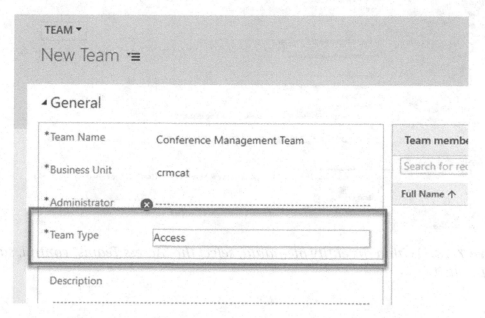

Figure 7-22. Creating an access team within Dynamics 365 CE

Access teams created by users allow team members to be added, and then the team can be given access to any number of records. User-created access teams are used in the same way as owner teams and sharing, giving access to individual records. The difference between a user-created access team and an owner team is that the access team does not have defined ownership nor does it have a security role applied, and its main purpose is to use sharing across the team to define and limit the security permissions on multiple records.

To create access teams per record, which are automatically created by the system, a small amount of setup is required per record type. Similar to queues, an entity/record type has to be enabled for use within access teams at the entity level. This can be configured within a solution and in the entity definition (Figure 7-23). While Teams can be accessed via the admin area of the Power Platform as highlighted at the beginning of the chapter, at the time of writing, only some areas of creating access teams can be completed by starting from this route. Entity settings and access team templates can be accessed by going via the Classic UI as shown at the start of the chapter.

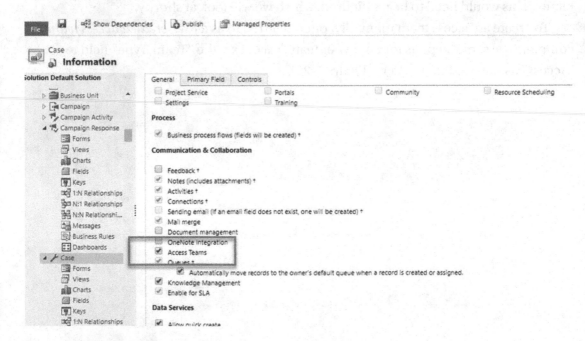

Figure 7-23. *Within the entity metadata, select the "Access Teams" control, save, and publish*

Access team templates allow for access teams to be automatically created per record using sub-grids within that record. This is particularly important for collaboration between users and to be able to dynamically provide access to a record that may be outside of a business unit without giving a larger scope to the whole entity than is necessary.

Task: Set up an access team.

1. Navigate to Security within the Classic UI and select "Access Team Templates" (Figure 7-24).

2. Ensure a record has been enabled for access teams (ensuring you have permissions to do so or are in a trial environment) or that you are using a record enabled by default, like the Account entity.

3. Create a new template for the record type just enabled.

4. Set "Entity" as the name of the entity selected in step 2.

Figure 7-24. *Creating an access team template within Dynamics 365 CE*

In the example in Figure 7-25, this would be the Case entity. (Only Account and Opportunity are enabled out of the box.) The "Entity" dropdown in the Properties window, as seen in Figure 7-25, is populated based on the entities that have "Access Team" enabled at the entity definition level.

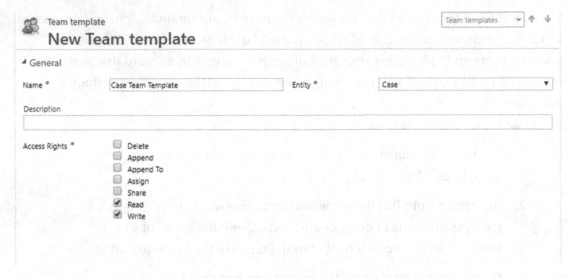

Figure 7-25. *Creating an access team within Dynamics 365 CE*

5. Within the entity form, add a sub-grid with the data source
    properties set in the following list and shown in Figure 7-26:

    •   **Records –** All Record Types

    •   **Entity –** Users

    •   **Default View –** Associated Record Team Members

    •   *Team Template –* <The one created in the previous step>

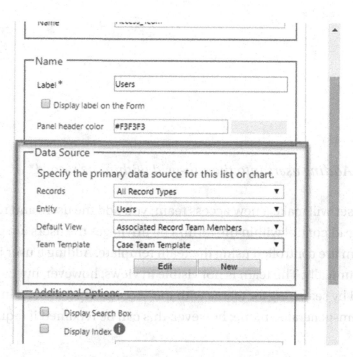

Figure 7-26. *Creating a sub-grid to allow for automatically generated access teams*

It is possible to create more than one access team template and have multiple sub-grids on the entity, creating different access teams based on specific permissions. This is a way to manage the security privileges given at a specific record level.

6. Once completed, ensure the customizations have been saved and published; then add a user to the sub-grid (Figure 7-27).

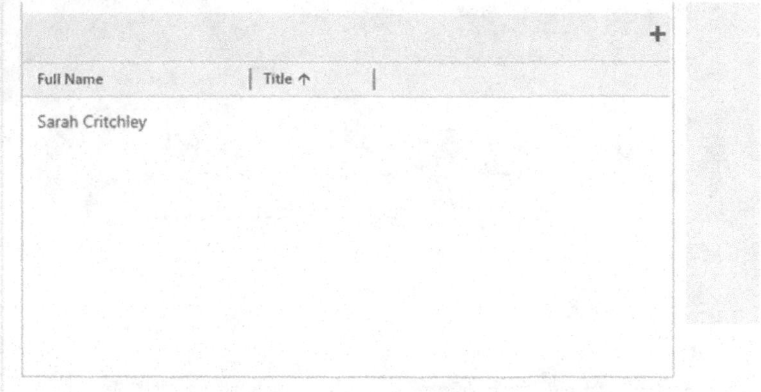

Figure 7-27. *Adding users into the sub-grid within the record*

Adding a user will make a new access team; you add the users and remove them using the sub-grid control within the form. The privileges the users are granted while within that team are controlled using the team template. Adding a user initially makes a new team dynamically. The team is not visible in views, however, but can be accessed via Advanced Find by searching for teams with the "Access" type, as seen in Figure 7-28. The name is a system-generated name; however, this can be renamed if required.

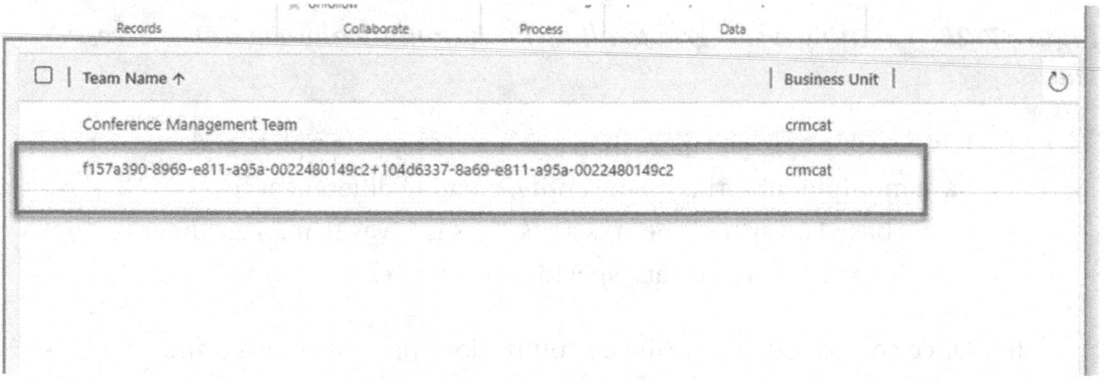

Figure 7-28. *Advanced Find of the system-generated access team*

It is not recommended to modify the team template while it is in use; however, sometimes this is required. If the template is modified, existing access teams will not be affected and must be recreated. They can be recreated by removing all members from the record and starting again, creating a new access team by adding the first user to the record (Figure 7-29).

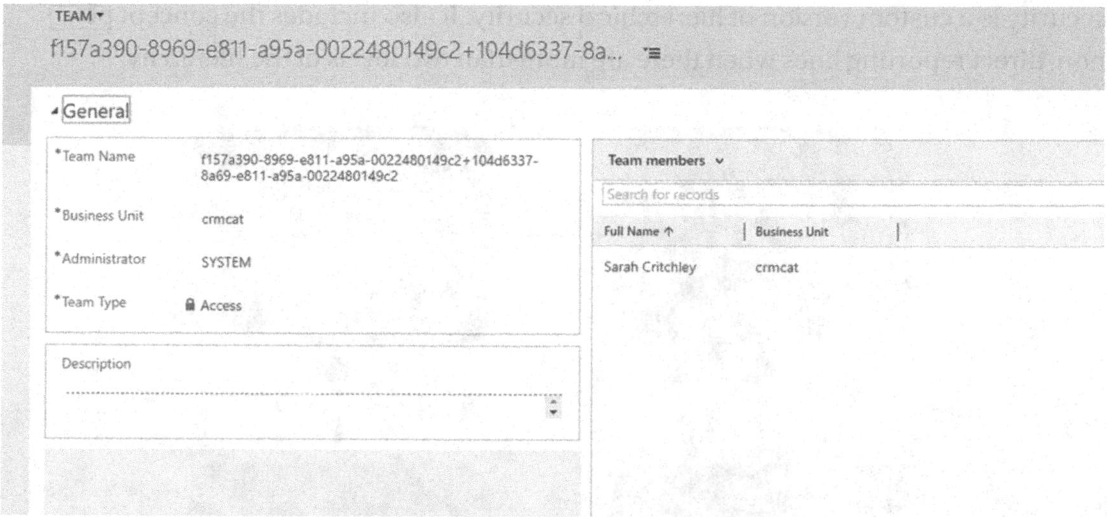

Figure 7-29. *System-created access team when the first user is added*

Access teams are a notable example of record-based ownership security within Dynamics 365 CE and are even used as standard within the Opportunity form in the Sales Team sub-grid. They should be considered within the security model; despite not being related to security roles, they provide reporting capabilities to organizations to see who has access to a given record above their set privileges at any time.

Hierarchical Security

So far, role-, record-, and field-based security has been discussed and demonstrated. Setup is primarily achieved using security roles and teams. Dynamics 365 CE has an extension to that current security functionality called *hierarchical security*. Hierarchical security can be used in combination with the previous methods and allows, in some cases, for a more "real-life" approach to security, especially with how it is reflected within teams through the managerial hierarchy in an organization.

Managerial hierarchy is based on the manager and direct reports. Being a named manager to a user gives the user referred to as the manager Read, Write, Update, and Append access to the user's data as if it was their own. (They must have Read access as an initial privilege.)

This type of access is only available within the same business unit. The subordinate and the manager must be within the same business unit or a child business unit, which is in contrast to positional security, which can be across multiple business units. Positional security is a custom version of hierarchical security. It also includes the concept of non-direct reporting lines when there are more than two levels of the hierarchy.

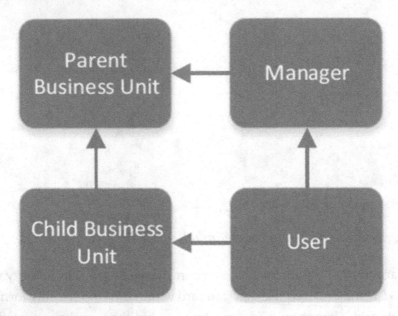

Figure 7-30. *Managerial security across a single business unit or child business unit*

Managerial security is shown in Figure 7-30, and positional security is shown in Figure 7-31; only one can be utilized. They are both set up in the same place within the system.

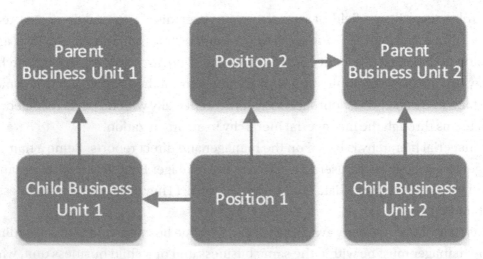

Figure 7-31. *Positional security across multiple business units*

Task: Set up hierarchical security.

1. Navigate to the Hierarchical Security screen using your choice of route as discussed at the beginning of the chapter (admin area of Power Platform or Classic Client).

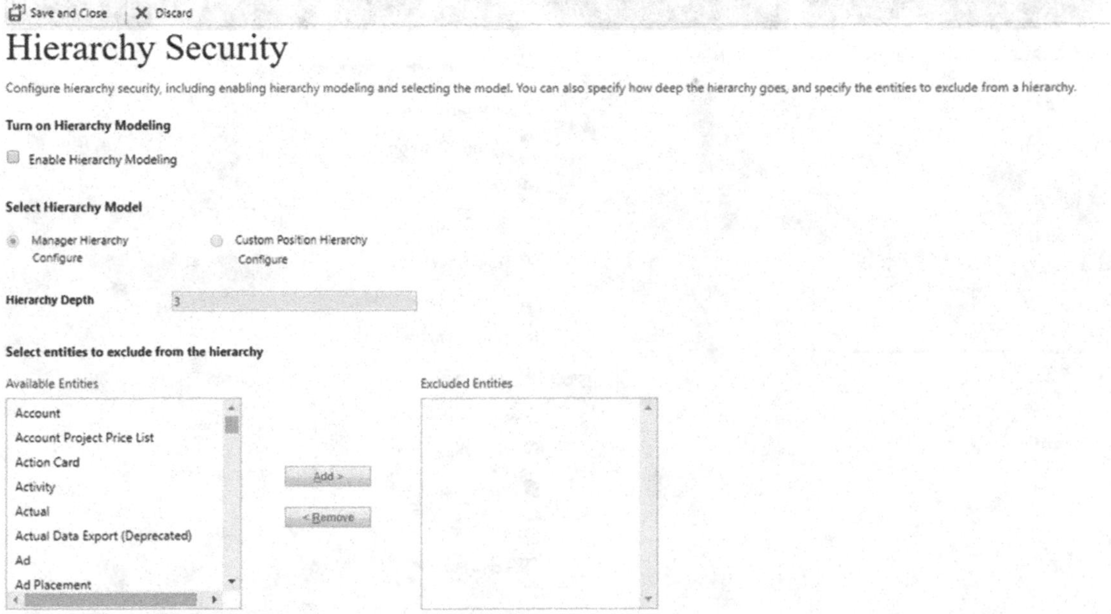

Figure 7-32. *Hierarchical security set up within Dynamics 365 CE*

From this screen, shown in Figure 7-32, you can select either "Manager Hierarchy" or "Custom Position Hierarchy."

2. Configure the depth (if you selected positional hierarchy).

3. Select which entities to exclude by moving the entities from left to right.

Not including an entity within the model means this will not be given any extra privileges through this structure, and those records would need to be reliant on other parts of an organization's security model.

Once the managerial hierarchy is set up, all that needs to be done to complete this setup is to set the managers up within the user record.

4. Navigate to a record (form or view) and select "Change Manager" (Figure 7-33). Another user within the same business unit can then be selected, and this is saved as the "Manager," giving them the elevated security privileges referred to earlier in the chapter.

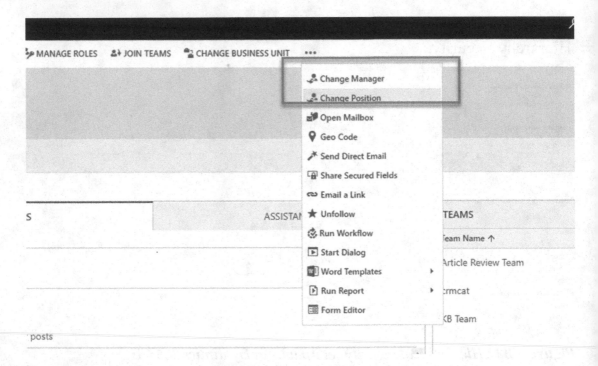

Figure 7-33. *Changing a manager position on a user record*

By selecting "Custom Position Hierarchy," a user can define the positions within that hierarchy. They can select "Configure" (once saved) or navigate to "Positions" from the Security section of the sitemap in the Classic Client or from the admin area of the Power Platform:

1. Select either "Configure" within the previous screen or "Positions" as seen in Figure 7-34 from the "Security" section of the Classic Client sitemap.

Figure 7-34. *Setting up positions within Dynamics 365 CE*

2. Click "New" to create a new blank Position record. You need to name this position, select the parent (multiple positions can refer to one parent; multiple users can be within one position), and save the record (Figure 7-35).

Figure 7-35. *Setting up a custom position hierarchy*

In the example in Figure 7-36, three positions have been created: CEO, CTO, and Technical Director. Selecting the hierarchy symbol on the left-hand side within the Position view opens up the hierarchy view to see the structure that has been created.

Figure 7-36. *Hierarchy View button within a view*

The hierarchy view, as shown in Figure 7-37, can give you a high-level overview of the current positional hierarchy, allowing you to easily make modifications, especially when initially creating the positions.

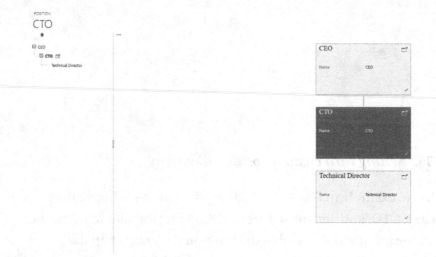

Figure 7-37. *Visualizing the positional hierarchy*

The final setup task is to assign the positions created to users within the system.

3. Navigate to a user record and select "Change Position," and then choose one of the positions from the view. This can be seen in Figure 7-38.

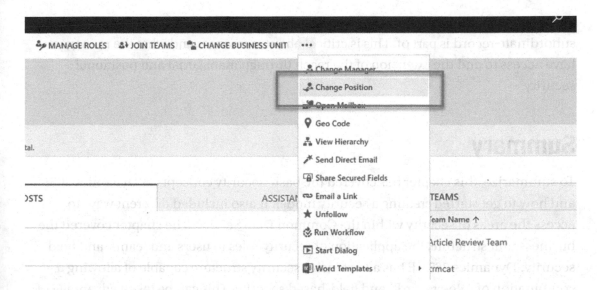

Figure 7-38. *Assigning a position to a user (a user can only have one position)*

Selecting "Change Position" gives you the choice of the positions created in the previous step, shown in Figure 7-39.

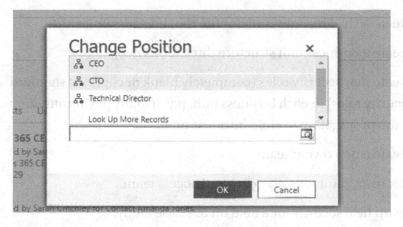

Figure 7-39. *Selecting a custom position for a user*

Positional security works in the same way as managerial security as far as the security rights it gives the reporting managers of those subordinates are concerned. It is important also to be aware that the manager's access extends to records shared with the subordinates and is inclusive to the records owned or shared with a team that the subordinate record is part of. This is critical about awareness and what the managers have access to and the extension of the reach through managerial and positional security.

Summary

To summarize, this chapter has covered the basic security concepts of Dynamics 365 and how to get started creating a security model. It also included different ways to access the areas of security within the Common Data Service. The chapter covered the business unit structure, the application of security roles to users and teams, and field security. Dynamics 365 CE has an extensive security structure capable of allowing a combination of role-, record-, and field-based security. This can be taken advantage of by organizations to give them the capability to comply with required data security and governance policies.

Chapter Tasks

1. Create a child business unit for the root business unit.

2. Create a business unit structure three levels deep.

3. Create new security roles (completely blank or copies of standard security roles) in each business unit, particularly paying attention to the propagation to child business units.

4. Create a new owner team.

5. Create an automatically generated access team.

6. Set up field security for a field on the Case entity.

7. Set up managerial hierarchy.

8. Set up custom positional hierarchy.

Further Reading

Security and Security Roles (Microsoft, 2018). URL: `https://docs.microsoft.com/en-us/dynamics365/customer-engagement/admin/security-roles-privileges`

Security Overview including a PDF by Microsoft on Scalable Security Modelling with Microsoft Dynamics (Microsoft, 2018). URL: `https://docs.microsoft.com/en-us/dynamics365/customer-engagement/admin/security-concepts`

Entity Metadata Browser (Microsoft, 2018). URL: `https://docs.microsoft.com/en-gb/dynamics365/customer-engagement/developer/browse-your-metadata`

Azure AD Groups. URL: `https://docs.microsoft.com/en-us/power-platform/admin/manage-teams`

CHAPTER 8

Mobile Application

The Unified Interface within Dynamics 365 CE expands its capabilities to give users a seamless experience across desktop and mobile. *Seamless* is a word often used to describe many things within technology, and in this case it reflects the ability to allow a user to use the same thought process whether using the application on a desktop, laptop, or mobile device. This is important because, as a result of restrictions on the number of fields and sections, forms within Dynamics 365 CE previously had to be designed separately depending on the device being used. This will no longer need to be the case with the Unified Interface, which will load forms optimally depending on the screen size of the application.

This functionality gives the application some distinct advantages. It means that, within the Unified Interface, the user experience is the same in any single form factor whether the application is being used on the Web (using different screen sizes, the tablet or the phone) or in a mobile application. User experience is very important across software development and usage. It often determines how much a user enjoys using the application and has a direct influence on their being able to perform an activity within the application, despite user experience being a difficult concept to measure consistently. What can be said to be consistent is that the Dynamics 365 CE application has a single user experience across all the devices it is used on. It has the same UI and, where possible, the same controls; if not, they are optimized to make usage easier (e.g., buttons easy to use with fingers, rather than a mouse click).

For all of this, it is easy to ask what the advantage is of using the downloadable Dynamics 365 CE app vs. using the browser on a mobile device. The mobile application has a strong road map of features. It is often used for mobile offline use, which is not possible via the web application. This is particularly useful in scenarios where the

© Sarah Critchley 2020
S. Critchley, *Dynamics 365 Essentials*, https://doi.org/10.1007/978-1-4842-5911-5_8

sales team is traveling and wants to update their appointments or review Dynamics 365 CE data without a guaranteed connection. Offline features will be returning to the application in the future and so won't be covered in this edition of the book. The downloadable app also offers an improved experience when switching between other apps on the mobile device, such as Microsoft Outlook, and provides additional unique features, such as pinch and zoom, easier-to-use navigation, and dedicated system settings. It is, however, personal preference and functionality-based decisions that push users toward using the downloadable app on Windows, iOS, or Android devices or simply using the web browser.

There are specific requirements for the application to run on phones and tablets, which can be found in the official Microsoft documentation, referenced in the "Further Reading" section at the end of this chapter.

Setup

To access the mobile application (not the web version of the app on mobile), download the app from the appropriate app store. It can be found by searching for the keyword "Dynamics 365." Read the terms and conditions, and download the app to your device.

When the app is opened for the first time, the user needs to enter the URL for the organization and authenticate with their login details, as shown in Figure 8-1.

Figure 8-1. *Mobile sign-in page*

If you wish to use the Dynamics 365 CE app from the browser on a mobile device instead, navigate to the URL home.dynamics.com or portal.office.com and sign in. There will be a prompt to select the app if home.dynamics.com was used. The only interface available for use on mobile devices is the Unified Interface and not the Classic UI. This includes accessing Dynamics 365 CE on the web browser; a user will still not be able to access the Classic UI application, including the full default application. There must be an "app" created that uses the Unified Interface forms or uses the standard "Customer Service Hub" or other related "Hub" apps as part of the current subscription (Figure 8-2).

Once logged in and with the app selected, the application is ready to go. There isn't any further setup required to begin using the mobile client.

Figure 8-2. App selector on mobile

Designing Dashboards and Forms for the Mobile Client

The responsive Unified Interface forms within Dynamics 365 CE are flexible and do not require a specific mobile form, as was the case in previous versions of the Dynamics 365 CE application. This gives distinct advantages to customers who wish to modify an existing form or create custom record types, as one form can be created and utilized across different form factors. Some items do need to be "activated" for mobile, such as controls like the editable grid (discussed later in this chapter).

This does mean that, depending on the device the form is viewed on, the placement of the form components may look slightly different, for example, there could be fewer columns in a smaller device as opposed to a larger desktop. The design of the form needs to take this into consideration, and organizations need to take a mobile-first approach to designing dashboards and forms going forward which is a common design approach when looking at a design to an application that needs to be adaptive across multiple form factors as there are often more mobile-specific decisions. Once an application can be used on a mobile, there is often less work to configure or make changes for use on larger devices. A mobile-first approach can be taken by designing the form for mobile use, where the form loads in specific sections from left to right before moving down.

It is important to see the difference and the adaptability of the forms. This section looks at the visual differences so as to help in the design of forms and to avoid having to rework them for each different form factor. This awareness will allow the forms to be built to meet the requirements of the application, whichever device is used.

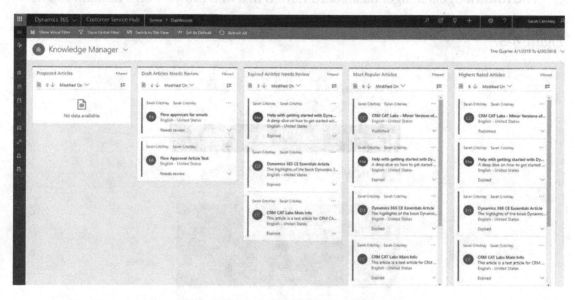

***Figure 8-3.** Knowledge Manager standard dashboard*

Figure 8-3 displays the Knowledge Manager dashboard within the Customer Service app. This is a dashboard that allows the user to see multiple streams of information and also to click the Tile view to see an aggregate list of those same records.

When the form is made smaller, the white space is reduced, and the controls on the page are reduced in size to give a consistent experience. Once the form is reduced to a mobile screen size, the application "snaps" into place and the form shrinks and adapts to the space, providing the default view of the aggregate Tile view. The same experience is consistent against the mobile app and the web client accessed on mobile. These examples can be seen in Figures 8-5 and 8-6.

Figure 8-4. *Tile view of the Knowledge Manager dashboard showing aggregates of the streams by clicking the Tile button*

The Knowledge Manager dashboard viewed in a web browser on a desktop can be reduced to a smaller screen size by adjusting the size of the browser window, shown in Figure 8-5.

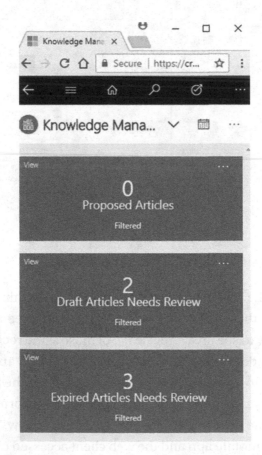

Figure 8-5. *Desktop application view on a smaller browser window*

On the mobile application, the same aggregated experience is the default experience due to the limited screen size, seen in Figure 8-6.

Figure 8-6. *Mobile app default dashboard*

Another relevant example is the Customer Service Performance dashboard, shown in Figure 8-7.

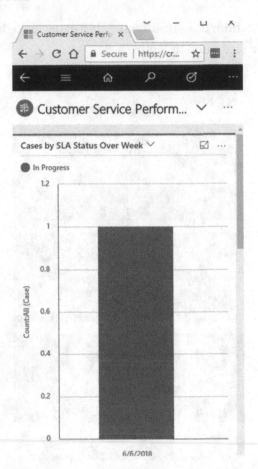

Figure 8-7. *Customer Service Performance dashboard in a small browser window*

This is also the same experience found within the app, as shown in Figure 8-8.

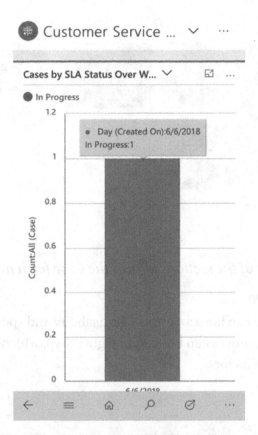

Figure 8-8. *The same dashboard in the mobile App*

Forms behave slightly differently. The sections of the form take up the available horizontal space, and should there not be enough space, they are stacked. This should be taken into consideration when designing forms so that, as a user, if they move from left to right, it would also make sense to move from top to bottom when those respective fields are accessed via mobile. This is visible in Figures 8-9 and 8-10, which display the standard Case form. This shows the sections "General Information," "Description," "Timeline," and "Related." The "General Information" section is loaded, followed by the "Description" section, *before* the "Timeline" and then "Related" sections, which are to the right.

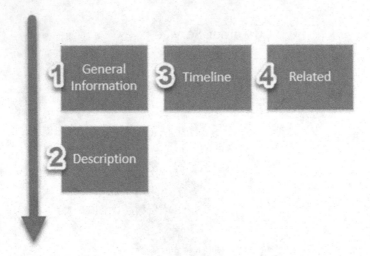

Figure 8-9. *The order of the sections within the Case form and how they load on mobile*

The order difference can have an impact on usability and speed of completing and retrieving data. The differences can be seen in Figure 8-10, which displays the same Case form with different form factors.

Figure 8-10. *The Case form in the web client on a desktop*

The header fields are visible first, followed by the "General Information" section within the Case, shown in Figure 8-11.

Figure 8-11. *The Case form displayed on a mobile client via the web application*

This is the same as within the app, where the header fields are visible, then followed by "General Information."

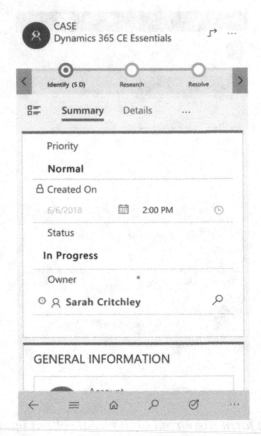

Figure 8-12. *The Case form displayed within the app on mobile*

Figures 8-11 and 8-12 show few differences in the available functionality once the screen size is reduced. This is a result of the smaller space on the form; certain controls are made to be smaller and more easily accessible when using a finger as a pointing device, which doesn't have the precision of a mouse. Aside from that, the forms are almost identical, and it is clear to see that the user experience is the same across the different forms. Even the relationships are viewed in the same way as on the web client by using the Related tab accessed from the action button and dynamically loading a sub-grid with the related records.

Some of the differences include the following:

- The user interface for the Business Process Flow is smaller and doesn't stay open.

- The additional "Semantic Zoom" control is available next to the first tab and not available on the web client.

- The number of tabs before the action button is used ("...") is reduced based on the available space.

There is also no longer any limit for displaying some fields on forms.

Dashboards for the Unified Interface vs. Classic Dashboards

Classic dashboards are still available within the Unified Interface. Classic dashboards allow embedded web resources, IFrames, Power BI tiles, views, and charts. With the Interactive Service Hub release in version 8, a new type of dashboard came, referred to as the "interactive experience," which could only be used within the first version of the Interactive Service Hub, a.k.a. the MoCA Client, later referred to as the Unified Interface Client.

In the latest version, the Unified Interface, including mobile, can run both standard dashboards and the more detailed and functional interactive dashboards. Customizers can select these different types when building solutions via the Solution screen or the App Designer, as shown in Figure 8-13, where standard, older-style dashboards are referred to as classic dashboards. The Classic UI, however, cannot run the interactive dashboards, which are exclusive to the Unified Interface.

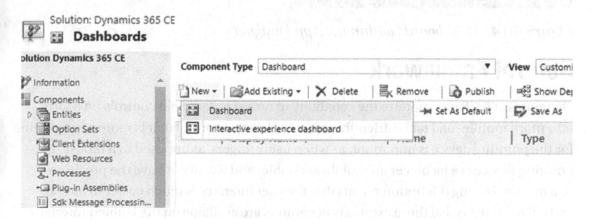

Figure 8-13. *Selecting the different dashboard types in a solution*

Interactive dashboards offer more functionality, such as being able to perform actions on records within a stream of data and see information by using the charts to filter that data. There are a lot more filter functions available to splice data according to requirements as well as the capacity to see aggregates of the data, which was previously not possible in classic dashboards.

From a mobile perspective, as the Unified Interface can display both classic and interactive dashboard types, this means that classic dashboards can still be used with the mobile client and are still responsive in the same way as the interactive dashboards are, albeit with less functionality (Figure 8-14).

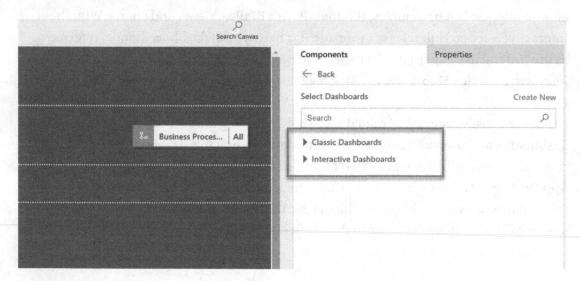

Figure 8-14. *Dashboards within the App Designer*

Control Framework

Dynamics 365 CE incorporates the capability to turn standard field controls on a form into more mobile- and tablet-friendly controls. Having a control that is more appropriate for the pointing device is important, as when using fingers, as opposed to a mouse, the pointing device is a lot bigger on mobile and tablet and we do not have the precision of a mouse. Having this option means that the user interface is much easier to interact with. The bonus is that these extra sets of controls are available on the Unified Interface for Dynamics 365 CE, which means they can be incorporated into the web experience as well and are not just for use on mobile. More details on the control framework are found in the "Further Reading" section at the end of this chapter.

The controls are available based on the specific type of field. This is similar to the controls that have been available in previous versions, such as the pen control on multiple-lines-of-text fields.

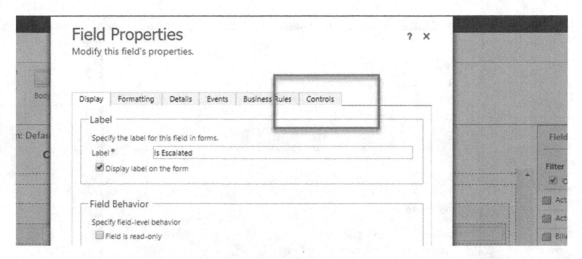

Figure 8-15. *The "Controls" tab on the Field Properties on a form*

Controls are added and configured in the specific field properties under the Controls tab (Figure 8-15). Customizers can navigate to this and select "Add Control," as shown in Figure 8-16.

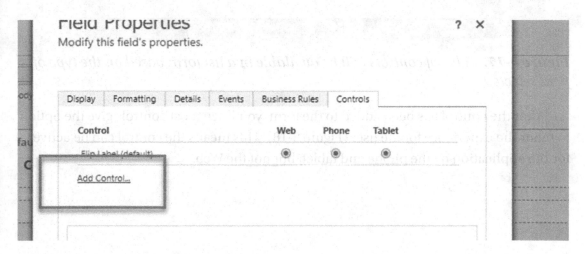

Figure 8-16. *Select "Add Control"*

The available controls will be visible to add (Figure 8-17). Some controls require additional configuration values to be entered; for example, the arc knob requires min and max values.

Figure 8-17. *A list of controls will be available in a list form based on the type of field selected*

After the control has been added to the form, you'll see most controls give the option to tailor the experience for the user (Figure 8-18). This means the control can be active for the application on the phone and tablet, but not the Web.

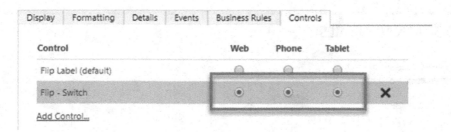

Figure 8-18. *The interfaces can be selected as to which the control appears on, giving a tailored approach to customizers*

The amended field would be changed from what it originally was. An example would be a "two-option" field type. This is displayed as a yes/no–type field, which could be kept as text, a checkbox, or a dropdown list where required. This is shown in Figure 8-19 with the "Is Escalated" standard field on the Case entity.

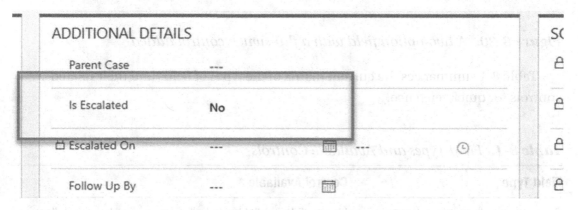

Figure 8-19. *Standard two-option field type with no control*

With the additional control, this field has been changed into something more visual and color-coded so the user can easily see the value of it without even having to read the text, as seen in Figure 8-20, where the "Flip – Switch" control has been added and has replaced the old control.

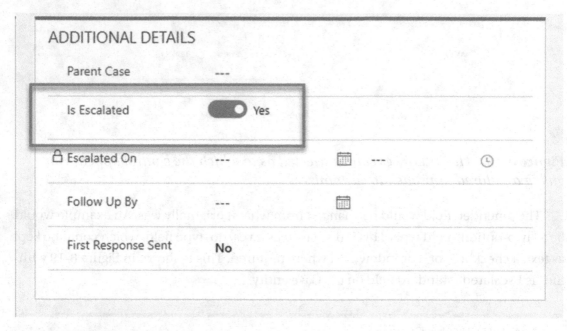

Figure 8-20. *A two-option field with a flip-switch control added*

Table 8-1 summarizes the current matrix of the types of fields and their related controls for quick reference.

Table 8-1. *Field Types and Available Controls*

Field Type	Control Available
Currency, whole number, decimal or floating point	Linear slider, radial knob, bullet graph, number input, linear gauge, arc knob
Option sets	Option-set control (two or three choices)
Two-option	Flip switch
Whole number	Star rating
Single line of text	Website preview (URL field only), auto complete, multimedia (URL only), input mask, barcode scanner
Multiple lines of text	Pen control

Testing the Mobile Application

Testing the mobile application has become much easier. However, it still shouldn't be underestimated when building custom applications. Designing for use on all form factors will allow for a more consistent user experience when a user switches from a laptop to a desktop or mobile. This is a natural experience when using software; and, based on the specifications of the app, it should be able to perform all functionality regardless of device.

When testing, ensure test cases include the following:

- Test across the mobile web interface (accessed via the browser) AND the mobile application.

- Test for user experience across multiple users and whether the information is displayed in the expected order.

- Test controls and if they match the availability as specified within the acceptance criteria.

- Test the full end-to-end process on a mobile form factor.

- If using offline, ensure this is tested and performs as expected and with a reasonable time frame specified by the acceptance criteria.

Summary

The Dynamics 365 CE application has come a long way from previous versions to become a mobile-first platform that allows users to work from anywhere and from any device. This chapter has focused on the consistency of the Unified Interface across desktop and mobile applications where specific features can be used within the mobile form factor. It covered task flows, which, especially for mobile, allow users to complete a set of tasks – that means a user does not have to navigate to multiple places across the application. It also reviewed the control framework within Dynamics 365 CE, which further adds to the commitment across the Unified Interface to promote using the application on mobile devices, allowing a greater level of control and visibility of the data for the user away from a desktop application.

Chapter Tasks

1. Download the Dynamics 365 application on mobile.

2. Perform basic tasks on the smartphone within the Customer Service Hub app, such as accessing records, creating new records, and updating fields.

3. Perform the same tasks on the Dynamics 365 web application on the Customer Service Hub app.

4. Reduce the size of the browser window so it is like a smartphone screen size and experiment with this across multiple screen types, for example, forms and dashboards.

5. Add a new control by changing a "Two-Value" field type on the "Escalated" field within the Case entity to a visual "Flip – Switch" control.

Further Reading

Mobile requirements for phones and tablets (Microsoft, 2018). URL: `https://docs.microsoft.com/en-us/dynamics365/customer-engagement/mobile-app/v8/set-up-manage/support`

Controls within the Unified Interface (Microsoft, 2018). URL: `https://docs.microsoft.com/en-us/dynamics365/customer-engagement/customize/additional-controls-for-dynamics-365-for-phones-and-tablets`

CHAPTER 9

Model-Driven Apps

Dynamics 365 CE modules went through a few stages of evolution. The first was when the core "Sales," "Service," and "Marketing" were separated out into their own Apps, and at around the same time, "Field Service" was also created as a new App. These were often referred to as "App modules" within Dynamics 365 CE. A single application could be visible to users without being distracted by possible nonrelevant ones. Customizations would be performed in the sitemap; areas would be hidden; and we would include workflows, new entities, and dashboards and create entirely new apps using the "XRM" capabilities of Dynamics 365. Since then it has evolved further, and now we have the concept of App "types." Currently in the maker experience, administrators have the ability to create three types of Apps:

- **Canvas Apps** – An App where the UI is created entirely by the user and is built using the Canvas Designer

- **Model-Driven Apps** – An app built on the Dynamics 365 Unified Interface (UI) and built using the Common Data Service and the App Designer

- **Portal Apps** – An app built on Microsoft Portals – an external-facing website – and built using the Portal Designer and the Portal Administration App

This book covers two out of three of these applications that can be built within the Power Platform. This chapter covers Model-Driven Apps. Those familiar with Dynamics 365 will be familiar with the interface of Model-Driven Apps because they use the same Unified Interface (UI). This interface cannot be modified in the same way as Canvas Apps, and there are some limitations should one wish to.

© Sarah Critchley 2020
S. Critchley, *Dynamics 365 Essentials*, https://doi.org/10.1007/978-1-4842-5911-5_9

Starting with Model-Driven Apps

A Model-Driven App is a grouping of components such as entities, dashboards, views, and charts; so each Model-Driven App can be specific to an area or function of the business. Model-Driven Apps can then be made visible with a specific set of security roles. Model-Driven Apps can contain the following (see Figure 9-1):

- Sitemap
- Dashboards
- Business Process Flows
- Entities
    - Forms
    - Views
    - Charts
    - Dashboards

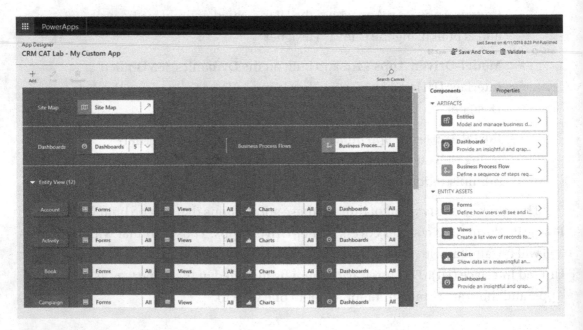

Figure 9-1. *The App Designer in Dynamics 365 CE*

Solutions

Model-Driven Apps are solution aware and utilize the Common Data Service. To migrate apps between environments, they need to be included in a solution. This means that the app can be exported and imported between environments, for example, development, QA, and production, using a "solution" package. Makers of apps have the option to create an app based on the default solution or on an existing solution. It is recommended to use an existing solution and the associated prefix before creating an app. A solution is linked to a publisher, which has a specific prefix, such as "D365CEEssentials_" or the name of the company or release. Prefixing allows other customizers to know which publisher has created the solution and is used to create unique names for fields and other assets. The app can be created from within the solution or from the "Apps" area within the sitemap and linked to the solution by selecting the option "Use the existing solution to create this App" at the time of creation (Figure 9-2). The app is then created under this prefix, which allows a user to create additional items under that specific app. Prefixes are discussed in more depth in the next section.

Figure 9-2. *Creating a new app from within a solution that has a publisher*

The App Designer can select which specific items to include in the app. It also gives users the capability to create additional items such as forms that can be created within the App Designer itself. When creating these items, if not created within a specific solution, it is easy to accidentally create them within the default solution. This means

317

the prefix of any additional item will be created with "new_" and will not be linked to the correct publisher. To avoid this, the app needs to be created within a solution and the option selected at the time of creation to ensure the prefix of a solution is linked to the app (Figure 9-3). It is easier to create components even sooner – within the Common Data Service inside a solution, which will be discussed later in this chapter.

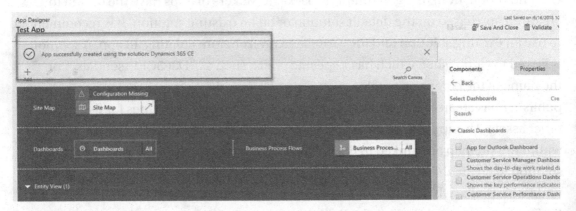

Figure 9-3. *Notification within the App Designer when successfully linked to the solution*

Solution Layering

In the previous section, solutions were highlighted as a great starting point for building an app and using it within the App Designer. Solutions are a great way of compartmentalizing functionality or releases, grouping components together to release to other environments as part of the software development lifecycle. There is a significant importance to not editing the default solution, which is the "base" solution within Dynamics 365 CE, and including customizations within it. This can be seen in Figure 9-4 where the "system solution" begins as the base for the user's experience.

The default solution is a combination of all the unmanaged and managed type solutions available within the system. As highlighted earlier, a new solution made by an organization is linked to a publisher, which has a specific prefix, such as "D365Essentials_" or sometimes something meaningful, such as the name of the company or release. Prefixing allows other customizers to know which publisher has created the solution and is used to create unique names for fields and other assets. Any changes made outside of this solution management method and within the default solution are hard to track and can also make releasing to other environments difficult (this is because the default solution would need to be exported and imported successfully in one go, which is normally unlikely to be successful).

There are also different types of solutions: managed solutions and unmanaged solutions (Figure 9-5). Many independent solution vendors (ISVs) use managed solutions as they provide extra capability to prevent target environments of the solution from modifying the components added by the solution. Solutions become managed by exporting the solution as a managed solution and installing that solution into an environment. It can then be patched and updated, or it can be deleted, taking all of its components with it. Unmanaged solution behavior is different from this. It is a reference to components within the default solution. When deleting an unmanaged solution, it does not delete the referenced components, and they remain within the default solution. To summarize, every Dynamics 365 CE system has a default solution; there are managed solutions (which are uneditable) and unmanaged solutions, both of which have publishers and specific prefixes which are linked to new entities and fields within Dynamics 365. It is not good practice to make edits within the default solution directly for the reasons stated earlier. The different types of solutions and the order in which they are installed influence how the platform is displayed to users. The next section looks at this layering in more depth.

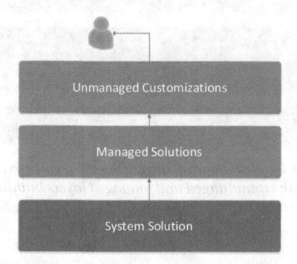

Figure 9-4. *The ordering of the application behavior, which is built upon unmanaged and managed components*

Solutions also have an influence on the application behavior that the user experiences. This can be seen in Figures 9-5 and 9-6. Managed solutions are loaded after the system solution, but before unmanaged solutions, which means a component can be edited in a managed solution and then an unmanaged customization and application behavior would show the last edit from the unmanaged customization.

The installation order of managed solutions also affects the application behavior. The latest managed solution installed is the solution that is loaded last out of the managed solutions before unmanaged customizations are loaded. More information on this layering can be found in the "Further Resources" section at the end of the chapter.

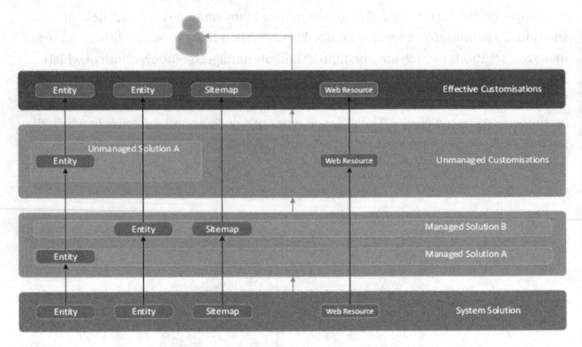

Figure 9-5. *A more detailed diagram displaying the segmented solutions and components within the unmanaged and managed layers building up to provide the application behavior*

Creating a Solution and Publisher

This next section will provide the steps to create a new solution:

1. To create a new solution, navigate to "Solutions" in the Common Data Service.

2. Click "New."

3. Enter a "display name" of your choice.

4. Select the Publisher lookup and select "Lookup More Records."

5. Select "New" on the new dialog window.

6. Enter a display name.

7. Enter a prefix. This prefix will be added to all new field names and entities within Dynamics 355 CE.

8. Click Save and Close.

9. Select "Add" to add the new publisher to the solution.

10. Add a Version Number as required.

11. Select "Save" to save the solution. Once saved, you can begin adding existing and new components within the Common Data Service.

Creating a New App

This section covers how to create a new app.

Task: Create an app.

1. Navigate to the Common Data Service, open your solution, and click "New." Select "Model-Driven App" (Figure 9-6).

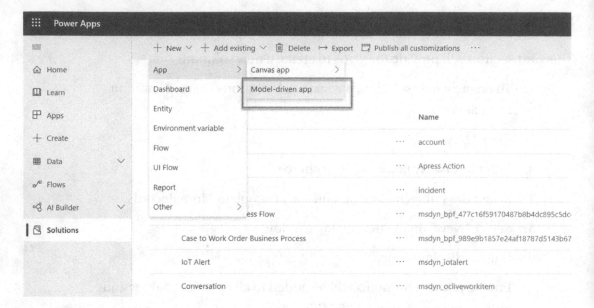

Figure 9-6. *Creating a new Model-Driven App*

2. This opens the App Designer as shown in Figure 9-7.

3. Follow the following points and enter related information for the app being created.

    When creating an application, the following information is needed:

    - **Name** – Manually enter the name of your app.

    - **Unique Name** – Automatically populates using the new_ prefix or the prefix of the publisher used in the solution selected in the "existing solution" step that follows.

    - **Description** – A short description of the application.

    - **Icon** – Use the default icon or an existing web resource image.

    - **Client** – Classic Interface (Web) or Unified Interface (available on mobile too).

    - **App URL Suffix** – Prepopulated based on the name; used for the app URL.

- **Use existing solution** – Use this for changing the prefix and telling new items made within the App Designer to use that prefix. Select it for this walk-through.

- **Choose a welcome page** – Option to add in an HTML web page as the welcome page when a new user opens the app.

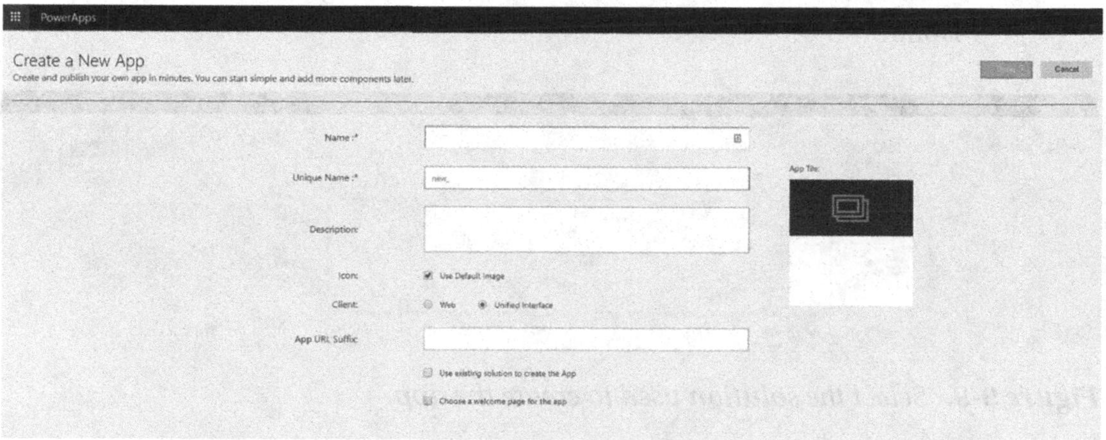

Figure 9-7. *Configuration details being entered for a new app*

Click the Next button once the initial app details have been completed, as shown in Figure 9-8.

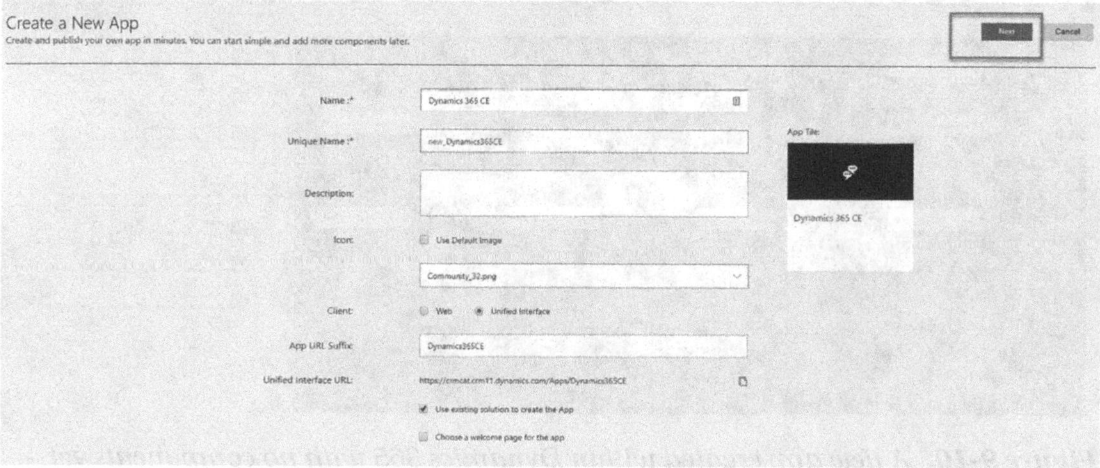

Figure 9-8. *Configuration details completed for the initial app information*

4. As the "Use existing solution" option was selected, the next page will be a solution selection prompt. If you have a sitemap component in the selected solution, you can choose to select this for the initial sitemap of the app and don't need to set it up within the App Designer, as it would be already made.

5. Once the solution has been selected, as shown in Figure 9-9, click "Done".

Figure 9-9. *Select the solution used to create the app*

This will create the app and load the App Designer, as shown in Figure 9-10, giving a success message that the solution has been used.

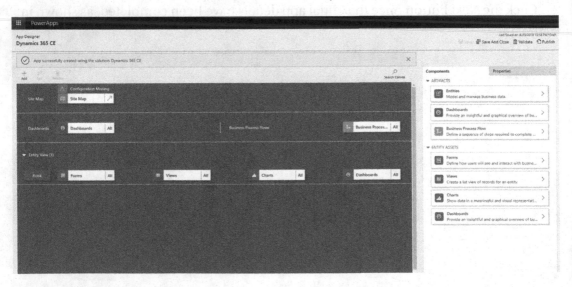

Figure 9-10. *A new app created within Dynamics 365 with no components yet configured*

Sitemap Designer

In a newly created app, the sitemap will display a "Configuration Missing" warning, as shown in Figure 9-11. This warning means that the app cannot be published since a sitemap does not yet exist, and one is required in order for a user to use the application; it must now be configured. Adding the sitemap should be the first task you complete in a newly built app because it saves time. By configuring the sitemap to include the components, such as entities, it automatically adds them to the application:

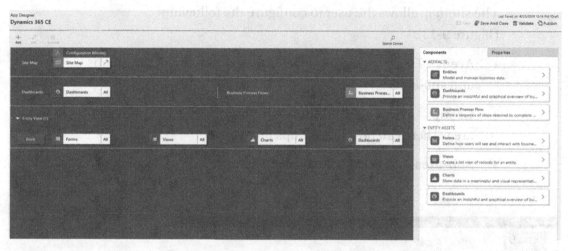

Figure 9-11. *"Configuration Missing" warning in the App Designer for the sitemap*

1. Click the diagonal arrow on the sitemap component within the App Designer, shown in Figure 9-12, to open the Sitemap Designer. This will allow users to configure the initial records to include in the navigational area of the app.

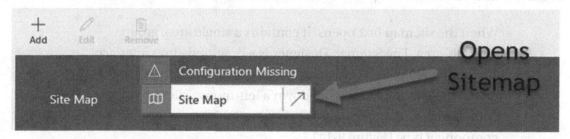

Figure 9-12. *Open the sitemap*

Clicking the diagonal arrow will open the Sitemap Designer so you can start adding components that users will be able to use to navigate the solution. The Sitemap Designer is displayed in the format of the Classic Interface, but for those apps that are configured using the Unified Client, it will be displayed differently, using a horizontal format. See Figures 9-22 to 9-28 later in this chapter for a comparison of the Classic Interface sitemap vs. the Unified Interface sitemap.

The sitemap allows the user to configure the following (Figure 9-13):

- **Areas** – These are the top-level "folders" that reveal the groups and sub-areas.

- **Groups** – These are collections of sub-areas that live under an area. There can be many groups in an area.

- **Sub-area** – A clickable item such an entity type or dashboard.

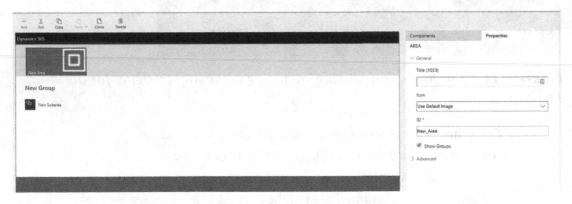

Figure 9-13. *Sitemap Designer with a single area, group, and sub-area*

When the sitemap first opens, it contains a single area, group, and sub-area. The Sitemap Designer is a drag-and-drop interface similar to the Process Designer. You can select the Components tab on the left-hand side, hold down a left-mouse click on a component, and drag it onto the next available space for that component type (Figure 9-14).

Figure 9-14. *Selecting a component in the Components tab on the left-hand side panel within the Sitemap Designer*

The minimum amount of information required when configuring an area or a group is the title on the right-hand side under "Properties" (Figure 9-15). When you configure a sub-area, you need to specify if that sub-area is a dashboard, entity, web resource, or URL. Here is a brief description of these types:

- **Entities** – All available entities are available for selection.

- **Dashboard** – Select a dashboard as well as which dashboard the item would take the user to by default when they select it.

- **Web resource** (e.g., an HTML page) – You must select the web resource. Parameters can be passed to it, for example, scripts.

- **URL** – A URL to another site or internal site to Dynamics 365 CE (e.g., another app, should the user have permissions). Parameters can also be passed here.

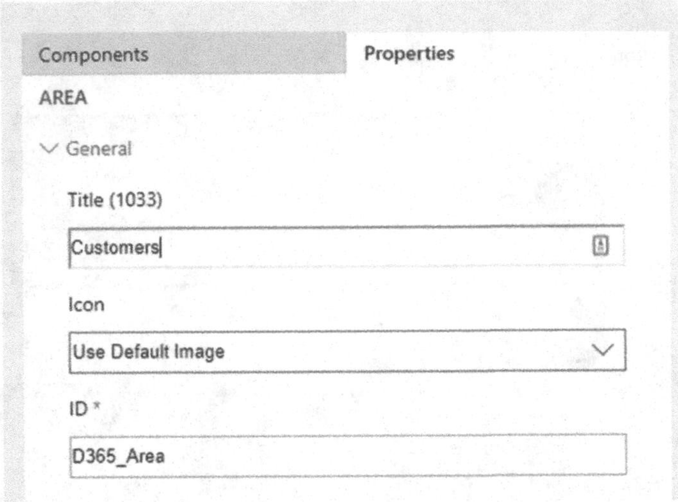

Components   Properties

AREA

∨ General

Title (1033)

Customers

Icon

Use Default Image

ID *

D365_Area

Figure 9-15. *Configuring a component's properties within the "Properties" pane on the right-hand side of the designer*

You can also use the toolbar at the top of the Sitemap Designer to edit and add components to the sitemap rather than using the drag-and-drop tool. In particular, the Clone and Copy/Paste tools are useful when editing larger sitemaps.

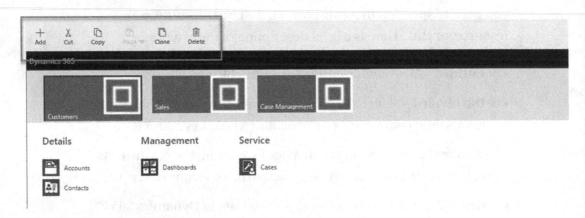

Figure 9-16. *Toolbar within the Sitemap Designer*

The Clone and Copy/Paste functions offer very similar functionality; however, Clone will copy and paste a group or sub-area in one click to the right or bottom of the selected item. Copy/Paste allows a user more control over where the pasted item will go, as seen in Figure 9-17.

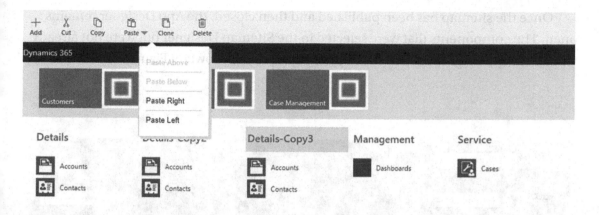

Figure 9-17. *Using Copy and Paste functions within the toolbar of the Sitemap Designer*

2. Configure three areas.

3. Configure a group per area.

4. Add two entities per group.

5. Once completed, click "Save" and then click "Publish" (Figure 9-18).

    Note: Even if the designer displays "Published," this still needs to be done when edits have been made.

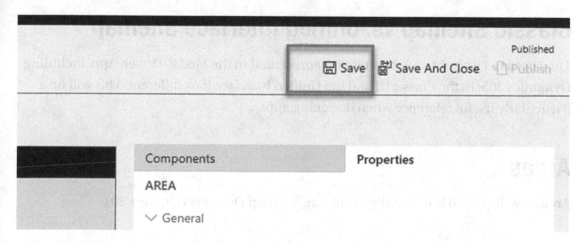

Figure 9-18. *Save and publish the sitemap using the Save button in the top-right corner of the screen*

Once the sitemap has been published and then closed, the App Designer remains open. The components that were selected in the Sitemap Designer but were not already within the app are now included within the Entity view, shown in Figure 9-19.

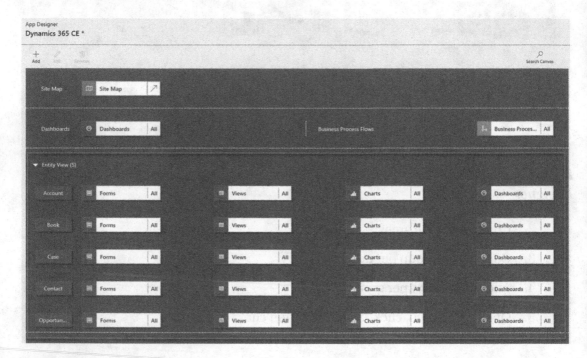

Figure 9-19. *Additional components added within the App Designer from the configuration of the sitemap*

Classic Sitemap vs. Unified Interface Sitemap

The Sitemap Designer and the sitemap represented in the Model-Driven App, including Dynamics 365, in the Classic UI and the Unified Interface look different. This will be a particularly useful reference when designing apps.

Areas

Areas are displayed horizontally within the Sitemap Designer (Figure 9-20).

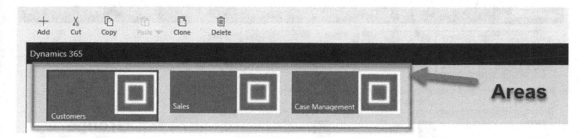

Figure 9-20. *Areas within the Sitemap Designer*

They are displayed vertically under the "..." button within the vertical sitemap in the Unified Interface (Figure 9-21).

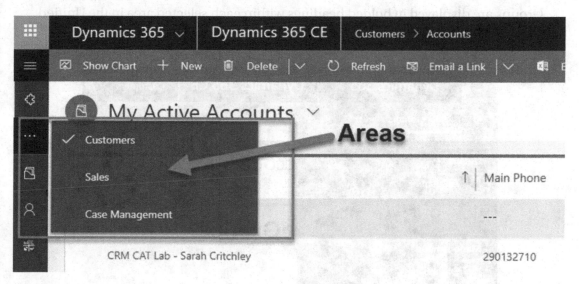

Figure 9-21. *Areas displayed in the Unified Interface*

Groups

Groups are displayed in columns within the specific area within the Sitemap Designer (Figure 9-22).

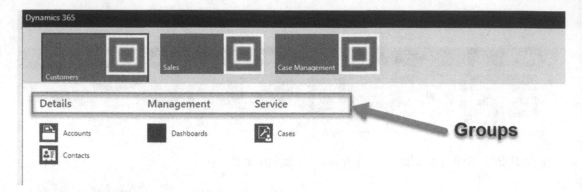

Figure 9-22. *Groups displayed in the Sitemap Designer*

Groups are displayed in bolded headings within each selected area in the Unified Interface, as seen in Figure 9-23.

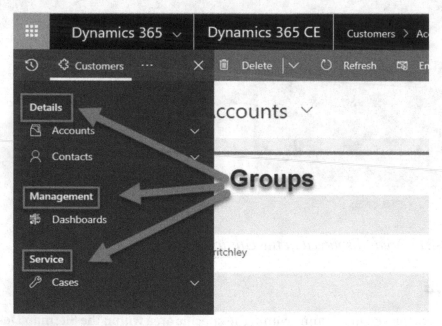

Figure 9-23. *Groups displayed in the Unified Interface*

Sub-areas

Sub-areas are specific items within each group that lead, normally, to an entity and are displayed within the Group column in the Sitemap Designer (Figure 9-24).

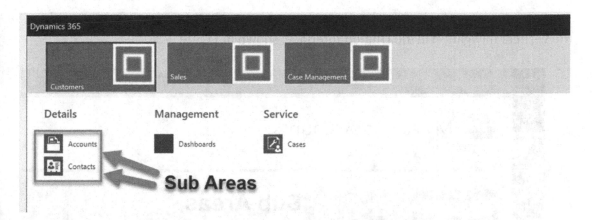

Figure 9-24. *Sub-areas defined in the Sitemap Designer*

Sub-areas are displayed under the group within the Unified Interface sitemap, as shown in Figure 9-25.

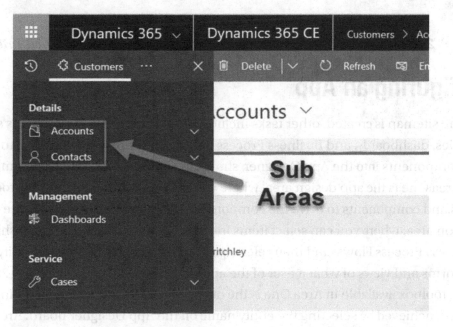

Figure 9-25. *Sub-areas displayed in the sitemap in the Unified Interface*

Sub-areas can also be found as their icon, as defined in the entity definition, within the vertical navigation in the Unified Interface, shown in Figure 9-26.

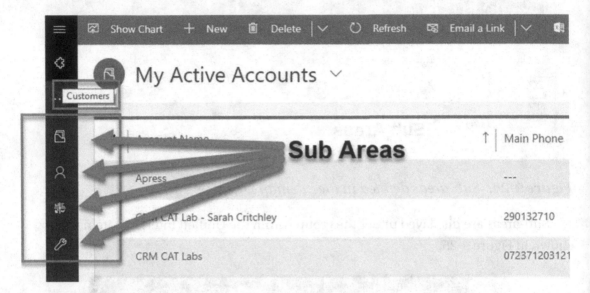

Figure 9-26. *Sub-areas are also displayed vertically within the Unified Interface*

Configuring an App

Once the sitemap is created, other tasks include adding additional components such as entities, dashboards, and Business Process Flows. There are two main ways to add these components into the App Designer, shown in Figure 9-27 as "Area One" and "Area Two." Area One is the app design area, where you can use controls such as the toolbar options and components to drive the component configuration. Area Two is the app definition area, where you can select items from Area One, such as entitles, dashboards, or Business Process Flows, and then select specific components to add or modify, such as the forms and views of what a user of the app would be able to use (Figure 9-28).

The toolbox available in Area One is the only area in which the entity definition can be edited, achieved by selecting the entity name on the App Designer board. Area Two is the only area where a new item can be created directly from the component area.

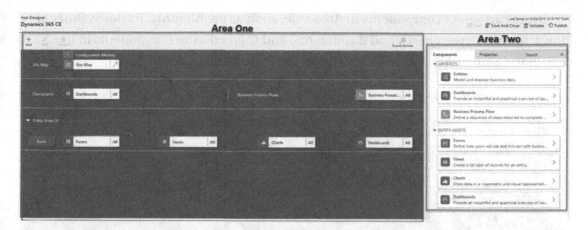

Figure 9-27.   App Designer breakdown

The "Edit" and "Remove" options within the toolbox in Area One are available only when selecting an entity name itself so you can edit the definition of the entity. (Note: Any changes made are reflected in all apps where this is available, not just the app being edited.)

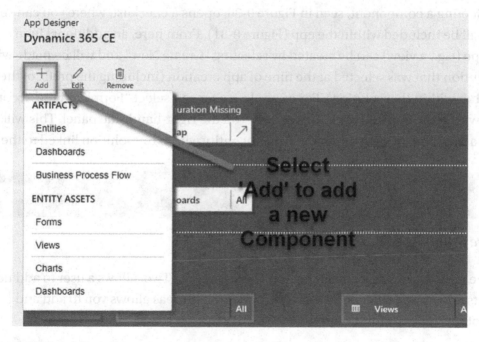

Figure 9-28.   Adding items to an app

Users can select components in Area One, such as dashboards, Business Process Flows, forms, views, charts, and dashboards, and then edit the components in the right-hand side of Area Two. This is shown in Figure 9-29.

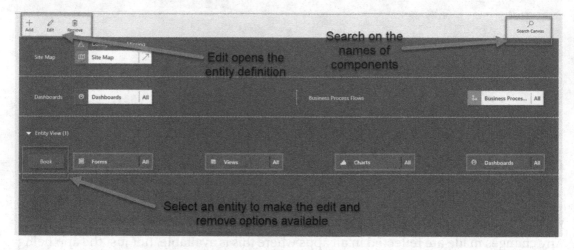

Figure 9-29. *Modifying components within an app*

Selecting a component, seen in Figure 9-30, opens a checklist, where you can select what will be included within the app (Figure 9-31). From here, an additional item of that type (e.g., a view) can be created by selecting "Create New" and will be made within the solution that was selected at the time of app creation (including the prefix of the publisher within that solution). For example, a user can select "Forms" on the Account entity within the app and click "Create New" on the right-hand side panel. This will create a new type of form under the Account entity within the solution linked to the app.

Figure 9-30. *Selecting a component*

The right-hand side pane in the App Designer, Area Two, allows a user to add new artifacts and assets. Selecting the arrows under these areas allows you to add and edit items of this type within the app.

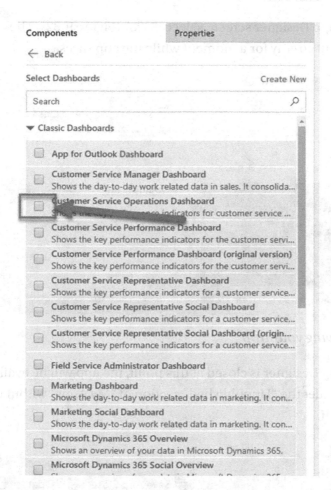

Figure 9-31. *Selecting items to be included within the app*

Task: Add various components to your app.

Using the information in the previous section, add more components to your app using the App Designer:

1. Add a Business Process Flow to your app.

2. Add an extra entity to your app.

3. Add two forms to your entity.

   Once the edits have been completed, it is recommended to review the sitemap once more to ensure the user experience is correct and contains all the record types and required components.

337

4. On the App Designer screen, select "Save" (Figure 9-32). The screen will go gray for a moment while the app saves.

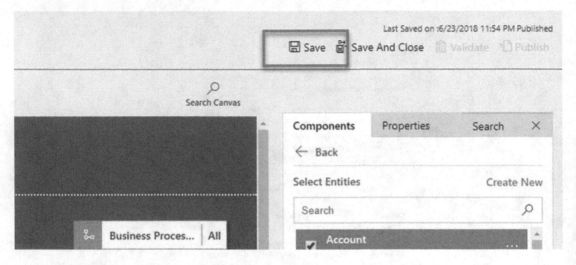

Figure 9-32. *Saving your app*

If the App Designer is closed at this point, the app will be available to edit under the "Unpublished" section of "My Apps" within the Classic UI.

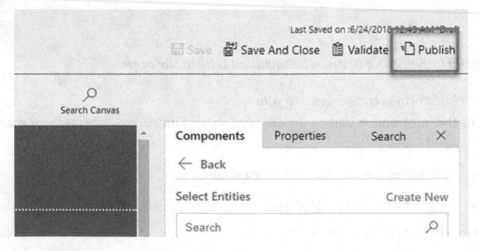

Figure 9-33. *Ensure the app is published for use by users of the system*

5. Once saved, the app can be published for use by other users. This can be done by clicking "Publish" (Figure 9-33). The app will now be available for use under the "Apps" area, **but only for system administrators.** The App has not yet been configured for a security, which is the next step.

App Security

When an app is in either an unpublished or published state, the security can be configured for the app from the App Designer screen.

Task: Configure security roles for an app.

1. Navigate to the maker experience and select "Apps."

2. Locate the app created in the previous section and select the expanded menu "…" to see the actions that can be completed on the App.

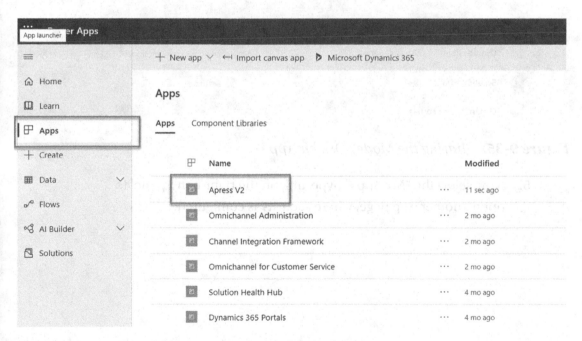

Figure 9-34. *Selecting the App in the maker experience*

3. Click "Share" in the extended menu to open a panel on the right-hand side of the screen. This opens the steps needed to be completed to share the app with other users. You must specify whom those other users would be by allocating a security role to the app and then to the user for the App to appear. To learn how to create Security Roles and assign them to users, navigate to Chapter 7 of this book.

4. Once you have created your security role, assign it to the user.

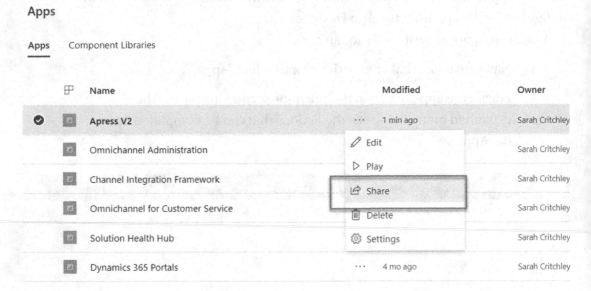

Figure 9-35. *Sharing the Model-Driven App*

5. Now select the "My Apps" hyperlink on the right-hand panel to open another App page, where security is configured.

Figure 9-36. *Right-hand-side panel that pops out when a user selects the "Share" button in the extended menu*

6.   In the My Apps page, locate your App and select the extended menu within the App selector, as shown in Figure 9-37.

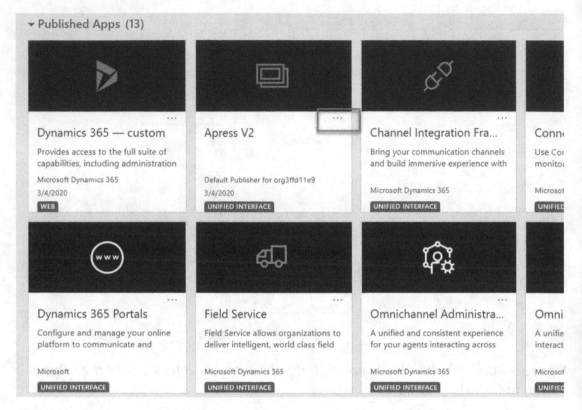

Figure 9-37. *Select the extended menu "..." on the app on the "My Apps" page*

7. Click "Manage Roles" to open another right-hand panel where you need to select the security role to give to the users whom you wish to grant access to the app.

8. Once complete, select "Done."

9. The configuration is now completed; you can go back to the previous app page, click "Share" on your app, and get the direct URL of your app from this page to send this to your users so they can access it directly.

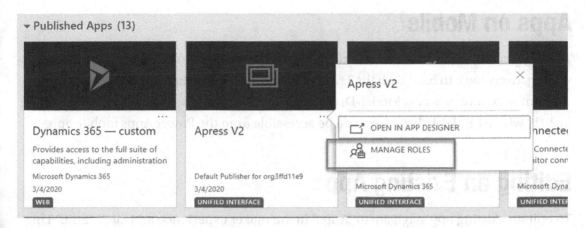

Figure 9-38. *Select Manage Roles*

For more information on security roles, please navigate to Chapter 7 of this book. This chapter covers what security roles are and how they can be configured and applied to users.

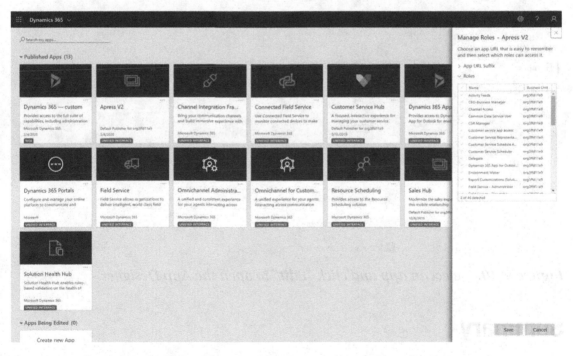

Figure 9-39. *Select the security role to apply to the App and click "Save"*

Apps on Mobile

The Application is, by default, available on the Dynamics 365 mobile App. At the time of writing, users have to have both the Dynamics 365 and the Power Apps apps from the relevant app store to access Model-Driven and Canvas Apps, respectively. This is changing in 2020 where Model-Driven Apps will be accessible from the Power Apps mobile app.

Editing an Existing App

To edit an existing app, navigate to "Apps" in the maker experience and click "Edit." This will open the App Designer covered earlier in the chapter and allow you to make your modifications, republish, and test the changes.

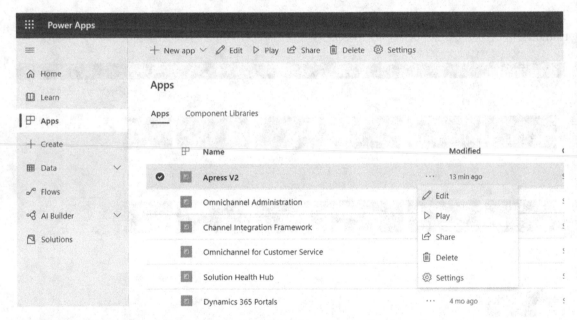

Figure 9-40. *Select an app and click "Edit" to open the App Designer*

Summary

Model-Driven Apps within the Power Platform are an exciting feature that allows for functionality to be encapsulated into purpose-built applications that can be enabled based on the organization's security model. First-party apps, such as those for sales and customer service, are presented in the same way as custom-built Model-Driven Apps, giving users a consistent experience. This chapter has covered the essentials of how to get started with Model-Driven Apps, add components, create a sitemap for your app, and publish your app to other users.

Chapter Tasks

1. Create a new unmanaged solution (and publisher).

2. Create a new Model-Driven App, linking the solution.

3. Modify and create the sitemap, using all the components.

4. Add more components into the app using the App Designer.

5. Publish the app.

6. Apply a security role to the App from the previous chapter.

7. Test the app.

Further Reading

Solutions in Dynamics 365 CE (Microsoft, 2018). URL: `https://docs.microsoft.com/en-us/dynamics365/customer-engagement/developer/package-distribute-extensions-use-solutions`

App Designer (Microsoft, 2018). URL: `https://docs.microsoft.com/en-us/dynamics365/customer-engagement/customize/design-custom-business-apps-using-app-designer`

Model Driven Apps (Microsoft, 2018). URL: `https://docs.microsoft.com/en-us/dynamics365/customer-engagement/customize/create-edit-app`

CHAPTER 10

Reporting: Views, Charts, and Dashboards

Dynamics 365 CE can be used by organizations as a system to run any part of their business concerning customer engagement. This can be done through the use of all or a combination of the apps that are available or by using extensions and customizations. Users create new data and update existing data through the continued use of the application, which creates a large store of transactional data over time. This data provides intelligence to the organization through quantitative and qualitative means. The data can indicate if a company is meeting sales targets and customer service SLAs and can be used to provide insights into trends of how services or products are being used. Data is a large source of potential insight for organizations to help improve their service, maintain their customers, and provide the direction of a company's future.

To obtain this insight, organizations must be able to report on the data available to them. This can be achieved in many ways using Dynamics 365 CE, which this chapter will cover. It is important to understand that the functionality itself is only a small part of being able to analyze and obtain insights from data. Having a clear and documented data model is essential, which can be easily created in Microsoft Excel or another tool. Understanding relationships between the data within Dynamics 365 by creating an entity relationship diagram (ERD) is also helpful. This chapter will review the capabilities and how to get started with the reporting methods available from within the application. When building an effective report, it is recommended that users look at the following actions:

1. Data model is understood – all data is captured or components are available (to perform calculations).

2. Use Unified Modeling Language (UML)-type diagrams, such as use case diagrams and sequence diagrams.

S. Critchley, *Dynamics 365 Essentials*, https://doi.org/10.1007/978-1-4842-5911-5_10

3. Relationships are understood for related information and aggregates.

4. Understand what the business goals or requirements are of the organization.

5. Functionality available within CE is understood.

6. Security requirements are reviewed.

7. Visual requirements are understood, for example, how that information is presented.

8. Create the report within Dynamics 365 CE and review.

9. Perform iterated testing (Create ➤ Test ➤ Improve).

Using the reporting methods within the Dynamics 365 CE platform, users will be able to see the information as and when they need it. It will be possible to utilize that data to make decisions and report on the company's operations both internally and externally.

Getting Started

This book often refers to *entities*. Entities are what can be described as a record *type*. In software development terminology, they can be referred to as a class or a table. They are a structure, or a blueprint, that contains descriptive data (metadata) about an object. An example of an entity in Dynamics 365 CE is an *Account* record. There are multiple instances of the Account record, which are represented as rows within a table. The fields within an entity represent columns within the table. Dynamics 365 CE is built upon a relational database structure that links entities using diverse types of relationships. There are many external resources through which to learn more about entity and relationship modeling. An older but still popular and useful technique for this is UML (Unified Modeling Language). UML is a way of modeling different diagrams that represent the data of an organization's structure in different states and is an effective way to understand the relationship structure and the functionality of a system.

Securing data is a critical part of the reporting process. Having access to operational data, especially in an aggregated or condensed form, can give insight into the business but can also break data governance policies if available to users who are not in the correct roles within the organization. Dynamics 365 CE utilizes security roles covered in Chapter 7, for various reporting functionality, but the functionality itself also has inbuilt mechanisms for security. Security roles allow users to run reports only on records available to them and not on records outside of their security role.

Dynamics 365 CE can include many customizations; however, even if an organization does not modify any processes or add any new custom fields, reviewing the standard views and dashboards is an important task that should be included in all implementations. What is set up as part of the standard platform might not be relevant or important to the organization. It is a small task to perform a review and remove or hide those fields. Doing so will ensure the standard CE system will be lean, easy to use, and quick to obtain information.

Dynamics 365 CE provides the capability for embedded Microsoft Power BI tiles within the standard dashboard. This chapter will not cover this functionality, as it introduces the complexity of another product. There are, however, many resources that do. Review the article by Microsoft that introduces this functionality, provided at the end of the chapter in the "Further Reading" section.

It is important to note that while Power BI integration can offer some benefits, there are also some drawbacks at the time of writing. Power BI capabilities are not yet available in the Unified Interface at the time of writing. In addition to that, the security models of Dynamics 365 and Power BI are separate, and by introducing an external component, there is a risk of displaying data to users who may not or should not have access. Take care when looking at integration between these two platforms.

There are currently some reporting features available only within the Classic UI and others only within the Unified Interface Client. These reporting features will be highlighted in each of the sections. There are new features in the October 2018 release of Dynamics 365, in which personal dashboards and charts and also the ability to run reports have become available.

Views

Dynamics 365 CE uses *views* to display a list of records (Figure 10-1). The list is often a filtered list of data, for example, Active Accounts, where the system obtains all of the Account records available in it that have their status set to "Active." Another example could be the Unassigned Cases view, where the "Owner" field on the Case entity is set to a team rather than a user. Views allow for the quick review and retrieval of information, enabling a user to focus on a set of data rather than on hundreds of potentially irrelevant records. A view is made up of columns at the top of the screen in the header from the entity and displays the data that is from the record within the row. Dynamics 365 CE can be customized to change these columns to what is required so only the most relevant information is displayed. Users can also search on the view (based on the Quick Find view), use an A–Z filter, and select records to contextually perform actions on those records, such as Delete, Resolve, Apply Routing Rules, and Add to Queue. Doing this saves the user from having to open the form and click a button instead.

Views are used in dashboards (both classic and interactive types) and are the basis of *streams* on interactive dashboards. They also form the basis for the initial information displayed within a chart, where the chart is driven by the grouping of data within the view that is selected by the user at the time of loading the chart.

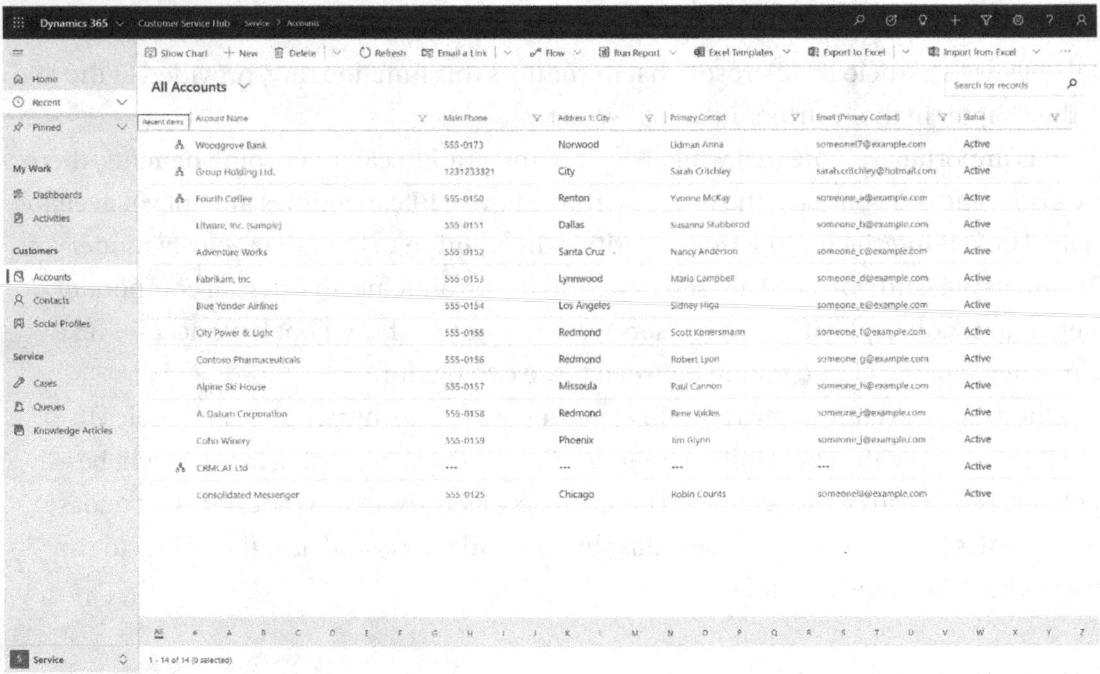

Figure 10-1. *Active Accounts view*

Users can also use filtering on the columns by selecting the filter and then modifying the criteria of the data to be returned, per column (Figure 10-2). This is very similar to the filter functionality within Microsoft Excel. Examples of filtering include if there is data within a column or not and specific option sets, and also this is where users can choose sorting features.

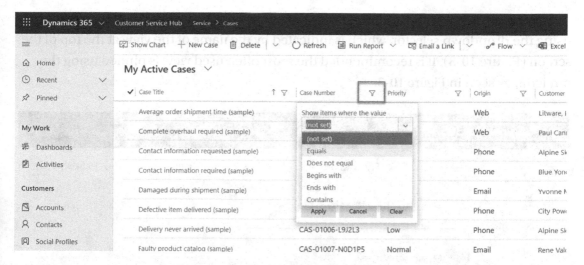

Figure 10-2.   *To use filtering within a view, click the Filter button and then select the dropdown on each of the columns to filter or add a custom filter*

Views are created and saved as Public, System, or Personal types, as follows:

- **Public views** are views created by the platform, such as Active Accounts or Inactive Cases. You can create new public views within the Common Data Service, and they would be available for all users given the correct security roles.

- **System views** are views created and used by the platform and often can be modified to make them more relevant. These include Quick Find, Advanced Find, Lookup, and associated views. Quick Find is particularly special as it influences what the search results are when searching not only on views but also on Lookup views of that specific entity on a record. The first three compatible columns are those that are displayed when the user is selecting an item from the "Lookup" field selector. You cannot create new forms of these types; you can only modify existing ones.

- **Personal views** are very similar to public views; however, they have been created by a specific user via the Unified Interface and are either kept with that user's space or shared with another user or team. They can be shared provided the user has "user"-level access for the Saved View entity. More information on the differences between the different views can be found in the "Further Reading" section at the end of the chapter.

Users have access to multiple views of data at any one time. They can be selected using the dropdown selector, which is indicated by the name of the view at the top of the screen (Figure 10-3). It is recommended the most often used view is pinned using the pin icon, as seen in Figure 10-3.

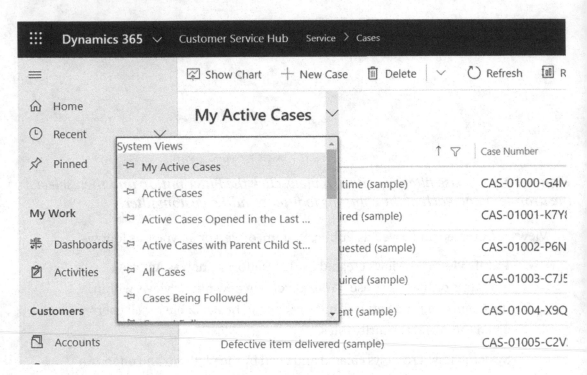

Figure 10-3. *View selector*

You can also use the Globally Most Recent Used button on the navigation area, which allows a user to pin views and records within the navigation area to avoid having to find them via the main sitemap (Figure 10-4).

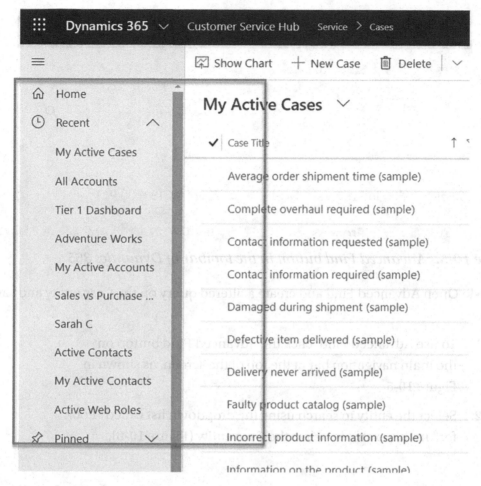

Figure 10-4. *Globally Most Recent Used list*

Creating a View

Views can be created in two ways, depending on the type of view being created. Personal views can be created from within the toolbar in the Unified Interface. System views are created and modified using the View Designer. Personal views are created using Advanced Find, which allows you to create a filtered query, configure sorting, and edit the columns that are displayed in the view using the Edit Columns button within the feature (Figure 10-5). The view is then saved as a personal view if made as a user, or if it was made via the Solution Explorer, it will be saved as a public view.

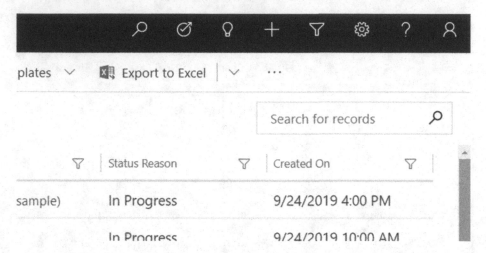

Figure 10-5. *Advanced Find button in the toolbar of Dynamics 365*

Task: Open Advanced Find and create a filtered query on the Case entity and save it as a view.

1. To use Advanced Find, click the Advanced Find button on the main navigation bar at the top of the screen, as shown in Figure 10-5.

2. Select the entity to search using the dropdown list called "Look for." In this example, select the Case entity (Figure 10-6).

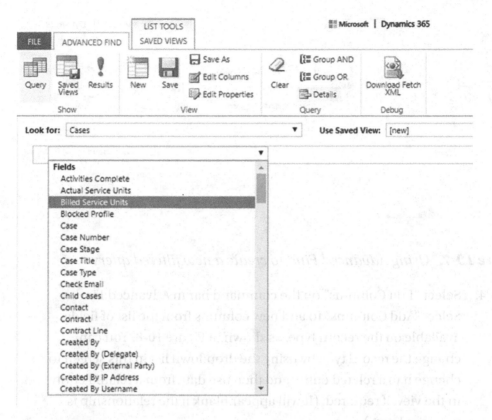

Figure 10-6. *Using Advanced Find within the Classic UI*

3. Select the "Status" field from that record type. Once the field is
    selected, you can perform a number of operators (such as "Equals"
    or "Contains Data") depending on the field type (such as "Single
    Line of Text" or "Two Options"). You would select a specific value
    or range where relevant to the operator. In this example, set the
    "Status" field as "Equals" and "Active" (Figure 10-7).

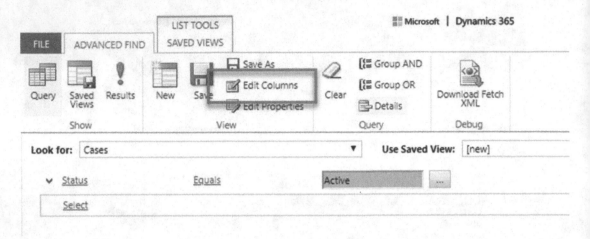

Figure 10-7. *Using Advanced Find to create a new filtered query*

4. Select "Edit Columns" on the command bar in Advanced Find.
    Select "Add Columns" to add new columns from the list of fields
    available on the record type, as shown in Figure 10-8. You can
    change the record type by using the dropdown list in this screen to
    change it to a related entity and then use data from a related entity
    in the view if required. (It will appear blank if the relationship is
    not populated.)

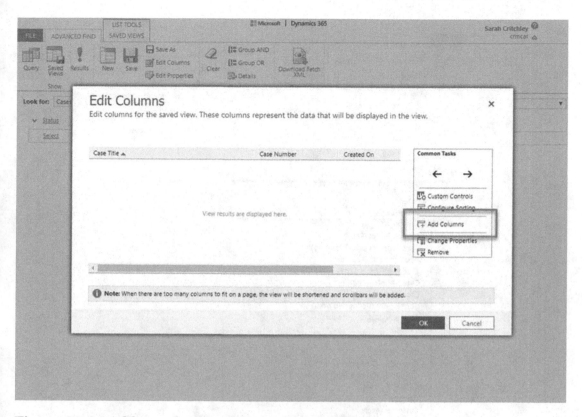

Figure 10-8. *Adding columns within Advanced Find*

5.   Click "OK" and "OK" again to save your column changes. To save the view, click "Save" on the command bar, and the system will prompt you for a name for the view. Enter a descriptive name and continue to save. This view is now available as a personal view if it was created via the main interface or as a public view if it was created using the Solution Explorer ("Views").

Advanced Find also allows you to create more complex queries using related entities defined in lookups. These relations are linked via a 1:N relationship from the entity specified in the "Look for" dropdown under the heading "Related," as shown in Figure 10-9. This is especially useful where queries are dependent on related data; for example, accounts where the primary contact lives in London would be set as "Looking for" the Account entity; however, it would be dependent on the related Contact entity as defined in the "Primary Contact" field on the Account record.

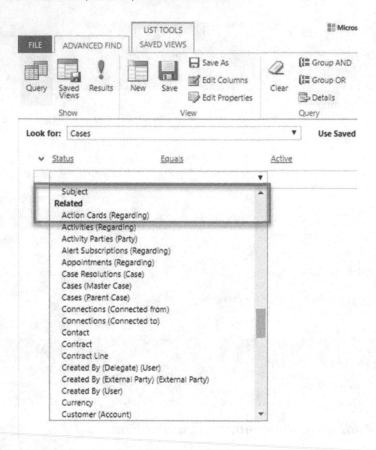

Figure 10-9. *Using the "Related" entities from Advanced Find*

Previous chapters covered activities and discussed using the "Sort Date" to filter on all activities. The "Sort Date" is a special field on the Activity entity that is designed to be populated using customizations (e.g., using workflows) so emails, tasks, and other activity types can be populated with the sort date specific to their activity type. The "Sort Date" field provides a single field to sort on within a view, so a priority list can be created at the activity level that includes all Activity-type entities. An example query that uses this field is shown in Figure 10-10; it uses the Activity entity in the "Look for" option and the "Sort Date" in the first line of the query.

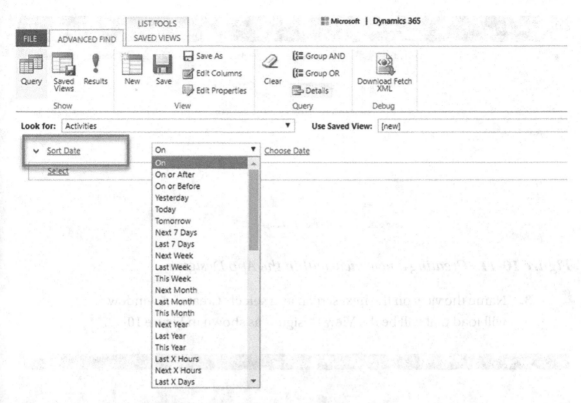

Figure 10-10. *Using the "Sort Date" field to filter activities*

There is an alternative to using Advanced Find as a customizer – instead, customizers can use the View Designer feature within the App Designer to create a public view. Personal views must be created using the Classic UI via Advanced Find as of the time of writing. However, it is expected that personal views in the Unified Client will be possible in the October 2018 release. In addition to that, modifications to the Quick Find view need to be completed within the Classic UI and do not appear in the App Designer (other system views do).

Navigate to the Common Data Service (see Chapter 1 on how to use the Common Data Service) and click the entity and then the "Views" component. From here, you can review the current views and create a new one by selecting "Create New." Views created in this way will be public.

Task: Create a new public view in the Common Data Service.

1. Open the Common Data Service, navigate to your entity in a solution, and click "Views."

2. Click "Create New" on the left-hand side of the screen under "Views" as shown in Figure 10-11.

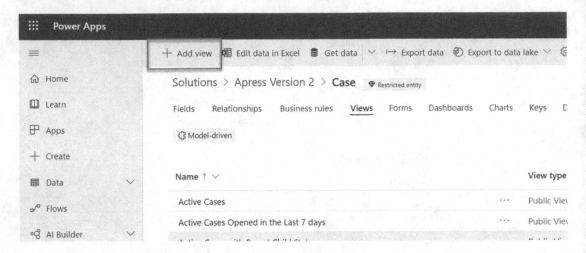

Figure 10-11. *Creating a new view within the App Designer*

3. Name the view on the next screen and select "Create." A window
   will load that will be the View Designer as shown in Figure 10-12.

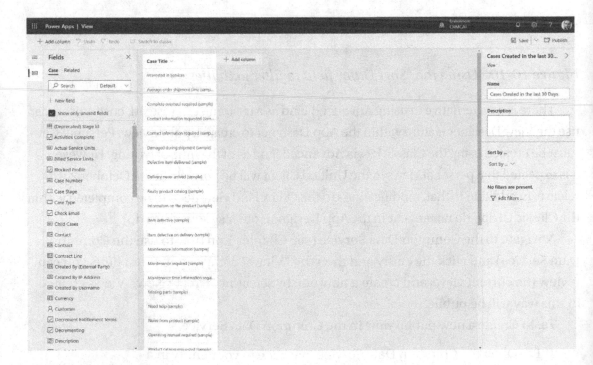

Figure 10-12. *View Designer in the Common Data Service*

4. Using the left column, you can drag fields over to the central View Designer so they "snap" into the columns. You can also rearrange the columns by clicking and dragging them.

5. On the right-hand-side panel, under "Filters," click "Edit Filters" to load an updated type of Advanced Find configuration.

6. Modify the filter by selecting "Created On" and "Less X Days" and type in 30 in the empty space to specify last "30" days as shown in Figure 10-13.

7. Save and publish the new view, and it will be available to use.

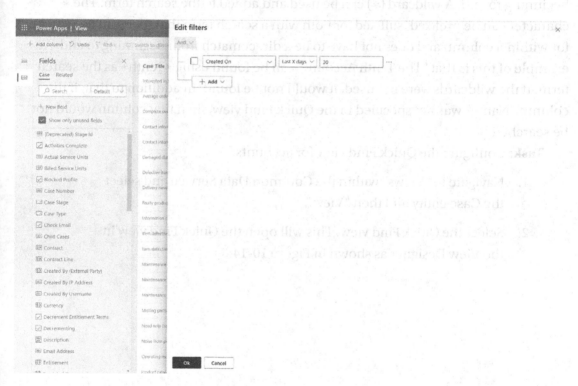

Figure 10-13. *View Designer within the App Designer*

Searching in a View

A Quick Find view is used on views to perform standard searching functionality (the alternative being a relevance search) and is enabled by default. More in-depth detail on Quick Find views can be found in the "Further Reading" section at the end of the chapter. Quick Find view configuration should always be considered in implementations to ensure the find columns (where the search will be performed on) and the view columns (data that will be returned) are correct for the organization.

When you begin typing in the search box within a view, the columns configured in the Quick Find's "Find" columns are searched for an exact match of the string from beginning to end. A wildcard (*) can be used and added to the search term. The * character can be prefixed, suffixed, or both with a search term that then can be searched for within a column and does not have to be a direct match from beginning to end. An example of this is that "The Tenth Account" can be found using *Tenth* as the search term. If the wildcards were not used, it would not be found. In addition to that, if the column "Name" was not specified in the Quick Find view, then that column would not be searched.

Task: Configure the Quick Find view for accounts.

1. Navigate to "Views" within the Common Data Service and select the Case entity and then "View."

2. Select the Quick Find view. This will open the Quick Find view in the View Designer as shown in Figure 10-14.

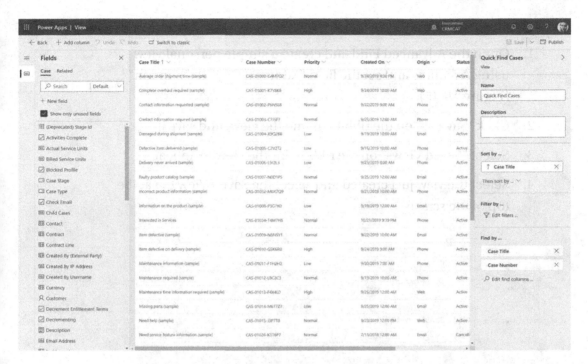

Figure 10-14. *View Designer of a Quick Find view within the Common Data Service*

3. Edit the columns returned in the same way as creating or modifying a system view in the Common Data Service specified in previous tasks.

4. Click the OK button and then click "Save and Close" and "Publish All Customizations."

5. Navigate to the entity and start using the search functionality to see the columns added to the view columns being output in the results of the search.

Managing Views

Views are managed by the system administrators and customizers who own the public and system views. Views are managed and edited via the Common Data Service. Users who create personal views are accessible via the Advanced Find menu. Users can edit their personal views (which appear alongside public views) by selecting and performing various operations on them, such as Delete, Assign, or Share.

Task: Review operations available on views.

1. Open the Advanced Find and create a simple personal view using Accounts and set the field "Address: City" to "London" (Figure 10-15).

2. Click "Save As" on the ribbon, name the view, and save it.

3. Select "Saved Views" on the ribbon for the view to appear.

4. Select the view just created and select the Saved View tab at the top of the screen.

Figure 10-15. *Saved personal views can be managed within the Advanced Find tab*

Various operations are now available, including Delete and Share. The sharing functionality is the same as sharing a record, which was covered in Chapter 4. The sharing functionality can be seen in Figure 10-16.

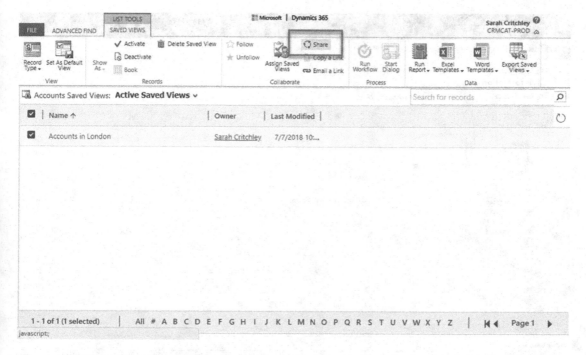

Figure 10-16. *Use the ribbon to perform various operations on selected saved views, including Delete or Share*

Editable Grids in Views

System and personal views have additional functionality to allow users to edit the records within the grid using the editable grid feature. Dynamics 365 CE as standard does not allow users to modify data in line within a view, and it is not until this feature is turned on that this is possible. Editable grids allow for quicker data entry and modification. This is added using the control framework, which is covered in more detail in Chapter 10.

Editable grids require a customizer to set up the editable grid control and modify its properties, including its available view, grouping amendments, and the lookup configurations on the available views.

Task: Add an editable grid to the Account entity.

1. Navigate to the Classic Client and select the Account entity, ensuring the name "Account" is selected and you are on the Entity Configuration screen.

2. Select the Control tab as shown in Figure 10-17.

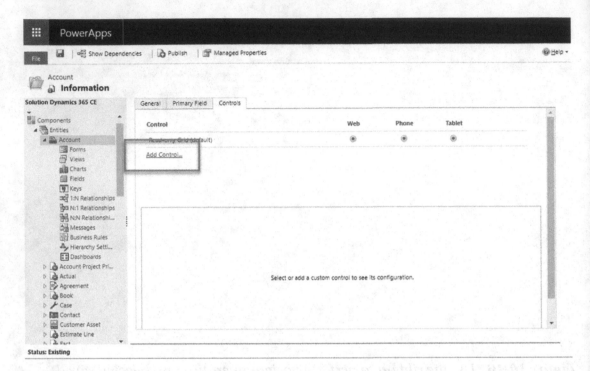

Figure 10-17. *Navigate to the Solution Explorer and click the Control tab to add a new control to the entity*

3. Select "Add Control." On the configuration page, scroll down and select "Editable Grid" making it available for the Web (Figure 10-18).

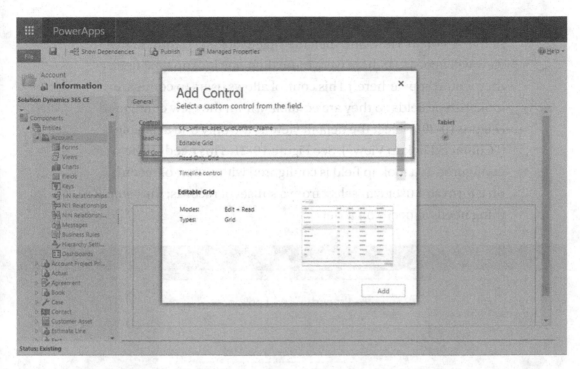

Figure 10-18. *Click "Editable Grid" on the Add Control window*

There is additional configuration required that manages lookups and grouping, highlighted in Figure 10-19.

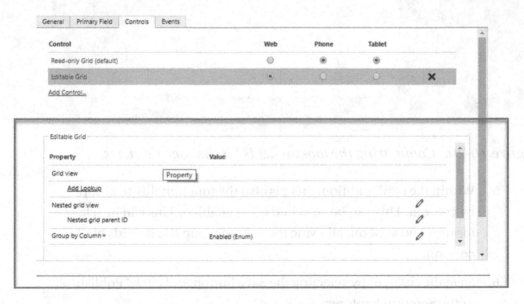

Figure 10-19. *Adding lookup fields within the editable grid so they can be used*

4. Select "Add Lookup" on the Grid View property. Select the My
   Active Accounts view, and then the single lookup column in that
   view will appear. (If there were more than one lookup type field,
   they would appear here.) This control allows users to configure
   lookup-type fields so they are editable within the view configured
   (Figure 10-20). Select the default view as the only one available
   ("Contacts Lookup View"). See Figure 10-21. This needs to be
   configured as a lookup field is configured with a view of records
   on a form so a user can select from a subset of records; the same
   thing needs to occur on a view.

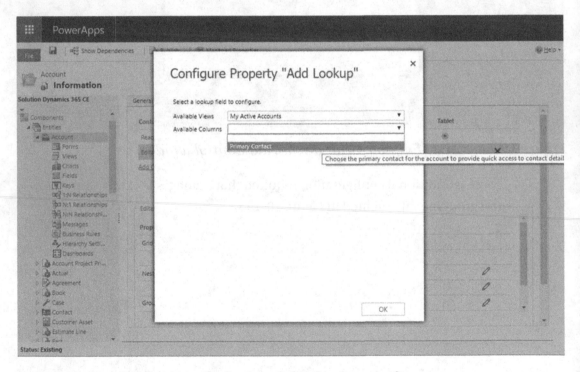

Figure 10-20. *Configuring the lookup fields for the specific views*

5. Within the configuration, there is also the functionality to group
   by column. This can be switched off or enabled. This can be left
   for now and kept on, allowing the user to group the records by
   column.

6. Save the changes by selecting the Save button and click "Publish"
   in the Solution Explorer.

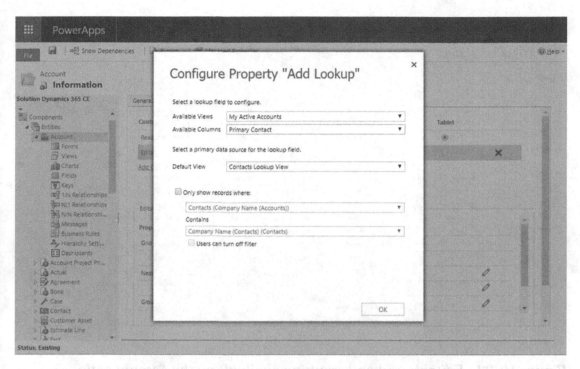

Figure 10-21. *Changing the default view for the lookup*

Once published, refresh the application and navigate to the Classic UI to see the new editable grid on the Accounts view. The user interface is different than standard; notice how the columns can now be edited in line without you having to navigate to the record itself. Grouping can also occur within the view of the fields available in the columns. Business rules, discussed in Chapter 12, also run within an editable grid view as all of the fields are present in the view (Figure 10-22).

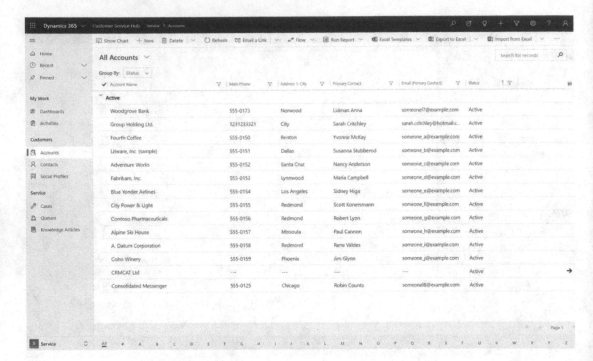

Figure 10-22. *Editable grid and grouping available on the Account entity*

Charts

Dynamics 365 CE allows for visualizations to be made that are based on a record type and a related view, creating a visual representation of a list based on the filtered information. This chart can be displayed while on the list view for the entity, embedded into a form, or seen from within dashboards. Charts can be created from within the Common Data Service, or personal charts can be created within the Unified Interface directly by a user and only available to them.

Charts have two types, as follows:

- **System** – A system chart is created in the same way as system views, which is by customizers via the Common Data Service.

- **Personal** – Personal charts are created via the Unified Interface.

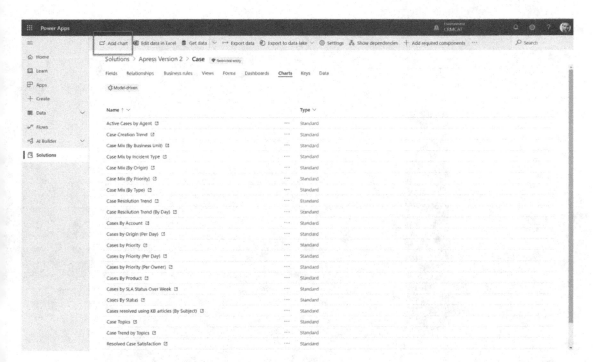

Figure 10-23. *Charts within the App Designer can be created when the "Chart" component is selected*

Charts can be created via the Unified Interface by selecting "Show Chart" as shown in Figure 10-23 and clicking the expanded menu in the Chart pane and then "New," as shown in Figure 10-24. This launches the Chart Designer.

Figure 10-24. *Charts can be created within the Chart pane in the Unified Interface*

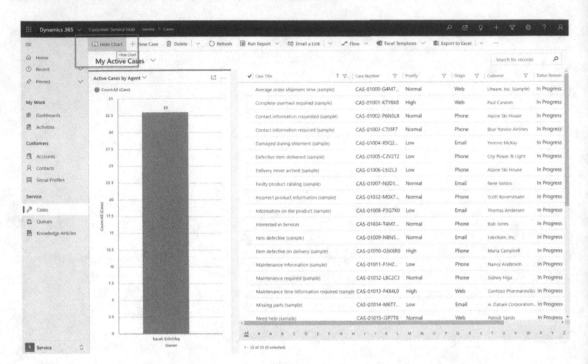

Figure 10-25. *Charts can be accessed using "Show Chart" and "Hide Chart"*

Charts can be accessed by users by selecting "Show Chart," on the view screen, shown in Figure 10-26.

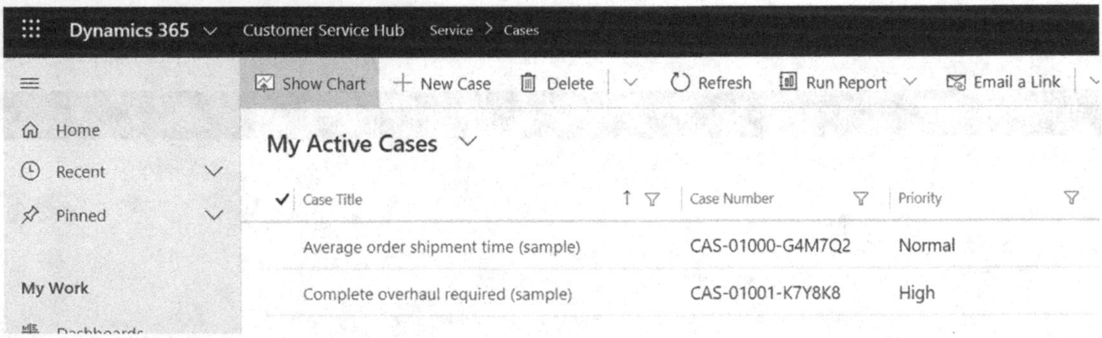

Figure 10-26. *In the Unified Interface, click a view and then "Show Chart" to see charts*

The Chart pane appears, and a user can select from the dropdown list of available charts for that record type (Figure 10-27).

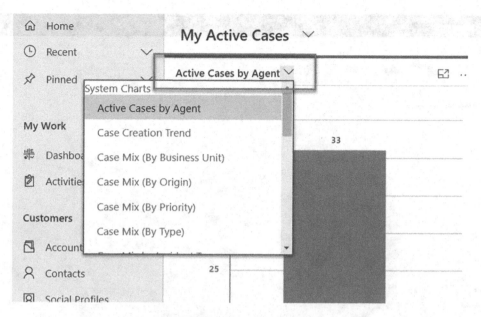

Figure 10-27. *Selecting Charts from the dropdown list, similar to Views*

Charts are built using the Chart Designer in Dynamics 365 CE for both system and public charts. The Chart Designer can be seen in Figure 10-28. The type of chart is selected from the ribbon bar.

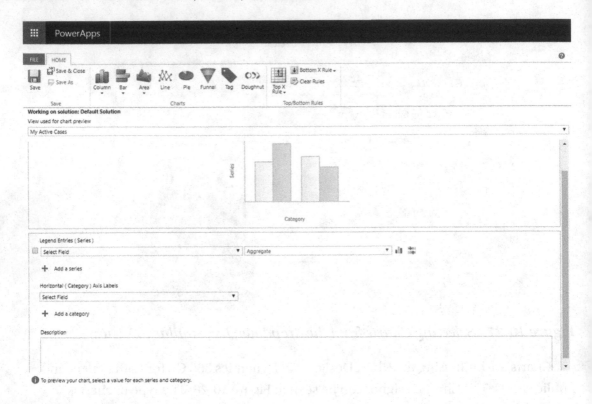

Figure 10-28. *Chart Designer*

The controls on the ribbon also allow for you to specify the "Top" and "Bottom" rules of a chart. This feature filters the results of a chart such that only the top or bottom 5, 3, or N number of records are used.

Task: Create a new public chart.

1. Navigate to the Common Data Service and select "New Chart." This opens the Chart Designer in a new window.

2. Name the chart (or leave it blank to be auto-populated by the fields used).

3. Select the view to be used by default and for preview purposes.

4. Add the legend or series for the vertical axis. This is normally a numerical type field, so it can perform an aggregate function. If a non-numerical type field is used, only the function "Count: All" or "Count: Non-Empty" is available. Use the "On Hold Time" in the Account entity as an example. This is a numerical field that can perform the "Sum" aggregation shown in Figure 10-29.

5. Add the category for the horizontal axis. This will be the cross-relationship based on the series selected in the previous step; for example, "On Hold Time" by "Modified On" date would display the sum of the total hold time cross-referenced by the Modified On date by month. This could potentially indicate spikes where accounts have had excessive amounts of hold time, in months.

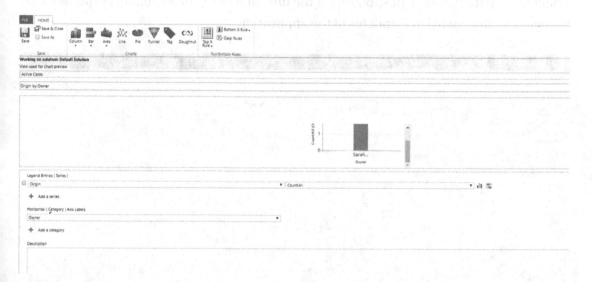

Figure 10-29. Adding legend and category to the Chart Designer

6. Save the chart and exit the Chart Designer.

7. Navigate to the entity selected (Cases, if the example was followed), expand the Chart pane, and select the chart from the list of charts.

Dashboards

Dashboards bring together views and charts to provide a single-screen experience for the user. A dashboard allows users to see information presented in a list format and perform operations on those records without having to navigate to the full records. It displays aggregates through tiles and visualization through charts, all while remaining in context with the records presented in the views.

Dynamics 365 CE has two types of dashboards at the time of writing. Classic dashboards from the legacy web client (which are visible in the Unified Interface) are available to be created as personal dashboards, and what is often referred to as "interactive" dashboards are available to be created by administrators (Figure 10-30). The creation of these types of dashboards can be achieved using the Common Data Service in the same way as views and charts are created. Classic dashboards are only available as personal-type dashboards at the time of writing; however, this experience is expected to change in later updates of the application.

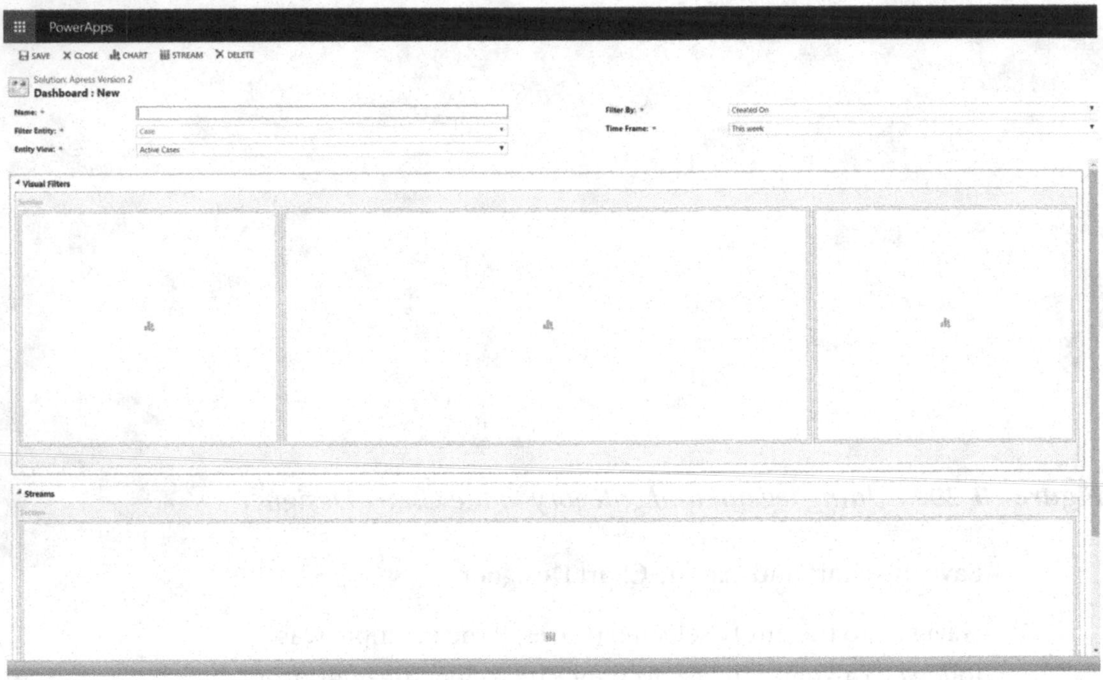

Figure 10-30. Dashboard creation experience from the Common Data Service

System dashboards, created via the Common Data Service for Apps, provide an enhanced dashboard experience compared to classic dashboards by displaying more contextual and modifiable information to the user, allowing them to act on items and filter information through tiles, views, and charts. Interactive dashboards are only available to be created at a system level.

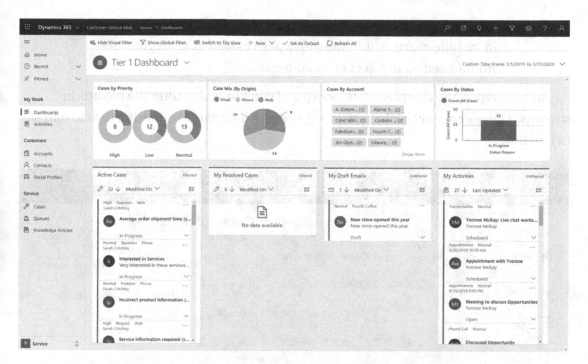

Figure 10-31. *Interactive dashboard within the Unified Interface*

This chapter will focus on creating system dashboards; however, this chapter does briefly cover how to create personal dashboards within the application.

Building a System Dashboard

At the time of writing, there are two ways to create system dashboards. Single-stream dashboards are available to be created via the Common Data Service for Apps (see Figure 10-32); however, single- and multi-stream dashboards can be created via the Model-Driven App Designer.

- **Multi-stream dashboards** allow for "streams" of information that are based on views or queues that are embedded and are based on any and multiple entities, for example, Accounts, Contacts, Opportunities, and so on. They include buttons for the user to switch to a Tile view, providing aggregates, or the user can open the visual filter to display visualizations on top of the streams.

- **Single-stream dashboards** are confined to one single entity and can include charts within the single page as well as aggregate tiles without needing to select extra buttons.

In both types, the charts are interactive and can be used to filter the records in streams. The user simply clicks certain segments of the chart to allow the data to refresh in real time.

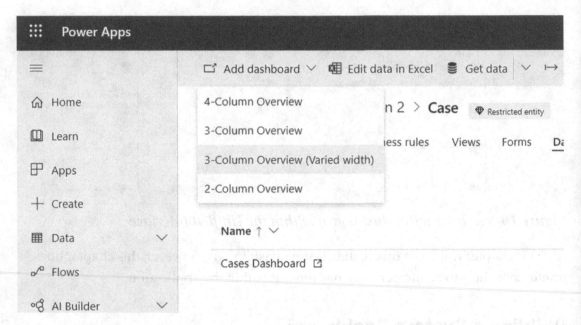

Figure 10-32. *Creating a single-stream dashboard via the Common Data Service*

More details on the specifics of dashboards can be found at the end of this chapter within the "Further Reading" section.

Task: Create an interactive multi-stream dashboard.

1. Navigate to the App Designer and select the "Dashboard" component.

2. Click "Create New" in the right-hand pane and select "Interactive Dashboards" (Figure 10-33).

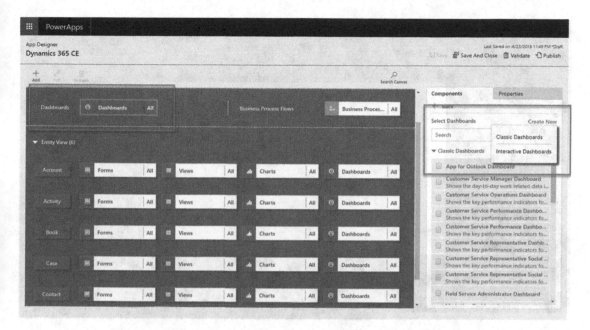

Figure 10-33. *App Designer "Dashboard" component*

3. Click the Multi-Stream tab and then "2 Column Overview,"
    as shown in Figure 10-34. This dashboard is designed to have
    multiple streams and two charts.

4. Select "Create" for the Dashboard Designer to open.

5. Select the dashboard to be created for the Case entity.

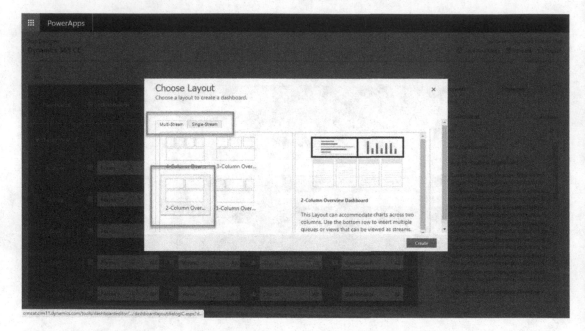

Figure 10-34. *Multi-stream and single-stream dashboard selectors*

6. There are three stages of creating a dashboard. Stage 1 includes setting up the initial information, which can be seen in the properties at the top of the screen, shown in Figure 10-35:

    • **Name** – Enter the name of the dashboard.

    • **Filter Entity** – The charts are based on this entity.

    • **Entity View** – The view of the selected entity.

    • **Filter By** – The field to filter on.

    • **Time Frame** – The time frame of the filtered field; this can be modified by the user in real time. (Note: Be aware of this field; it can make it appear as if there is no data within the dashboard.)

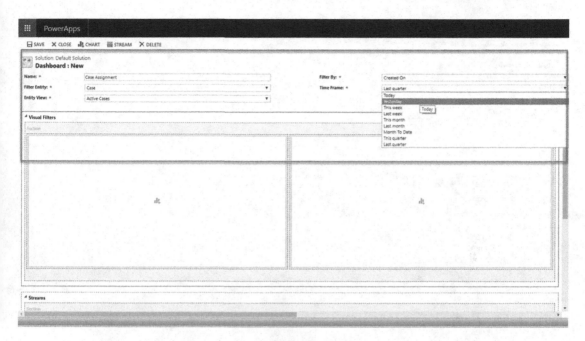

Figure 10-35. *Multi-stream Dashboard Designer*

7. Stage 2 is to add the "streams" of information, which are
    represented by views and queues. Select the "Streams" space at
    the bottom half of the designer for the stream selector to appear.
    Select if it is based on a view or a queue (view, in this example)
    and select which entity. Examples in Figure 10-36 are Active Cases
    (View), All Activities (View), and All Phone Calls (View).

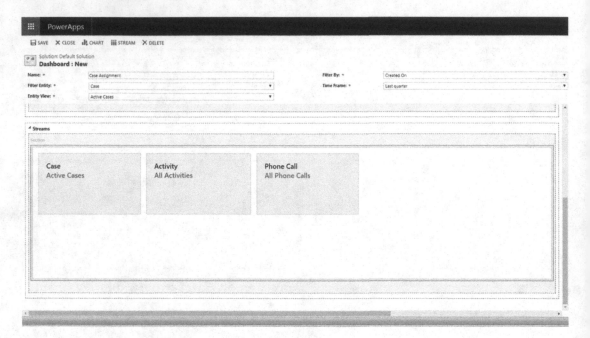

Figure 10-36. *Add streams within the dashboard*

8. Select the Visual Filters tab for the last stage. Selecting the Chart
    button on the Dashboard Designer opens the chart selector. This
    will be locked as the same record type and view as for the "Filter
    Entity" selected in the dashboard configuration. Select the charts
    from the standard charts available for the Case entity by clicking
    "Add." Visual filters, or charts, are used to filter down the records
    within the views selected (Figure 10-37).

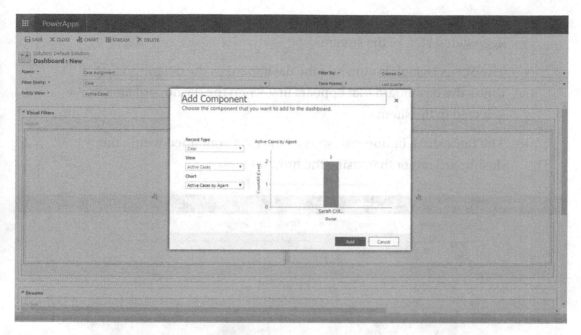

Figure 10-37. *Adding visual filters*

9. Once completed, click "Save," "Validate," and then "Close."

10. Ensure the dashboard is selected to be included in the app (or all of them) and click "Save" and "Publish" on the App Designer.

11. Refresh the app, and the dashboard will then be visible to users.

Using Interactive Dashboards

When a dashboard is open, there is various functionality available from the single-page view. This functionality can assist in performing operations and tasks quickly without having to navigate to a view or even a record. Some basic functions are listed here (Figure 10-38):

- Select the Show Visual Filter button on the ribbon to display the charts in the multi-stream dashboard based on the Filter entity.

- Select the Show Global Filter button on the ribbon to filter on the records, like in Microsoft Excel.

- Select the Switch to Tile View button on the ribbon to see an aggregated view of the streams.

- The Set as Default button sets the dashboard as the default so that this is the dashboard that appears first when the dashboard area is selected in the sitemap.

- The Refresh All button refreshes all the data contained within the dashboard rather than using the browser button.

Figure 10-38. *Using dashboards: the ribbon control*

You can click the action button on a card view to perform various actions on a single record or on multiple records at one time, as shown in Figure 10-39.

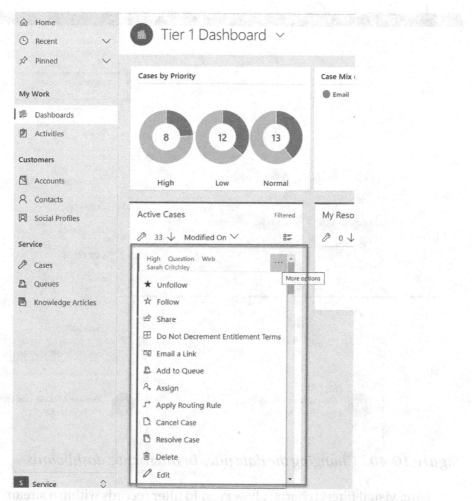

Figure 10-39. *Select the action button on a card view to perform operations*

Interactive dashboards by default have a filter date set against them upon creation. This can be modified or changed to a custom time frame to load the records within that range (Figure 10-40). The custom time frame cannot be saved within the properties of the dashboard at the time of writing.

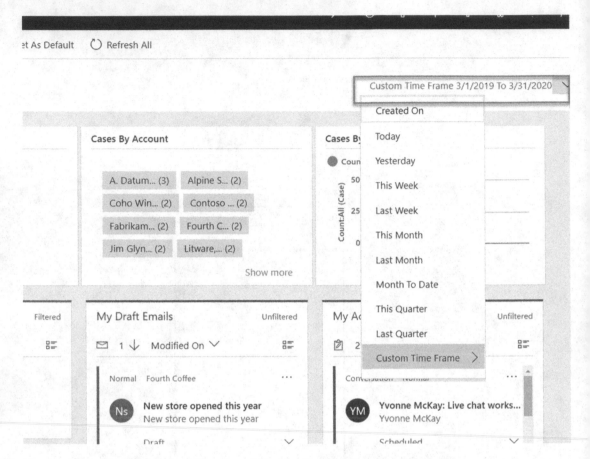

Figure 10-40. *Changing the date filter in interactive dashboards*

Using visual filters (charts) allows you to filter records within a stream based on those charts, removing unnecessary data and allowing you to focus on data you are reviewing or searching for (Figure 10-41).

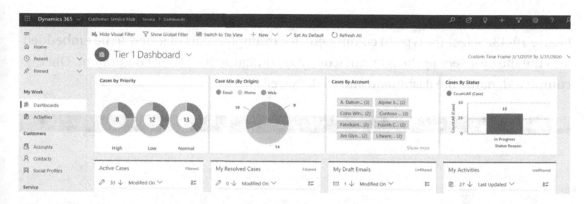

Figure 10-41. *Use the visual filter and click the charts to filter the records within the streams*

Building a Personal Dashboard

To build a personal dashboard using a classic dashboard type, navigate to the Dashboard area within the Unified Interface and select "New" and then select "Dynamics 365 Dashboard." Select the layout as shown in Figure 10-42.

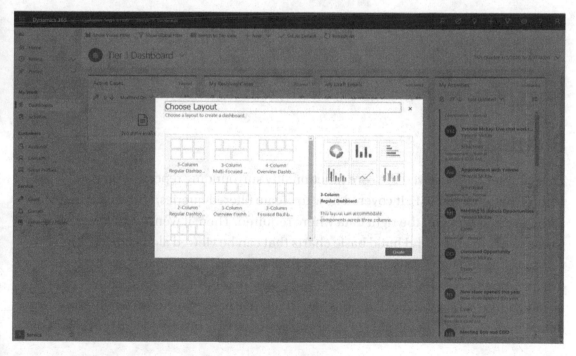

Figure 10-42. *Creating a personal dashboard*

Once you have selected the layout, the Dashboard Designer will appear as shown in Figure 10-43. Select the type of component, for example, chart of a view to be embedded into the tile by selecting the relevant icon, and configure the type of component. Once completed, name the dashboard and click "Save."

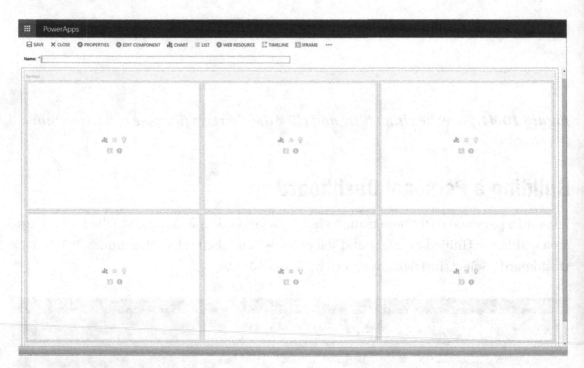

Figure 10-43. *Selecting components on a personal dashboard*

Summary

This chapter has reviewed the core functionality surrounding reporting on data within Dynamics 365 CE. It covered how to create filtered queries, known as views, to allow users to focus on the right data where required. Then, it went on to cover how to use views in charts and build basic charts that can be viewed alongside data in a view, embedded into forms, and used within dashboards. Dashboards are critical for organizations to be able to offer a single-page view of more than one stream of data, see visualizations alongside the data, and filter data so users can focus on small subsets of data where required. Being able to modify how the data is displayed to users across the organization is critical to using Dynamics 365 CE effectively. This chapter has covered how to get started in this area to help you learn the core principles of modifying views, charts, and dashboards to display data in the most effective way.

Chapter Tasks

1. Create a new view.

2. Modify an existing view, changing the columns and sorting criteria.

3. Create a new chart.

4. Create a dashboard via the Common Data Service.

5. Create a dashboard via the App Designer – selecting "Multi-Stream"

6. Become familiar with all the components of using an interactive dashboard, such as "visual filter."

Further Reading

Standard Entities and exporting the ERD of the standard Dynamics 365 CE System (Microsoft, 2018). URL: `https://docs.microsoft.com/en-us/dynamics365/customer-engagement/developer/use-metadata-generate-entity-diagrams`

Power BI Integration with Dashboards (Microsoft, 2018). URL: `https://docs.microsoft.com/en-us/dynamics365/unified-operations/dev-itpro/analytics/power-bi-integration`

Quick Find Search vs Relevance Search (Microsoft, 2018). URL: `https://docs.microsoft.com/en-us/dynamics365/customer-engagement/basics/relevance-search-results`

Classic and Interactive Dashboards (Microsoft, 2018). URL: `https://docs.microsoft.com/en-us/dynamics365/customer-engagement/basics/start-your-day-dashboard-chart`

Interactive Dashboard features (Microsoft, 2018). URL: `https://docs.microsoft.com/en-us/dynamics365/customer-engagement/customize/configure-interactive-dashboards`

Reporting within Dynamics 365 using the Report Wizard (Microsoft, 2018). URL: `https://docs.microsoft.com/en-us/dynamics365/customer-engagement/basics/create-edit-copy-report-wizard`

Personal Views and Sharing (Microsoft, 2018). URL: `https://docs.microsoft.com/en-us/dynamics365/customer-engagement/customize/create-edit-views`

CHAPTER 11

Forms, Views, and UI Customizations

This chapter will cover the core UI customizations available within Dynamics 365 CE. Customizing the user interface gives users the capability to modify how data is displayed, which, in turn, influences how they update the information as well. In addition to that, learning how the records are connected to each other through relationships gives greater understanding of the information held within Dynamics 365 CE, empowering users to get more value out of the system by using reporting and navigational features.

Forms are used within Dynamics 365 CE to display fields to users (Figure 11-1). They hold information about where fields are placed and the format in which they are viewed and are one of the main areas where a user will interact directly with data. It is important to understand the different terminology involved in creating forms, how to create new fields, relationships, adding components to forms, and the different types available. This chapter will focus on these topics to ensure you can design a positive user experience where users can add data to and retrieve data from the system with ease.

© Sarah Critchley 2020

S. Critchley, *Dynamics 365 Essentials*, https://doi.org/10.1007/978-1-4842-5911-5_11

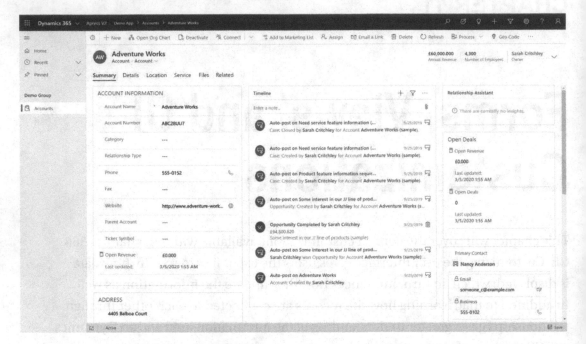

Figure 11-1. *An example of a form on an Account record*

Many of the actions being performed in this chapter will be done so in the maker experience within the Common Data Service. This will be highlighted in the relevant sections. In some areas, the classic experience will be used; however, it is expected that those areas will be updated to be possible in the maker experience in future updates.

Entities and Fields

As discussed in Chapter 2, record types are often referred to as *entities* within Dynamics 365 CE. Entities are used to categorize types of records and in database terms are the same as a table within a database. Users and processes create records of a type either within the user interface or programmatically, creating rows within that table. Entities have related metadata linked to them, such as fields, views, and forms. Fields are columns within the database linked to the entity and are the descriptive information that is stored within the row. Dynamics 365 CE comes with many entities already pre-created and used within defined business processes, such as the Account and Contact entities. There is also the ability to create custom entities that can be used to support existing processes or, instead, to create entirely new processes.

Entities and related information, such as fields, are added through *the Common Data Service* within the maker experience at make.powerapps.com directly in solutions or through the Data area (solutions are the recommended approach, which are covered in more depth in Chapter 11). Fields represent data within the system and, from a database point of view, represent at least one column within the Dynamics 365 CE database. The standard record types, such as Case, Account, Contact, and Opportunity, all come with fields already created against them. New fields can be created if required. Fields are added to a form; however, not all fields have to be added to a form (Figure 11-2). A form provides the user experience and the ability for the user to enter data. The form is also used operationally for business processes, such as workflows, and for business rules to operate, including where form scripts, such as JavaScript, are added. Entities can have multiple forms that users can switch between when viewing a record. Multiple forms can be added via the App Designer for a single record type – for example, a Case – and users can switch between the forms available. A field can then exist on any number of forms within the record type.

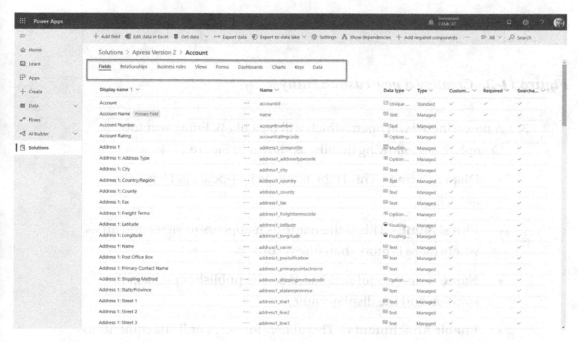

Figure 11-2. *Where fields can be added within the maker experience via the solutions*

Task: Create a new entity within Dynamics 365 CE.

1. Navigate the maker experience and open a solution (solutions are covered in depth in Chapter 11).

2. Click "New" and "Entity," as shown in Figure 11-3.

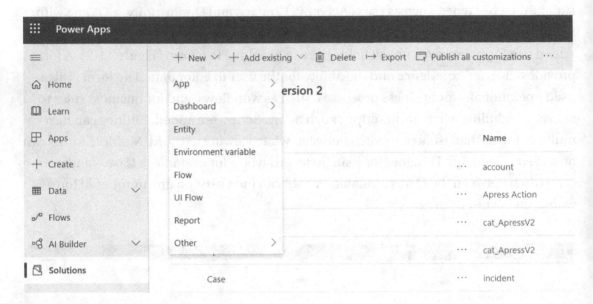

Figure 11-3. *Creating a new custom entity*

3. A new window will open, which will be a blank Entity window. Complete the following details, as shown in Figure 11-4:

- **Display Name** – This is the name as it appears in Dynamics 365 CE.

- **Plural Name** – This is the name as it appears in views and areas where there is more than one record.

- **Name** – Auto-populated based on the publisher prefix in the solution and the display name.

- **Enable Attachments** – This allows for notes and attachments to be added into the timeline component of the form.

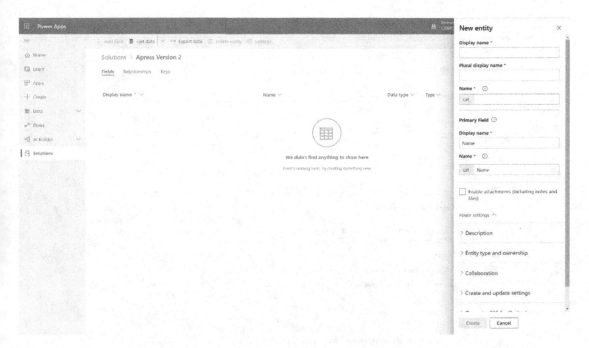

Figure 11-4. *Where the entity can be configured at creation*

There are some areas which can be expanded on this panel –
some notable items are highlighted in the following (Figure 11-5):

- **Define as an activity entity** – Defining an entity as an Activity entity
  means it will be a child of the Activity Pointer entity and will be
  available to create from the timeline in all other entities.

- **Ownership** – If this entity should be owned by a user or a team or by
  an organization (organization ownership is outside of the security
  role structure).

- **Description** – A short description of the entity.

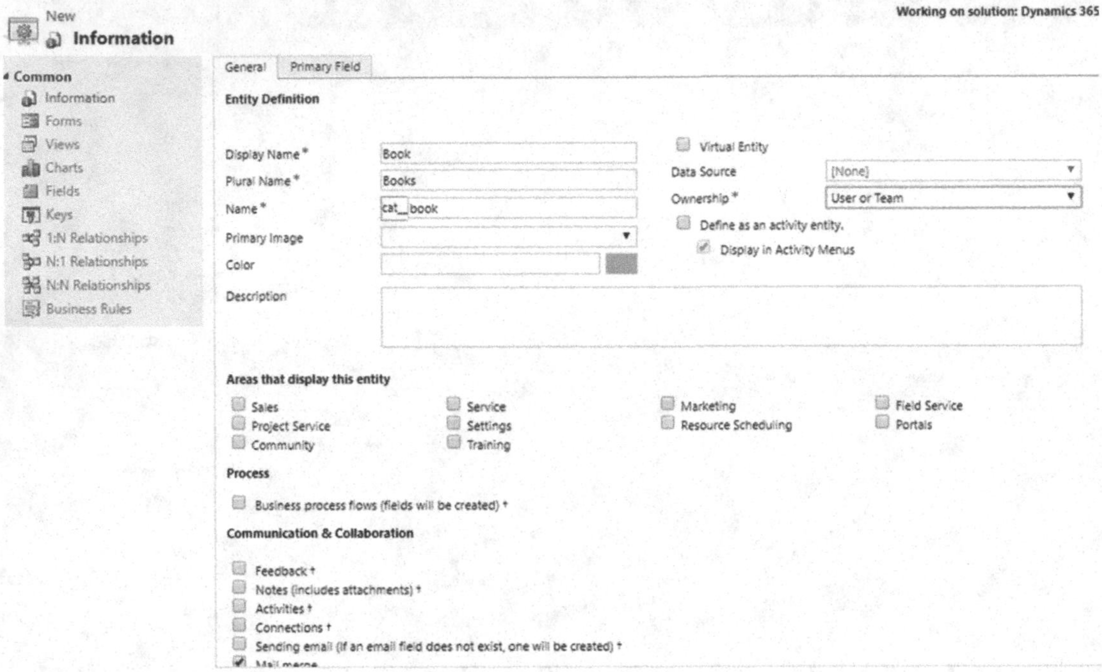

Figure 11-5. *Classic experience of creating an entity*

Some configuration is still not possible in the maker experience, such as creating Virtual Entities. This can be achieved by opening the classic experience and configuring the entity from this area. This can be seen in Figure 11-6.

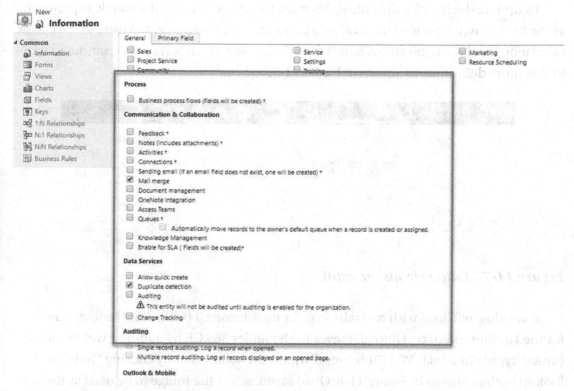

Figure 11-6. *Entity configuration options*

These options are sometimes enabled and cannot be disabled, such as "Activities" fields. This area is where the entity is enabled for many out-of-the-box functionalities, such as feedback, activities, and Business Process Flows. For more information on all of these options, see the "Further Reading" section at the end of this chapter.

A special note for activities: To enable activities, such as Tasks and Phone Calls, to be added to a custom entity, this must be configured via the classic experience at the time of writing.

4. Do not add any extra configuration options to the entity definition, and click "Save." The entity will be created in the system and may take a moment to load.

5. Once saved, the options on the left-hand pane will become available, such as forms, views, and charts.

To update the icon for the entity, this must be achieved using the classic experience at the time of writing and is not available in the maker experience. Navigate to the classic experience and open the entity. Select the "Update Icons" option on the command bar in the entity definition, as shown in Figure 11-7.

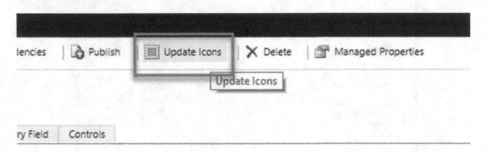

Figure 11-7. *Editing icons for entities*

A window will load with two tabs, one for the Classic UI (web client) and another for the Unified Interface. Upload images to Dynamics 365 CE by adding a web resource (image type) either via "Web Resources" within the solution or by clicking "New" in the lookup option, shown in Figure 11-8. Once saved, select the image to be used as the icon and publish the changes.

Figure 11-8. *Adding a web resource image for entity icons*

The new entity should now be created, with an optional icon. Icons add a professional look and feel to records, as a puzzle piece or cog icon can look "unfinished" to a user of the system, especially when it is used multiple times for custom entities within an app. It is best practice to upload an icon for all entities that is relevant to what it represents within the system.

The following sections will look at creating new fields and other entity components.

Task: Create a new field.

1.   To add new fields to an entity, select the entity you want to modify in the solution and open it. Navigate to "Fields" within the Common Data Service (Figure 11-9).

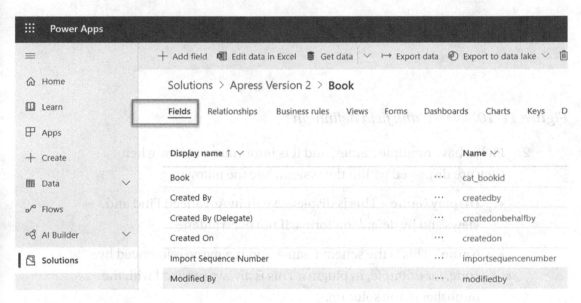

Figure 11-9. *Adding a new field*

A window will open to define the configuration for the field on the right-hand side of the screen as shown in Figure 11-10.

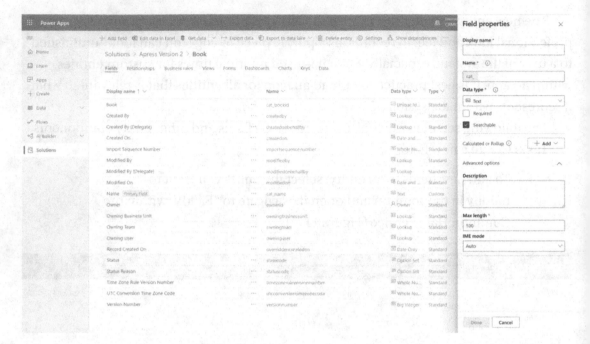

Figure 11-10. *New blank field definition*

2. Fields have multiple names, and it is important to know where
    they are displayed within the system. See the following:

    - **Display Name** – This is displayed within Advanced Find and
      views and by default on forms, if not overridden.

    - **Name** – This is the schema name and is a name referenced by
      code, for example, in plugins. This is always prefixed with the
      publisher of the solution.

    A field has a requirement level (Figure 11-11). The requirement
    level can be one of the following:

    - **Optional** – The user can choose to input data or not. If not, it is
      left empty.

    - **Business Required** – On the form, this is a required field and
      must be entered. It is displayed with a red asterisk.

- **Business Recommended (only available to select via the classic experience)** – This displays with a blue asterisk next to the field name and is used to prompt the user that they should fill it in but are not required to. If not, it is left empty.

Figure 11-11. *Types of fields*

The field can be set as "Searchable," which means this field is displayed within Advanced Find and can be used on Quick Find views. The field can also be switched on for field security (see Chapter 4 for more information) and also auditing. The record type itself must be switched on at the entity definition level for auditing to be enabled. You also have the opportunity to add a description, which appears as a "tooltip" to the user to give them more description about what the field is used for when the cursor hovers over the field within the form.

Fields have a data type, which refers to the type of data the field holds and that can be entered within the field (Figure 11-11). Table 11-1 briefly explains the data types; however, for more information, see the "Further Reading" section at the end of this chapter.

Table 11-1. *Field Data Types*

Data Type	Brief Description
Single Line of Text	Used for brief text entry, often referred to as a "string," and can be numerical and alphabetical.
Option Set	A defined list of option-set values that are created by the user. Local or global option sets are available. Global is often used where the values are needed in more than one field. Only one option can be selected.
Multi-Select Option Set	Same as previous except more than one option can be selected.
Two Options	Often referred to as a "Boolean," this is the type of field that is a "yes/no"-type field; however, any two options can be defined, not necessarily yes and no.
Image	Used to configure the image of the entity if it supports images.
Whole Number	Integers with a value between –2,147,483,648 and 2,147,483,647 can be in this field.
Floating Point Number	Up to five decimal points of precision can be used for values between –100,000,000,000 and 100,000,000,000 in this field.

(continued)

Table 11-1. (*continued*)

Data Type	Brief Description
Decimal Point Number	Up to ten decimal points of precision can be used for values between −100,000,000,000 and 100,000,000,000 in this field.
Currency	Displays values as money in the default currency. This creates four fields, which include the base currency value and the currency value entered by the user, transaction currency field, and exchange rate field.
Multiple Lines of Text	Same as a single line of text except the maximum length of this field is longer, different controls can be added, and the text box or area can be made into multiple lines on the form it is used on.
Date and Time	Displays a date picker with an optional time picker. Can be date-only and also has many options for the local time zone.
Lookup	A lookup field that references another record.
Customer	A type of lookup field that references both a contact and an account.

Depending on the selected data type – for example, Single Line of Text – the types of field and format available are determined. Maximum length should be considered for text-based fields as this limit will prevent a user from entering any more data (and also if used programmatically).

Use the following reference table to review the different types of fields available within Dynamics 365 CE and the Common Data Service.

There are also additional types of fields called "calculated" and "rollup" fields, which are types of fields available on specific data types (Table 11-2). Calculated and rollup fields rely on extra definitions to operate successfully. These will be covered in the next section.

Table 11-2. *Field Type Reference for Calculated and Rollup Fields*

Type	Where available
Calculated Field Type	A single line of text, options, whole number, currency, date time, Boolean (two options), decimal number
Rollup Field Type	Decimal number, currency, date time, whole number

3. Select the type and related options for a field, such as "Two Options"; and once all the options have been selected and the field has been configured, select "Done." The field is now ready to use on a form (Figure 11-12).

Figure 11-12. *Save the new field by clicking "Done"*

Fields can also be created from within the form itself. If this route is used, always remember to open a form directly from a solution and not from the default solution accessible from within the application for administrators. This is so the prefix is correctly assigned for the field and is not "new_." Solutions are covered in Chapter 9.

Rollup Fields

Rollup fields are a special type of field that allows you to create aggregate functions of related child records. Child records and relationship types are covered more in the next section; however, briefly, child records are where there are multiple records (N) associated with one parent record (1) in a hierarchical relationship. An example of this is found in the Case record and some of its standard functionality. The case has a self-referential relationship, which is a one-to-many type. One Case record acts as a "parent," while others can be associated with the Case record as its "children," creating a "child case"-like structure. This type of relationship infers a relevancy that the child records have to the parent.

Different types of aggregation can be performed, such as sum, count, min, max, and average. Examples of rollup fields are that the last activity date on a Case record could be related to an Activity entity and be the max of the associated activity. Another example, which the following walk-through covers, could be a count of the child cases related to a parent case that does not exist as standard (but the relationship does).

Using these fields in views and dashboards can display important overview data within a parent record, which will be useful at a glance, removing the need for a user to navigate to a record and count associated records.

Task: Create a rollup field.

1. Create a new field of type "Whole Number" on the Case entity, naming it "No of Child Cases" (Figure 11-13). Do not save the record.

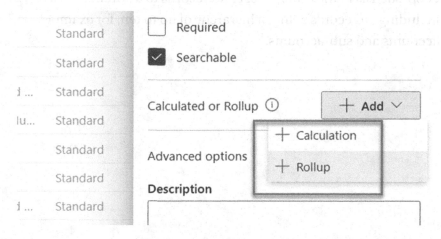

Figure 11-13. *Create a new field where the "Field Type" field is "Rollup"*

2. Select the "Field Type" as "Rollup." A warning will appear to save the field first. Save the field, and a new window will open which is the rollup and calculated Field Designer (which differs slightly). It is important to note that selecting this button saves the record, so be sure to be happy with the schema name and the current configuration of the field which opens the rollup Field Designer, as you cannot change the schema name once saved.

Figure 11-14. *Creating a new rollup field definition*

The Field Designer will open (Figure 11-15). The "Hierarchy" option refers to the ability to aggregate beyond just one record deep, such as in the example of child records to a parent, including *all* records within a hierarchy of up to ten, for example, accounts and sub-accounts.

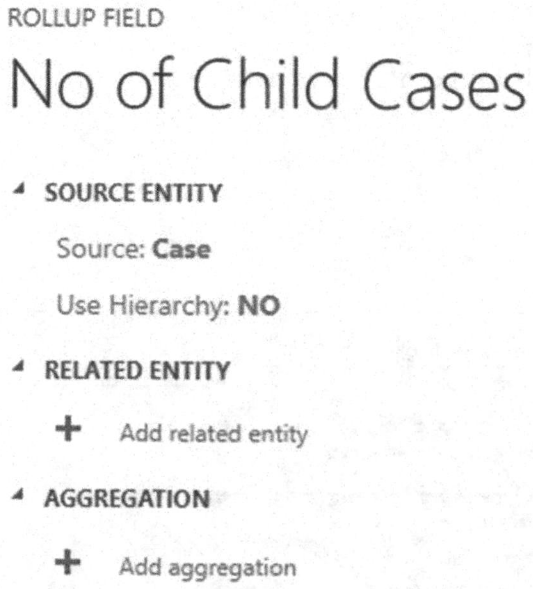

ROLLUP FIELD

No of Child Cases

⊿ **SOURCE ENTITY**

Source: **Case**

Use Hierarchy: **NO**

⊿ **RELATED ENTITY**

✚   Add related entity

⊿ **AGGREGATION**

✚   Add aggregation

Figure 11-15. *Defining the rollup configuration*

3. Leave the "Hierarchy" setting as "No."

4. Set the "Related Entity" to "Case" by selecting the plus icon (Figure 11-16). The field that defines this relationship is called "Cases (Parent Case)." All child relationships define the parent by using a lookup field that references the parent record, and this field has a name. The name is "Parent Case." This defines the relationship we are using for the aggregate.

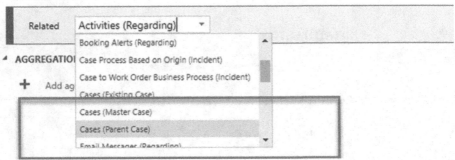

Figure 11-16. *Adding the related entity in the Field Designer for a rollup field*

5.   Click the checkbox on the right-hand side of the logic block to
continue to confirm this edit to the field business logic definition.

6.   Now define the aggregate function (Figure 11-17). Select the plus
icon and select "COUNT." The case will be the only value available
for the related entity. There is the option to add filters within the
definition. This is particularly useful if the aggregate function
should only be looking at cases with a particular value, such as
status, subject, or case type.

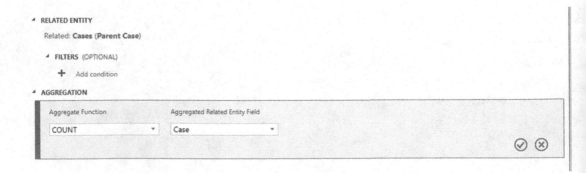

Figure 11-17. *Configuring the aggregation business logic for the rollup field*

7. Select the checkbox on the right-hand side of the logic block. There will be a yellow warning that mentions the rollup field at the bottom of the Field Definition window referring to how these fields are calculated.

   Rollup fields "roll up" and calculate initially 12 hours after creation and then every hour after that. This is to ensure the rollup job is not impacting the user experience or the performance of the system as the system could potentially be counting through lots of records to perform the defined function. Having multiple types of these fields could cause issues if they were all operating at the same time. A system job is created for each rollup field that can process up to 50,000 records and updates two new fields created behind the scenes in addition to the field itself displayed to the user. These extra fields define the last date and time it was updated and the state the aggregation is in, for example, running.

   You can manually update rollup fields' scheduled time runs, which is normally advisable so as to run out of operating hours if possible. To do this, navigate to the system job menu and locate the name of the job. Select it and edit its configuration through the user interface.

8. Click "Save and Close" on the Field Definition window and also "Save and Close" on the Field window.

The rollup field has now been made and can be added to a form.

Calculated Fields

Calculated fields allow you to add business logic within a field definition that performs calculations or operational logic – for example, to add days and hours to the values contained within a field – to create a more useful or relevant value that is displayed to the user. Calculated-type fields can often replace custom code and are a great way to add in operational-type business logic.

In the walk-through that follows, a new calculated field will be created that will set the "Next Activity Date" to +2 days from the "Modified On" date from the Case entity.

This will give users a target date to always provide a follow-up activity by and also allow users to sort on that field in columns, allowing the prioritization of cases based on interactions, preventing cases from going "stale."

Task: Create a calculated field.

1. Create a new field of type "Date Time" on the Case entity and name it "Next Activity Date." Ensure this is a "Date Only"-type field by selecting this option in the "Format" field. ("Date Only"-type fields remove the "Time" portion of the field from the user interface.) Do not save the field just yet.

2. Set the "Field Type" to "Calculated." The same warning will appear as the rollup. Save the field and the new tab will open.

   The same Field Designer appears in which you can configure the business logic as part of the field, with some modified options available, as shown in Figure 11-18.

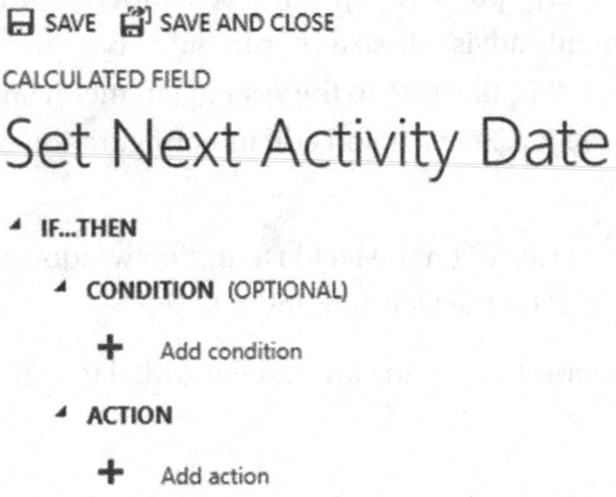

Figure 11-18. *Calculated field definition*

Optional conditional "if" operators can be added if the field should only be operating under certain circumstances. Complex branches can be created should there need to be. In this walk-through, there is no requirement to add any conditional operators.

3. Select "plus" in the "Action" heading, and a number of operations will become available (Figure 11-19). It is a good idea to become familiar with these types of formulas as they define the functional scope of calculated fields and what can be achieved, such as Add Hours, Add Days, and Add Weeks. For a more comprehensive list, see the "Further Reading" section at the end of this chapter.

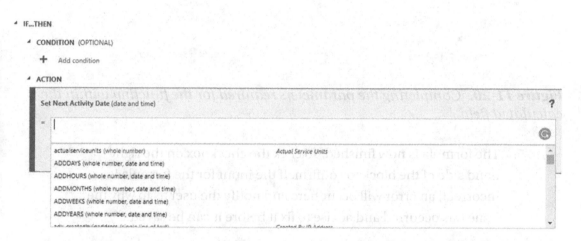

Figure 11-19. Selecting the action for the calculated field

4. The format of the operation is the function name and, in brackets, the input values. For this example, use "ADDDAYS (whole number, date and time)" – the whole number, which is the number of days to add, and the target date and time. The input can be specifically defined values – for example, 2 – or it can be dynamically based on fields in the context of the record the calculated field is placed upon. To use field names, start typing the display name of the field to see it appear within the action dropdown. For this example, select "ADDDAYS," enter "2," and then start typing "modified" for the field "Modified By" to appear and then select it. It should automatically be enclosed in brackets. See Figure 11-20 for reference.

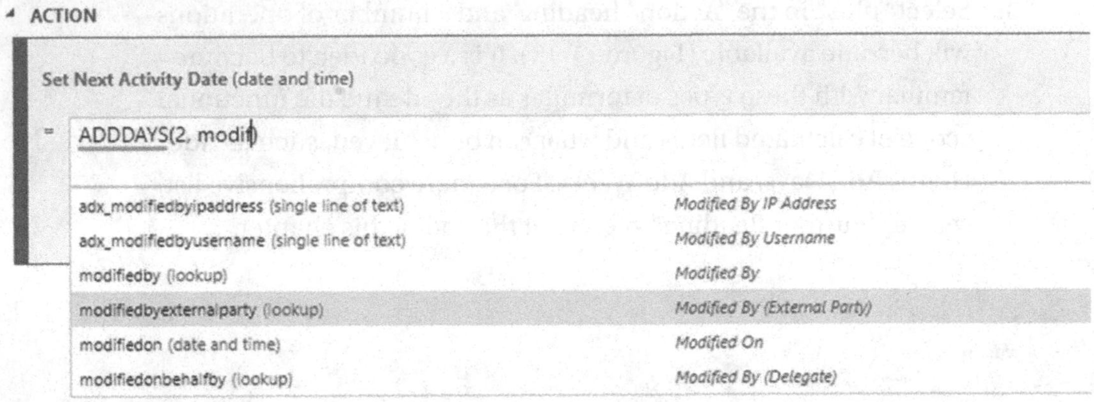

⁴ ACTION

Set Next Activity Date (date and time)

= ADDDAYS(2, modif|)

adx_modifiedbyipaddress (single line of text)	*Modified By IP Address*
adx_modifiedbyusername (single line of text)	*Modified By Username*
modifiedby (lookup)	*Modified By*
modifiedbyexternalparty (lookup)	*Modified By (External Party)*
modifiedon (date and time)	*Modified On*
modifiedonbehalfby (lookup)	*Modified By (Delegate)*

Figure 11-20. *Completing the parameters required for the function within the calculated field*

5. The formula is now finished, so click the checkbox on the right-hand side of the block to confirm. If the input for the formula is incorrect, an error will occur here and notify the user as to why the issue has occurred and advise to fix it before it can be saved.

6. Click "Save and Close," and then "Save and Close" again on the Field window, and the field is now ready to be used on a form (Figure 11-21).

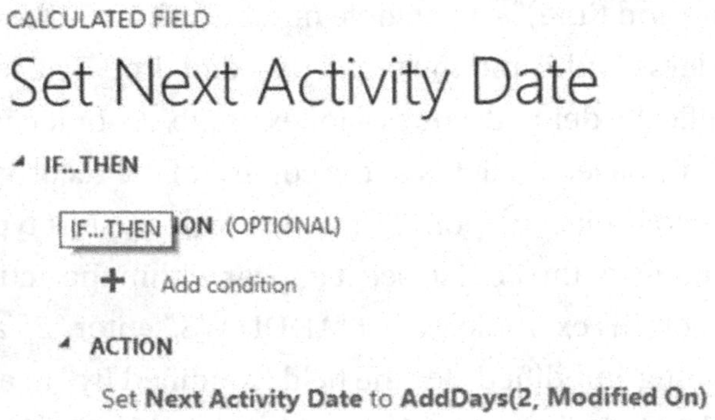

CALCULATED FIELD

Set Next Activity Date

⁴ IF...THEN

IF...THEN |ON (OPTIONAL)

+ Add condition

⁴ ACTION

Set **Next Activity Date** to **AddDays(2, Modified On)**

Figure 11-21. *Completed calculated field definition*

Relationships

Dynamics 365 CE is built upon a standard relational database structure. There are many resources on relational databases available on the Internet; however, this section will briefly discuss the types of relationships available within the platform and how they are represented to the Dynamics user.

There are three types of relationships visible from the maker experience within the entity definition:

- **1:N** – One to many

- **N:1** – Many to one

- **N:N** – Many to many

Figure 11-22. *How to access relationships in the maker experience*

1:N and N:1 are the same relationship, but with the primary entity switched around depending on the perspective that is being looked at (e.g., the one or the many). To see this in action, select 1:N within the Solution Explorer for the Case entity and look for a relationship. The column "Primary entity" will always be the Case. Click the N:1, and the primary entity will be the referred-to entity, and the Case entity is the inferred entity (Figure 11-23).

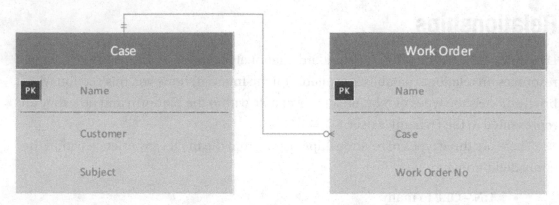

Figure 11-23. *An ERD or "crow's foot" diagram of a 1:N relationship of a case and a work order*

A 1:N relationship is defined as a lookup field, as shown in Figure 11-24, and is visible to the user as a lookup field on a form from the referred-to entity. The referred-to entity is visible on the parent or primary entity, on the navigational area of the form under the "Related" section, or can be made available within a sub-grid, as there can be more than one related record that must be displayed as a list.

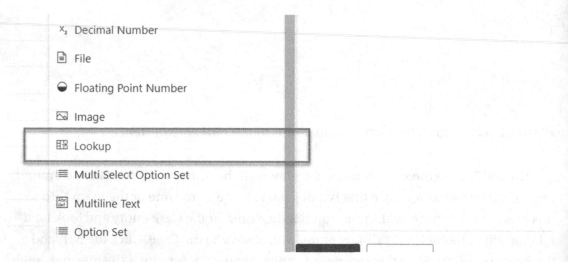

Figure 11-24. *A lookup field, which creates the relationship automatically*

This type of relationship infers that one entity can be referred to by many other entities. The related entities can only refer to one primary entity.

Another type of relationship is a many-to-many type. This type of relationship is not available as a field and is instead only available under the "Related items" within the tab menu on the UCI or within the extended menu in the Classic UI.

Many-to-many (N:N) relationships are where an entity can be linked to any number of secondary entities, and the second entity can be linked to any number of primary entities, and there is no constraint on the number. It is important to note that for one-to-many relationships, it will have a specific relationship name and reference reason. A commonly referenced example in software development is authors and books. Authors would have an N:N relationship with books, as there could be more than one author to a book; however, it would not be defined as a 1:N as it would be restricting the author to only writing one book. Lookups are restricted to only one record. Another example of a many-to-many relationship is where doctors have many patients and patients have many doctors.

When a many-to-many relationship is created in the Dynamics 365 CE user interface, an intersect entity is created within the database that is not visible to the user. This makes these types of relationships harder to report on than those with a 1:N relationship. It is often a design consideration to make two 1:N relationships and manually create an "Intersect" table to ensure reporting can be achieved by the user with ease. Examples of manual intersect entities within the standard system include Order Products and Opportunity Products entities, which are intersect entities between the Product and the Opportunity and Order entities.

Creating and Modifying Relationships

In the previous section, field creation was covered, which can include lookup type fields. 1:N and N:1 relationships can also be created via the maker experience within the entity metadata, as shown in Figure 11-21.

While they can be created within a lookup field, relationships have defined behavior that in some cases can be modified. These settings can be found under the relationship within the Solution Explorer, within the correct type, as highlighted in Figure 11-25.

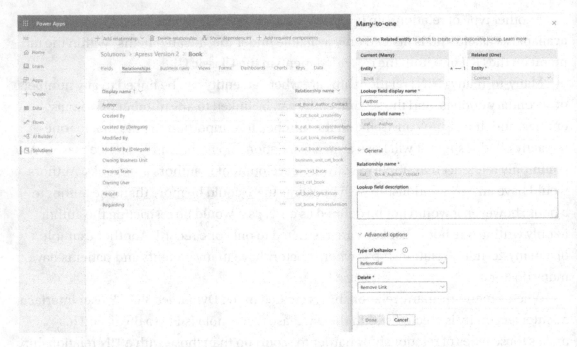

Figure 11-25. *Relationship configuration*

Relationship configuration can vary depending on the type of relationship. Here is an overview:

- **Searchable** – Available in Advanced Find

- **Hierarchical** – Used to define hierarchy visualizations in a 1:N relationship (configured in Hierarchy Settings within the entity metadata) – *not available in the maker experience at the time of writing, only in classic*

- **Type of behavior**

  - **Parental** – An action performed cascades to its children.

  - **Referential** – Not directly linked and only referred.

  - **Referential, Restrict Delete** – Not directly linked; however, delete is restricted if there are child entities.

  - **Configurable Cascading** – Custom settings.

The types of behavior operate on an action that is performed within the system – for example, when a record of this type is "assigned" or "re-parented" – and define what behavior should happen in this scenario. The types of behavior are covered extensively in the "Further Reading" section of the chapter.

Modifying the behavior of a relationship is critical as it determines what happens to related records, especially child records, if a parent is deleted. In parental-type relationships, a cascade delete occurs, which means child records are deleted along with their parent. It is recommended that relationships are reviewed when created to ensure the configured behavior is as expected.

Relationships can also be used to map fields when new records are created within the context of another. An example of this is when an Opportunity record is created as part of the lead-to-opportunity Business Process Flow or when a child record is created directly from a sub-grid. Configuring the mappings, as shown in Figure 11-26, allows you to configure which fields are automatically copied from the parent record to the new record being created, reducing manual data entry and errors.

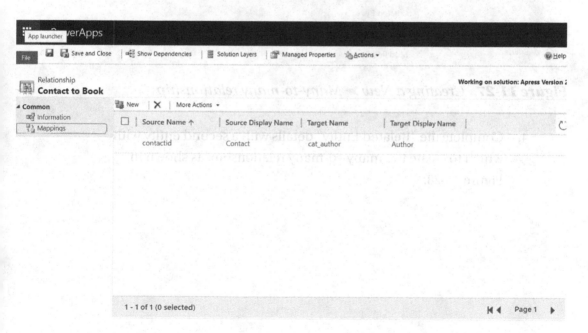

Figure 11-26. *Relationship mapping*

Task: Create a N:N relationship.

1. Navigate to the entity metadata via the maker experience for the custom entity you made in the earlier steps.

2. Select "N:N Relationships."

3. Click "New ➤ Many-to-many" as shown in Figure 11-27.

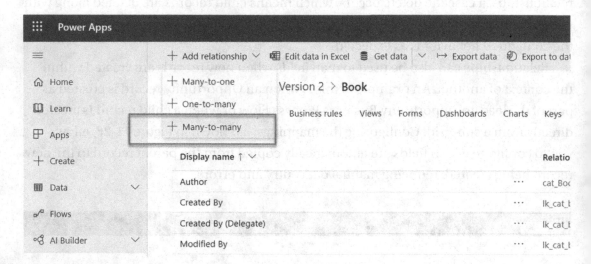

Figure 11-27. *Creating a New ➤ Many-to-many relationship*

4. Complete the "Related Entity" details with a second entity with which to create the many-to-many relationship, as shown in Figure 11-28.

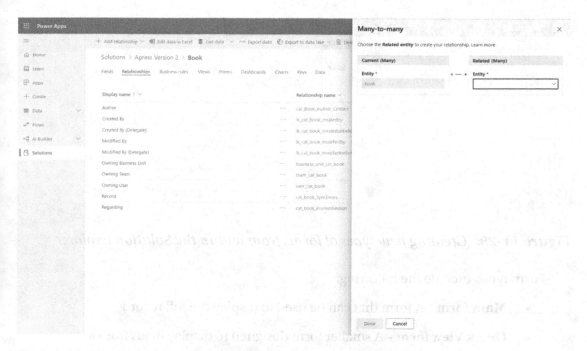

Figure 11-28. *Creating a New ➤ Many-to-many relationship*

5. Set the display options to use the plural names of the entities.

6. Select "Save and Close."

The relationship has now been made and can be used within the system.

For more information on relationship configuration, see the "Further Reading" section at the end of this chapter.

Forms

Forms within Dynamics 365 CE are the visual representation of the data fields. They also allow for other controls and visuals to be created. Their primary purpose is to display data and allow data to be created and modified by the user.

There are four main types of forms available (Figure 11-29). Entities can have multiple forms, and they are defined per app according to what is included in the App Designer.

Figure 11-29. *Creating new types of forms from within the Solution Explorer*

Form types include the following:

- **Main form** – A form that can be used to display the full record

- **Quick View form** – A smaller form designed to display fields from a parent entity (1:N) field referenced on the form

- **Quick Create form** – A form used by the Quick Create button on the navigation (the plus button) or using sub-grids from related entities

- **Card form** – A UCI client–only form used to configure how the "cards" appear within dashboards in the Unified Interface

For more information and a deep dive on forms, see the "Further Reading" section at the end of this chapter.

The form design experience is the same type of experience for each type of form. However, the design itself should be different depending on the type. The design for Quick Create forms, for example, should contain fewer fields for users to complete given that the purpose of the Quick Create form is to quickly create records as opposed to providing the full main form. The Card form, as it is used in dashboards, should only contain a small number of entities for high-level visibility as it is not meant to be used as a "full form" experience:

- The Card form type is aimed at displaying a high-level overview of information to a user. This is used on dashboards, for example.

- The Quick Create form definition is slightly larger compared to the Card form and is designed for users to quickly enter information.

- The Quick Create form can be used from the main navigation screen to quickly create new records.

- The Main form types are designed to see the full record and edit more details.

- The Quick View form is designed to also be smaller and display a collated view of details of a related record.

A great standard example is the "Contact" Quick View form in the Account entity by default. Within a Model-Driven App or in the maker experience itself, open an Account record with the primary contact record holding a value, as shown in Figure 11-30.

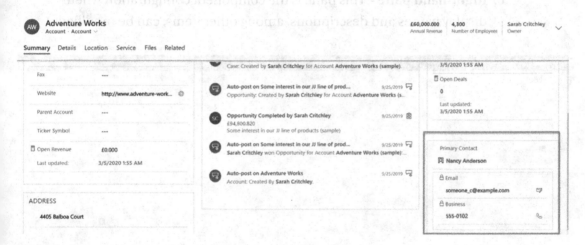

Figure 11-30.   *Quick View form of the Contact record on an Account entity*

Creating and Modifying Forms

This section will walk you through how to create and modify forms in Dynamics 365 CE.

Forms are created and modified using the Form Designer. This Form Designer is a drag-and-drop interface which allows you to easily configure the forms in a visual way. Only Main forms can be configured in this way; the other types of forms use the Classic Designer experience (more details can be found in the "Future Reading" section at the end of this chapter).

Task: Review and modify an existing form.

1. Open the "Main Form" for the entity you made in the previous step. This opens the Form Designer as shown in Figure 11-31:

    a. **Left-hand pane** - This is a list of the fields that can be dragged into the main central visual representation of the form. There is also an area selector on the far left to switch between adding components and fields and to see the tree view as shown in Figure 11-32.

    b. **Central form** – This is the main form and how it would be visible to users. You can drag the fields on the left panel over to the central form.

    c. **Right-hand pane** - This pane is the component configuration where display names and descriptions, among other items, can be modified.

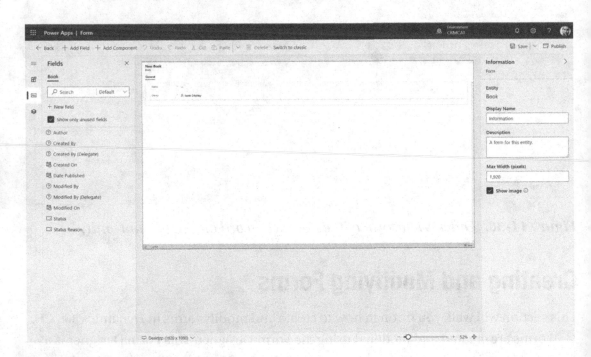

Figure 11-31. *The Form Designer*

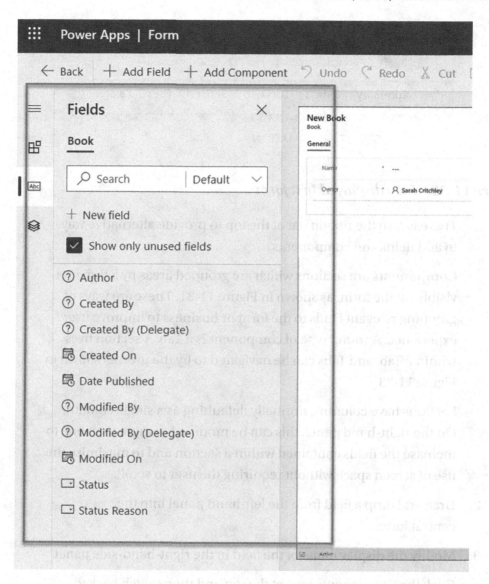

Figure 11-32. *The Form Designer in Dynamics 365 CE*

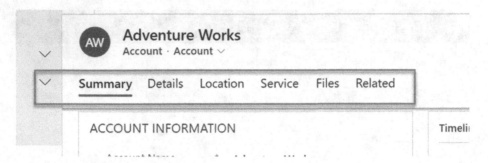

Figure 11-33. *Tabs displayed in a form*

There is also the ribbon bar at the top to provide alternative ways to add fields and components

Components are sections which are grouped areas by a thin line visible on the form, as shown in Figure 11-31. These are ways of grouping relevant fields to the form or business to improve user experience. Another type of component is a Tab. A section lives within a Tab, and Tabs can be navigated to by the user, as shown in Figure 11-33.

Sections have columns, normally defaulting as a single column. On the right-hand panel, this can be modified to more than one to increase the fields contained within a section and to maximize the use of screen space without requiring the user to scroll.

2. Drag and drop a field from the left-hand panel into the central form.

3. Modify the display name of the field in the right-hand-side panel.

4. Click the Components area at the top and then switch back to Fields.

5. Click the Components area on the left-hand-side panel.

6. Click one column Tab. Notice where the Tab was created and the name "Tab."

7. Select the Tab name ("Tab") and on the right-hand panel, name the Tab.

8. Select Components and click 1 Column Section.

9. Drag a number of fields into this section.

10. Continue to familiarize yourself with the Form Designer.

11. Click Save and publish your changes.

The available configurations in the Form Designer are extensive, so it is recommended to review each of these as a separate task in the Dynamics 365 CE system to see what is available and how it displays on the form. Further details to assist with this can be found in the "Further Reading" section at the end of this chapter.

Common options available in these areas include the following:

- Changing the width of a field

- Changing the form display name of fields

- Adding the name of tabs or sections

- Changing the column and field label alignment

- Making a field read-only

- Adding custom events on fields

- Adding business rules on fields

- Adding custom controls on fields

- Adding events on tabs (this is for developers using JavaScript)

To add a new form, navigate to "Forms" and click "New," using the dropdown to select which type (Figure 11-34). Quick Create forms can be disabled if the entity is not enabled for Quick Create (which is required to be switched on in the additional configuration of an entity). Click "Main Form" to create a new form a user would use in an Application such as Dynamics 365 or a Model-Driven App. An almost-empty form will open, allowing you to add in fields from the Form Designer in the same way as in the previous section.

Figure 11-34. *Creating a new form*

Sometimes it is quicker to use the "Save As" function on an existing form, especially when you need to make a form similar to one that exists already. If this is done, be aware of any events/scripting that will be copied over to the new form. Always check "Form Properties" and review them when using "Save As."

Additional Form Controls

There is a range of different controls on the form that enable you to add other data and operations.

The header options allow you to add in a header-type form feel to the record, keeping the fields there in view while the user navigates around different areas of the form.

Figure 11-35. *The header in the form via the Unified Interface*

You can add a sub-grid using the Insert tab and "Sub-grid" component (Figure 11-36). Sub-grids allow you to see related child records and can display specific views and configurations. This can help users review related records and perform actions upon them without having to open the individual records, potentially saving them large amounts of time. Sub-grids can also be made into "editable" grids. (For more information on editable grids, see Chapter 10.)

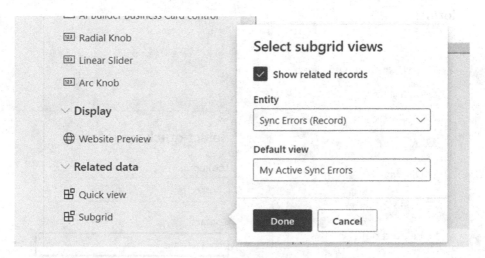

Figure 11-36. *Adding a sub-grid component*

Other types of components that can be added into a form are as follows (some may not be available via the latest Form Designer at the time of writing, and you must navigate to the classic experience by clicking "Switch to Classic" in the Form Designer) (Figure 11-37):

- **Bing Maps** – Adds in the Bing Maps component. A Bing Maps Key needs to be added, and this is enabled in the General tab in system settings.

- **Navigation Link** – Available when the user is in the "Navigation" area. Adds a web resource or external URL to the navigation items.

- **Social Insights** – Requires Social Engagement integration, and this is turned on in the administrative settings. Allows the user to specify social insight functionality for particular feeds.

- **Knowledge Base Search** – Adds the knowledge base search for any entity enabled for knowledge management (includes custom entities).

- **ACI Control** – Previously Azure Customer Insights; not usable at the time of writing.

- **Relationship Assistant** – Adds the relationship assistant control to forms.

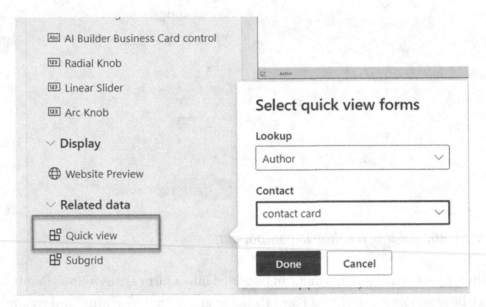

Figure 11-37. *Quick View form control on the Form Designer*

Quick View Forms

Quick View forms are designed to be embedded into a related entity's form where there is a lookup to a parent record from a 1:N relationship. They allow a user to see related fields from the record within the lookup field without having to select the record and load the form. The fields are displayed in a read-only state. The forms are particularly useful for quick reference and are normally designed with a small number of fields to give the user a snapshot of information.

Task: Add a Quick View form to a record.

1. Create the Quick View form for the related record that is being referenced (or use an existing one, e.g., from the Case entity).

2. Add a lookup field to make the reference to the record on the related entity, for example, Account. This is the entity that will show the form.

3. Once this has been created, while in the related entity's form in the Form Designer, click Components and select "Quick View Form" as shown in Figure 5-37.

4. Configure the name of the component, the referring entity, and the name of the Quick View form from that entity. Click "OK" and "Done."

5. Publish all customizations before navigating to the entity and seeing the Quick View form in action.

Quick View forms are empty and are not visible until the referencing lookup field holds a value.

Navigation Pane and Related Items

The navigation pane is only available in the Classic Form Designer at the time of writing. Navigate to this area by clicking "Switch to Classic" on the Form Designer.

The navigation pane is available on every entity under the "Related" tab. This shows all related child entities which are referencing the parent record which is being viewed. This tab is shown in Figure 11-38.

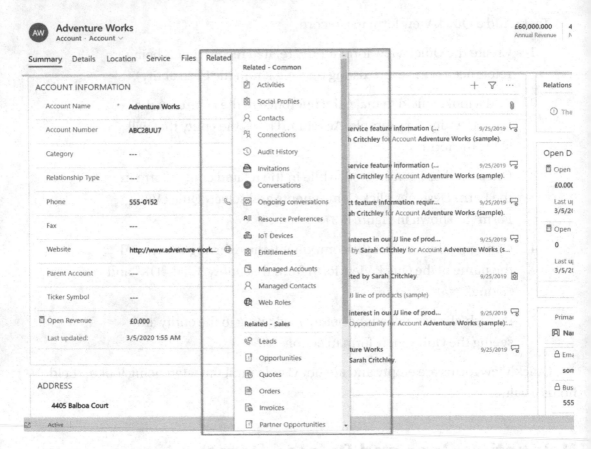

Figure 11-38. *The Related tab in an entity shows the related child records*

The following instructions relate to the Classic Designer, which has not been covered in this book. To learn more about the Classic Designer, see the "Further Reading" section.

The left-hand side of the Classic Form Designer allows you to change what users see under the Related tab within a form. When a user clicks the Related tab, they see the list of the entities visible in the navigation in a tab. These are the "many" records that are referencing the "one" record in a relationship (and equally can also include N:N) and are displayed in a list form when they are selected in this tab.

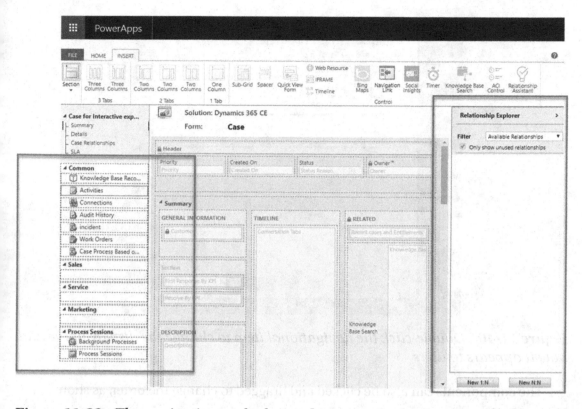

Figure 11-39.   *The navigation and relationship panes in the Form Designer*

In the Classic Form Designer, you can double-click the navigational component – for example, "Activities" – and change how it is displayed in the "Related" dropdown view. This is particularly useful to add a display name relevant to the business function.

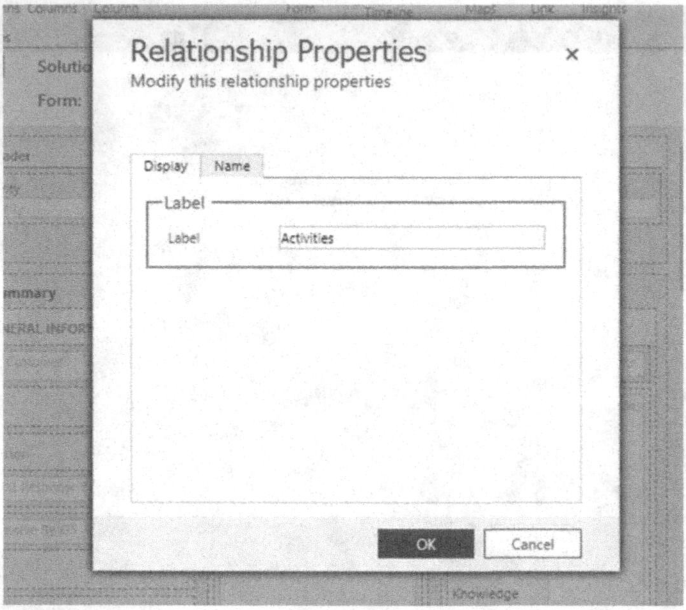

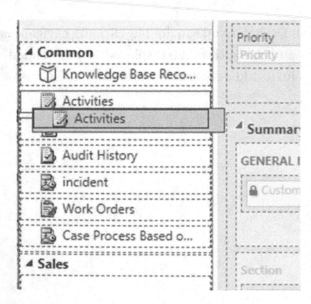

Figure 11-40. *Double-click the navigational item to change the display name and how it appears to users*

The components can also be clicked and dragged to change the order, as shown in Figure 11-41.

Figure 11-41. *Drag and move the navigational components*

On the right-hand side of the Form Designer is the Relationship Explorer. This pane allows users to create a new 1:N relationship (with the primary entity being the main entity the user is on) or an N:N relationship. Users can also select from available relationships that are not being used to add to the navigation pane. Relationships can only be used once on the navigational area and cannot be duplicated.

Updating the navigation is important to ensure a user navigating on the form has access to the most relevant records and that these are positioned near the top of the list for easy access.

Summary

UI customizations within Dynamics 365 CE have the potential to influence how a user interacts with the data within the system. This chapter has covered the numerous ways the user interface can be modified using the features of the platform. It covered creating new entities to store data, how to add new fields to those entities, and the extensive types of data that can be stored within Dynamics 365 CE, as well as the different types of forms that can present that data to the user and what controls can be added to make it easier to review and add data. Relationships and navigation between related records can assist users in how they see information that can influence decision-making and the next action a user takes, influencing the end customer experience. In summary, this chapter has covered ways to get started with the available UI customizations within Dynamics 365 CE to create a positive user experience for users of the platform and also the end customers.

Chapter Tasks

1. Create a new custom entity.

2. Create a range of new fields for the custom entity that includes all of the different field types.

3. Create a rollup field.

4. Create a calculated field.

5. Create a new form.

6.   Modify an existing form.

7.   Create a new N:N relationship.

8.   Configure a 1:N relationship.

9.   Add a reference panel to a form.

10.   Add a sub-grid to a form.

Further Reading

Virtual Entities (Microsoft, 2018). URL: `https://docs.microsoft.com/en-us/dynamics365/customer-engagement/developer/virtual-entities/get-started-ve`

Entities in Dynamics 365 CE (Microsoft, 2018). URL: `https://docs.microsoft.com/en-us/dynamics365/customer-engagement/customize/create-entities`

Types of Field (Microsoft, 2018). URL: `https://docs.microsoft.com/en-us/dynamics365/customer-engagement/customize/types-of-fields`

Rollup Field Reference (Microsoft, 2018). URL: `https://docs.microsoft.com/en-us/dynamics365/customer-engagement/customize/define-rollup-fields#rollup-calculations`

Calculated Field Reference (Microsoft, 2018). URL: `https://docs.microsoft.com/en-us/dynamics365/customer-engagement/customize/define-calculated-fields`

Relationship Behavior (Microsoft, 2018). URL: `https://docs.microsoft.com/en-us/dynamics365/customer-engagement/developer/entity-relationship-behavior#BKMK_CascadingBehavior`

Types of Forms (Microsoft, 2018). URL: `https://docs.microsoft.com/en-us/dynamics365/customer-engagement/customize/main-form-presentations`

CHAPTER 12

Processes

Processes are a way to implement custom business logic within Dynamics 365 Customer Engagement and the wider Power Platform in some cases. This business logic can include automation and Business Process Flows that are built within the application and that can be achieved often in a drag-and-drop control without the need for external tools or development. Using these tools to customize the system allows organizations to add operational value and provides the opportunity for more implementation of business processes, often reducing large maintenance overheads and the requirement for organizations to have development knowledge.

It is considered best practice within Dynamics 365 to review the standard features of the platform and then the capabilities of customization, before considering development for building more complex automation and processes. One of the best and most important practices when customizing the platform is to review the routes by which a requirement can be achieved using these three practices. Of course, custom code is not the enemy, and certainly a complex string of processes should not be created compared to logic that may be achieved using a few lines of code. All this is shown in Figure 12-1.

© Sarah Critchley 2020
S. Critchley, *Dynamics 365 Essentials*, https://doi.org/10.1007/978-1-4842-5911-5_12

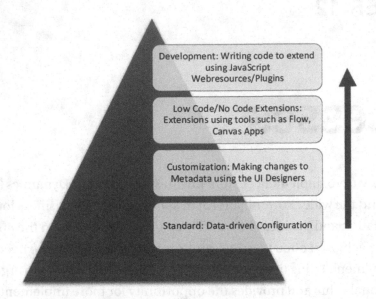

Figure 12-1. *Customizing Dynamics 365 CE*

The processes covered in this chapter are configurable for the most part within the maker experience, with only one on the Classic UI. They have an initial learning curve to begin using and maintaining them within the system. That said, the complexity is not the tools available but instead the implementation of the business logic. While Dynamics 365 CE provides a vast number of tools with which to implement powerful processing for businesses with relatively small amounts of effort, the business logic itself still requires thought, planning, documentation, and testing after implementation. The process should still be treated as a software project using implementation methodologies.

Starting with Processes

The types of processes covered in this chapter are as follows:

- **Business Process Flows** – Used to create guided processes for the user, configurable via the maker experience

- **Workflows** – Used to create real-time or background automation (see the following note; planned to be deprecated)

- **Actions** – Used to create platform operations and implement reusable logic used in workflows and Business Process Flows, configurable via the Classic UI

- **Business Rules** – Implements field-level-based logic via the maker experience

---

Dialogs are a process within Dynamics 365 CE; however, Microsoft has announced they will be deprecated. Look at using Business Process Flows, or canvas apps, to implement this type of workflow.

Since the Common Data Service and Dynamics 365 Unified Interface, the maker experience of processes has significantly been updated. Business Rules and Business Process Flows can still be seen using the classic experience; however, where possible, utilize the new experience in the Common Data Service.

In this updated version of *Dynamics 365 Essentials*, the examples in this chapter have been refreshed to be the latest Common Data Service Interface for Business Process Flows and Business Rules. Workflows have been moved to the end of this chapter for reference purposes (e.g., supporting a legacy system) and should not be used to create new processes where possible.

Business Process Flows

Business Process Flows are a guided process that allows users to be prompted for certain information required at specific steps in the process. Business Process Flows can include mandatory fields so that it becomes a gated process where such fields must be completed before allowing a user to move on to the next stage.

There are many Business Process Flows already in the system being used for standard processes. These include the Case entity, the lead-to-opportunity process, and opportunity management. The standard Case entity Business Process Flow can be seen in Figure 12-2. Business Process Flows are available on both the Classic UI and the Unified Interface with minor cosmetic and functional differences.

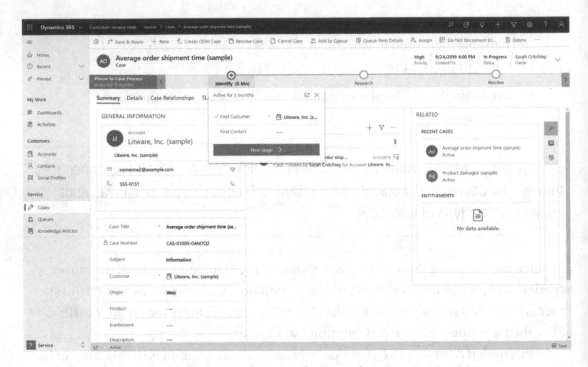

Figure 12-2. *Standard Business Process Flows within Dynamics 365*

To use a Business Process Flow, fill in the fields required at each named stage (in the Unified Interface, the stage name needs to be selected). In the example of the Case entity, the "Identify" stage is asking for the "Customer" field to be completed and also "Contact" if required. You would complete these, with the minimum being the "Customer," and then click the Next Stage button. The Next Stage button moves the Business Process Flow's active stage to the next stage, in the Case example, to "Research."

Business Process Flows can branch based on the type of data entered within the fields. You can get directed to different stages based on the data entered, presenting you with additional or various stages based on this. You do not have to be aware of the change in the branches themselves and can continue using the Business Process Flow based on the information required at the stage presented to you at the time. Related records can also be used within the Business Process Flow. An example of this is the standard lead-to-opportunity process flow, which uses both the Lead and the Opportunity entities, guiding the user from one to the other within a single screen. This experience can be created for up to five other standard or custom-enabled entities.

Within a record, you can utilize more than one Business Process Flow at once. You can use the Switch Process button (under the "Process" dropdown in some forms) and change to another active Business Process Flow available for your security role.

This means you can begin in one Business Process Flow, switch to another, and move back and forth as required so that more than one process is running at the same time. The first Business Process Flow you will see on a record will always be the first one in the list by default, even if you have switched to another instance. Business Process Flows are based on an entity. When they are created, a reciprocating entity is created in the background, and when you begin a Business Process Flow on a record, an instance of the Business Process Flow entity is created. This instance stores information related to the current state of the Business Process Flow.

Business Process Flows are finished once they reach the end and the user clicks "Finish." Various information is available for reporting on Business Process Flows, including the current stage, the time the process has taken to complete, and the time within each stage. This information can be found on the specific instances and can be used to trigger further automation processes, such as workflows or the basis of an organizational SLA.

One of the main operational differences in the Unified Interface is you can click the "popout" button in a Business Process Flow, which opens a pane on the right-hand side of the window, which you can use in the "docked" state (Figure 12-3). This reduces the need to keep clicking the stage name to check the fields, and you can review the form while having the stage information and fields locked in the right-hand side pane (Figure 12-4).

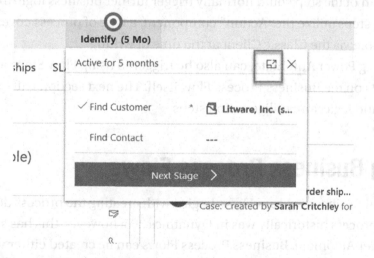

Figure 12-3. "Popout" button within the Dynamics 365 Unified Interface

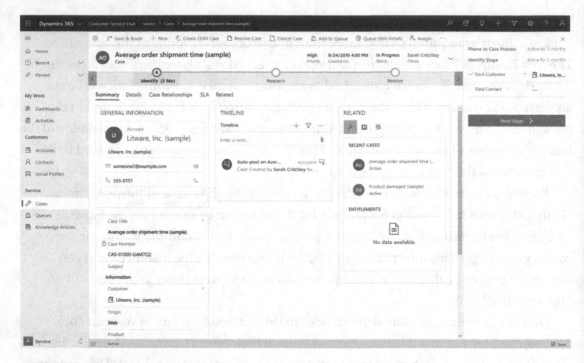

Figure 12-4.   *The docked Business Process Flow within the UCI*

Action steps can be embedded within Business Process Flows. Action steps are displayed as a button available within the Business Process Flow stage for you to select. They can also optionally prompt you to complete information to complete the step. The completion of the step could normally trigger further business logic from within the action. Action steps utilize the "Action" component, a type of process covered later in the chapter available via the Classic Client at the time of writing.

Flows, using Power Automate, can also be triggered using Flow Steps and from changing fields on the Business Process Flow itself. The next section will look at how to create them, add logic, and utilize action steps.

Creating Business Process Flows

The creation of Business Process Flows begins with creating the process definition. The creation process historically was in Dynamics 365; however, this has since been moved to Power Automate. Business Process Flows can be created either via the App Designer or directly from the maker experience in the Power Platform. It is recommend you use the maker experience route, which is the modern experience for creating Business Process Flows, as shown in Figure 12-5, where the user is prompted to enter the name, category (Business Process Flow), and record type (e.g., Case).

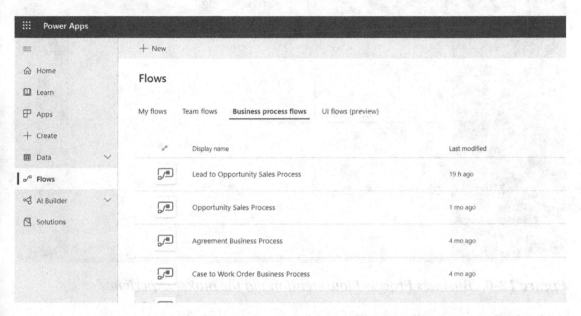

Figure 12-5. *Creating Business Process Flows from within the App Designer*

When a new Business Process Flow is made, a new entity is created behind the scenes. This can be seen in Figure 12-6, where the name of the entity is visible and can be modified. Instances of the Business Process Flow entity are created when a user begins a Business Process Flow or uses the switch process to select it. Information about that specific instance of Business Process Flow is then stored on that record.

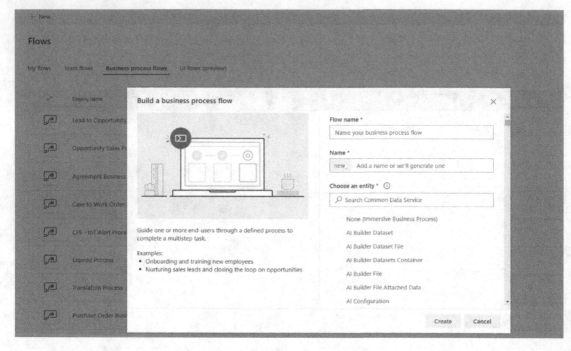

Figure 12-6. *Business Process Flow creation via the maker experience*

Task: Create a new Business Process Flow.

1. Navigate to the maker experience and click "Flows."

2. Select "Business Process Flows."

3. Click "New."

4. Enter a descriptive name for the process, select the entity, and click "Create." This opens the Business Process Flow Designer.

   A selection of the entity should open which is shown in Figure 12-7. This is where the entity to link with the Business Process Flow is selected. (There are also immersive Business Process Flows which require no entity – more on that later!)

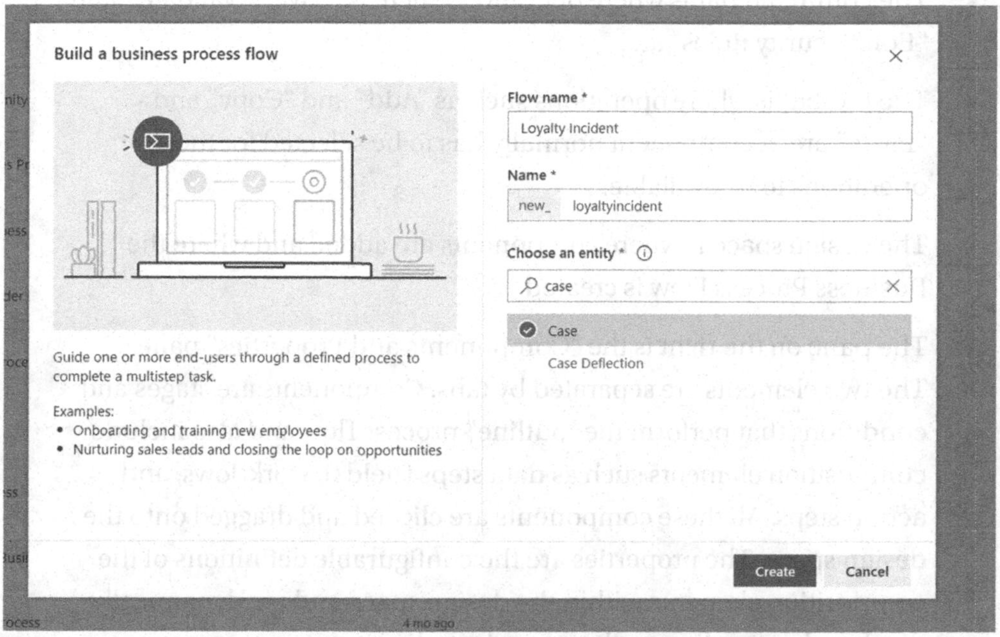

Build a business process flow   ×

Flow name *

Loyalty Incident

Name *

new_   loyaltyincident

Choose an entity * ⓘ

🔍 case   ×

✓ Case

Case Deflection

Guide one or more end-users through a defined process to
complete a multistep task.

Examples:
- Onboarding and training new employees
- Nurturing sales leads and closing the loop on opportunities

Create   Cancel

Figure 12-7. *Entity selection when creating a Business Process Flow*

The diagram shown in Figure 12-8 displays a breakdown of the
main components of the Business Process Flow Designer.

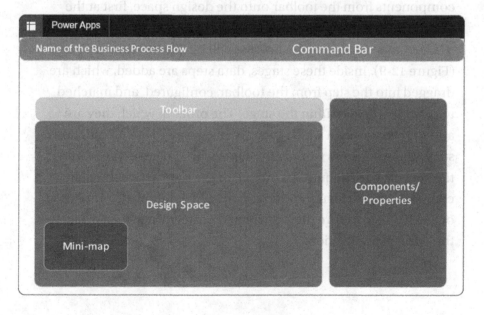

Figure 12-8. *Business Process Flow Designer overview*

- The command bar is where operations such as "Save," "Validate," and "Edit Security Roles" are.

- The toolbar is where operations such as "Add" and "Copy" and "Paste" are. A component normally has to be selected for these operations to be available.

- The design space is where components are added and where the Business Process Flow is created.

- The pane on the right is the "Components and Properties" pane. The two elements are separated by tabs. Components are stages and conditions that perform the "outline" process flow and also include composition elements such as data steps (fields), workflows, and action steps. All these components are clicked and dragged onto the design space. The properties are the configurable definitions of the composition elements within the design space and are dynamically displayed depending on the one selected.

- The *minimap* allows for a high level of visibility, which is useful for more complex or larger Business Process Flows.

To begin Business Process Flow design, click and drag the components from the toolbar onto the design space, first at the stage level, including any conditional components, to create a "flow" that the user of the process will be guided through (Figure 12-9). Inside these stages, data steps are added, which are dragged into the step from the toolbar, configured, and matched to reference fields within the stage. The order in which they are added is the order in which they are displayed to the user. Action steps and workflows work in the same way and are dragged into the specific stage required. Once all of the stages have the right components, the final step should include defining the properties on each one to ensure they are named correctly and are correct to the design specification.

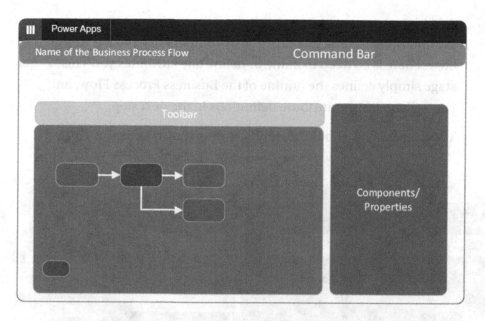

Figure 12-9. *Business Process Flow components added to the design space*

5. The designer has one stage set up at the time of creation. Click the Components tab.

6. Click and drag the "Condition" component into the design area and connect it with the stage by dropping it onto the plus icon (Figure 12-10). The plus icon displays when a component is dragged into the design area to indicate the connecting points for a component and where they can be added.

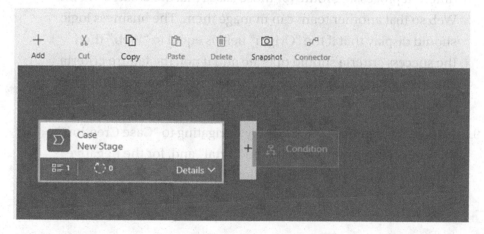

Figure 12-10. *Adding a "Condition" component on a Business Process Flow*

7. Add two more stages for the positive and negative exit points to the condition by dragging the "Stage" components into the design area. There is no need to name or define any attributes yet. This stage simply defines the outline of the Business Process Flow, and you will modify the attribute definitions in the next step.

The process flow should currently look as shown in Figure 12-11.

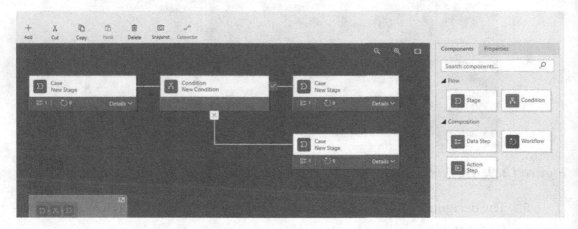

Figure 12-11. *A basic Business Process Flow with a conditional component branch*

8. Enter the conditional business logic on the "Condition" component as "If Origin" which equals "Value" of "Web," as shown in Figure 12-12. The purpose of this logic is to offer a different processing route for those cases that are created via the Web so that another team can manage them. The business logic should display that if the "Origin" field is equal to "Web," then the success criteria should operate and if not, the failure criteria should operate, indicated by the "cross" on the routing line from the condition.

9. Update the names of the stages by navigating to "Case Creation" ➤ "Check Origin" ➤ "Respond on Portal" and, for the negative conditional outcome, "Email Follow Up."

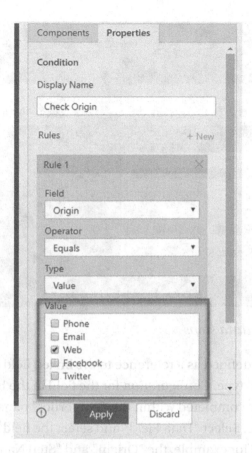

Figure 12-12. *Adding conditional logic*

10. The stages will have a single data step (field) already created within them automatically. Add the fields for the user to complete per stage. The same process occurs where the "Data Step" component is dragged, but this time it gets dragged into the stage itself. Click and drag, and the stage will have the same plus icon as the larger stage components did when connecting the condition.

11. Move two data step components into the "Case Creation" stage, the "Respond on Portal" stage, and also the "Email Follow Up" stage (Figure 12-13).

447

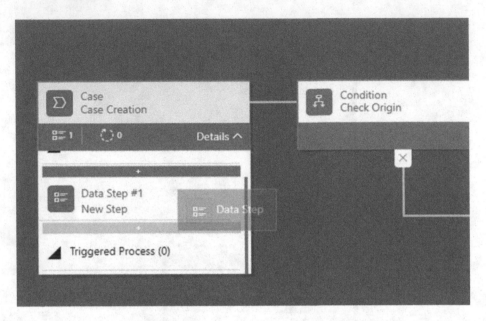

Figure 12-13. *Adding data steps*

12. Data steps are defined as a reference to the linked field on the
     selected record type. Configuration for the field in the Business
     Process Flow is completed within the "Properties" pane on the
     right-hand side. Select "Data Field" and select the field from the
     dropdown list; for example, the "Origin" and "Step Name" fields
     are automatically populated with the same name (Figure 12-14).
     It can be modified as required, often because a shorter name or
     a task-based label is needed. If the field is required and the user
     must be prevented from moving forward until this is complete,
     set "Required" to "Yes." The order can be changed using the
     "Sequence" dropdown without having to drag and move them.

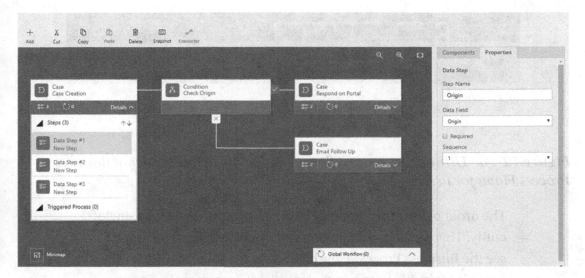

Figure 12-14. *Configuring the "Data Step" fields in the properties*

Important!   If the field is changed from the one originally set, the step name does not change.

---

13.   Complete the field definitions as shown in the table in Figure 12-15.

Case Creation Stage	Process on Portal Stage	Email Follow Up Stage
Origin	First Response By	Email Checked
Find Customer	First Response Sent	First Response Sent
Subject		

Figure 12-15. *Business Process Flow field reference*

The Business Process Flow design and definition are now completed. Workflows and action steps can be added in the same way as the data steps, where they are clicked and dragged from the right-hand-side panel onto the definition in the design space (Figure 12-16).

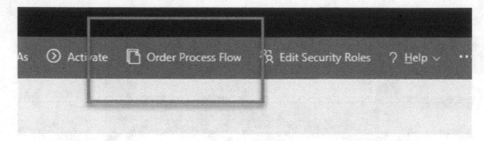

Figure 12-16. *Using order process flow to define the default order of Business Process Flows for users*

The order of Business Process Flows can be prioritized on a single entity. This works in conjunction with security roles. The user will see the Business Process Flow highest on the list first (which will be their "default") based on their available security role. To move the Business Process Flows higher or lower, use the up and down arrows on the dialog box (Figure 12-17).

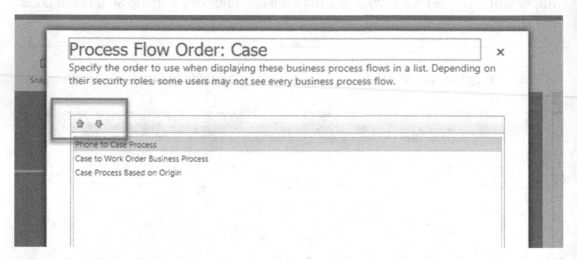

Figure 12-17. *Use the up and down arrows to configure the default order*

The Business Process Flow Designer also includes a shortcut to the security role list if you need to modify the security roles and control which roles have access to this entity. The Business Process Flow must be saved, validated, and activated before its name will correctly display in the Business Process Flow list within the security role.

Click the "Edit Security Role" button and select the security role
to modify (Figure 12-18). Navigate to the Business Process Flows
tab within the security role to see the process with the name just
created, modify the security privileges as required, and save the
role (Figure 12-19).

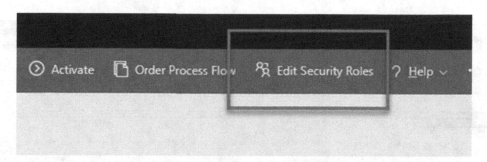

Figure 12-18. *Click "Edit Security Roles" to configure the security role and security
for the Business Process Flow just created*

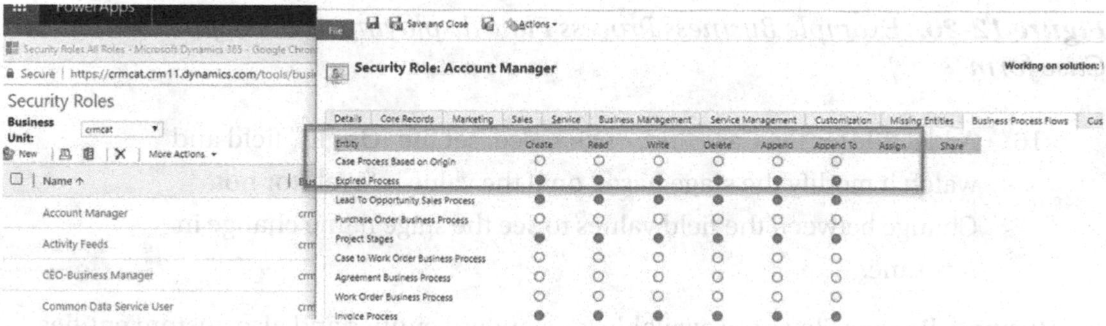

Figure 12-19. *The business process is defined as an entity, and privileges can be
defined within the security role definition under the Business Process Flows tab*

For single-entity Business Process Flows, Create, Read, and Write
privileges are required within a security role. Delete is required
if an instance of a Business Process Flow (where one has been
started) needs to be deleted. Append and Append To privileges
are used for cross-entity Business Process Flows that utilize more
than one entity. For more information on security, please see
Chapter 4.

14. Save and publish the Business Process Flow and navxigate to the app and the Case entity.

15. Create a new Case entity to see the Business Process Flow in action (Figure 12-20). (If it is not displaying, ensure it is included within the app.)

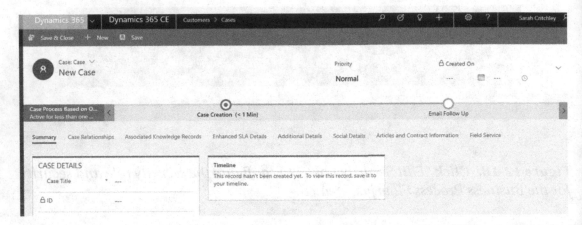

Figure 12-20. *Example Business Process Flow displaying as the default within the Case form*

16. Add a title for the Case and, once saved, set the "Origin" field and watch it modify the stage based on if the value is "Web" or not. Change between the field values to see the stage name change in real time.

Business Process Flows are available for standard entities and also custom entities. The "Business Flow" flow option needs to be selected within the entity metadata (Figure 12-21). Once this option is selected, it cannot be turned off.

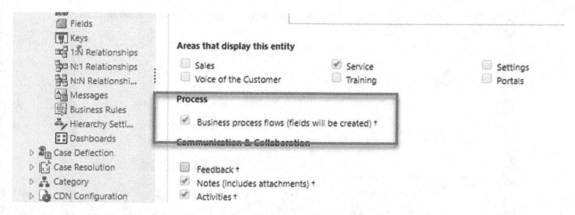

Figure 12-21. *Configuring an entity to use Business Process Flows*

This section has covered what Business Process Flows are, how to use them, and how to get started building a new Business Process Flow. Business Process Flows can be created for custom or existing entities, and their ordering and security roles are defined, giving organizations the capability to manage users in different departments and display the correct process. They are an excellent way of implementing custom-guided processes that can include mandatory gateways and conditional branching.

Immersive Business Process Flows

In the previous section which explored Business Process Flows, there was the option when creating a new process to select no Common Data Service entity. In the past, Business Process Flows have been reliant on an entity to be "attached" to them. This is no longer required and allows a user to choose to select the immersive experience to create a process without the entity reliance.

When new Business Process Flows are created, a new entity is created in the background which then users can build upon. To do this, select "None (Immersive Business Process)" when selecting the entity when you create a new Business Process Flow.

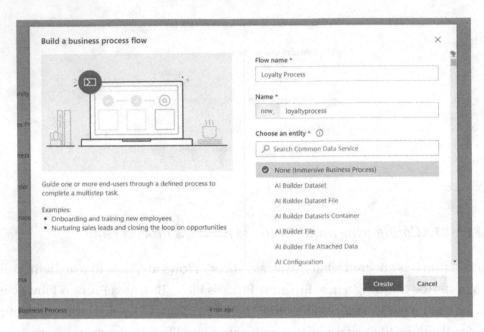

Figure 12-22. *Configuration for an immersive Business Process Flow*

Calling Other Processes from a Business Process Flow

Actions can run within a Business Process Flow using an Action Step within the Stage. If that Action requires user input, it can be configured to request input within a popup when a user selects the Action Step button. To configure an Action for a Business Process Flow, specify this on the "Available to Run" section on the configuration in an Action, as shown in Figure 12-23.

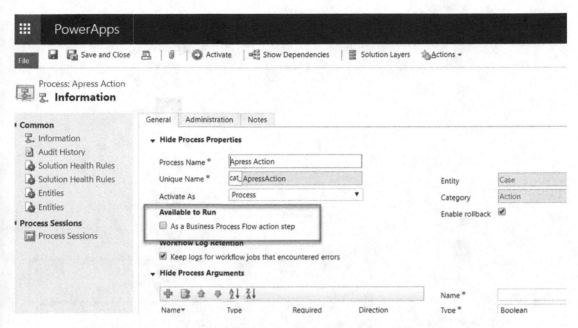

Figure 12-23. *Setting an action to run as a Business Process Flow step*

Flows, from Power Automate, can also be called from a Business Process Flow in a similar way. A user would select the button on a Business Process Flow which links to a Flow. Select the "Flow Step" (in preview at the time of writing) and select your Flow to use this feature.

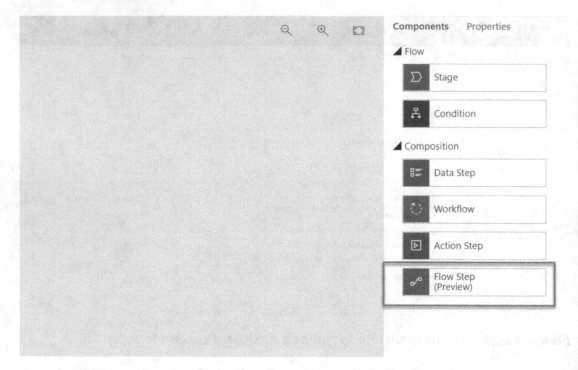

Figure 12-24. *A Flow Step component in a Business Process Flow*

Actions

Actions within Dynamics 365 CE are a type of process that acts as a reusable component to be utilized by workflows and Business Process Flows. Actions can optionally take an input, perform business logic, and produce an output. Custom actions can be built using the UI or can perform more complex business logic within code and be saved and imported into the platform to be used within workflows. Actions are particularly useful because they are an encapsulated piece of business logic that can then be used by customizers of the system without ever having to use the code. For this reason, they are a great investment to utilize within projects.

Actions, unlike classic workflows or "Flows" in Power Automate, have no trigger. Actions are the input, logic, and output only and are expected to be used within other processes like workflows and Business Process Flows that do have a trigger. What is useful about actions is that the more generic they are, the more they can be utilized within the platform.

There are a set of standard action processes that are available with Dynamics 365 CE and can be used by customizers right away. Using Classic Workflows, they used to be found within the "Perform Action" step within a workflow under the heading "Command Actions," as shown in Figure 12-25. Now they can be used in Flow under the "Perform action" Action in any automated Flow. These actions are the same actions utilized with the functionality of many of the standard processes of Dynamics 365 CE, such as "ResolveQuote" and "QualifyLead."

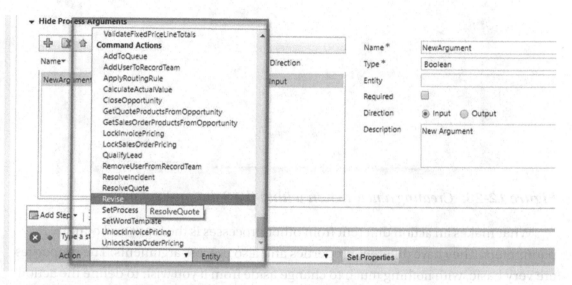

Figure 12-25. *Standard actions available within the system*

Creating Custom Actions

Creating an action needs to be completed using the Classic Client at the time of writing. From within the Solutions area of the maker experience, select the expanded menu and select "Switch to Classic." Select "Processes" and specify the category of a new process needs to be set to "Action," and the entity needs to be specified, as shown in Figure 12-26. This opens the Action Designer and the definition.

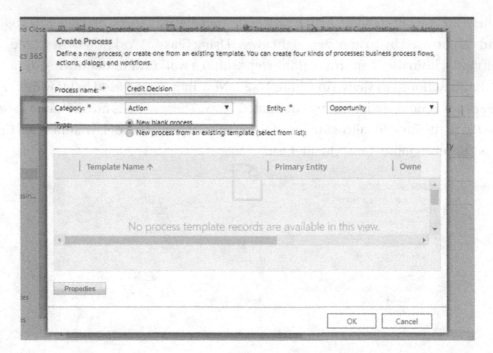

Figure 12-26. *Creating a new action within the Solution Explorer*

What makes an action different from other processes is the input and output parameters. They have different properties and also process arguments. The properties are very basic, with nothing much to change aside from if you wish to define the action as an action step as shown in Figure 12-27.

Action steps are a feature that allows for an action to be embedded inside a button in a Business Process Flow stage (Figure 12-28). When selected, a dialog window opens presenting the input parameters to the user to be completed. This is especially useful for incorporating manual processes within a guided Business Process Flow, with the "trigger" being manual. The output and follow-up action are self-contained within the action rather than reliant on a secondary process, such as a workflow, to finish the work.

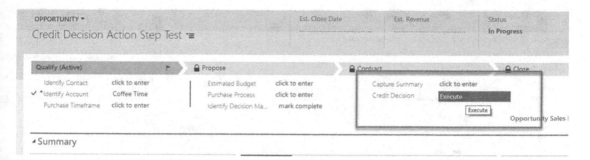

Figure 12-27. *Action step within a Business Process Flow*

The process arguments within an action are specified as an object, which can be an input or an output, and also have a type (Figure 12-28). The type is very similar to the type of the fields within Dynamics 365, for example, text and numerical (for more information on fields, see Chapter 11).

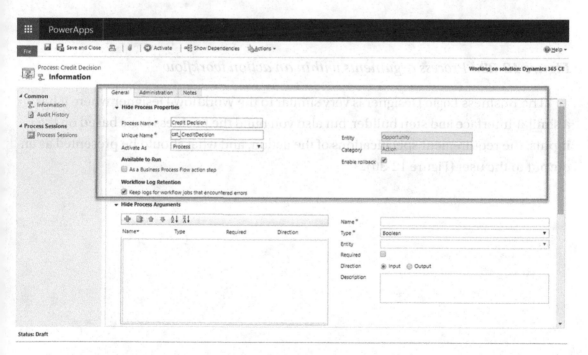

Figure 12-28. *Process properties within an action*

Other configuration elements can be added, including if the argument is required and the description. The arguments are used to store information either entered by the user as input or to perform operations on within the business logic and then provided as an output to the user (Figure 12-29).

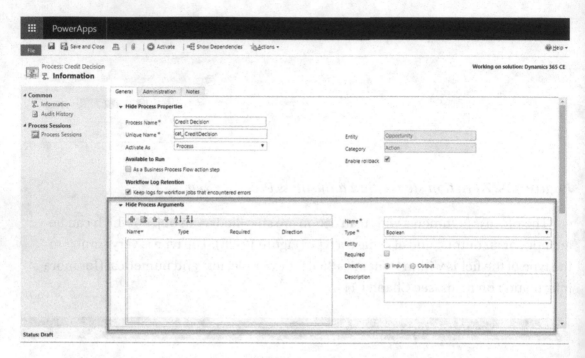

Figure 12-29. *Process arguments within an action workflow*

The Business Logic Designer is very similar to the Workflow Designer where it has a similar interface and step builder, but also you build the business logic based on the inputs, the requirement specifications of the action, and what should be presented as an output to the user (Figure 12-30).

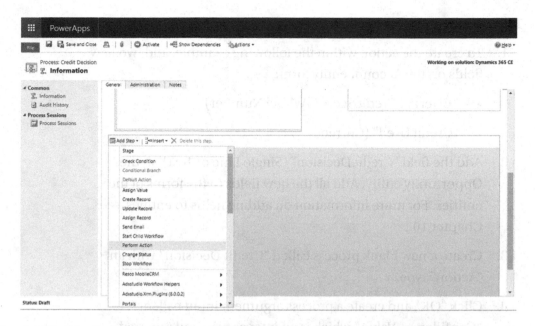

Figure 12-30. *Steps available within an Action Designer differ slightly from the Workflow Designer*

Arguments specified within the process are available to be used, as seen in Figure 12-31, to perform conditional checks and within updates to records.

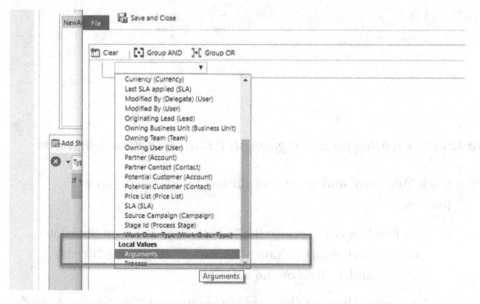

Figure 12-31. *Arguments are available within the Process Designer under "Local Values"*

Task: Create a custom action.

1. To create the action within the following example, add two new fields on the Account entity form:

   - "External Credit Score" (Whole Number)

   - "Credit Used" (Currency)

2. Add the field "Credit Decision" (Single Line of Text) on the Opportunity entity. Add all the new fields to the forms of the entities. For more information on adding fields to entities, see Chapter 10.

3. Create a new blank process called "Credit Decision" with an "Action" type.

4. Click "OK" and create a process argument input called "Confidence_Value," which is an integer type and required.

5. Select "Available to Run" as an action step in the properties (Figure 12-32).

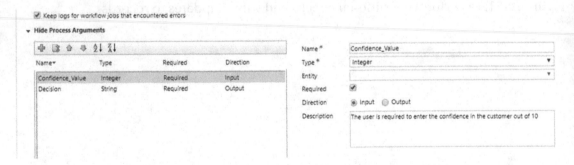

Figure 12-32. *Creating process arguments within an action definition*

6. Click "Add Step" and select "Condition." Build the condition as follows:

   - The first line is a check for the "Credit Used" field on the related account (Potential Customer (Account)) against the "Credit Limit" standard field on the account.

   - The second line is a check that the argument "Confidence_Value" is greater than 6.

- The third line is to check that the external credit score for the related account is greater than 5. See Figure 12-33.

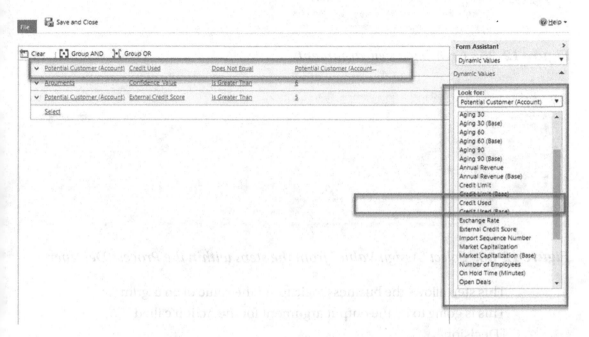

Figure 12-33. *Use the Form Assistant to add dynamic values into the "Value" field on the first line*

All of the lines have to equal to true for the next business logic to execute, as shown in Figure 12-34.

⌑ Clear	[•] Group AND	}•[Group OR	
∨ Potential Customer (Account)	Credit Used	Does Not Equal	Potential Customer (Account...
∨ Arguments	Confidence Value	Is Greater Than	6
∨ Potential Customer (Account)	External Credit Score	Is Greater Than	5
Select			

Figure 12-34. *The final condition should appear in three lines*

7. Create a new argument that is an output argument of type string called "Decision" (Figure 12-35). Click "Add Step" and select the "Assign Value" step (Figure 12-36).

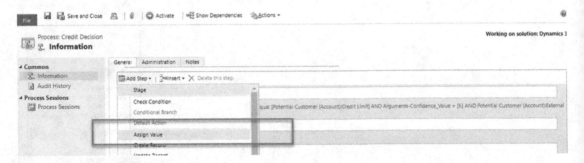

Figure 12-35. *Creating a new argument*

Figure 12-36. *Select "Assign Value" from the steps within the Process Designer*

This step allows the business logic to set the value of an argument. This is going to be the output argument for the Action called "Decision."

8. Click "Set Properties" (Figure 12-37).

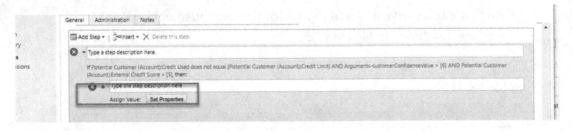

Figure 12-37. *Set properties of the value within the Process Designer*

9. A new window will appear in which to configure the properties of the value. Name it "Statement Label" and enter the value for the argument as "Passed." The "Name" field is a dropdown of all the arguments of the type "output" defined within the action.

At this point in the design, the action process could be finished and then utilized in a workflow. The workflow would "call" the action and enter the input decision in its properties, and then the action would have an output decision that the workflow could then use and update a record with. The action created here as an example can be utilized within a workflow by selecting "Perform Action" on a workflow definition that is linked to the Opportunity entity (or related entity).

When the action is used in other areas, such as action steps, it can hold the extra steps so as to update the opportunity with the value from the output argument. The next steps in this walk-through add in follow-up actions.

10. Click "Update Record" and "Set Properties" on the Opportunity record.

11. On the Form Assistant, click "Look for" and then "Local Values" and "Arguments" (Figure 12-38).

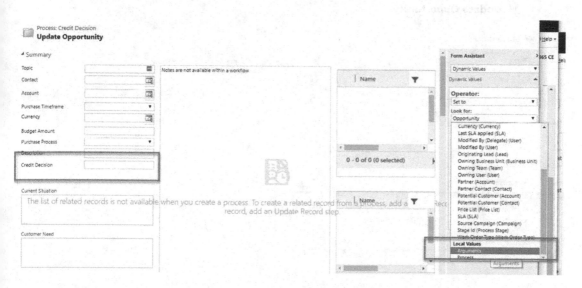

Figure 12-38. *Update the record with the dynamic values from "Local Values" within the Form Assistant*

The arguments available are "Decision" and also the input argument "Confidence_Value" (Figure 12-39).

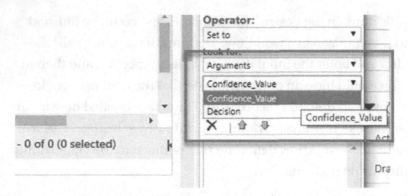

Figure 12-39. *Both arguments are available in the "Local Values" area of the action*

12. Click the "Decision" value and select "OK."

13. Move the cursor into the "Credit Decision" field on the Opportunity form and then select "OK" on the Form Assistant to add the dynamic value into the field (Figure 12-40).

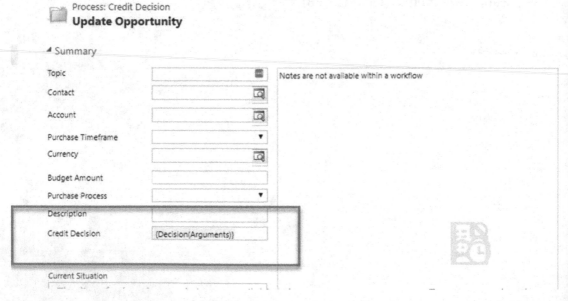

Figure 12-40. *The argument's value can be utilized as a dynamic value within a Create or Update step*

14. Save and close the properties and activate the action.

Task: Add the action into a Business Process Flow as an action step.

This section will take the action made in the previous steps and add it into an existing Business Process Flow:

1. In the solution, under "Processes," click "Add Existing" and select "Opportunity Sales Process" (Figure 12-41).

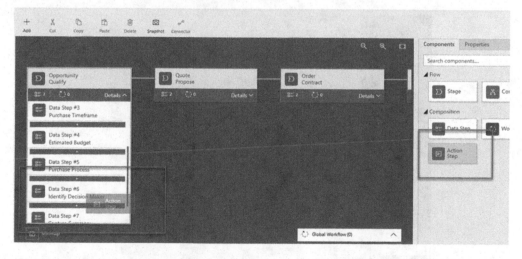

Figure 12-41. *Select an existing process to add into the solution via the Solution Explorer*

2. Open the "Opportunity Sales Process" Business Process Flow and expand the "Opportunity: Qualify" stage.

3. Drag the "Action Step" component over to the stage from the component list, as shown in Figure 12-42.

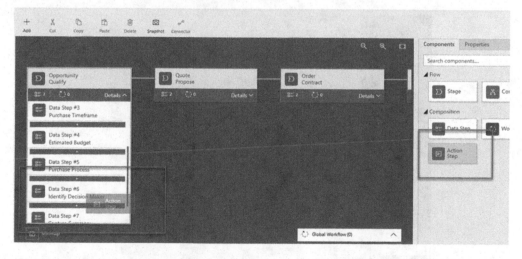

Figure 12-42. *Add an "Action Step" component within the existing Business Process Flow*

4. On the properties of the action step, name the component "Credit Decision," which will be the name that appears to the user.

5. Select the action made in the earlier step within the "Execute Process" lookup (Figure 12-43).

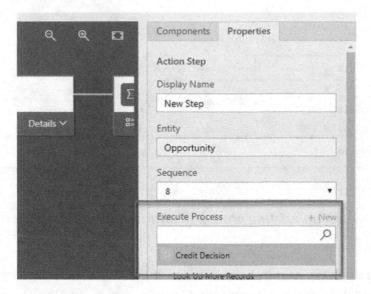

Figure 12-43. *Add the Credit Decision action within the "Execute Process" field*

6. Do not manually enter any input or output arguments; leave them empty, as shown in Figure 12-44.

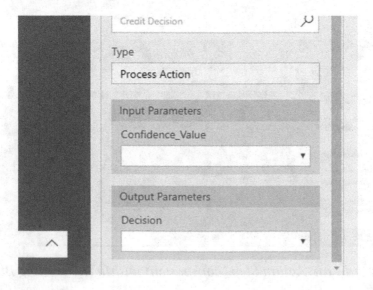

Figure 12-44. *Leave the input and output parameters for the action blank*

468

7. Update the Business Process Flow by selecting "Update."

Task: Test the action step.

This last section will cover testing the action step:

1. Open an Account record and add the following details into the custom fields added at the start of this section:

    - **"Credit Limit"** – 2,000

    - **"Credit Used"** – 100

    - **"External Credit Score"** – 9

2. Save the record.

3. Create a new Opportunity record and associate the Account record, naming the Opportunity record and saving it.

4. Within the first stage of the Business Process Flow should be an action step called "Credit Decision." Click "Execute," and the input parameter dialog should appear requesting the input (Figure 12-45).

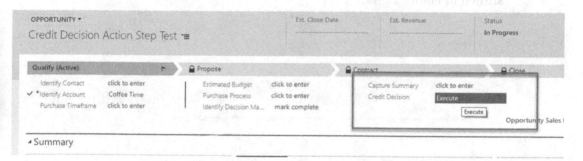

Figure 12-45. *The action step has been added within the Business Process Flow*

5. Enter "8" in the "Confidence_Value" field when this is prompted and click "Execute" (Figure 12-46).

Figure 12-46. *Selecting the action step opens the input dialog request for the user to complete*

6. The "Credit Decision" field should now be updated to "Passed," as shown in Figure 12-47.

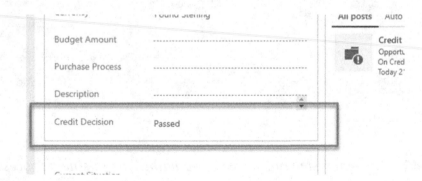

Figure 12-47. *Completing the action performs the final logic and updates the "Credit Decision" field*

Action steps are a robust way to add processes that require a manual input into a Business Process Flow (Figure 12-48). At the time of writing, they are still in preview and are not supported in production environments. Actions allow organizations to create encapsulated business logic so that it can be reused by other processes.

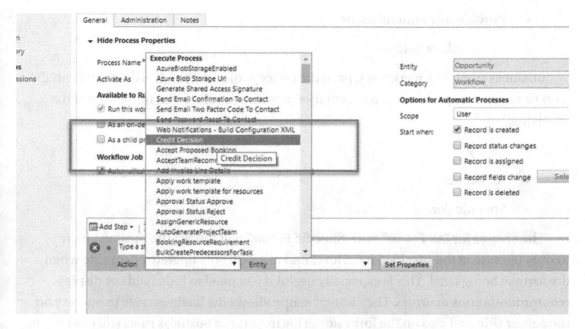

Figure 12-48. Using the action within a workflow using the "Perform Action" step

Business Rules

Business rules are not strictly a type of "process" within Dynamics 365 CE. That said, they are a feature within the Common Data Service that allows you to create business logic at the form level. Form-level business logic allows organizations to implement instant logic and can help guide the user with decisions or prevent errors that would normally be implemented by custom scripting. Using business rules enables a no-code approach that can be adopted and owned by more people within the organization and is often quicker to change should there be need to.

Users can use the same **Process Designer** as was used for Business Process Flows to create business logic on fields that allow the following:

- Fields to be set with values or cleared

- Set requirements (mandatory)

- Show or hide fields

- Validate and check data

- Display error messages

- Provide recommendations

- Lock/unlock fields

Business rules, like workflows, have the concept of a "scope." It is different from the workflow-type scope. Instead, a user can set a business rule to run under one of the following:

- Entity

- All Forms

- Specific Forms

The scopes for "All Forms" and "Specific Forms" will restrict the business logic to only operate at the specified form level and also will only operate client side when the form is being used. This is especially useful if you need to hide fields or display recommendations or errors. The "Entity" scope allows the business rule to operate on the server side and also on the form side. This means the business rules will operate on any operation that involves updating that entity. In addition to that, the "Entity"-scoped business rules operate in real time, which means the changes will apply to the form instantly for the user to see. It is important that all the fields that a business rule uses are available on the form so they are able to trigger. In the same way as if you were using an editable grid, all fields need to be available on the view used in order for a business rule to activate.

Business rules can be created directly from the Common Data Service via the entity as shown in Figure 12-49.

Figure 12-49. *Access Business Rules in the Common Data Service*

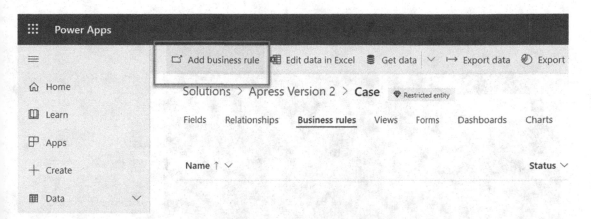

Figure 12-50. *Create a new Business Rule*

Task: Create a new business rule from the Common Data Service.

The following example will add a basic condition on the Case form to set the "Resolution" field as mandatory if a resolution date has been set:

1. Navigate to the Common Data Service and select the entity (via a solution ideally) and select "Business Rules" as shown in Figure 12-49.

2. Click "New" to create a new blank business rule as shown in Figure 12-50.

3. The empty Process Designer will open, as shown in Figure 12-51. This is the same designer as the Business Process Flow Designer. For a more detailed explanation of the user interface, please refer to the previous section in this chapter, which covers it in depth.

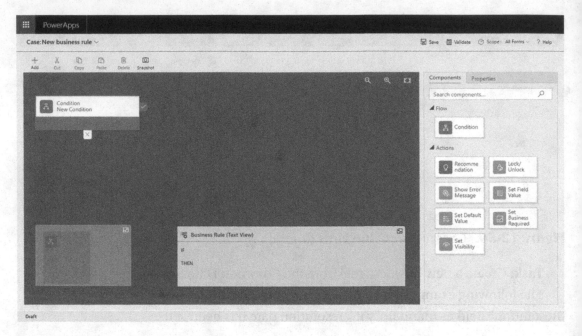

Figure 12-51. *Business Rule Designer*

4. Set the business rule scope to "Entity" by changing the "Scope" dropdown field in the top right-hand corner of the Process Designer.

5. Set the condition on whether the "Resolution Date" field contains data (Figure 12-52). Add this condition using the "Properties" pane on the right-hand side, with the condition block selected in the design space.

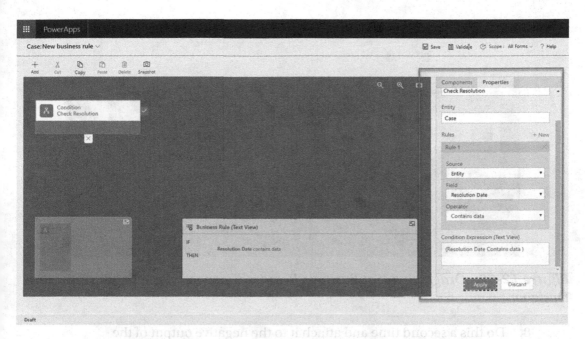

Figure 12-52. *Adding in the condition for the business rule in the "Properties" pane*

6. Add a name to the business rule by selecting the dropdown next to the name.

7. Click the Components tab and drag the "Set Business Required" component onto the design space, attaching it to the positive output of the condition. This is shown in Figure 12-53.

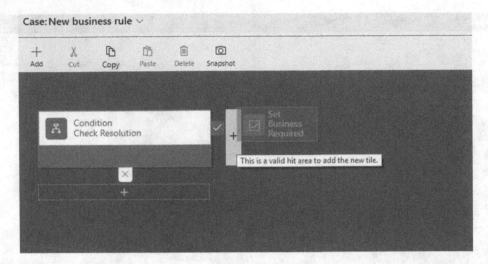

Figure 12-53. *Dragging a "Set Business Required" property into the Business Rule Designer*

8. Do this a second time and attach it to the negative output of the condition. These will set the field to "Business Required" for the positive case and to "Optional" for the negative case.

9. Click the components in the design space and set the properties so the field is related to the "Resolution" field for both components and the status is set to "Business Required" and the negative outcome of the condition is set to "Not Business Required" (Figure 12-54).

Figure 12-54. *Defining the condition for the Business Required action in the "Properties" pane*

10. Ensure the display names of all components are descriptive for actions they are performing.

11. Name the business rule by selecting the "Business Rule Name" field at the top of the screen and entering the name, as shown in Figure 12-55.

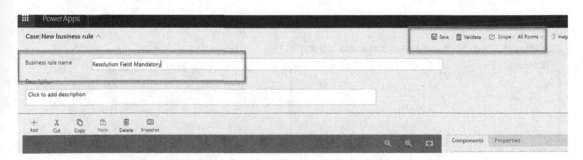

Figure 12-55. *Naming the business rule*

12. Click "Save" and then "Validate." Validation checks for any errors within the process and will highlight them in an error list at the top of the design space.

13.   Click "Activate" (Figure 12-56).

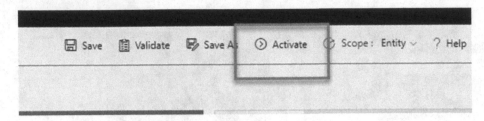

Figure 12-56. *Select "Activate" in the Business Rule Designer*

Task: Test the business rule.

1.   Open a Case entity in which to test the field in action. Once a
       resolution date is entered, the field "Resolution" now becomes
       mandatory. If the "Resolution Date" field is empty and contains
       no data, the resolution date now is no longer mandatory
       (Figure 12-57).

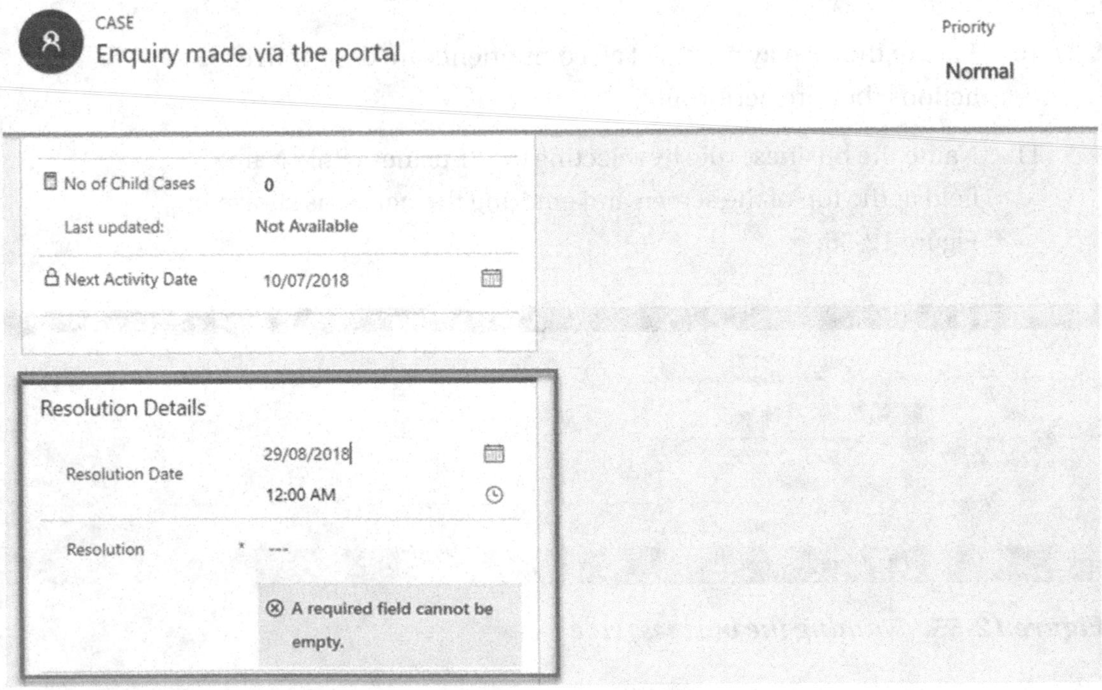

CASE
Enquiry made via the portal   Priority

                                                                                           Normal

No of Child Cases   0

Last updated: Not Available

Next Activity Date   10/07/2018   📅

Resolution Details

                           29/08/2018   📅
Resolution Date
                           12:00 AM   🕐

Resolution   *   ---

                           ⊗ A required field cannot be
                              empty.

Figure 12-57. *Testing the business rule*

This section has reviewed Business Rules and what they are capable of. The preceding example would have normally required scripting within the platform, and business rules allow this to be done using basic logic.

Workflows

As highlighted at the start of this chapter, **workflows have been announced as being deprecated from the Dynamics 365 system**. Power Automate is being recommended as the alternative, and as a maker, you will see this recommendation in the system if you are to create a new Workflow using the classic experience.

This section of the chapter has been kept and moved to the end for purposes of managing workflows in a legacy system and support. It is not recommended to create new workflows or utilize workflows when creating new processes. It does however contain some useful information regarding the thought process that would assist a user in creating any type of automation, especially when using Power Automate, covered in later chapters.

Workflows are a type of process within Dynamics 365 CE that allows users to create automated business logic in real time or within the background of the application. Workflows are created via the Solution Explorer (not the App Designer, at the time of writing) and can contain conditional steps and perform actions based on contextual data from the record it was triggered from.

Workflows can be executed from the actions a user performs within the system, which are as follows:

- Creation of a record

- Update of a record and update of specific fields (including status changes and assignment)

- Deletion of a record

Workflows can also be run via Business Process Flows automatically on stage entry and exit. They can be triggered manually by a user using the "Run Workflow" operation (this is only available in the Classic UI at the time of writing; however, it will be available in the Unified Interface as part of the October 2018 release).

Complex nested conditional business logic can be achieved using workflows, including the concept of scheduled workflows using background workflows that have "wait" conditions (Figure 12-58).

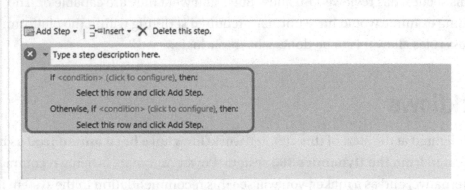

Figure 12-58. *Example conditional logic within a workflow*

Workflow templates can be made where business logic is created within the workflow and saved as a template against the entity. This is a very similar process to creating email templates. It is a great way to create complex reusable business logic, saving effort in the long term.

Dynamics 365 CE has an operational way of processing data within workflows and actions. The operations of the platform can be summarized into the following areas:

- Pre-operation

- Database operation

- Post-operation

The "operation" can be a Create, Update, or Delete. There is the concept of a state *before* the change, the change itself, and the state *after* the change (Figure 12-59). The important part is that the states before the change and after the change are likely to be different. Having this information and being able to utilize this in custom operations is important. Workflows can also perform database operations, such as Create and Update. The main limitation of workflows is that they are unable to perform a Retrieve Multiple function. This drawback is often a reason for using extensions by third parties or implementing custom code using plugins.

Figure 12-59. *Platform operation overview*

When creating a new workflow or modifying an existing one, you have the option to define the workflow as either "real-time" or "background." Background workflows are often attributed to better performance as they allow the system to determine when the resources become available within a time frame to operate (normally between 1 and 2 minutes). See Figure 12-60.

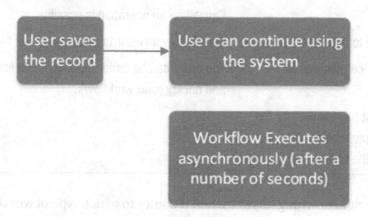

Figure 12-60. *Background workflows trigger action*

Real-time workflows are advantageous as the action defined within the workflow happens instantaneously (Figure 12-61). Real-time workflows will result in a user having to wait until the action is completed before the screen refreshes and the save is completed. This also means that you see any changes that the workflow has made to the current record or related records within sub-grids. There are some advantages and disadvantages to each of the types, which are summarized in Table 12-1.

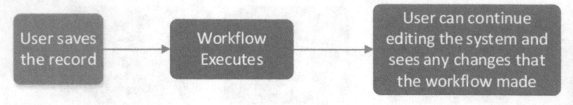

Figure 12-61. *Real-time workflows trigger action*

Table 12-1. *Advantages and Disadvantages of Workflow Types*

Background Workflows	Real-Time Workflows
Can perform "Wait" operations.	Cannot perform "Wait" operations.
Cannot operate before a Save operation.	Can perform logic before a Save operation (pre-operation).
Can fail silently.	Cancelling an operation is possible.
Can be attributed to better performance.	Can display an error to a user.
The order cannot be guaranteed.	The order can be better managed with linked real-time and background workflows.
The user does not have to wait for the workflow to complete before they can continue editing the record after the save.	

There is no right or wrong answer when it comes to which type of workflow is better. It depends entirely on the business logic required, if there are any dependencies, and what user experience is required (e.g., is the user expecting the information immediately?).

Workflows also run within a "scope" of privileges. These can be summarized as follows:

- **User** – Workflow will only run on records owned by the same owner as the workflow.

- **Business Unit** – Workflow will only run on records owned by a user in the same business unit as the owner of the workflow.

- **Parent-Child Business Unit** - The workflow will only run on records owned by a user in the same business unit or child business unit of the owner of the workflow.

- **Organization** – Any user can execute the workflow.

The most restrictive is keeping the scope to a user. However, most of the time this is too restrictive for organizations, and instead they set it to the Business Unit or Parent–Child Business Unit if these are being utilized. The Organization scope is the least restrictive. With this in mind, there are some security considerations of workflows, as seen in Figure 12-62.

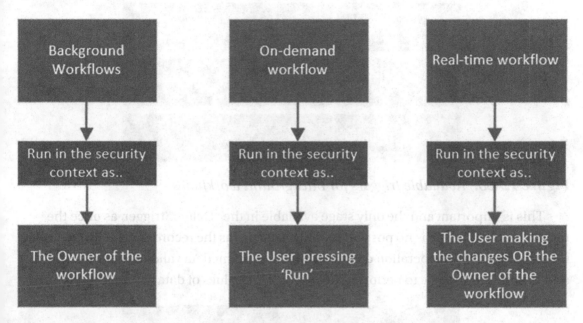

Figure 12-62. *Security considerations for the context of workflows*

There are also different options available for the background and real-time workflows for the available triggers. The main difference is the option of "Execute As" for real-time workflows. This option allows the use of "impersonation" of another user and their security roles and is not necessarily the user executing the changes or the owner of the workflow. Impersonation is where an operation is run in the context of another user who is normally not the user who has triggered the operation. This is often used to get around the security constraints of the implemented organizational security without having to modify the structure itself.

Real-time workflows and background workflows have different trigger points available, as shown in Figures 12-63 and 12-64. Background workflows only have the option for after the operation has happened within the database. Real-time workflows have the option for after and also before the database operation to have access to the "pre-operation" stage of the platform.

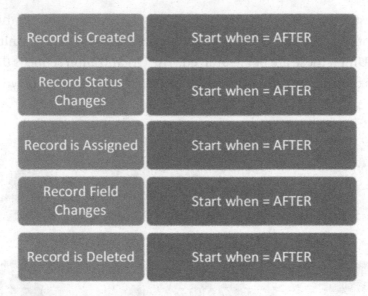

Figure 12-63. *Available triggers for background workflows*

This is important and the only stage available in the "Delete" trigger, as once the record is deleted there is no post-operation available (as the record is deleted!). Reasons for requiring the pre-operation data would be to perform data validation checks and to add in conditional logic to perform operations if the values of data are not correct.

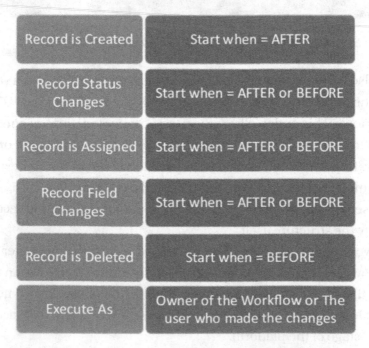

Figure 12-64. *Available triggers for real-time workflows*

Creating Workflows

Workflows are created from the Classic UI within the Solution Explorer (Figure 12-65).
Please note workflows should no longer be used to create business automation in modern experiences of the Dynamics 365 platform and Power Automate should now be used.

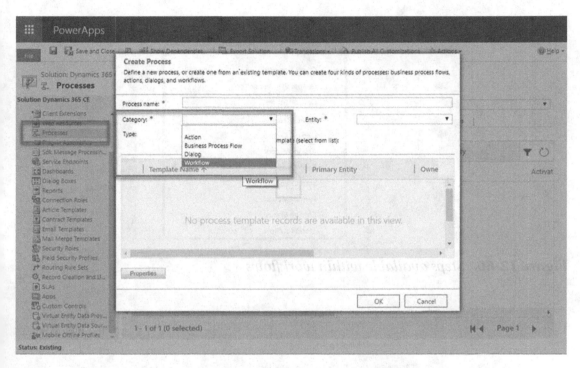

Figure 12-65. *Creating a workflow within the Solution Explorer*

Once the workflow is created and the scope, triggers, and type of the workflow have been defined, the business logic needs to be built. Workflows have a large level of business logic available to them. This chapter will review the functionality available that is essential to get started with workflows.

These questions should be the starting point when constructing business logic within the platform:

- What does it need to do?

- Are there conditions or requirements I need to enforce?

- What are the record types involved?

485

The answers to these three questions will give you enough information to get started building a workflow.

Workflows are made up of steps, as shown in Figure 12-66. The step that was used previously normally defines the next required step (Figure 12-67). Steps are built upon one another, especially when using conditions, so "branching" and conditional branching can occur.

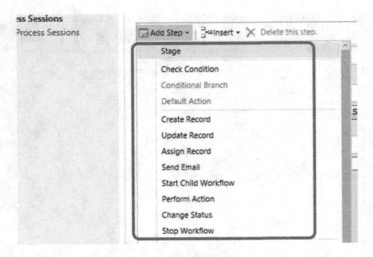

Figure 12-66. *Steps available within workflows*

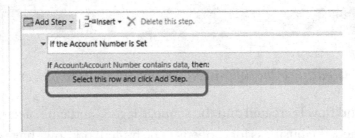

Figure 12-67. *Selecting the next line beneath a step to add a next step in the flow*

The available steps and their functionality are summarized here:

- **Stage** – Used to organize your business logic into sections.

- **Check Condition (If, Then)** – Adds a conditional statement (*if x is true, do this*).

- **Conditional Branch (Otherwise, If Then)** – Used directly after a check condition *(if x is true, do this; otherwise, do this)*.

- **Default Action (Otherwise)** – Inserts logic for action if the condition or conditional branch fails *(if x is true, do this; otherwise, do this; else, do this)*.

- **Wait** – Waits until a condition is met and then performs the step. Not available in real-time workflows.

- **Parallel Wait Branch** – Adds a wait branch that is running at the same time as your previous wait branch.

- **Create Record** – Allows the creation of an entity, or related entity, record (can use dynamic values).

- **Update Record** – Allows the update of an entity or related entity (can use dynamic values).

- **Assign Record** – Assigns the entity.

- **Sent Email** – Creates an email activity in CRM and sends it.

- **Start Child Workflow** – Starts a child workflow (normally a different entity).

- **Change Status** – Changes the status of the entity record.

- **Stop Workflow** – Stops the workflow with a completed or cancelled status. In real-time workflows, this reason is reported to the user in the user interface, and the save does not take place.

When a record is created or updated, the properties of that operation must be set (Figure 12-68). This includes populating mandatory fields, for example, in a "Create" operation. Using these operations allows the use of dynamic data from within the operation of the workflow so that a workflow can retrieve values from another area of the system linked to the context and populate it within the entity being created or updated.

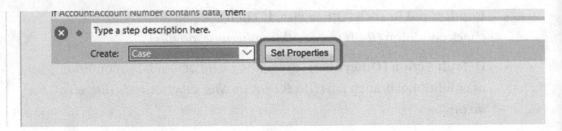

Figure 12-68. *Select "Set Properties" to define the data to be used in operations performed by the workflow*

Workflows have a concept of *context*. The context is created from the trigger point. In the example that follows, it is the Account that has triggered the workflow. From the start of that operation, the information from the Account record available when the workflow was triggered (not after) is available to use and to perform conditional business logic – that is what the context is. In addition to that, related entities defined in lookup values on the Account can be utilized within that business logic, also within its operational context.

Workflows can also trigger *child workflows*. Child workflows are available for background and real-time workflows. They allow workflows to be "chained" together so the initial triggering context can be retained and expanded upon through multiple different entities that may not be available in the initial workflow.

When a user navigates to the properties of an entity definition, they will see what looks like a new, blank record. The frame is not based on any form and contains all of the visible fields on forms, including those that are not visible on the forms near the bottom. There is a pane on the right-hand side called "Form Assistant" that allows a user to use the following:

- **Operation Functionality** – This allows the user to set numerical values and dates dynamically, for example, +2 days or +12 months.

- **Dynamic Data using "Look For"** – Via the parent and child entities, field data can be retrieved and then selected to be used within the fields. This operation adds the dynamic value within the field in yellow highlight in Figure 12-69.

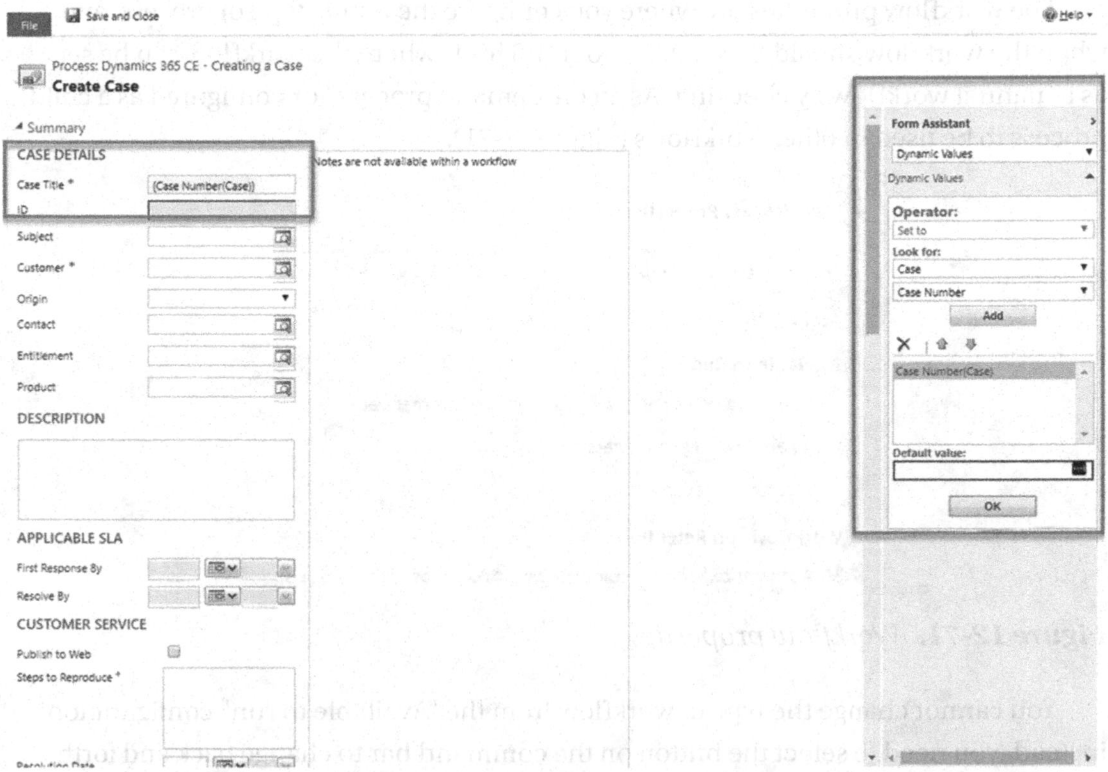

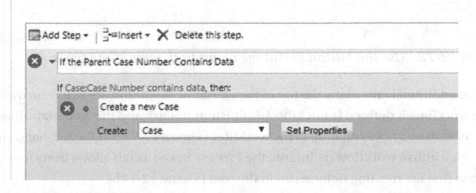

Figure 12-69. *Using the Form Assistant to set dynamic values within the entity in a workflow*

Where all steps are not completed for the workflow to be activated, errors will appear. Errors are indicated within workflow creation by the red "x" that appears next to a step (Figure 12-70).

Figure 12-70. *Selecting the next line beneath a step to add a next step in the flow*

The workflow properties are where you configure the name, type of process, and when the workflow should be available to run. This is where the workflow can be set as a manual workflow by checking "As an on-demand process" or configured as a child process to be used in other workflows (Figure 12-71).

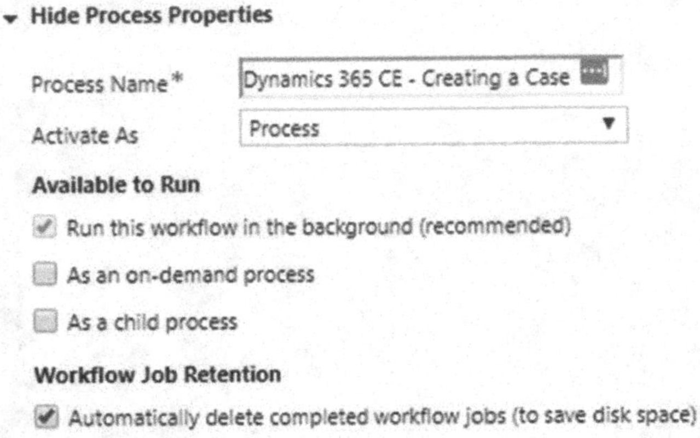

▾ **Hide Process Properties**

Process Name *   Dynamics 365 CE - Creating a Case

Activate As   Process   ▾

Available to Run

☑ Run this workflow in the background (recommended)

☐ As an on-demand process

☐ As a child process

Workflow Job Retention

☑ Automatically delete completed workflow jobs (to save disk space)

Figure 12-71. *Workflow properties*

You cannot change the type of workflow from the "Available to run" configuration; instead, you need to select the button on the command bar to change back and forth between a background and a real-time workflow, as shown in Figure 12-72.

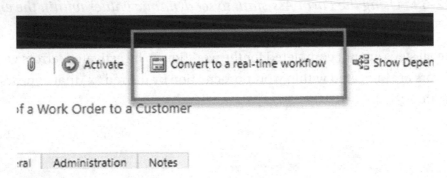

Figure 12-72. *Use the button to change between the workflow types*

The additional tabs along the top of the workflow definition are where an owner of the workflow is defined (under the Administration tab), and the Notes tab allows customers to add notes relating to the workflow (Figure 12-73). At the left-hand side of the pane within a workflow definition, the Process Sessions tab allows users to see the sessions that are running or have run in the past (Figure 12-74).

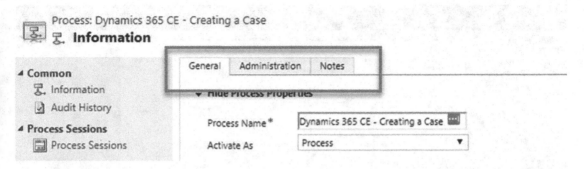

Figure 12-73. *Administrative tabs within the workflow definition*

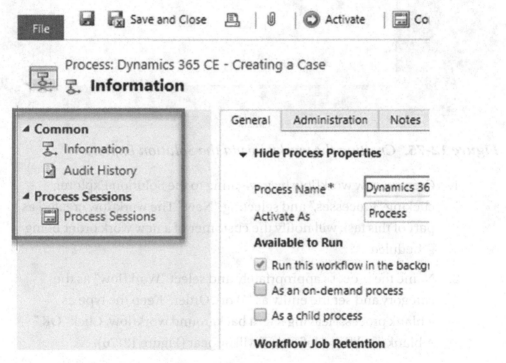

Figure 12-74. *Process Sessions tab within the workflow definition*

By default, the workflow job retention option is automatically set to delete the workflow jobs, but this can be unchecked. System jobs that are in an error state or pending will be visible from this area under "Process Sessions."

The next step is to get started and begin building a new workflow. The workflow task within this chapter walks you through how to create an email notification that is sent to the customer when a work order is set to "Scheduled."

Task: Create a background workflow (Figure 12-75).

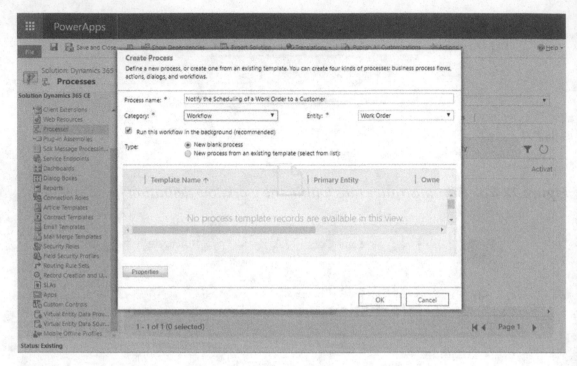

Figure 12-75. *Creating the workflow via the Solution Explorer*

1. Create a new workflow by navigating to the Solution Explorer, clicking "Processes," and selecting "New." The workflow created as part of this task will notify the customer of a new work order being scheduled.

2. Name the process appropriately and select "Workflow" as the category and set the entity as "Work Order." Keep the type as a blank process, leaving it as a background workflow. Click "OK." A blank workflow definition will appear (Figure 12-76).

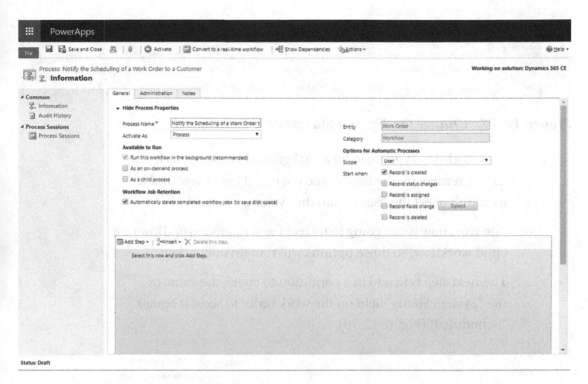

Figure 12-76. *Empty workflow definition is created*

3. The next step is to configure the scope and trigger and to confirm the type of workflow to be used (real-time or background).

4. The scope should be configured for "Organization," as any user can trigger this workflow and it is not security restricted (in this fictional scenario).

5. The trigger for the workflow occurs on change of the status field on the Work Order entity. Change the "Start When" field to "Record Fields Change" and click "Select" to open a popup. Select the "System Status" field and then click "OK" (Figure 12-77). Notice a value has not been specified. This will need to be specified within the condition to ensure the business logic is set up correctly.

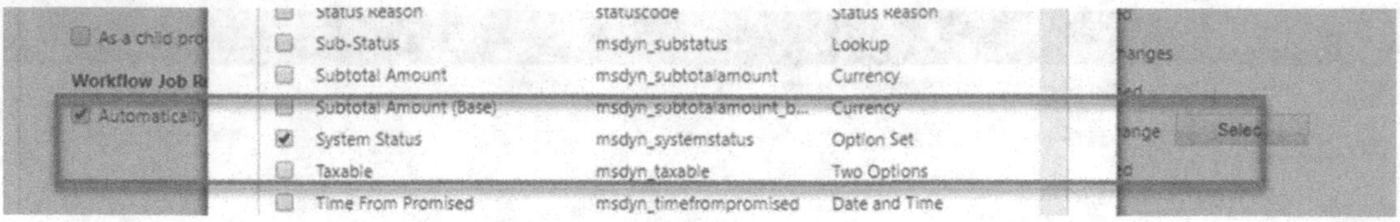

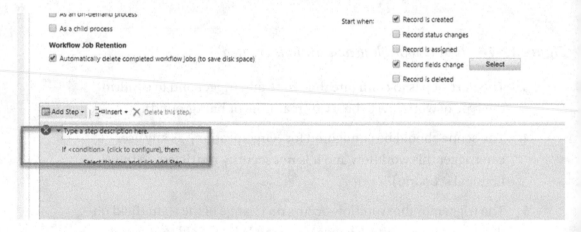

Figure 12-77. *Change the "System Status" field to be the trigger*

> This workflow is going to be a background workflow as it is not a requirement for the user to see the email being sent and it wouldn't affect the user within the system.

6. The workflow is not going to be used as a manual workflow or a child workflow, so those options will remain unchecked.

> The next step is to add in a condition to check the value of the "System Status" field on the work order to see if it equals "Scheduled" (Figure 12-78).

Figure 12-78. *Select the empty condition to configure it*

7. Click "Add Step" and select "Check Condition" (Figure 12-79). This will add an empty conditional clause with an empty condition.

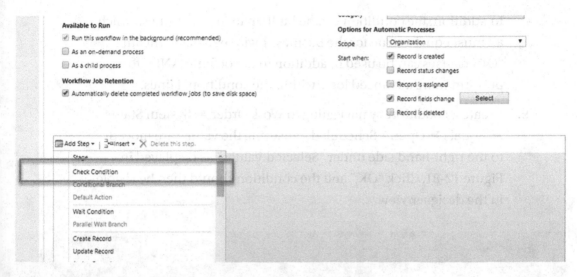

Figure 12-79. *Click "Check Condition" to add this step*

8. Click the empty condition name to open a popup window. The
    window will look very similar to Advanced Find (Figure 12-80). The
    purpose of this window is to select the entity and the field followed
    by the operator and what the values available will be based on the
    operator. It is possible from here to not select the primary entity – for
    example, the work order in this case – and select related entities.

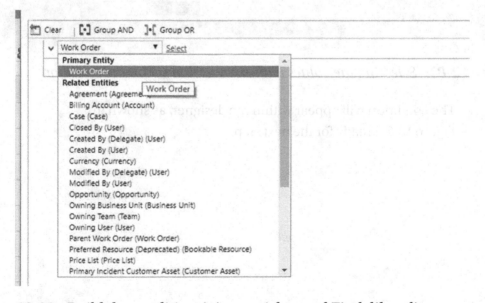

Figure 12-80. *Build the condition using an Advanced Find–like editor*

In addition, the condition can be built up to multiple lines, which all must equal to true for the business logic specified beneath. "OR" clauses can be used in addition to the default "AND" to perform more advanced logic within the conditional lines.

9. Create a condition by navigating to Work Order ➤ System Status ➤ Equals ➤ Open – Scheduled - ensuring the values are moved to the right-hand side under "Selected Values" as displayed in Figure 12-81. Click "OK," and the condition should then be visible in the designer view.

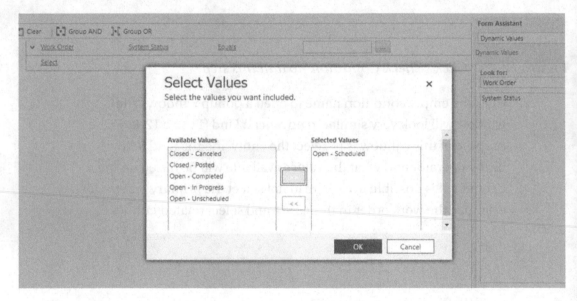

Figure 12-81. *Selecting the values within an option set on the operator*

The condition will appear within the designer, as shown in Figure 12-82, ready for the next step.

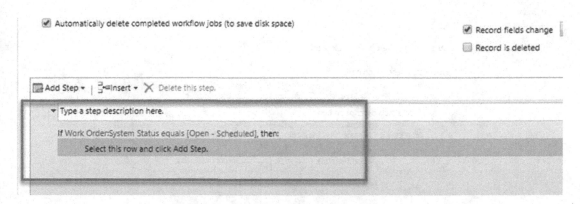

Figure 12-82. *Select the next row and add the next step*

10. Select the next row, where the text "Select this row and click Add Step" is selected in blue, and select "Add Step." Now that the condition has been added, the workflow definition needs to create the email record to send.

11. Select "Send Email." This will create a new block (Figure 12-83).

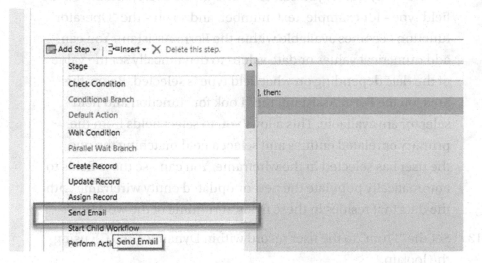

Figure 12-83. *Click "Send Email" to create a new email to send from Dynamics 365 CE*

12. Select "Create New Message" from the dropdown. This is where you can also choose to select an email template (Figure 12-84).

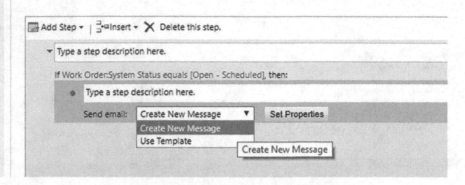

Figure 12-84. *Configure the Send Email options and properties on the "Send Email" step*

With a blank instance of the Email record open, the "Form Assistant" appears on the right-hand side. This pane gives users the functionality to add dynamic data in the fields selected within the entity frame.

On the entity frame, you can click into the field. Depending on the field type – for example, text, number, and so on – the "Operator" function becomes available within the Form Assistant. You can add numerical values or date values to dynamically set the value of the date depending on what field type is selected. Below this area, on the Form Assistant, the "Look for" function and field selector are available. This allows you to select fields from the primary or related entities and select a field matching the one the user has selected in the wireframe. You can use these fields to automatically populate the new or updated entity wireframe with the data that resides in these fields at runtime of the workflow.

13.   Set the "From" to the user record within Dynamics 365 CE using the lookup.

14.   Select the "To" field and click the Form Assistant to the right-hand side, selecting "Look for" ➤ "Work Order," and select the field "Reported By Contact."

15. Select "Ok" and it will now appear in blue in the box, as shown in Figure 12-85. This is often referred to as a "dynamic field" and will be based on data within the record that the workflow is run from (Figure 12-86).

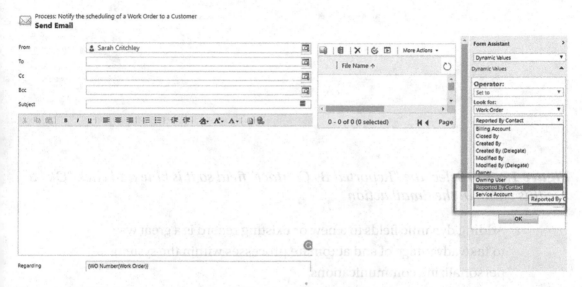

Figure 12-85. *Form Assistant within the email sent action in a workflow definition*

16. Select the blue highlighted text "Reported By Contact" and click "Ok." It will now appear in the "To" field in a yellow highlight (Figure 12-86). The yellow highlight shows this is a dynamic field and is retrieving the data from the related information held in the context of the workflow.

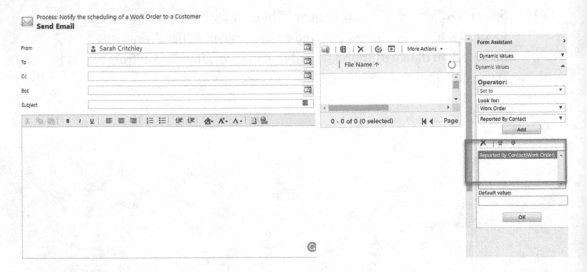

Figure 12-86. *Select the "Reported By Contact" field so it is blue and click "Ok" to use this value in the Email action*

Adding dynamic fields to a new or existing record is a great way to take advantage of and automate processes within the system, personalizing communications.

When editing workflows, they are easily identifiable by the yellow highlight in the blank entity form, as seen in Figure 12-87.

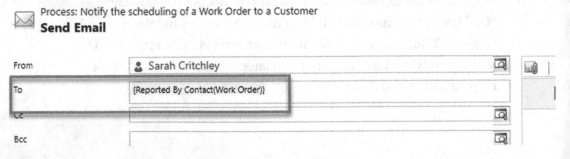

Figure 12-87. *Yellow highlight indicates this field will be populated with data from the primary or related entity field at runtime*

17.   Enter "Your Work Order has been Scheduled" in the "Subject" field.

In the body of the email, you can also use dynamic values just as the previous task did for the "To" field. Within an Email record, dynamic values are denoted by curly braces and not yellow highlight.

18. Create an email body that uses dynamic data, including the fields from the work order in the same way as in the previous step (Figure 12-88):

   • "Reported By Contact"

   • "Word Order Number"

   • "Time To Promised"

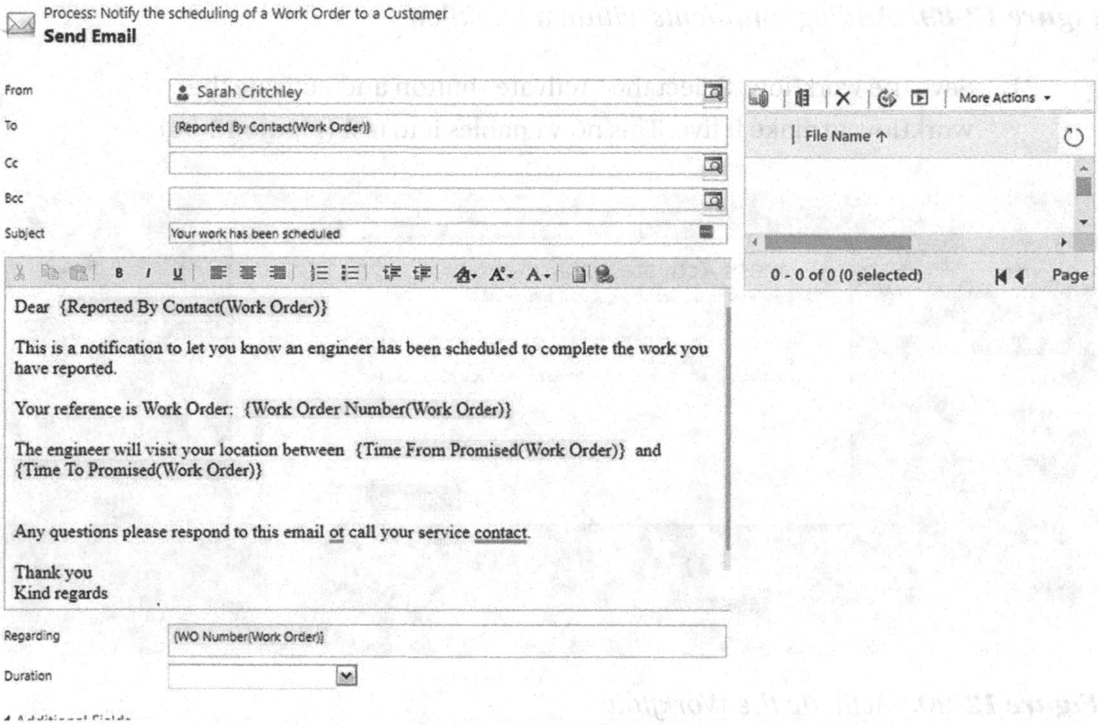

Figure 12-88. *Creating an email using dynamic data within a workflow*

19. Once completed, select "Save and Close" to close the email record.

20. Add in comments for each of the logic blocks within the workflow. The comments should describe simply what is happening within that step. This is to help other customizers know what that step is intended to be doing (Figure 12-89).

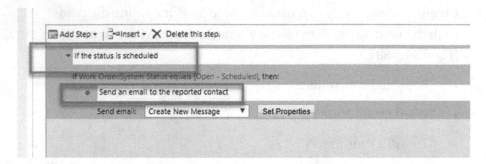

Figure 12-89. *Adding comments within a workflow*

21. Save the workflow. Select the "Activate" button and activate the
    workflow to make it live. This now enables it to test (Figure 12-90).

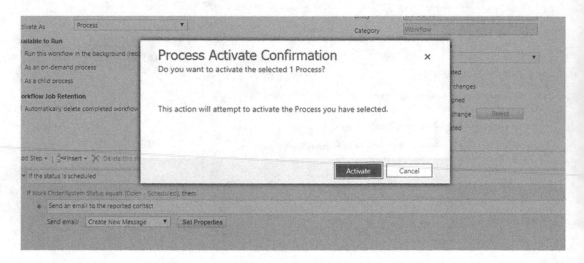

Figure 12-90. *Activate the Workflow*

To test the workflow, create a new work order and complete the basic details,
including the "Reported By Contact," the "Time To Promised," and any other fields
used within the workflow. If there is no data within dynamic data fields used within
the workflow definition, the related fields will be blank. This could look unprofessional
for external communications, such as emails, if there are placeholder texts and empty
spaces. To deal with this, you can add a fallback value in the value selector so that if the
first value is null, the fallback value will be used. Change the work order to "Scheduled"
by booking it manually (which is the easiest way to change the status) on the schedule
board. This will trigger the workflow, and in a few moments, something like Figure 12-91
should appear in the Activities.

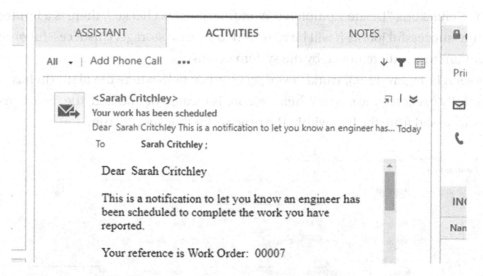

Figure 12-91. *Email activity within the "Activities" of the work order*

Troubleshooting

When a workflow is triggered, it creates a system job record. The system job record contains information about the process and the business logic. For background workflows, the system job can be seen in its waiting state under the Process Sessions tab within the workflow definition. Here, you can see the business logic and what step the current process is at. This is a great way to review workflows paused or stopped due to errors, as they would also be displayed here if an error occurred (Figure 12-92).

Figure 12-92. *Accessing Process Sessions of the workflow within the definition*

If the checkbox "Delete Completed Workflow Jobs" is checked, there is a limited time to see the successful job, as it will be removed to save on storage. Unsuccessful processes will remain here until removed by the system or a user.

As seen in Figure 12-93, workflows display green ticks where the platform has successfully executed the steps. When a record is created or updated, the record instance can be accessed from the link within the process for that specific run.

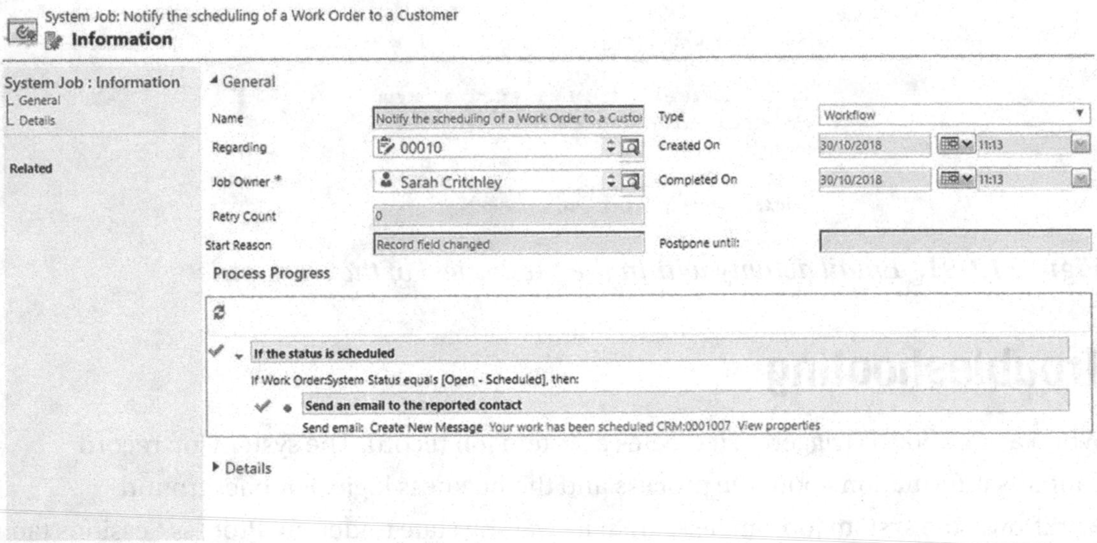

Figure 12-93. *Accessing the system job within the workflow definition and reviewing the steps*

Summary

This chapter has covered the core processes within Dynamics 365 CE. Processes provide easy-to-use functionality to customize the system to suit the requirements of organizations. Being able to create complex business processes using just the user interface gives organizations a large amount of capability, ownership of the platform, and the capability to change those processes as and when they change within the organization itself. Business Process Flows and task flows offer a guided process for users to follow prompts step-by-step, with added business rules where required to automate tasks even further. Workflows offer an extensive capability to provide external and internal automation, which can be performed in the background or in real time, displaying changes immediately to the user. Finally, business rules offer an extra layer of processing, which can be on both the client and server side of the application, offering the capability to perform error checking and various other tasks to speed up data entry and enforce rules where required. This chapter has covered these core processes within Dynamics 365 CE to allow you to get started implementing more customized and specific business logic to the platform.

Chapter Tasks

1. Create a new Business Process Flow in the maker experience.

2. Create a business rule.

3. Create a new action in the Classic Client.

4. Use the action within a Business Process Flow as an action step.

Further Reading

Workflows in more depth (Microsoft, 2018). URL: `https://docs.microsoft.com/en-us/dynamics365/customer-engagement/customize/workflow-processes`

Business Rules (Microsoft, 2018). URL: `https://docs.microsoft.com/en-us/windows/desktop/secauthz/business-rules`

A guide to Actions (Microsoft, 2018). URL: `https://docs.microsoft.com/en-us/dynamics365/customer-engagement/customize/actions`

`Automated Flows calling Actions` (Microsoft, 2019) URL: `https://docs.microsoft.com/en-us/business-applications-release-notes/april19/microsoft-flow/automated-flows-call-common-data-service-action`

CHAPTER 13

Power Automate

Power Automate is a workflow tool that allows for the event-to-action-style automation of processes inside and outside of the Microsoft 365 suite of technologies. It offers external connectors and the capability for custom external connectors to be built to and from other technologies (Figure 13-1). This chapter will review the basics of Power Automate and how to get started with Dynamics 365 and the Common Data Service.

To assist with terminology, Power Automate is previously known as Microsoft Flow. There are still the concept of "**Flows**" being created within Power Automate.

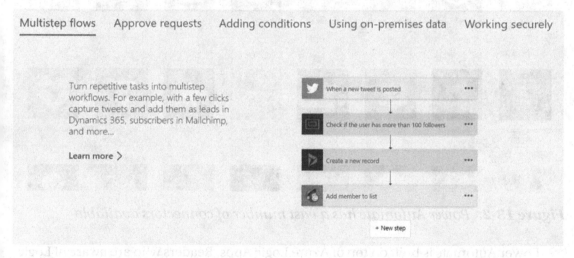

Figure 13-1. *Power Automate*

Power Automate can automate small tasks owned by the user as well as larger organizational tasks that are based around software implementations involving platforms such as Dynamics 365 CE (Figure 13-2). There is a large amount of flexibility within Power Automate due to its capability to allow users to automate tasks, such as when an email is flagged to create a to-do item or even to send a notification to the user's phone when an email is received from their manager. Equally, utilizing it to perform more complex tasks, such as to send HTTP requests and manage the response messages

S. Critchley, *Dynamics 365 Essentials*, https://doi.org/10.1007/978-1-4842-5911-5_13

507

or connect to third-party providers such as MailChimp or Twitter, allows for a wider application of services, including using it in the context of Dynamics 365 CE. Its most recent addition to its capabilities includes Robotic Process Automation in both attended and unattended forms. This means tasks can be recorded and automated, across both web and local applications, allowing them to be triggered from numerous events. Power Automate contain "Flows" – respective of its previous name "Microsoft Flow."

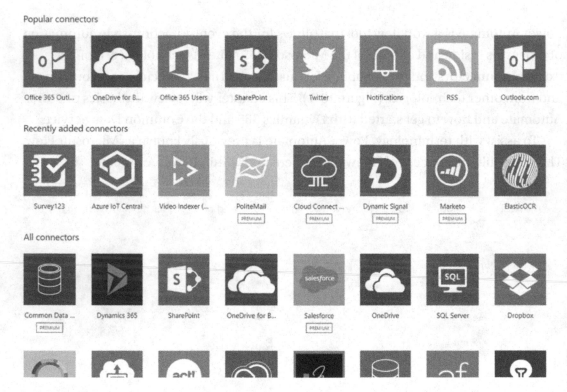

Figure 13-2.   *Power Automate has a vast number of connectors available*

Power Automate is built on top of Azure Logic Apps. Readers who are aware of Logic Apps can bring their existing knowledge and easily get up to speed on using Power Automate with a minimal learning curve. The core differences between the two are the licensing models, the run limits, and the availability of connectors in different plans for Power Automate.

A flow within Power Automate begins with a trigger. The trigger can be a manual trigger, where a user selects a button within the application (including the Common Data Service) or on their mobile. Alternatively, a trigger can also be an event within an application, such as an email is received or a record is created in the Common

Data Service. The trigger kicks off an action. An action would normally either connect to another service to get information, post information, or otherwise do something. Before, after, or during the action, conditional modifiers can be added for each loop for managing multiple records and other logic to create more complex automation within the application. There are also actions that convert information to different formats. An example of this is "Parse JSON," which converts JSON-formatted data, often used over HTTP requests, into fields that can be used in Flow. Various mathematical functions can also be performed on the data outside of the action context and within the context of the content blocks being used within the flow logic (Figure 13-3).

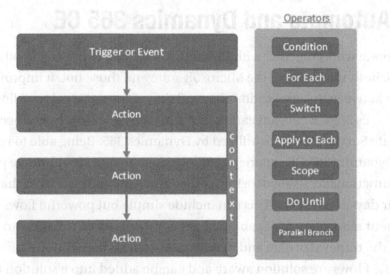

Figure 13-3. *Overview of a flow within Power Automate and what can be achieved within*

You can create a blank flow and start building business logic from scratch. Alternatively, you can use a predefined template, where the trigger, action, and sometimes a follow-up action have already been defined and only minor pieces of setup information require configuration.

Power Automate also includes approval functionality. Approvals allow for a self-contained "approval board" that displays pending approval items that have been assigned to an Office 365 user (normally a user or team). Within a flow, an approval item can be created and assigned to a user. The user can get a notification on their email, approval board, or phone (provided they have the Power Automate mobile app) and approve the item with a small number of clicks. Business logic and rules can be added around the approval creation once it has been approved to further automate the process.

For example, approval can trigger actions within Dynamics 365 CE, Outlook, or other systems that can then lead to further processes. Approvals simplify the mechanism of functionality for approving something within any scenario or industry and allow simple to more complex approval workflows to be built and easily modified should business requirements change over time.

The goal of Power Automate is to automate tasks that take time up for users and organizations in order to connect applications that would otherwise take development effort and possibly substantial amounts of time.

Power Automate and Dynamics 365 CE

Power Automate works together with Dynamics 365 CE to connect it to other applications, both those part of the Microsoft suite and those not. It improves the connectivity between the applications beyond that of the standard workflow processes within Dynamics 365 CE covered earlier in the book. It does this by connecting to the Common Data Service, the store utilized by Dynamics 365. Being able to run flows from within the Dynamics 365 CE experience allows users to quickly automate processes and expand the functionality using data from other applications or services that can assist them in their day-to-day tasks. This can include simple but powerful flows that automate their document management capabilities, get approvals for permission and sign off, or even trigger the retrieval of data and iterate upon collections of information.

Automatic Flows are solution aware and can be added into a solution and moved across environments as a solution with other components relating to your app. They do not rely on solutions to move between environments, and makers can export the .zip file of the flow to transition it from one environment to the other, albeit disconnected from the other customizations done within Dynamics 365 CE or the Common Data Service for Apps.

Business Process Flows are also managed under Power Automate and can be found within the flow maker experience. They were historically a Dynamics 365 process and are covered in Chapter 12 of this book, as well as how to get started with it.

Use Cases for Power Automate Within Dynamics 365 CE

It has been highlighted in this chapter that Power Automate can be used for individual productivity, such as flagging emails as high priority from external triggers. It can also be used for organizational productivity and automation to enhance Dynamics 365 implementations. Dynamics 365 implementations often don't include just the Customer Engagement platform, but also other Microsoft products, such as SharePoint, OneNote, OneDrive, PowerBI, and Azure. For example, Power Automate can be used to enhance document management within SharePoint and OneDrive, such as creating an approval item when a new SharePoint item is created. A similar use case could be that, within Dynamics 365 CE, when a new record (of any type) requires approval, it triggers an action. Power Automate does not exclusively work for Microsoft-based applications. It has available external connectors to other products, such as DropBox, Gmail, Twitter, Google Sheets, and more. Use of the external connectors can expand the reach and capability of the Dynamics 365 CE application to provide more value and more data within the system from other sources across the Internet and organization. This results in increased productivity by saving time usually spent performing actions manually and reducing the errors of those manual actions. It can also provide more useful information and empower users in their roles to quickly identify trends and provide an improved level of service to customers by having more information from multiple areas together in a single place.

Power Automate also expands the previous capability of Dynamics through enhancing what is now possible using workflow automation. Examples in this area are actions such as HTTP requests. These types of requests allow Power Automate to connect to external services or serverless components such as Azure Functions that would otherwise need to be developed using code. There are also functions and parsing functionality that can be achieved using Flow as well as generation of audio using Microsoft Translator and other third parties, such as Marketo, Basecamp, and WordPress. These features further enhance the capability to enable loosely coupled integrations. For enterprise integrations, it is the recommendation to use Logic Apps as an integrator or developer for advanced integration scenarios; further resources on this comparison can be found within "Further Reading" at the end of this chapter.

Beyond integrations, another great example of a flow within the realm of document management is one that copies files from one folder to another within SharePoint. Power Automate can be used to automate actions within the same application.

In summary, there are many different use cases that can be met using Power Automate, such as using it to enhance document management solutions, to connect to HTTP endpoints, and to approve items within Dynamics 365 CE. It is the low-code workflow engine of the modern business application platform.

Getting Started with Power Automate: How to Create a Flow

This section will walk you through on how to create a basic flow using Power Automate and Dynamics 365 CE. Ensure there is at least a trial subscription of Dynamics 365 CE and Power Automate active on the environment.

To avoid any confusion, this chapter uses the "Common Data Service (Current Environment)" connector. This connector has additional capability than the older version which is called just "Common Data Service." It is useful to be aware of newer and older versions of the same connector as the platform updates. This is how you will work with data displayed in the Dynamics 365 applications.

Task: Create a basic flow.

1. Navigate to your solution from either `make.powerapps.com` or `<yourregion>.flow.microsoft.com`. Select "New" and select "Flow." This will open a new window.

2. In the new window, it will prompt you for a trigger. Type in "Common Data Service." There may be more than one connector that appears; select the "Current Environment" connector.

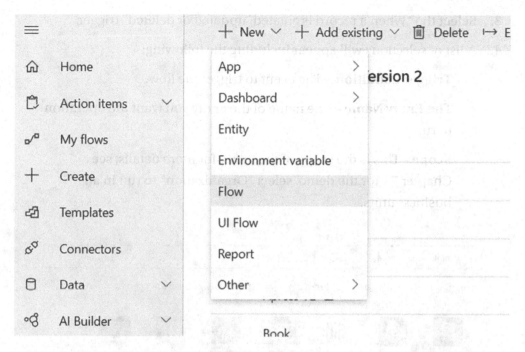

Figure 13-4. *Select "Flow" from within a solution*

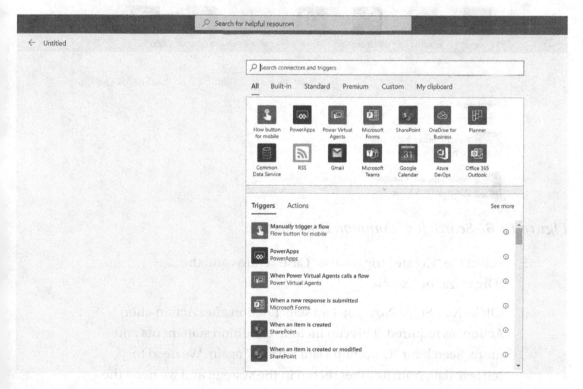

Figure 13-5. *Specify the trigger for the Flow*

3. Select the "When a record is created, updated or deleted" trigger.

4. A list of selections will appear including the following:

    - **Trigger Condition** – The event to trigger the flow.

    - **The Entity Name** – The name of the entity you want the operation to run.

    - **Scope** – This is the scope of the flow – for more details, see Chapter 7 – for the demo, select "Organization" to run in all business units.

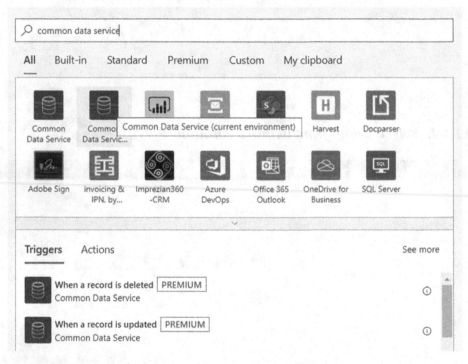

Figure 13-6. *Search for "Common Data Service"*

5. Select the "Create" trigger, the "Case" entity, and the "Organization" scope.

6. Click "New Step." Now you can select Action after Action after Action, as required. This can include condition statements and more. Search for "Common Data Service" again. We need to retrieve data from another record in the system, and we need the "Get Record" action.

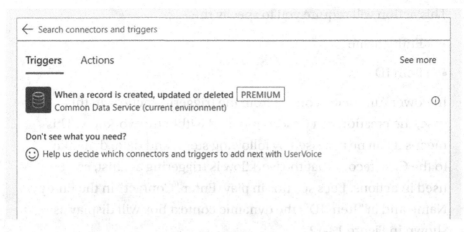

Figure 13-7. Select "When a record is created, updated or deleted"

7. These options will be different than the options before, as these
    are actions. Select "Get Record."

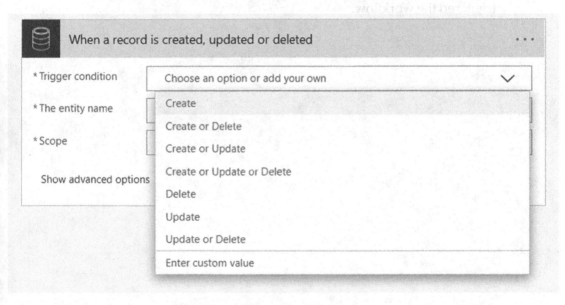

Figure 13-8. Select "Create" for the Trigger Condition

8. This action will require you to specify the

    •   Entity name

    •   Item ID

    In Power Automate, context from the triggering action, in this case, the creation of a Case, is retained within the workflow. This means it can be accessed by following steps, and data, dynamic to the Case record that the workflow is triggering against, can be used in actions. Let's see this in play. Enter "Contact" in the Entity Name and in "Item ID"; the dynamic context box will display as shown in Figure 13-12.

9. In the dynamic content box, type "Customer" and select "Customer (Value)." This enters the unique identifier into this action to retrieve the Contact record associated to the Case which triggered the workflow.

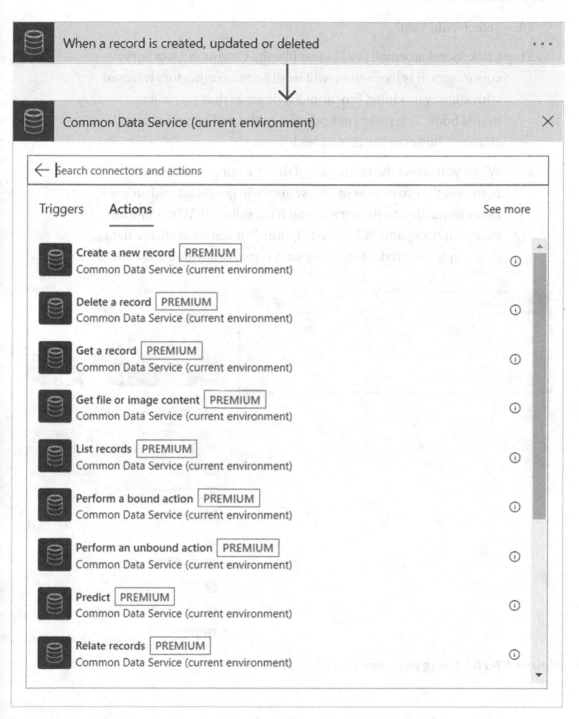

Figure 13-9. *The available actions in the Common Data Service connector (at the time of writing)*

10.   Select "Add Step."

11.   Click "Send an email (V2)" – just like the Common Data Service connectors, it is likely there will be different connectors released with slightly modified functionality or areas that you will see in this book. The platform updates rapidly and some areas will change – however the principles less so.

12.   When you select the connector, if this is a connector not used before in the environment, the system will go ahead and create a new connection to the service you have selected. When this has completed, expand "Advanced Options" to see all available data that can be entered. Mandatory data is marked with a red asterisk.

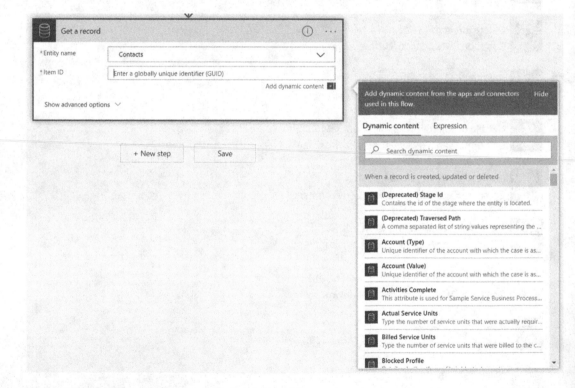

Figure 13-10.   *Using dynamic data in a Flow*

13. For this specific action, details for the "To," "Subject," and "Body" fields are required. In Power Automate, context from the triggering action, in this case, the creation of a Case, is retained within the workflow. This means it can be accessed by following steps, and data, dynamic to the Case record that the workflow is triggering against, can be used in actions. Let's see this again in play. Select "Add Dynamic Content" under the "To" field.

14. Select "Email" from the Action "Get Record." The Actions are stacked in the dynamic content, and each has its own data available from its return value when the workflow is in progress.

15. Enter the text "A new case has been created."

16. Enter the following text in the body. This email is to notify you that a new case has been created and we are currently investigating the issue. The case number is :" keeping your cursor a space after the word 'is :' .

17. In the dynamic data, search for "Case Number" and select this – it should enter the dynamic data as a tag called "Case Number." At runtime, this would populate with the data held within the Case Number field.

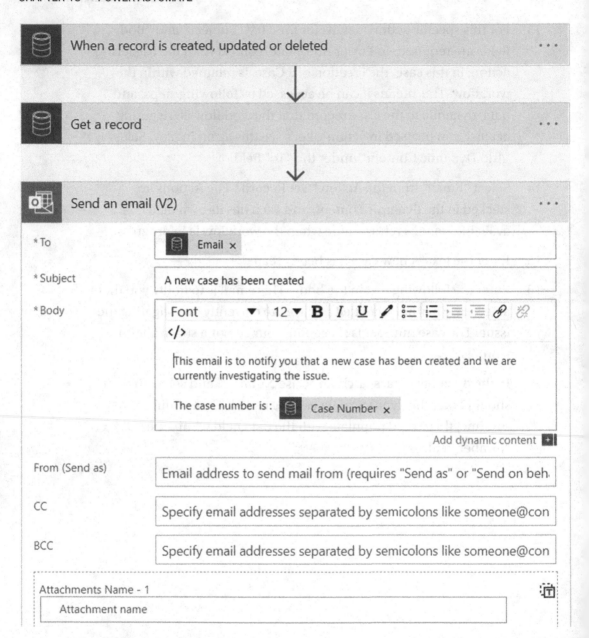

Figure 13-11. *A new action – using the Office 365 connector (Outlook)*

18. The business logic is finished; however, before we save it, name the flow at the top of the screen before navigating away.

19. It is best practice to test your workflows – to do this once it is saved, click "Test." As the flow has never run, you will need to perform the trigger action yourself. Select this option, as shown in Figure 13-12.

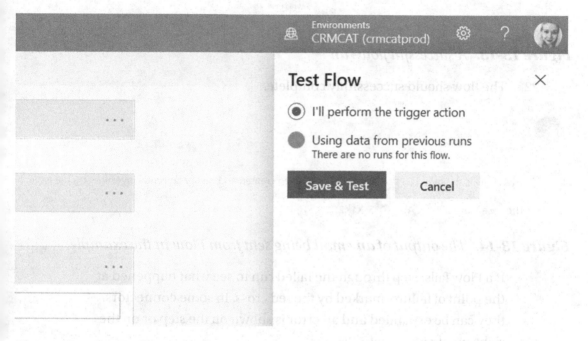

Figure 13-12. *Testing your flow in Power Automate*

20. Open a new tab, open the Dynamics 365 Customer Service app, and create a new Case. This will perform the trigger action. Enter you are testing against test data, and the contact entered in the Customer field is a Contact record and has a test email address.

21. When the trigger action is performed, you can see the workflow begin and the runtime in action. Ticks or red crosses will appear against each step.

Figure 13-13. *A successful flow run*

22. The flow should successfully complete.

 Sarah Critchley

You ⌄

This email is to notify you that a new case has been created and we are currently investigating the issue.

The case number is : CAS-01035-X1K2C1

Figure 13-14. *The output of an email being sent from Flow in the example*

If a Flow fails, step through the failed run to see what happened at the point of failure, marked by the red cross. In some connectors, they can be expanded and an error is shown on the step or on the right-hand-side panel.

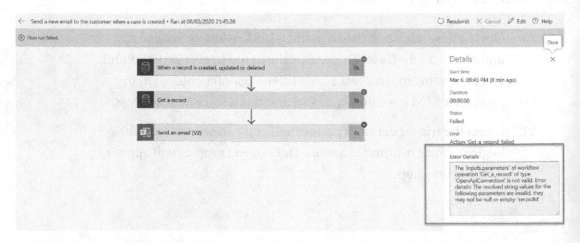

Figure 13-15. *A failed Flow run shows the point of failure and, in most cases, an error*

Each flow has an area where several actions can be performed upon it, including switching the Flow off. This means it will not be triggered even when the triggering action happens. Other actions include deleting the flow, saving a copy, and seeing analytics on the flow runs. You can also see the run history of the flow, each time the triggering action has started the workflow automation.

Figure 13-16. *A flow homepage as such, which details a number of actions and a view of the historical runs*

Summary

Power Automate has the potential to be a powerful tool in business system implementations and for personal productivity. The features of Power Automate take down the barriers of complexity and cost of system integrations, inside and outside of the Microsoft 365 platform. This chapter has covered the essentials of the Power Automate and using it within Dynamics 365 via the Common Data Service. It has walked you through how to create a new flow using the Common Data Service connector – the connecter being used to create workflow automation in the Dynamics 365 CE Apps. It has also covered using other connectors, including the Outlook connector alongside the Common Data Service. Using Power Automate to perform automation logic using Dynamics 365 CE extends the capabilities of the system to increase productivity through automation, and this chapter gives you all the tools necessary to get started.

Chapter Tasks

1. Create a Flow that uses the Common Data Services connector.

2. Create a Flow that uses another connector (outside of the Common Data Service).

3. Create a Flow that uses a non-Microsoft service.

Further Reading

Azure Logic Apps and Power Automate (Microsoft, 2018). URL: `https://docs.microsoft.com/en-us/azure/azure-functions/functions-compare-logic-apps-ms-flow-webjobs`

Change Tracking in Power Automate (Microsoft 2018). URL: `https://docs.microsoft.com/en-us/dynamics365/customer-engagement/admin/enable-embedded-flow-in-your-organization`

Embedded Flow in Dynamics 365 CE (Microsoft, 2018). URL: `https://docs.microsoft.com/en-us/dynamics365/customer-engagement/admin/enable-embedded-flow-in-your-organization`

CHAPTER 14

Power Apps Portals

This book has focused on Dynamics 365 CE Apps, first-party applications created and managed by Microsoft on the Power Platform. There was also a chapter on Model-Driven Applications, providing the capability to go beyond those first-party apps and build custom applications using the same interface. This chapter covers an introduction to the third type of application available on the Power Platform, a Portal app.

Figure 14-1. *Microsoft Power Apps Portals*

© Sarah Critchley 2020
S. Critchley, *Dynamics 365 Essentials*, https://doi.org/10.1007/978-1-4842-5911-5_14

Power Apps Portals provides a different capability to Model-Driven and even Canvas Apps. They provide access to create an application which is externally facing on the Internet, in the same way a website functions – providing customers of organizations the ability to sign in and access and view their data, stored within the Common Data Service.

This capability is useful, especially as many organizations are moving to a self-service-driven model of customer service, regardless of industry. It also provides organizations with the ability to allow customers to perform tasks that, historically, only internal staff could do – freeing them up to work on other processes while significantly improving customer satisfaction.

What Power Apps Portals allows is to build a website application which has the Common Data Service as the central data store without needing to know extensive web development compared to building, maintaining, and hosting, for example, a custom ASP.net website.

A Short History

Power Apps Portals is not a new feature available to organizations. Power Apps Portals is built from Microsoft Portals, previously only available to just Dynamics 365 CE customers. Microsoft Portals came from an acquisition of a company called "ADX Studio" – this company specialized in creating websites using Dynamics 365 and related technology and was the original company to develop the feature of Power Portals as we see today.

How a Portal Works

When a user selects to make a Portal App, as seen in Figure 14-2, from the "Apps" screen (a Portal App is not solution aware at this time), the supporting solutions used in Power Apps Portals are installed. This includes the Portal Administration App, which is represented as a Model-Driven Application. This results in two applications – one being the portal and the other being Portal Administration, which shows the Portal page and underlying structure in Model-Driven form.

This only happens for the first Portal app. Once a second Portal App is created, this will be also configured via the Dynamics 365 Portals or Portal Administration App. (The apps are the same, named differently depending on the licensing.)

Apps

Apps   Component libraries (preview)

	Name		Modified	Owner	Type
	Apress V2	...	4 d ago	Sarah Critchley	Model-driven
	Omnichannel Administration	...	2 mo ago	Sarah Critchley	Model-driven
	Channel Integration Framework	...	2 mo ago	Sarah Critchley	Model-driven
	Omnichannel for Customer Service	...	2 mo ago	Sarah Critchley	Model-driven
	Solution Health Hub	...	4 mo ago	Sarah Critchley	Model-driven
	Apress Self Service	...	4 mo ago	Sarah Critchley	Portal
	Dynamics 365 Portals	...	4 mo ago	Sarah Critchley	Model-driven
	Customer Service Hub	...	4 mo ago	Sarah Critchley	Model-driven

Figure 14-2. *Two Applications as part of Power Apps Portals*

A Portal works by creating Entity records which represent a web page – the web page that an external user interacts with. These pages (records) are configured by updating several controls on the page to reference entities and related records, resulting in a web-like experience.

Authentication in Power Apps is supported by ASP.net authentication capabilities, similar to if you were to create a templated or scaffolded ASP.net portal. Customers can be invited to the portal with an invitation code or choose to sign up using Azure AD B2C, Google, Facebook, or Micorosft authentication they are familiar with, further increasing their use of the portal to submit their information securely. From an organization's perspective, this can be administered via the "Contact" record using the "Portal Contact" form, where users can also perform features such as reset the password and manage roles via the Portal App.

Power Apps Portals is still a website underneath. Portals use a language called Liquid – a proprietary language, now managed by Microsoft, used to code the portal. In addition, portals use JavaScript, HTML, and CSS, web-based technology languages used to build traditional websites.

Creating a New App

To create a new Portal App, navigate to the maker experience and select "Apps." Select "New App" and select Portal.

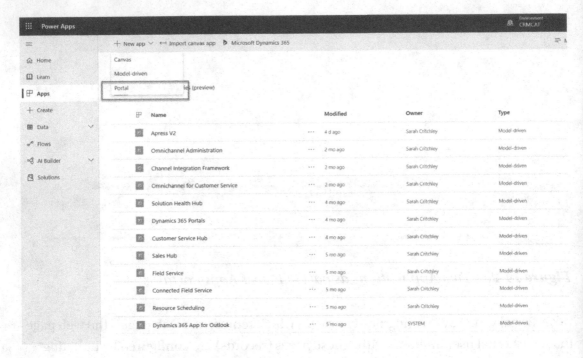

Figure 14-3. *Creating a new Portal App*

A window will appear, as shown in Figure 14-4. This will be where the App is named and the URL for customers will be set. Enter the details, select the language, and click "Create." The App will be created behind the scenes. This can take up to an hour to be created, especially if this is the first portal in the environment.

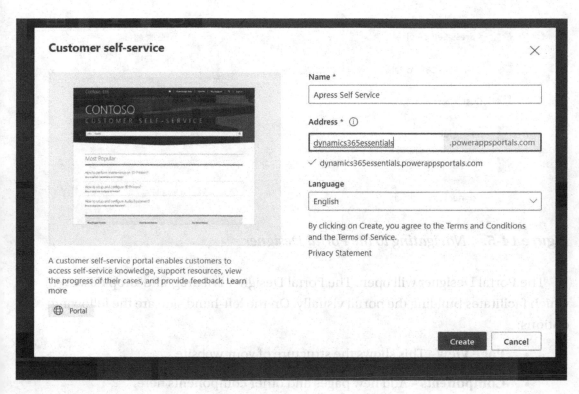

Figure 14-4.   Naming a new Portal App

Portal Designer

Once a Portal is created, navigate to the Portal Designer by selecting the App and selecting "Edit," as shown in Figure 14-5.

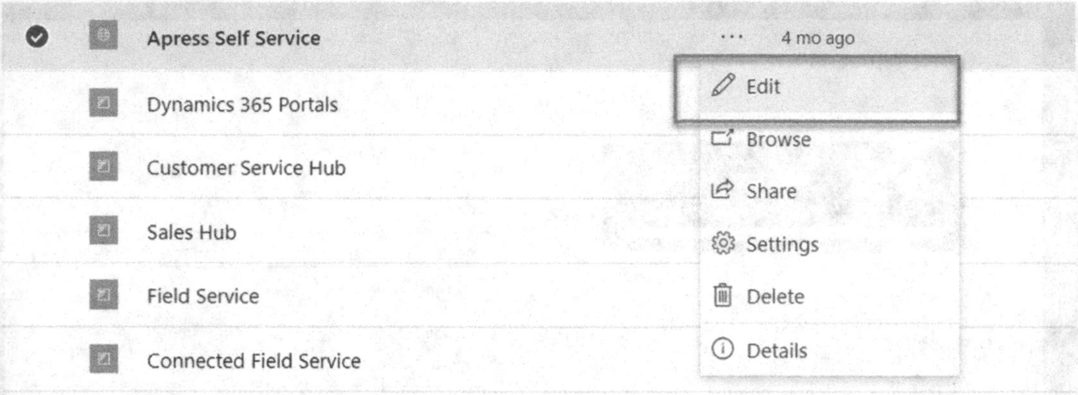

Figure 14-5.   Navigating to the Portal Designer

The Portal Designer will open. The Portal Designer is a drag-and-drop designer which facilitates building the portal visually. On the left-hand side are the following options:

- **Page View** – This shows the structure of your website.

- **Components** – Add new pages and other components here.

- **Theme** – Shows the CSS. The CSS is the styling component of the website and its own language. Using the drag-and-drop designer changes this.

- **Templates** – These are starting points for some pages which allow you to build prebuilt components.

Figure 14-6. *Portal Designer*

When a component is selected in the main central designer, the right-hand side panel is where that component can be configured such as the name, text, and color.

There are limitations to what the Portal Designer can do at the time of writing without having to use Liquid and web-based languages to configure it. For many cases, there will be the need to configure the App from the Administration App (more details can be found in "Further Reading").

Power Apps Portals does a brilliant job of providing the capability to create basic externally facing applications which utilize the Common Data Service.

Deploying a Portal

A Portal is not just the application, but mostly the configured data based on the configuration and entities behind the scenes. This means the data cannot be moved from development to other environments in the same way as other apps (using solutions). To move a portal, the data must be moved. An easier way of doing this is using the **Configuration Migration** tool provided by Microsoft. The tool comes with already created schema definitions of this data, depending on if the portal was created with a template or not (it provides schemas for both instances). More information on deploying a portal can be found in "Further Reading."

Summary

This chapter has provided a starting point to Power Apps Portals. It covered what the application is made up of, including how it is different from other types of applications within the Power Platform. It summarized how to create a portal, configure it, and deploy it in other environments. Power Apps Portals is built on existing technology available from the legacy Dynamics 365 platform, and so the technology has been used for a long period of time, where the Power Platform has refreshed the maker experience providing an easier way of getting started with building Portal Apps.

Chapter Tasks

1. Create a Portal application in your environment.

2. Once ready, edit the portal and get familiar with the Portal Designer.

3. Open the Administration Model-Driven App and familiarize yourself with the sitemap and the entity structure of your portal (do not delete anything!).

Further Reading

Learn more about Portals (Microsoft). URL: https://docs.microsoft.com/en-us/learn/modules/introduction-to-dynamics-365-portals/

What are Portals? (Microsoft). URL: https://docs.microsoft.com/en-us/powerapps/maker/portals/overview

Portal Migration using Configuration Migration Tool (Microsoft). URL: https://docs.microsoft.com/en-us/powerapps/maker/portals/admin/migrate-portal-configuration

Index

533

© Sarah Critchley 2020
S. Critchley, *Dynamics 365 Essentials*, https://doi.org/10.1007/978-1-4842-5911-5

S

Printed in the United States
By Bookmasters